Estonia, Latvia & Lithuania

⊕ HELSINKI
(FINLAND)
p144

Estonia
p47

Latvia
p157

Lithuania
p232

**Anna Kaminski,
Leonid Ragozin, Angelo Zinna**

CONTENTS

Bear, Estonia (p347)

Curonian Spit (p278)

Rīga (p162)

Toolkit

Storybook

Curonian Spit (p278)

ESTONIA, LATVIA & LITHUANIA

THE JOURNEY BEGINS HERE

My family's story is interlinked with Estonia, Latvia and Lithuania. My paternal grandparents used to spend their summers on the beaches of Pärnu, while my mother spent the warmer months, along with her mother and sister, of her childhood and then later years berrying, swimming in the lakes and walking the forest trails of Aukštaitija National Park, or else sunning herself on Jūrmala's sand. My parents saw Tallinn's tall spires and Rīga's zeppelin sheds, and trod the cobblestones of Vilnius long before I was born, when the three countries were still subjugated by the Soviet Union. For me, personally, it's been fascinating to witness immense changes during the past 20 years: the resurgence of national character through art, music and architecture, the proliferation of imaginative restaurants and creative hotels, the consignment of Soviet detritus to junkyard theme parks, the futuristic elements. Yet underneath it all, there's still something achingly familiar to me since childhood.

Anna Kaminski

@ACKaminski

Anna is a writer about travel and culture, and the author of Eyeball Tacos and Kangaroo Stew, a food-driven travel memoir that includes her early travels in the Baltic states. Anna wrote the Lithuania chapter.

My favourite experience involves hiking among the giant sand dunes and pine forest on Lithuania's **Curonian Spit** (p278), one of the most peaceful corners of the world.

WHO GOES WHERE

Our writers and experts choose the places which, for them, define Estonia, Latvia and Lithuania.

RANDREY/GETTY IMAGES ©

Time slows down in the **West Estonian Archipelago** (p132), a collection of islands scattered in the Baltic Sea largely occupied by a UNESCO-listed biosphere reserve. Cycling is an ideal way to discover this region where craters, cemeteries and churches hide. Start from Kuressaare's castle and get all the way to Tahkuna Lighthouse, Hiiumaa's northernmost point, for a trip across Estonia's remote archipelago.

Angelo Zinna

@angelo_zinna

Angelo is a writer and photographer based in Florence, Italy. Angelo wrote the Estonia and Helsinki chapters.

TANYA KEISHA/SHUTTERSTOCK ©

The high, pine-covered **Bālta Kāpa** (White Dune, p188) in Saulkrasti – with the view of a dark meandering river cutting through the golden sands on its way to the sea – is what I consider to be the essence of the Baltic experience. I can never get enough of it, so I keep coming here again and again.

Leonid Ragozin

@leonidragozin

Leonid is a Rīga-based journalist mostly covering political subjects; he has co-authored a book about the Russo-Ukrainian war. Leonid wrote the Latvia chapter.

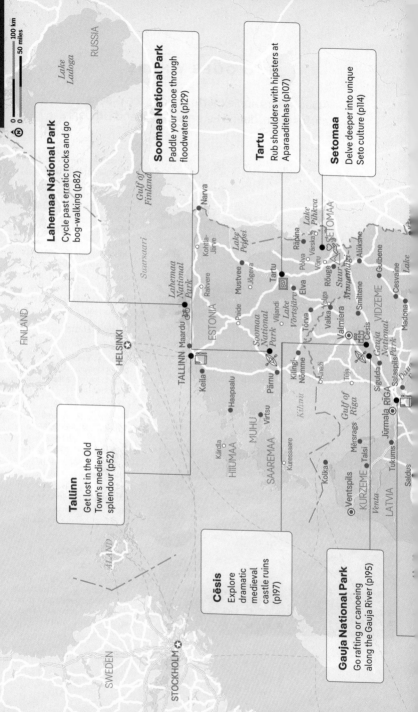

Lahemaa National Park
Cycle past erratic rocks and go bog-walking (p82)

Soomaa National Park
Paddle your canoe through floodwaters (p129)

Tartu
Rub shoulders with hipsters at Aparaaditehas (p107)

Setomaa
Delve deeper into unique Seto culture (p114)

Tallinn
Get lost in the Old Town's medieval splendour (p52)

Cēsis
Explore dramatic medieval castle ruins (p197)

Gauja National Park
Go rafting or canoeing along the Gauja River (p195)

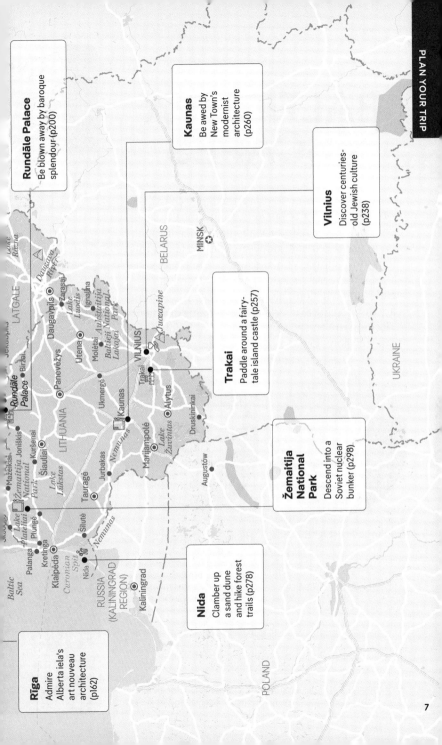

Rundāle Palace
Be blown away by baroque splendour (p200)

Kaunas
Be awed by New Town's modernist architecture (p260)

Vilnius
Discover centuries-old Jewish culture (p238)

Trakai
Paddle around a fairy-tale island castle (p257)

Žemaitija National Park
Descend into a Soviet nuclear bunker (p298)

Nida
Clamber up a sand dune and hike forest trails (p278)

Rīga
Admire Alberta iela's art nouveau architecture (p162)

LATGALE

Lake Rāzna

Daugava River

Daugavpils
Zarasai
Lake Luodis
Ignalina
Aukštaitija National Park
Utena
Molėtai
Lakajai
Biržai
Panevėžys
Rundāle Palace
Ukmergė
LITHUANIA
Kaunas
Nemunas
VILNIUS
Trakai
Alytus
Marijampolė
Lake Žaurintus
Druskininkai
Kuršėnai
Šiauliai
Joniškis
Mažeikiai
Žemaitija National Park
Lake Lūkstas
Jurbakas
Tauragė
Šilutė
Plungė
Palanga
Kretinga
Klaipėda
Curonian Spit
Nida
Lake Plateliai
Baltic Sea

BELARUS

MINSK

UKRAINE

RUSSIA (KALININGRAD REGION)
Kaliningrad

Augustów

POLAND

7

BALTIC SEA ESCAPES

Stretching for over 2000km, the Baltic coastline offers all manner of pursuits, from sunbathing at sedate resorts such as Pärnu and glitzier Jūrmala and playing arcade games in brash Palanga, to enjoying solitude on windswept Cape Kolka and searching for a secluded patch of white sand to call your own along Lithuania's coast. Kitesurfers are discovering Svencelė in the Nemunas Delta or flocking to Ventspils and other Latvian hotspots, while offshore, Estonia's many islands provide extra adventures.

For the Love of Lighthouses

Of the Baltic coast's many lighthouses, Estonia has the most; and the world's oldest continuously operated lighthouse is in Kõpu, Hiiumaa. Some, like Viirelaid, offer overnight stays.

Hiking the Coastal Route

Divided into day-sized chunks, easily accessible by public transport, the 1419km-long Coastal Trail spans the Baltic coastline, allowing you to explore its varied ecosystems.

Baltic Beach Etiquette

Pay attention to beach signs along the Baltic coast: some beaches are official naturist hotspots, while others are women-only, men-only or regular beaches.

BEST COASTAL EXPERIENCES

Base yourself in the fishing village of ❶ **Nida** (p278), clamber up the giant Parnidis Dune and seek solitude along pine-forest trails.

Take kitesurfing lessons, then spend a week or two catching the wind at Lithuania's new kitesurfing hotspot of ❷ **Svencelė** (p291).

Spend lazy days on the beach and go for sunset walks along Latvia's stunning pine-covered dunes in ❸ **Saulkrasti** (p188).

Live it up at ❹ **Jūrmala** (p180), the Baltics' posh beachside spa resort with numerous restaurants and swathes of white sand.

Grab a bicycle and take to the quiet seaside trails of ❺ **Kihnu Island** (p130) with its long beaches and traditional Estonian culture.

ANDREI NEKRASSOV/SHUTTERSTOCK ©

Haapsalu Castle (p132), Estonia

FANTASTIC FORTS

Dotting the countryside and the coast, the Baltics' castles and fortresses testify to centuries of conflict withcompeting civilisations. Estonia weathered invasions by Danes, Swedes and the Germanic Teutonic Order. The latter, along with the Russian Empire, also accosted Latvia, along with the Polish-Lithuanian Commonwealth.

Oldest Castle

Tallinn's Toompea Castle – the Baltics' oldest – was originally built of wood in the 10th century, and rebuilt in stone in 1227 by the German Knights of the Sword.

Island Redoubt

Its seemingly impregnable island location in the middle of Lake Galvė notwithstanding, Trakai Castle was damaged during wars with Muscovy in the 17th century.

BEST CASTLE EXPERIENCES

Paddle around the fairy-tale red-brick castle on an island within a lake in ❶ **Trakai** (p257), and explore its museums.

Head into the atmospherically lit tunnels of ❷ **Klaipėda Castle** (p290), built by the Teutonic Order in the 13th century, for historical exhibits.

Get two fortresses in one in ❸ **Cēsis** (p198): dramatic ruins left from medieval crusaders and an elegant home of their 18th-century descendants.

Admire the turreted tower of ❹ **Haapsalu Castle** (p132), then venture into its eerie tunnels to check out medieval weaponry.

Visit ❺ **Narva Castle** (p90), a chess match writ large, facing off with its Russian counterpart across the river.

QUIRKY MUSEUMS

Every Baltic town worth its salt has a museum or two, with the capitals – Vilnius, Rīga and Tallinn – featuring the lion's share of excellent repositories of history, art and more. Some are futuristic and combine striking architectural design with wonderfully interactive content, while others pay tribute to quirkier interests, from devils and amber to vintage gas masks.

LEFT: KALUM/SHUTTERSTOCK ©; RIGHT: LN TEAM/SHUTTERSTOCK ©

Amber Museum

Nida's Mizgiris Amber Museum is the region's best, with an engaging voiceover, unparalleled collection of amber pieces and plenty of interactive elements.

Houses of Horror

Each of the Baltic capitals has a museum devoted to occupation – essential for learning about Soviet repressions and mass deportations suffered by each respective country.

Cool for Kids

Across the Baltics, outdoor ethnographic museums preserve old homesteads, frequently have petting zoos and offer kid-friendly, hands-on farming experiences.

BEST QUIRKY MUSEUM EXPERIENCES

Peruse the carvings, masks and other images of Lucifer throughout world mythologies at Kaunas' ❶ **Museum of Devils** (p271).

Dine on 17th-century Latvian recipes at ❷ **Hoijeres Krogs** (p217), a historic inn that once hosted a tsar now turned into a museum.

Don a vintage gas mask and peruse KGB murder weapons, replica atomic bombs and Soviet memorabilia at Lithuania's ❸ **Atomic Bunker** (p264).

Visit the room of whispering heads at the ❹ **Kumu Museum** (p68), a futuristic edifice housing Estonia's best contemporary art collection.

Learn about Estonia's seafaring heritage in the Bond-villain-lair-like space of ❺ **Seaplane Harbour** (p74); don't miss the ice yachts!

A DESIGN FOR LIFE

There are few corners of Europe where you'll find such a wealth of design and architectural styles. Soviet brutalist constructions aside, craft-rich Lithuania has long leant towards elaborate baroque, Gothic and Renaissance embellishments, and has a centuries-old tradition of woodcarving and ironwork. Besides its own baroque and Renaissance masterpieces, Latvia is renowned for the art nouveau of its capital, while Estonia combines contemporary, modernist design with an eco-conscious, sustainable approach to infrastructure and public spaces.

Art Nouveau Explosion

Latvia's economic prosperity in the late 19th century coincided with the construction of new buildings in Rīga according to Western Europe's art nouveau trend.

Contemporary Glass

Estonia's glass art surged since the establishment of Tallinn's first furnace in 1991. Merle Kannus and Maret Sarapu hold their own internationally with their unconventional creations.

Kaunas: Creative City

As of 2023, Kaunas has been recognised as one of UNESCO's Design Cities for its modernist architecture that reflects the optimism of the interwar period.

⑤

②

④

③ ①

BEST ARCHITECTURE EXPERIENCES

Wander the streets of
❶ **Vilnius' Old Town** (p238),
with its Renaissance buildings,
baroque domes and pillars,
and flamboyant Gothic church
spires.

Sip craft beer at
❷ **Aparaaditehas** (p107),
Tartu's Soviet-era industrial
complex turned into a hip,
stencil- and graffiti-covered
cultural hub.

Step inside Kaunas' ❸ **Art
Deco Museum** (p268) to
admire a beautifully recreated
example of an interwar
apartment, complete with
vintage furniture.

Stroll down Rīga's ❹ **Alberta
iela** (p167), an art nouveau
gem of a street filled with
whimsical ornaments, Greek
drama masks and sphinxes.

Get lost amid the serpentine
cobbled lanes, mighty
medieval walls and sturdy
defence towers of ❺ **Tallinn's
Old Town** (p53).

Palmse Manor (p84), Estonia

MIND YOUR MANORS

When they weren't at war with one another, the Baltic aristocracy preferred to spend their time in comfortable country piles, dating from the 15th to early 20th centuries. There are around 400 manors and palaces in Estonia; 570 in Lithuania, and over a thousand in Latvia. Some have been turned into museums, others into sumptuous historical hotels.

Bartolomeo Rastrelli's Legacy

If you've been to St Petersburg's Winter Palace, you might do a double take at Latvia's sumptuous Rundāle Palace, designed by the same Italian architect.

Manor Stays

It's easiest to live like nobility in Latvia and Estonia, where dozens of manors have either been converted into hotels or are available to rent.

BEST PALACE EXPERIENCES

Marvel at devils, witches and other elaborate Mardi Gras masks from the Samogitia region inside the barn at ❶ **Plateliai Manor** (p301).

Admire traditional woodcarvings, metalwork and contemporary art within the 19th-century ❷ **Oginski Palace** (p299) in Plungė.

Be awed by the baroque splendour to rival St Petersburg, built for the greatest adventurist in Russian imperial history at ❸ **Rundāle Palace** (p200).

Live like a noble at Estonia's ❹ **Alatskivi Manor** (p112), a neo-Gothic creation rebuilt in the 19th century to resemble Scotland's Balmoral Castle.

Explore ❺ **Palmse Manor** (p84) in Estonia's Lahemaa National Park, fully restored along with its many outbuildings.

ELVIS ANTSON/SHUTTERSTOCK ©

LEGACY OF COMMUNISM

The Baltics have seen more than their share of bloodshed, most recently during WWII that saw the Nazi extermination of most of the region's Jewish population (often with active local participation in the atrocities). After 1945, when the three countries were forcibly incorporated into the USSR, political repression in the form of imprisonment, deportations and executions followed.

Forest Brotherhood

Lithuania offered robust anti-Soviet resistance in the form of its partisan movement, the Forest Brotherhood, from 1944 to 1953.

Open Prisons

Some of the former communist prisons are open to visitors. Experience life as a Soviet detainee overnight in Karosta or Liepāja, or tour Vilnius' Lukiškės Prison.

Holocaust Sites

Lithuania's countryside is dotted with over 250 *žydų genocidas* signs, pointing to modest memorials that commemorate the execution sites of Jewish communities in WWII.

BEST HISTORY & WAR EXPERIENCES

Wander amid statues of Lenin and Stalin with martial music on the loudspeakers at the ❶ **Grūtas Park** (p314) near Druskininkai.

Descend into the former bunkers of the first Soviet nuclear silo and current ❷ **Cold War Museum** (p301) in Žemaitija National Park.

Pay your respects at ❸ **Salaspils Memorial** (p179), a piece of Soviet brutalism commemorating the inmates of a Nazi concentration camp in Latvia.

Admire the concrete avenues of Tallinn's ❹ **Maarjamäe Soviet Memorial Complex** (p72) with its monuments to fallen Estonian soldiers.

Learn about WWII battles at the former Soviet border post turned ❺ **Hiiumaa Military Museum** (p136) in Estonia.

15

WILD THINGS

Back in the early 1970s, Estonia, Latvia and Lithuania took a lead on their fellow Soviet Republics in establishing the first national parks in the USSR. The 15 national parks (plus additional regional parks) in the Baltics, comprising pine, spruce and birch forests, are home to big beasts such as brown bears, lynxes, wolves, elk and wild boars. Extensive marshlands, coastal sand dunes, countless lakes and rocky seashores provide vital habitats for wading birds and seabirds.

Kings of the Forest

While brown bears, lynxes and wolves are found across the Baltics, the greatest numbers live in Estonia thanks to its extensive forest cover (52% of the country).

Horned & Hooved Creatures

Elk sightings are fairly common in the Baltics, while roe deer and wild boar tend to be shyer. To spot bison, head for Lithuania's Pašiliai Forest.

Twitcher Features

Its key location makes the Baltics a birding paradise. Spot 270 of Lithuania's 300 species in the Nemunas Delta Regional Park during spring and autumn.

❺
❷
❹
❶   ❸

BEST NATIONAL PARK EXPERIENCES

Spot elk and wild boars in the pine forests of Lithuania's ❶ **Curonian Spit** (p278), and bring your binoculars for close-ups of black cormorants.

Paddle your canoe through the floodwaters of ❷ **Soomaa National Park** (p129) during the 'fifth season' and spot numerous waterfowl.

Wander the trails through pine forest, forage for berries, or take to the lakes in a canoe or paddleboard in ❸ **Aukštaitija National Park** (p304).

Go rafting down the Gauja River that meanders past enchanting forested hills in ❹ **Gauja National Park** (p195).

Cycle the forested trails past giant erratic rocks, go bog-walking, and spot bears and boars in ❺ **Lahemaa National Park** (p82).

AN ETHNIC MELTING POT

With the ebb and flow of country borders, it's little surprise that the Baltics have long been home to assorted ethnic and religious minorities. The largest and most prominent of those was the thriving Jewish communities that had contributed to Baltic life for centuries before WWII, though after the war only a shadow remained. Besides a recent Jewish revival, the Karaim, the Seto and Old Believers are among those that make up the Baltics' rich cultural tapestry.

The Karaim

A Turkic-Judaic sect adhering to the Law of Moses and originating in Baghdad, the Karaim were brought to Lithuania in the 1400s; only about 200 remain.

The Seto

A distinct religious and linguistic minority whose language belongs to the Finnic group, the Seto number around 12,500; their ancestral lands are in Estonia's Setomaa region.

Old Believers

Splitting from the Russian Orthodox Church in the 17th century and facing persecution, Eastern Orthodox Christians found refuge in Estonia and Latvia.

Choral Synagogue (p170), Latvia

⑤

④

❶

❷❸

BEST MINORITY EXPERIENCES

Learn the stories of Russian religious dissidents at the carefully restored ❶ **Slutiški Old Believers' Farmstead** (p226) in the far corner of Latvia.

Taste *kibinai*, then trace Karaim ancestry, and peruse traditional dress, photographs and everyday items at Trakai's ❷ **Karaite Ethnographic Museum** (p258).

Delve deep into Lithuania's centuries-old Jewish history and culture using multimedia expositions at the evocative ❸ **Samuel Bak Museum** (p249) in Vilnius.

Pay your respects at the ruins of Rīga's ❹ **Choral Synagogue** (p170), burned down by Latvian Nazi collaborators with the congregation still inside.

Hear the Seto language, taste the distinctive local cuisine and delve into Seto culture in ❺ **Setomaa** (p114), in Estonia's southeastern corner.

COUNTRIES & CITIES

Find the places that tick all your boxes.

Helsinki

UNIQUE BY DESIGN

The Baltics' northern neighbour, scenic Helsinki beckons with its striking archipelago setting on the Gulf of Finland. Its mixture of contemporary architecture, design shops, waterside saunas and bars, and plethora of art galleries make it a appealing city-break destination. You can arrive in style by taking the two-hour ferry from Tallin.

p144

HELSINKI (FINLAND)
p144

Estonia
p47

Estonia

A CULTURAL CROSSROADS

Nordic-leaning design and industrial warehouses repurposed as art galleries and microbreweries meet mighty medieval walls and labyrinthine alleyways in Tallinn, Estonia's forward-looking capital. Further afield, the university town of Tartu buzzes with student life, and Pärnu offers beachside relaxation, while the islands of Saaremaa and Hiimaa are best explored on two wheels.

p47

Latvia
p157

Latvia

DUNES AND FORESTS

Few countries pack in as much as Latvia. Riga's elaborate art nouveau buildings and its UNESCO-protected Old Town contrast dramatically with gritty, coastal Liepāja's Soviet tenements and lively bar scene. Beyond lie Jūrmala's beach scene, the aristocratic decadence of Rundāle Palace, Sigulda and Cēsis castles and windblown, remote Cape Kolka.

p157

Lithuania
p232

UNSPOILED NATURE
MEETS MILLENNIAL HISTORY

Its countryside dotted with elaborate wooden carvings, Lithuania is more agricultural than its neighbours. Beyond the cobbled streets, art galleries and confection-like churches of Vilnius and the craft-beer bars of Kaunas, its attractions range between Baltic beaches, lakes, forest trails, and cultural and music festivals rooted in its pagan past.

p232

ITINERARIES

Baltic Capitals

Allow: 4 days **Distance:** 697km

Hit the three Baltic capitals, taking in Vilnius' hilltop castle and cobbled Old Town, then crossing rolling countryside and forest to reach Rīga with its zeppelin hangars and art nouveau buildings. Explore Tallinn's beguiling Old Town, ringed by medieval fortifications, then hop on a ferry for a bonus stay in design-forward Helsinki.

①

VILNIUS ⏱ 1 DAY

Start your tour in **Vilnius** (p238), Lithuania's capital. Marvel at the Cathedral Square with its impressive bell tower, take a funicular up Gediminas Hill for lofty views from the castle, detour to the arty breakaway 'republic' of Užupis, and grapple with Lithuania's wartime history at the Museum of Occupations and Freedom Fights. Dine on Lithuanian staples at Etno Dvaras or splurge on a meal at Amandus.

Tallinn (p52), Estonia

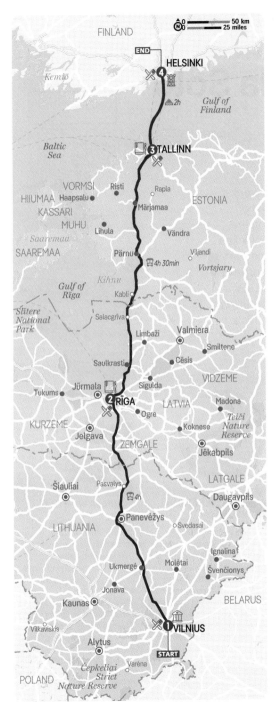

② RĪGA ⏱ 1 DAY

Continue to **Rīga** (p162) and devote the day to exploring Vecrīga (Old Rīga) with its cobbled streets and important buildings such as the Three Brothers. Stop by the Rīga History and Navigation Museum for an overview of Latvia's history, stroll along central Rīga's Alberta iela to admire art nouveau architecture, drink in the bustle at the Central Market and dine at 3 Pavaru.

③ TALLINN ⏱ 1 DAY

Press on to **Tallinn** (p52) and focus your energies on the cobbled narrow lanes of the beautifully preserved medieval Old Town. Ascend a defence tower or two, perhaps visit the Tallinn City Museum, take a bus to Kadriorg Park for an immersion in Estonian art at the Kumu Museum, then head for Telliskivi Creative City for craft beer and street art. Dine at refined NOA.

④ HELSINKI ⏱ 1 DAY

Take a ferry to **Helsinki** (p144), then fortify yourself with coffee near the market square before packing a picnic and hopping on another ferry to explore the UNESCO-protected fortress of Suomenlinna. Then make your way to the city's world-famous Design District, before sweating it out at the legendary Kotiharjun Sauna. Finish off with classic Finnish cuisine at Ravintola Nokka.

MISTERVLAD/SHUTTERSTOCK ©

ITINERARIES

Lithuania Solo

Allow: 7 days **Distance**: 843km

You can pack a lot into a week's travel in the southernmost of the Baltic states, including the lively capital and a 'land of lakes' national park, a handsome port town, a beach resort, hiking and cycling Lithuania's unique sliver of dune-covered land jutting into the Baltic Sea, and Lithuania's second city.

❶ VILNIUS ⏱ 2 DAYS

Start in the capital, **Vilnius** (p238). Stroll the cobbled streets of Old Town, delve into millennia-old history at the Palace of the Grand Dukes of Lithuania and visit the MO Museum for an infusion of contemporary art. Meet the renegade artists' 'republic' of Užupis, and dine on creative cuisine at Amandus.

⚓ *Detour: Head to scenic Trakai (p257), and explore its picturesque island castle.*
⏱ *4 hours*

❷ AUKŠTAITIJA NATIONAL PARK ⏱ 1 DAY

Spend a day in the densely forested **Aukštaitija National Park** (p304), paddleboarding or canoeing on lakes near Palūšė, hiking or cycling the myriad trails through fragrant pine forest, or summiting Ladakalnis Hill for scenic, lake-filled panoramas. Poke your head into the Ancient Beekeeping Museum to check out the vintage tree-trunk beehives, and dine on traditional Lithuanian fare at Romnesa Ignalina.

❸ KLAIPĖDA W ⏱ 1 DAY

Head for the appealing port city of **Klaipėda** (p289), with its enchanting historical centre, Germanic half-timbered buildings, an absorbing castle museum and a large park dotted with contemporary sculptures.
⚓ *Detour: For some classic Baltic beachtime fun, hit nearby Palanga (p290), sun yourself on its white sand, play arcade games along its pedestrian strip, and admire the 'Baltic gold' at the Amber Museum.*
⏱ *5 hours*

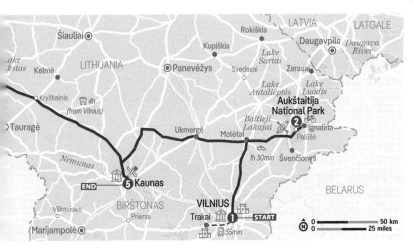

4 CURONIAN SPIT ⏱ 2 DAYS

Base yourself in Nida, the prettiest of the **Curonian Spit**'s (p278) fishing villages. Summit the giant Parnidis Dune to admire the Sahara-like landscape, visit the superb Mizgiris Amber Museum, cycle to Juodkrantė, and peruse wooden sculptures of witches and devils along Juodkrantė's Witches' Hill. Alternatively, spend two days walking some of the Coastal Trail's most scenic sections and chow down on smoked eel.

5 KAUNAS ⏱ 1 DAY

Finish in Lithuania's second city, **Kaunas** (p260), exploring the cobbled Old Town with its quirky museums devoted to medicine, basketball and traditional music. Don't miss New Town's UNESCO-protected modernist architecture, two superb apartments decked out with interwar furnishings, a brutalist church, and museums devoted to Lithuania's best-known artist, devils and a Japanese diplomat who saved Jews, as well as the city's best dining.

Luscious Latvia

Allow: 6 days **Distance**: 585km

A week in Latvia takes in diverse attractions beyond the show-stealing capital: from the country's premier beach resort, a buzzy port city with more Baltic beaches and a historic town with an impressive waterfall, to a former seat of aristocratic decadence, a medieval castle and epic outdoor adventures in Latvia's top national park.

❶ RĪGA ○ 2 DAYS

Begin in buzzy **Rīga** (p162), strolling around Old Rīga and its medieval merchants' residences. Learn about Latvia's struggle for independence at the Museum of the Barricades of 1991, admire the art nouveau architecture along Alberta iela and go shopping inside WWII zeppelin hangars. *↝ Detour: Head to the magnificent **Rundāle Palace** (p200), designed by Italian architect Bartolomeo Rastrelli, famous for St Petersburg's Winter Palace.* ○ *5 hours*

❷ JŪRMALA ○ 1 DAY

Centred on the affluent townships of Majori and Dzintari, strung along a beautiful white-sand beach, **Jūrmala** (p180) is Latvia's top beach resort to 'sea' and be seen. Check out its genteel 19th-century wooden villas, stroll along its 24km-long stretch of sand, attend a fish-smoking demonstration at the Jūrmala Open-Air Museum, or hit the walking trails through the forest and dunes of Ragakāpa Nature Park.

❸ KULDĪGA ○ 1 DAY

Its Old Town wonderfully preserved, lovely **Kuldīga** (p204) has venerable historical buildings including 17th-century gems such as the Old Town Hall, Old Wooden House and Duke Jacob's Pharmacy. The town is also renowned for 249m-wide Ventas Rumba, allegedly Europe's widest waterfall – a spectacular sight, particularly in spring, when you can watch *vimba* (migratory bream) jump the falls en route from the Baltic.

FROM LEFT: LN TEAM/SHUTTERSTOCK ©, DANIEL BOND/SHUTTERSTOCK ©, TATJANA SIKA/SHUTTERSTOCK ©

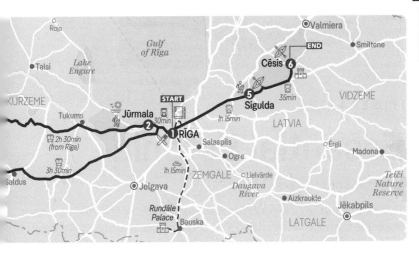

④ LIEPĀJA ⏱ 1 DAY

Throughout its centuries of existence, gritty **Liepāja** (p216) has worn many hats: major trade centre, vast naval port, Soviet military base. Its industrial heritage is still visible in its red-brick warehouses, though many have been repurposed as live-music venues and lively bars. Immerse yourself in the extremes of Soviet experience at the Karosta Prison, and sun yourself on some of the Baltics' most attractive beaches.

⑤ SIGULDA ⏱ 1 DAY

The spread-out gateway town to the Gauja Valley, **Sigulda** (p190) is a terrific springboard for hiking the forested trails of Gauja National Park, canoeing or floating down the slow-flowing Gauja River, or engaging in more adrenaline-packed activities: hurtling down a bobsleigh track or soaring above a giant fan in a skydiving simulator. The scenically situated, centuries-old Sigulda and Turaida castles also clamour for your attention.

⑥ CĒSIS ⏱ 1 DAY

Another good base for exploring Gauja National Park, cobbled-laned **Cēsis** (p197) is famed for its two castles. Atmospheric dark-stone towers are all that's left of a 13th-century Livonian stronghold that was sacked by Ivan the Terrible. Nearby, peruse the 18th-century castle-manor with fin-de-siècle interiors or take to the Gauja River to paddle the scenic stretch between Cēsis and Līgatne, lined with sandstone outcrops and forest.

Tallinn (p52), Estonia

ITINERARIES

Essential Estonia

Allow: 7 days **Distance**: 641km

This week-long jaunt around Estonia proudly showcases the country's diversity, from the wonderland that is Tallinn and the university town of Tartu to Estonia's biggest national park, the genteel beach resort town of Pärnu, one of the country's many islands, evocative castle ruins, and remote villages with a fascinating minority culture.

➊ TALLINN ⏱ 2 DAYS

Kick off in **Tallinn** (p52), with its UNESCO-listed Old Town – one of Europe's best-preserved walled cities, with its cobbled lanes, merchants' houses, defence towers, museums and dining scene. Give yourself another day for attractions further out: Kumu Museum, Kadriorg Palace, and Telliskivi Creative City complete with craft-beer bars and a photography museum.

➋ LAHEMAA ⏱ 1 DAY

Spend a day cycling around **Lahemaa** (p82), Estonia's largest national park, featuring rolling countryside, an indented coastline, and pine-fresh hinterland encompassing forest, lakes, erratic boulders, rivers and peat bogs, and areas of historical and cultural interest. Visit the centuries-old Palmse Manor and Sagadi Manor, and break for lunch in Võsu, with its long beach and summertime bars.

➌ TARTU ⏱ 1 DAY

Head south to Estonia's intellectual capital and premier university town – not to mention the 2024 European Capital of Culture. **Tartu**'s (p98) charms include the handsome city centre, lined with 18th-century buildings, superb museums, atmospheric 19th-century Supilinn neighbourhood, and Aparaaditehas – a former Soviet complex turned hip dining, shopping and cultural hub.

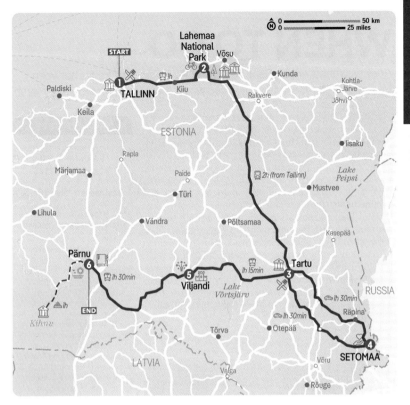

❹ SETOMAA ⏱1 DAY

You'll want some wheels to explore **Setomaa** (p114), Estonia's southeastern corner that's culturally distinct from the rest of the country and home to around 15,000 Seto people, with their own language and unique traditional dress, a highly local cuisine and cluster-like villages. A good place to kick off your exploration is Värska, with therapeutic minerals springs, Farm Museum and an excellent restaurant.

❺ VILJANDI ⏱1 DAY

One of Estonia's most appealing towns, **Viljandi** (p110) overlooks a picturesque valley with the teardrop-shaped Lake Võrtsjärv at its heart. It's centred on the atmospheric 13th-century castle built by the Teutonic Order, aka the Brothers of the Sword. Viljandi is ideal for time-travelling rambles and is particularly lively in late July when it hosts the Viljandi Folk Music Festival – Estonia's biggest annual music festival.

❻ PÄRNU ⏱1 DAY

Turn-of-the-20th-century villas dot the streets of **Pärnu** (p123), Estonia's premier seaside resort. In Soviet times, it was synonymous with rest, rejuvenation and healing mud treatments, and its golden beach still attract both local families and holidaymakers from abroad. *◢ Detour: Take a boat to **Kihnu island** (p130), a living museum of Estonian culture and long, quiet beaches. ⏱4 hours*

WHEN TO GO

Answer: whenever you want. You can enjoy summery pursuits between May and September and snow-filled winter thrills from December to March.

The Baltics' mild, sunny summers, long days, beautiful beaches, water sports on the Baltic Sea and numerous lakes, and forest trails leading to bilberry and wildwstrawberry patches are just some of the reasons to visit Estonia, Latvia and Lithuania during the warmer months. Beach-hopping is on the agenda along the Curonian Spit, Palanga, Jūrmala, Pärnu and other Baltic Sea resorts, and summer is also the ideal time for hiking the long-distance Coastal Trail and Forest Trail (as is late spring and early autumn). While the warmer months are also busiest when it comes to music and other festivals, there's something to celebrate in the Baltics year-round. Inland, the continental climate requires layers and a raincoat if travelling outside the winter months, and plenty of warm gear in wintertime. Winter brings its own pleasures, from a plethora of snow sports to lively Christmas markets.

⊕ I LIVE HERE

TALLIN FOR ALL SEASONS

Liisi Rannast-Kask is Head of Collections at Tallinn's Vabamu Museum of Occupations and Freedom.

I love Tallinn's beaches not only during the summer but also for the pleasures of winter swimming. During the colder months, my husband and I enjoy Telliskivi Creative City with its buzzy cafes, bars and events. A great thing about Tallinn is how easy it is to enjoy nature: in summer, we take our daughter berrying on Aegna island; in autumn, I hike on the Paljassaare Peninsula to watch birds or enjoy the silence of Nõmme bog.

WHITE NIGHTS, DARK NIGHTS

The Baltics' latitude means up to 18½ hours of daylight in June and long evenings of pearlescent light during summer. Conversely, winter brings ample darkness, with the sun setting as early as 3.20pm in Tallinn in December.

Tallinn (p52), Estonia

Weather through the year

JANUARY	FEBRUARY	MARCH	APRIL	MAY	JUNE
Average daytime max: **-4°C (25°F)**	Average daytime max: **-5°C (24°F)**	Average daytime max: **1°C (33°F)**	Average daytime max: **5°C (41°F)**	Average daytime max: **12°C (53°F)**	Average daytime max: **16°C (60°F)**
Days of rainfall: **16**	Days of rainfall: **14**	Days of rainfall: **12**	Days of rainfall: **10**	Days of rainfall: **11**	Days of rainfall: **12**

COLD WINTERS, SNOWY DAYS

The coldest month in the Baltic states is January, when average daily temperatures hover around 0°C (32°F) and have been known to plummet as low as -30°C (–22°F) inland. January is also the snowiest month, with average snowfall of 23cm.

The Baltics' Biggest Festivals

Kaziukas Crafts Fair (p245) Vilnius's biggest bash takes over the medieval streets and squares, with tens of thousands of attendees, artisans from all over Lithuania and beyond, and music, dance and food. 🌂 **March**

Midsummer's Eve (p276) All over Estonia, Latvia and Lithuania, it's celebrated in a big way, with huge bonfires lit across the countryside and revellers in traditional dress looking for love. 🔆 **June**

Summer Sound (p217) Liepāja hosts various festivals all summer long; during this two-day event, rock, hip-hop and electronic music reverberate off the dunes near the beach. 🔆 **August**

Viljandi Folk Music Festival (p110) Estonia's largest music festival and one of Europe's largest folk fests attracts 20,000 music fans with an impressive international lineup spread over 100 mini-concerts in four days. 🔆 **July**

Quirky Festivals

Shrove Tuesday (Mardi Gras) (p276) In the villages of Samogitia, Lithuania, local revellers dress up in traditional costume and wooden masks depicting devils and other folk-tale characters, and go door to door with musicians to chase away the winter darkness. 🌂 **February**

Treski Music and Inspiration Festival (p117) This new alternative festival in Setomaa combines African rhythms and

bands across four stages with ice baths and the Wim Hof Method instruction. 🔆 **August**

MJR Alternative Music Festival (p271) Attracting 5000 to 6000 people per year to an island near Zarasai, 'Mėnuo Juodaragis' celebrates Lithuania's pagan roots and features alternative and experimental music, as well as historical re-enactments and artisan demonstrations. 🔆 **August**

Palanga (p290), Lithuania

FEELING HOT, HOT, HOT

Summers in the Baltic states are largely sunny and mild (on the coast) and hotter inland, with Lithuania hitting record highs of up to 36°C (97°F) on some days. The Baltic Sea is warmest in July with temperatures of up to 20°C (68°F).

JULY	AUGUST	SEPTEMBER	OCTOBER	NOVEMBER	DECEMBER
Average daytime max: **17°C (63°F)**	Average daytime max: **17°C (63°F)**	Average daytime max: **12°C (53°F)**	Average daytime max: **8°C (46°F)**	Average daytime max: **3°C (37°F)**	Average daytime max: **-2°C (28°F)**
Days of rainfall: **13**	Days of rainfall: **14**	Days of rainfall: **14**	Days of rainfall: **16**	Days of rainfall: **16**	Days of rainfall: **17**

LEFT: ANASTASIA SOTCHENKO/SHUTTERSTOCK ©; COLLECTION CHRISTOPHEL/ALAMY STOCK PHOTO ©

Gauja National Park (p195)

GET PREPARED FOR ESTONIA, LATVIA & LITHUANIA

Useful things to load in your bag, your ears and your brain

Clothes

Layers As locals say, 'there's no such thing as bad weather, just bad clothing'. Bring a sweater and a waterproof jacket if travelling during any season, since even in summer you might face downpours and cool nights. For winter travel, bring thermal underlayers and a warm coat.
Footwear Waterproof snow boots are essential in winter; the rest of the time, trainers, sandals and other practical footwear will do. Estonians, Latvians and Lithuanians dress up to go out, so pack a pair of dress shoes or high heels, but watch your step on the cobblestones in the latter!
Swimwear You'll want to pack swimming gear and a quick-drying towel to take

Manners

A reserved demeanour is common across the Baltics, but people become more effusive as you get to know them.

Inviting people home for dinner is widespread, and the cooking often eclipses the restaurant scene.

Sensitive conversation topics include the active participation by Lithuanian and Latvian civilians in Nazi atrocities, and criticism of anti-USSR war heroes.

advantage of the Baltic coastline's white-sand beaches as well as numerous lakes, plus saunas found in many Estonian hotels and holiday apartments.

📖 READ

Silva Rerum (Kristina Sabaliauskaitė; 2008) Four-part historical novel about the Grand Duchy of Lithuania.

The Man Who Spoke Snakish (Andrus Kivirähk; 2007) This Estonian story speaks of the country's relationship with nature.

Salt to the Sea (Ruta Sepetys; 2016) This novel touches on painful episodes in Lithuanian history by exploring WWII and its aftermath.

Touched by Eternity (Aleksandrs Čaks; 2016) Ballads dedicated to the riflemen who fought in wars and stood at the heart of Latvian independence.

Words

Estonian:
Tere (te-rre) – 'hello'
Jah (yah) – 'yes'
Ei (ay) – 'no'
Tänan (ta-nahn) – 'thank you'
Palun (pah-lun) – 'you're welcome'
Vabandage (vah-bahn-dah-ge) – 'excuse me' (if you're trying to squeeze past people) or 'sorry' (if you bump into someone)
Appi! (ahp-pi) – 'Help!'

Latvian:
Sveiks/Svelka (svayks/svay-kuh) – 'hello' (the former if you're male, the latter if you're female)
Jā (yah) – 'yes'
Nē (neh) – 'no'
Lūdzu (loo-dzu) – 'please'
Paldies (puhl-deas) – 'thank you'
Nav par ko (naav pahr koh) – 'you're welcome'

Atvainojiet (uht-vai-naw-yeat) – 'excuse me'
Piedodiet (pea-doad-eat) – 'I'm sorry' (if you've bumped into someone)
Palīgā! (puh-lee-gah) – 'Help!'

Lithuanian:
Sveiki (svay-ki) – 'hello'
Taip (tayp) – 'yes'
Ne (neh) – 'no'
Prašau (prah-show) – 'please'
Dėkoju (deh-kaw-yu) – 'thank you'
Prašom (pra-shom) – 'you're welcome'
Atsiprašau (aht-si-prah-show) – 'excuse me'
Atleiskite (aht-lays-ki-teh) – 'I'm sorry' (if you've bumped into someone)
Gelbėkite! (gal-beh-ki-teh) – 'Help!'

📺 WATCH

Vanishing Waves (pictured, Kristina Buožytė; 2012) A scientist connects with a comatose young woman's subconscious.

Whisper of Sin (Algimantas Puipa; 2007) A suicidal woman confesses love for a priest.

Smoke Sauna Sisterhood (Anna Hints; 2023) The Tartu-born director celebrates southern Estonia's traditional saunas.

Four White Shirts (Rolands Kalniņš; 1967) A rock band tries to bypass Soviet censorship.

Is It Easy to Be Young? (Juris Podnieks; 1986) Documentary about the last Soviet generation trying to break out from the totalitarian prison.

🎧 LISTEN

Klakokancios Kanklės/ Wandering Zithers (Agota Zdanavičiūtė; 2021) Eleven Lithuanian musicians utilising the traditional *kanklė* (zither) in their music.

Dzeguses Balss (The Menuets; 1996) Top album by a band that's Latvia's Beatles and Jefferson Airplane, all in one.

Warriors of Thunder (Thundertale; 2009) Fine example of Lithuania's power-metal/folk-metal genre by the Kaunas-based band.

Lätsi Pitto (Zetod; 2022) Estonian folk band blending traditional and contemporary sound in tribute to the musical heritage of their native Setomaa.

CHATHAM172/SHUTTERSTOCK ©

Traditional Lithuanian dishes

THE FOOD SCENE

From belly-warming stews and dumplings to globally inspired fine dining, the Baltics' food scene has something for everyone.

Did someone say 'stodge'? Baltic gastronomy has its roots planted firmly in the land, with livestock and game forming the basis of a hearty diet that developed to sustain bodies performing hard rural labour. The seasons have traditionally played a crucial part in Baltic cuisine, with potatoes, rich stews, and dumplings with myriad different fillings, plus all manner of preserves (jams, dried mushrooms) sustaining the Baltic population during the long, cold winters; vitamin-starved palates embracing all manner of greens in springtime; summer feasts of fruit and forest berries; and autumn foraging for mushrooms.

These days, there's a lot more to the Baltic repertoire than hearty home cooking. Refined restaurants in the big cities champion inno-

vative dishes that transform seasonal ingredients into new forms, while a thriving international food scene spans the globe, from the Caucasus to Japan by way of India and South America. Speciality coffee shops and craft-beer bars are popping up like mushrooms in the rain, replacing hard liquour and mass-produced beer as tipples of choice.

The Baltic Pantry

Step inside a Baltic kitchen and you'll typically find a loaf of rye bread, a cupboard full of homemade berry jams, fermented vegetables and dried or pickled mushrooms, and another brimming with grains and pulses: pearl barley, spelt, millet, buckwheat, and all manner of beans. There'll be potatoes and other vegetables and a freezer full of

Best Baltic Dishes	RŪKYTAS UNGURYS	ŠALTIBARŠČIAI	VÜRTSIKILU SUUPISTE	PIRUKAD/ PELMEŅI/ KOLDŪNAI
	The Curonian Lagoon's smoked eel is wonderfully fatty and flavourful.	Lithuania's kefir-based summer cold borscht comes with new potatoes.	Estonia's smoked or pickled sprats, served with rye bread and cheese.	Meat, potatoes, mushrooms or berry dumplings.

wdumplings. In the fridge you'll find some herring, some cuts of meat, offal, eggs and assorted dairy products (butter, mild cheeses, kefir, milk). The spice rack isn't complete without dill, caraway seeds, cinnamon and bay leaves.

Regional Specialities

Fish is a traditional staple of seaside communities, and since smoking, salting and drying fish to get through the winter has been a way of life for centuries, you'll encounter a great wealth of smoked fish along the Baltic coast (particularly Lithuania's Curonian Spit), from mackerel and eel to pikeperch, smelt and bream. Latvians and Lithuanians are prolific beekeepers, with excellent honey for sale in summer months. Until recent years, vegetarians have had to make do with potatoes and vegetable side dishes, but that's changing, with restaurants catering to both vegetarians and vegans in the big cities. Of the three countries, Lithuania is the most offal-loving, while Estonia liberally uses blood in its cooking. Game is widely consumed, particularly in rural areas.

Time for a Drink

All three Baltic countries have a long-standing coffee-drinking tradition, with excellent speciality shops found in all major cities. The craft-beer revolution has found fertile ground particularly in Tallinn and Tartu in Estonia, Rīga and Liepāja in Latvia, and Kaunas, Vilnius, and Panevėžys in Lithuania, with microbreweries specialising in American-style craft brews. On top of that, Lithuania's farmhouse ale-brewing tradition goes back centuries and has been resurrected around Biržai. Latvia and Estonia also have long brewing traditions. Besides high-quality vodka, look out for Lithuania's fruit wines, Latvia's Rīga Black Balsam and Esto-

FOOD & DRINK FESTIVALS

Vilnius Gastronomy Week In early November, restaurants participating in this food festival wow diners with specially created dishes.

Klaipėda Sea Festival Lithuania's biggest seaside bash in July, with street food and stalls selling smoked fish, honey and bread.

Rīga Restaurant Week In March, the capital's top restaurants offer set menus – an excellent deal, especially at high-end establishments.

Carnikava Lamprey Fest August festival dedicated to a slightly monstrous-looking fish that's one of Latvia's top delicacies.

Tallinn Street Food Festival (p75) Each year in June, food trucks cook up international flavours, best enjoyed outdoors.

Tallinn Craft Beer Weekend (p76) For two days in June, local and international breweries serve hundreds of beers in the capital's Kultuurikatel.

Latvian rye bread sandwiches

Tallinn Street Food Festival (p75)

RYE BREAD	BLINY	PELĒKIE ZIRŅI	POTATO PANCAKES
Nutritious, aromatic, wonderfully flavourful rye bread is popular across the Baltics.	All Baltic countries riff on thin crepes with a sweet or savoury filling.	Grey peas cooked with bacon: a traditional Latvian Christmas dish.	Potato pancakes, served with sour cream or stuffed with meat.

Local Specialities

Savoury Dishes

Cepelinai Lithuania's rugby-ball-shaped potato-dough dumplings with assorted fillings.

Šiupinys Pork snout stew with pork tail, trotter, peas and beans is Lithuania's winter warmer.

Smoked fish Hugely popular across all three Baltic countries.

Snacks

Kibinai Mutton-, mushroom- or vegetable-filled pastry from Trakai, Lithuania.

Kiaulės ausis Smoked pigs' ears – beer snack, particularly in Lithuania and Latvia.

Kepta duona Lithuania's deep-fried garlicky bread sticks.

Sweet Treats

Šakotis Lithuania's sweet, spit-roasted batter.

Rupjmaizes kārtojums Latvia's answer to Black Forest cake.

Kama Estonia's toasted barley, rye and wheat flour mixed with kefir, berries and sugar.

Debesmanna Egg whites whipped with chocolate or pureed fruit in Latvia.

Traditional Drinks

Midus Mead, the honey-tinged nobleman's drink.

Kibinai

Rīga Black Balsam Tar-black, 45%-proof concoction with herbs and spices.

Gira/kvass Mildly alcoholic Baltic beverage made from fermented rye bread.

Vana Tallinn Sweet and strong syrupy liqueur.

Rūgušpiens/kefir Fermented super-yogurt.

Dare to Try

Alionių skilandis Lithuania's minced meat smoked in pork bladders.

Vedarai Pig intestines stuffed with mashed potato are a filling Lithuanian staple.

Verivorst Estonia's Christmas sausage, made of pig intestine.

Verikäkk Balls of blood rolled in flour and eggs with bits of pig fat thrown in for taste.

Sült Estonia's jellied pork – an umami-rich, gelatinous treat.

MEALS OF A LIFETIME

Amandus (p255) Lithuania's larder is transformed into off-the-wall creations by the high priest of modern Lithuanian cuisine in Vilnius.

Uoksas (p262) In Kaunas, seasonally changing tasting menus and à la carte dishes make the most of sustainable ingredients from the Baltics.

NOA (p57) Tallinn's renowned fine-dining destination follows the Nordic drive to continuously innovate, with views to match its award-winning dishes.

3 Pavaru (p167) Not just a meal, but a culinary show staged by three celebrity chefs in Rīga's Old Town.

Inara Vanavalgõ Kohvitarõ (p116) The homey cafe of politician turned chef Inara Luigas is dedicated to preserving Estonia's Seto traditions.

THE YEAR IN FOOD

SPRING

Winter stodge is replaced by lighter fare as market stalls burst forth with radishes, beetroot, young nettles, sorrel and other spring greens. Look out for bottles of nutrient-heavy birch sap, sometimes mixed with fruit juices.

SUMMER

Fresh hazelnuts, honey, currants, gooseberries, plums, watermelons, cherries, apricots and chanterelles grace market tables. Lithuania's restaurants serve *šaltibarščiai* (kefir-based borscht).

AUTUMN

Game (deer, hare, wild boar) dishes appear on restaurant menus. Ask a local to show you where best to pick boletus, red pine mushroom, milk cap and other edible fungi. Berry preserves make an appearance.

WINTER

Oven-baked root vegetables and meaty stews are popular. Munch on *cepelinai* and *koldūnai* (dumplings) in Lithuania, *mulgipuder* (porridge) in Estonia and grey peas with bacon and blood sausage in Latvia.

Market, Riga (p162), Latvia

YEVGEN BELICH/SHUTTERSTOCK ©

Curonian Spit (p278), Lithuania

BALTIC TRAILS

The most epic adventure in the Baltics is hiking along the two trails that cut through all three countries – the Coastal Trail and the Forest Trail. Spanning hundreds of kilometres, they traverse majestic dune landscapes and fairy-tale forests, passing by lakes, marshes, quaint villages and vibrant cities.

The Routes

COASTAL TRAIL

The 1419km-long trail begins near the Russian border on the Curonian Spit and leads all the way to Tallinn with detours to Estonian islands. The Gulf of Rīga creates an enormous loop in the middle of an otherwise straightforward meridional route. In Lithuania and Latvia, you'll be mostly walking along pine-covered dunes and wide sandy beaches and an occasional lagoon-type lake. In Estonia, brace for Nordic-type landscapes with granite boulders on the beach and green meadows lining the seafront. The route passes through major coastal cities – Klaipėda, Liepāja, Ventspils, Rīga and Pärnu.

FOREST TRAIL

This trail is longer, at 2141km, and the route is more convoluted, starting at the Polish border and running through western Lithuania and Latvia, then turning east via Gauja National Park towards Lake Peipsi in Estonia. Having reached the Gulf of Finland near the Russian border, it turns sharply to the west and runs along the coast towards Tallinn, thus complementing the Coastal Trail. On the way, it passes through nearly all the main national parks in the three countries and follows the course of major rivers – Nemunas, Abava and Gauja. The route passes through several major cities – Kaunas, Rīga and Tartu – as well as a few small-town gems, such as Kuldīga.

RUSLANSTRELNIK/SHUTTERSTOCK ©

Gauja National Park (p195), Latvia

Hike in the Baltics

Of course, no one expects you to hike for 114 days in a row, which is the estimate for the entire Forest Trail route. Instead, both trails are divided into 10km to 25km sections doable in a day. Consult baltictrails.eu for detailed itineraries. Trailheads in each of the sections are located in proximity to bus or train stations as well as accommodation clusters. If you want to hike just one section to give it a try, you can always chose one that's doable as a day trip out of a capital city, with no overnight on the trail at all. That said, if you are into camping, you'll find dedicated places for pitching tents all along the way.

Greatest Hits

Where to begin? Just go to baltictrails.eu and find the most doable and appealing section of the trails.

If you're in Tallinn, you can get a taste of the trails by walking through the **Viimsi Peninsula** (Forest Trail, section 49). With a bit more time, check out the **North Estonian Klint**, a limestone escarpment on the northern coast (Forest Trail, section 36) or the austere Nordic landscape in the Swedish villages area near **Haapsalu** (Coastal Trail, sections 51 and 52). If in Tartu, you're close to the Forest Trail that runs along **Lake Peipsi**. Consider hiking sections 27 or 28, bracing for onion cakes and smoked fish in Russian Old

Believers' villages. In Rīga, the coast between **Vecāķi** and **Saulkrasti** stations is uniformly beautiful and very easily accessible at any point along the route (Coastal Trail, sections 25 and 26). For a proper forest adventure, catch a morning bus to Līgatne in **Gauja National Park** and trek out of there either towards Sigulda or Cēsis (Forest Trail, sections 5 and 6) – both routes are picturesque.

If you find yourself in Klaipėda, the **Curonian Spit** is an obvious choice. For a sample itinerary out of Nida (p278). In the area of Kaunas or (especially!) Druskininkai, hit the trails in the blueberry- and mushroom-filled forests of **Dzūkija National Park** (Forest Trail, sections 55 and 56).

STEAMY DELIGHTS

A steaming sauna comes as the cherry on the cake after a hard day of hiking in the forest or along the coast. Thankfully, saunas are a crucial part of culture in all three countries and there are plenty on offer. Just look for accommodation options – be it forest lodges or campgrounds – that come with a sauna. These are particularly ubiquitous in Estonia, but you'll find many options in the other two countries as well. The sauna experience in the Baltics includes elements of Finnish and Russian traditions, with twig beating commonly used as a form of massage. Cold beer can be great après sauna, but strong liquor and sauna aren't really compatible.

F-FOCUS BY MATI KOSE/SHUTTERSTOCK ©

Soomaa National Park (p129), Estonia

THE OUTDOORS

With its lakes, extensive coastline, national parks and dense forest, the Baltic states are a playground for land- and water-based fresh-air fiends.

Lapped at by the Baltic Sea, Estonia, Latvia and Lithuania share a coastline hundreds of miles long that attracts kitesurfers, windsurfers, sailors and other water-sports enthusiasts. Inland, paddleboarders, kayakers and canoeists take to the lakes and rivers, while hikers and cyclists can challenge themselves by tackling the long-distance Coastal Trail and Forest Trail, with the latter connecting the national parks of the interior. In winter, cross-country and downhill skiers traverse the landscape, while ice skaters and ice surfers seek their thrills on frozen bodies of water.

Hiking & Cycling

Whether you're a trekker or a day rambler, the Baltics have trails for all hiking abilities, including two long-distance Baltic Trails (p38).

The hiking season is May to October. Shorter hikes are found in Žemaitija and Aukštaitija national parks in Lithuania, Gauja National Park in Latvia and Lahemaa National Park in Estonia. Good bases for exploration include Otepää and Rõuge in Estonia; Valmiera and Cēsis in Latvia; and Lithuania's Nida, Juodkrantė, Visaginas and Ignalina.

Mostly flat, the region offers superb cycling territory besides the Baltic Trails. In Lithuania, take to the cycling trails of the Curonian Spit, the lake-studded Dzūkija National Park and around Lake Plateliai. The forest trails in Aukštaitija National Park and Labanoras Regional Park draw mountain bikers, with fatbikes in Visaginas used for the boggier sections. In Estonia, pedal among the erratic rocks, bays and countryside of

---

Bigger Thrills In The Baltics

BIRDWATCHING
Watch birds pass overhead in spring and early autumn at **Ventės Ragas Ornithological Station** (p294) in the Nemunas Delta.

BLOKARTING & ICE SAILING
Go blokarting (windsurfing on land) along Nida's airstrip or take to the ice of the **Curonian Lagoon** (p278) in winter.

BOG WALKING
Take to the boardwalks above the marsh flora along Lahemaa's **Viru Trail** (p82) to appreciate some of the oldest landscapes in Estonia.

FAMILY ADVENTURES

Wander amid fairy-tale wooden carvings at **Witches' Hill** (p281) in Juodkrantė. **Hike woodland trails** and go paddleboarding in **Aukštaitija National Park** (p304). **Climb a giant sand dune** and build sandcastles on white-sand beaches in **Nida** (p278).

Let the kids loose on the water slides in **Druskininkai** (p312). **Explore historical homesteads** at the **Estonian Open-Air Museum** (p77) west of Tallinn. **Learn about Estonia's early days** at Äksi's Ice Age Centre in **Vooremaa** (p118) and check out

the wildlife at Elistvere Animal Park. **Embark on a slow-motion canoeing** or rafting adventure on the **Gauja** (p196), Latvia's most beautiful river. **Meet a bear**, an elk, or a boar while rambling along the **Līgatne Nature Trails** (p195).

Lahemaa National Park, or try the back roads of Muhu, Saaremaa and Hiiumaa islands. In Latvia, two wheels are the best way to explore Liepāja, Ventspils, Sigulda and Jūrmala, as well as the windswept Cape Kolka, while the Latgale Lakelands trails offer longer adventures.

On the Water

A long coastline, several rivers and countless lakes make the Baltics a fantastic water-sports destination. Persistent breezes on the Curonian Lagoon draw kitesurfers to Lithuania's Svencelė and Palanga, and Pāvilosta in

Latvia. In Lithuania's interior, Aukštaitija National Park is excellent for lake swimming, as well as paddleboarding and canoeing. Other water sports hotspots include Lithuania's Labanoras Regional Park and Dzūkija National Park, as well as Latvia's Latgale Lakelands. Latvia's Gauja and Abava rivers offer days-long paddling routes. In southwest Estonia, canoes, kayaks or traditional *haabjas* (Finno-Ugric log boats) are a superb way to explore Soomaa National Park, particularly in early spring when it's completely flooded, while Otepää is another good spot to organise and access canoe trips, along with Haanja Nature Park, Masalu and Vilsandi.

Winter Sports

Between December and April, the Baltics' forests are beribboned by cross-country skiing trails. Otepää in southeast Estonia – the best of the Baltic winter resorts – offers limited downhill skiing, countless cross-country trails and a ski jump. At the heart of Latvia's winter-sports scene, Cēsis comprises short-but-sweet downhill runs, cross-country trails and an adrenaline-infused 1200m-long artificial bobsleigh run. Besides the huge indoor slope in Lithuania's Druskininkai, there's exceptional cross-country skiing amid deep, whispering forests and frozen blue lakes of Aukštaitija National Park.

MORE ACTIVITIES

See our map on page 42

DAINA VARPINA/SHUTTERSTOCK ©

Cesis (p197), Latvia

BEAR-SPOTTING
Spend the night in a forest hide in **Alutaguse** (p81) to spot some of the 900 brown bears resident in Estonia.

SANATORIUM VISIT
Dip into the curative mineral waters and healing mud of **Värska** (p114), surrounded by the natural beauty of the southern borderlands.

BOBSLEIGH RUN
Hurtle down Sigulda's **Bobsleigh and Luge Track** (192), reaching speeds of up to 130km per hour.

LEVITATION SPREE
Also in **Sigulda** (p190), levitate in a stream of pumped air, an effect akin to parachuting or skydiving.

0 100 km
0 50 miles

Kayaking/Canoeing
1. Pāvilosta (p221)
2. Svencelė (p29)
3. Gauja National Park (p195)
4. Soomaa National Park (p129)
5. Aukštaitija National Park (p304)

Walking/Hiking
1. Curonian Spit (p278)
2. Aukštaitija National Park (p304)
3. Gauja National Park (p195)
4. Lahemaa National Park (p82)
5. Kiidjärve (p120)

FINLAND

Lake Ladoga

Gulf of Finland

Suursaari

Narva

HELSINKI

Kohtla-Järve

Lake Peipsi

Rakvere

Lahemaa National Park

Maardu

Mustvee

Rāpina

Lake Pihkva

TALLINN

Paide

Jõgeva

Põlva

Varska

SETOMAA

Keila

ESTONIA

Tartu

Võru

Haapsalu

Soomaa National Park

Viljandi

Elva

Rõuge

Suur Munamägi

Kärdla

Pärnu

Lake Võrtsjärv

Otepää

HIIUMAA

Kilingi-Nõmme

Tõrva

Valga

MUHU

Virtsu

Ainaži

Valka

Valmiera

Smittene

Alūksne

Kuressaare

SAAREMAA

Kihnu

Tūja

VIDZEME

Cēsis

Gauja National Park

Gulbene

Gulf of Riga

Mērsrags

Sigulda

Salaspils

Cesvaine

Kolka

Talsi

Tukums

JŪRMALA

RĪGA

Ventspils

KURZEME

Venta

Pāvilosta

LATVIA

Madona

RUSSIA

STOCKHOLM

SWEDEN

ÅLAND

Pāvilosta

42

National Parks

1 Aukštaitija National Park (p304)
2 Lahemaa National Park (p82)
3 Gauja National Park (p195)
4 Curonian Spit National Park (p278)
5 Žemaitija National Park (p298)

Cycling

1 Latgale Lakelands (p228)
2 Nemunas Delta (p292)
3 Dzūkija National Park (p316)
4 Hiiumaa (p136)
5 Kihnu (p130)

Skiing/Snowboarding

1 Rīga (p162)
2 Sigulda (p190)
3 Druskininkai (p312)
4 Otepää (p113)
5 Aukštaitija National Park (p304)

ESTONIA, LATVIA & LITHUANIA

THE GUIDE

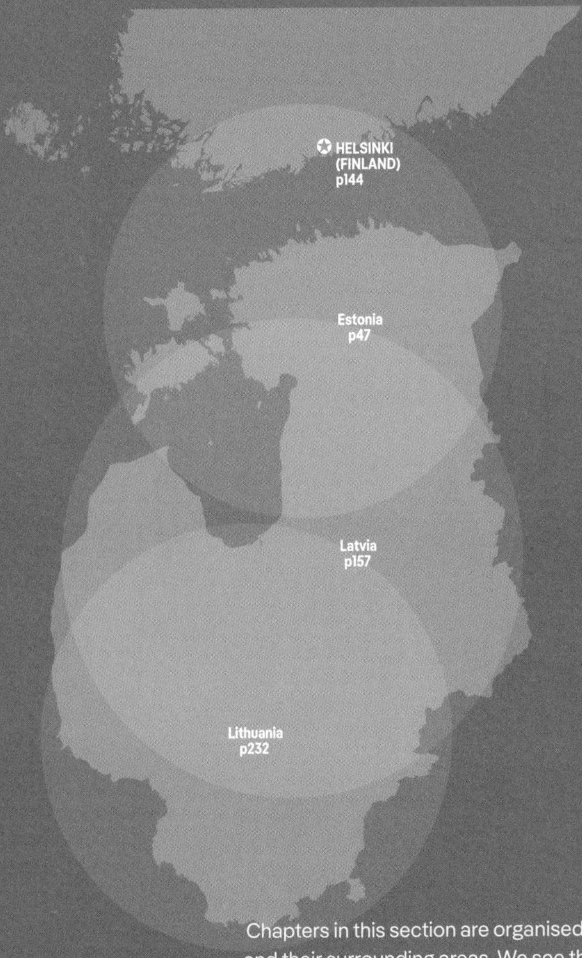
HELSINKI
(FINLAND)
p144
Estonia
p47
Latvia
p157
Lithuania
p232

Chapters in this section are organised by hubs and their surrounding areas. We see the hub as your base in the destination, where you'll find unique experiences, local insights, insider tips and expert recommendations. It's also your gateway to the surrounding area, where you'll see what and how much you can do from there.

Lahemaa National Park (p82), Estonia

Above: Tallinn (p52); Left: Tartu (p98)

Estonia

A CULTURAL CROSSROADS

Ruled and influenced by different empires throughout its history, Estonia developed a distinct character that defies easy definition.

Estonia has long been defined by its strategic position at the crossroads of northern Europe's sea routes. Part of the Hanseatic League trading bloc during the Middle Ages and later absorbed into the Swedish kingdom, Estonia's identity grew increasingly tangled as the Russian Empire conquered its territory in the early 18th century. Independence followed the Russian Empire's collapse in 1917, but Estonia's larger neighbours never ceased to view this small country as an essential pawn on their geopolitical chessboard. Estonians would have their nationhood removed by both Nazi and Soviet forces during WWII, a conflict followed by nearly five decades of USSR rule. Today, most Estonians tend to resent the 'post-Soviet' label, although a large portion of the population – over 20% – is composed of ethnic Russians who either moved in Soviet times or descend from migrants.

Despite its convoluted past, Estonia is a nation looking forward. In cities, folk music festivals go hand in hand with a thriving contemporary art scene, and former industrial districts live a second life as design-centric creative hubs filled with galleries and international restaurants. Outside urban areas, nature maintains a central role in the local way of life. Half the country is covered by forests and 2000 islands spill from the coastline. Whether you're visiting to escape the crowds or to decipher its layered culture, Estonia awaits discovery.

ARCADY/SHUTTERSTOCK ©

THE MAIN AREAS

Tallinn	Narva	Tartu	Pärnu	Haapsalu
Modern capital, with a medieval heart. p52	Borderland fortress. p87	Cradle of culture. p98	The summer capital. p123	Resort town and island gateway. p132

Find Your Way

Over half of Estonia is covered by forests and a third of the population is concentrated in the capital, leaving the majority of the country dotted with small settlements surrounded by nature.

FINLAND

HELSINKI

Tallinn, p52
Dynamic, tech-driven capital with a UNESCO-listed Old Town. Discover medieval roots, some of the best museums in the Baltics and parks filled with art.

TALLINN

Keila-Joa
Paldiski
Keila
Nõva
Riguldí
Tahkunanina
Kärdla
VORMSI
Hullo
Rapla
HIIUMAA
Haapsalu
Märjamaa
Käina
Heltermaa
E67
KASSARI
Sõru
MUHU
Lihula
Võhma
Kuivastu
Pärnu-Jaagupi
Orissaare
Virtsu
Saaremaa
Pärnu
SAAREMAA
Sakla
Kuressaare
Pootsi
E67
Gulf of Rīga
Kihnu
Sääre

Haapsalu, p132
Rural at its core, this resort town in northwestern Estonia is your gateway to the wild islands of the surrounding archipelago.

Pärnu, p123
Estonia's summer capital is the country's prime beach destination, a wellness-centred, family-friendly town with resorts and 19th-century villas.

0 — 40 km
0 — 20 miles

CAR

Driving your own vehicle is the fastest way to move around the country, which can be crossed from north to south in just three hours. Major rental companies operate in Tallinn and Tartu.

BUS

With some patience, all of Estonia can be visited using public transport. Cheap and reliable buses run regularly between cities and smaller towns.

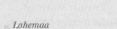

TRAIN

Moving around by train is easy. The northern line links Tallinn to Narva and Paldiski, while two lines travel south to Pärnu and Tartu, then onwards to Valga. All tickets can be booked via elron.ee

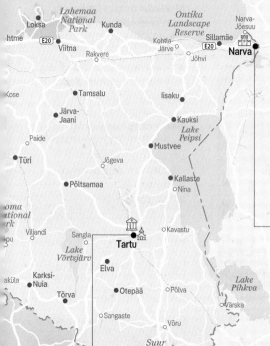

Narva, p87

The third largest city in Estonia sits right on the border with Russia. Reconstructed almost entirely after WWII, it's the quintessential Soviet city.

Tartu, p98

Home of Estonia's first university, Tartu is a friendly place, kept vibrant by its seasonally changing student population.

Plan Your Time

With its long list of cultural attractions Tallinn tends to grab all the attention, but make sure to save some time to explore the islands and rural towns of the south, where centuries-old traditions remain alive and well.

Toompea (p58)

If You Only Have One Day

● Spend your morning exploring Tallinn's Old Town, from the **Town Hall Square** (p52) in the lower part to elevated **Toompea** (p58). Seek traces left behind by the Hanseatic League in the **Great Guild Hall** (p57), then enter onion-domed **Alexander Nevsky Cathedral** (p59), before lunch in the creative hub of **Telliskivi** (p62).

● In the afternoon, stroll **Kadriorg Park** (p66) and enter the **Kumu Museum** (p68) to enjoy a century of Estonian art. Pay a visit to **Maarjamäe's monumental memorials** (p72) to understand Estonia's troubled past, then finish with a seaside dinner in **Noblessner** (p75) or a drink in the **Rotermann Quarter** (p77).

Seasonal Highlights

The winters are harsh in Estonia, but the endless summer days and short distances allow for deep explorations.

MARCH

In late March/early April, Soomaa National Park experiences a 'fifth season' as floods transform it into a **kayaking** playground.

APRIL

Birdwatching season in Matsalu National Park as migratory birds pass through these wet plains.

JUNE

Estonia celebrates **Jaanipäev** (Midsummer) on 21 June: one of oldest festivities in the country sees huge bonfires welcome summer.

Three Days to Travel Around

● Dedicate a few days to discovering the fascinating culture of southern Estonia. In Tartu, the country's second city, walk through Old Town and climb up **Toomemägi** (p102) to admire the remains of **Tartu Cathedral** (p102). Rent an e-bike and head to **Aparaaditehas** (p107) for a paper-making workshop at Typa and a tour of this refurbished industrial area's galleries.

● Spend day two touring the **Setomaa** region (p114), home of the musical Seto minority. Start in **Värska** (p114) with a Lake Lämmi cruise along the Russian border, and continue to the **Piusa Caves** (p122). On day three head to charming **Viljandi** (p110).

If You Have More Time

● After a few days in Tallinn, head west towards the resort city of **Haapsalu** (p132) and its **castle** (p132), making a short detour on the way to visit the impressive relics of the **Rummu limestone quarry** (p81).

● From Haapsalu travel to Rohuküla and take the ferry to **Hiiumaa** (p136), your first encounter with the biosphere reserve of the West Estonian Archipelago. Visit quirky lighthouses and remnants of WWII before moving on to Estonia's largest island, **Saaremaa** (p138), where mysterious craters, an impenetrable fortress and a century-old ship await. Back on the mainland, finish your trip in **Pärnu** (p123).

JULY	**AUGUST**	**SEPTEMBER**	**DECEMBER**
Viljandi holds its **Folk Music Festival**, one of the most anticipated music events in southern Estonia.	The warmest month of the year is festival season in Setomaa, which celebrates its **Kingdom Day** and the open-air **Treski Music Festival**.	Narva's **Station Festival** takes place at the end of summer, bringing international musicians and performers to the city.	**Christmas markets** light up the main squares of Tallinn and Tartu, serving steaming mulled wine to warm chilly days.

Tallinn

HISTORY | A TOWERING CITADEL | OLD TOWN CHARM

GETTING AROUND

Tallinn's Old Town is best explored on foot, but to reach many of the sights in the suburbs you'll need to get on a bus or rely on the electric scooters that seem to have taken over the city. Bus tickets can be purchased with contactless cards directly on the bus (cash is not accepted) or online via tallinn.pilet.ee. Timetables are available at transport.tallinn.ee.

Soon after Tallinn entered the Hanseatic League mercantile alliance in the late 13th century, it became the most important port of the Gulf of Finland and a crucial junction on the Baltic Sea's trade routes. The resulting wealth led to the construction of the best preserved medieval city of Nordic Europe, still contained within its original walls and guarded by 26 red-roofed watchtowers. This Old Town is a gem of stone architecture and cobbled alleys, even if at times it feels like a theme park. But Estonia's culturally vibrant capital extends beyond its ancient borders – stretching along the coast are neighbourhoods of traditional wooden houses, post-war high rises and glass office towers housing an ever-growing tech sector. From the creative district of Telliskivi to the imperial art park of Kadriorg, getting to know Tallinn rewards a few days of any visitor's time.

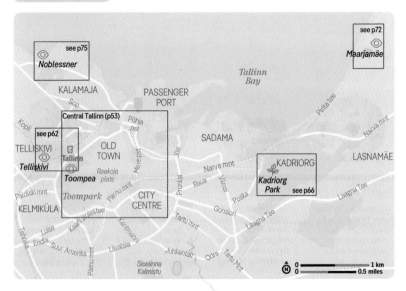

GADAG/SHUTTERSTOCK ©

Town Hall Square

The Heart of Old Town

MAP P54

Under the eye of Old Thomas

As one of northern Europe's best preserved medieval towns, the historic core of Tallinn calls for slow strolls through narrow lanes that sit between tall towers and gothic cathedrals. The Old Town (Vanalinn) is divided into two sections: Toompea, on the hill; and the Lower Town. **Town Hall Square** (Raekoja Plats) is the epicentre of the latter, an open space all roads seem to lead to. Photogenic, pastel-coloured buildings surround the square that for centuries housed Tallinn's main market where Hanseatic traders would meet to exchange goods, now occupied by the terraces of restaurants that cater to day trippers who arrive on cruise ships at the nearby port. In December, one of Tallinn's Christmas markets lights up the square, watched over by the **Town Hall**, a gothic structure whose early-15th-century origins place it among the oldest municipal buildings in northern Europe. The Town Hall welcomes visitors on weekends in December and every day from late June through August. Outside these periods, tours are available exclusively by appointment. A visit inside gives access to the **Council Chamber** and the **Citizens' Hall** where

Continues on p57

☑ **TOP TIP**

Tallinn's train station sits northwest of Old Town. Buses depart from the station 2km southeast of the centre. The compact inner city is walkable, while trams and intercity buses link the suburbs. You can purchase one-hour public transport tickets by tapping your contactless card on the vehicle, or via tallinn.pilet.ee.

THE OLDEST PHARMACY IN EUROPE?

The exact opening date of Tallinn's Town Hall Pharmacy remains a mystery, but records showing its activity as early as 1422 have led to the self-awarded title of oldest continuously working chemist in Europe. This establishment found long-term stewards in the Burchardt family, who managed it through ten successive generations, from 1583 to the early 20th century. Today, the pharmacy houses a small exhibition that chronicles its rich history and legacy. Enter to see the collection of healing concoctions and remedies once sold there. Open Monday through Saturday, from 10am to 6pm.

 WHERE TO STAY IN TALLINN —

Old Town Backpackers
Small hostel that gets messy at times, but a great place to meet new friends in a homely atmosphere. €

Fat Margaret's Hostel
Near Fat Margaret tower and the train station, with dorms, private rooms, a sauna and a small pool. €

Three Crowns Residents
Some of the cheapest private Old Town rooms, in a historic building on Vene Street. Cheaper options are small. €

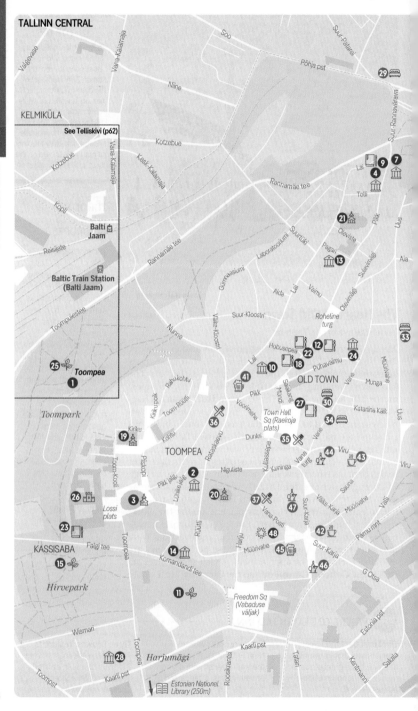

TALLINN CENTRAL

KELMIKÜLA

See Telliskivi (p62)

Balti Jaam

Baltic Train Station
(Balti Jaam)

Toompea

Toompark

TOOMPEA

OLD TOWN

Town Hall
Sq (Raekoja
plats)

KASSISABA

Hirvepark

Wismari

Harjumägi

Freedom Sq
(Vabaduse
väljak)

Estonian National
Library (250m)

TOP SIGHTS
1 Toompea

SIGHTS
2 Adamson-Eric Museum
3 Alexander Nevsky Cathedral
4 Children's Literature Centre
5 Contemporary Art Museum
6 Estonian Museum of Architecture
7 Fat Margaret
8 Gallery Seek
9 Great Coastal Gate
10 Great Guild Hall
11 Harju Hill
12 House of the Blackheads
13 KGB Prison Cells
14 Kiek in de Kök
15 Lindamäe Park
16 PoCo Pop And Contemporary Art Museum
17 Rotermann Quarter
18 St Canute's Guild
19 St Mary's Cathedral
20 St Nicholas' Church
21 St Olaf's Church
22 St Olaf's Guild
23 Tall Hermann Tower
24 Tallinn City Museum
25 Toompark
26 Toompea Castle
27 Town Hall Pharmacy
28 Vabamu Museum of Occupations and Freedom

SLEEPING
29 Fat Margaret's Hostel
30 Hotel Telegraaf
31 Hotel Viru
32 Nordic Hotel Forum
33 Old Town Backpackers
34 Three Crowns Residents

EATING
35 Ill Draakon
36 Peet Ruut
37 Pegasus
38 RØST Bakery
39 Tai Boh

DRINKING & NIGHTLIFE
40 Chicago 1933
41 Koht
42 Kohvik Lummus
43 RUKIS
44 Sessel
45 Valli Bar
46 Whisper Sister
47 Winkel

ENTERTAINMENT
48 Sõprus Cinema

SHOPPING
49 Tallinn Design House

The colourful flower market extending from ❶ **Viru Gate** is your starting point. Pass the double towers that lead into Old Town and take a right onto Müürivahe Street at the Black Angus bull sculpture to reach the ❷ **Hellemann Tower**, where a steep climb leads to a 200m walkway built on the former defensive walls. Once you're back at ground level stroll through ❸ **St Catherine's Passage** (p65) then turn right on Vene Street. Between ❹ **Sts Peter and Paul's Cathedral** (p64) and ❺ **St Nicholas' Orthodox Church** (p64) find the ❻ **Banned Books Museum** (p65) dedicated to censored literature. As Vene splits, take a left, then a right, then a left again to reach Pikk Street from where it's a short walk to ❼ **Fat Margaret**, housing the Estonian Maritime Museum. Turn back, walk on Pikk past the 14th-century, pastel-

painted ❽ **Three Sisters**, and turn right on Tolli Street to get to ❾ **St Olaf's Church**, Old Town's tallest structure, whose viewing platform awaits at the top of a 258-step staircase. You're just a few minutes away from the Short Leg Gate that leads to Toompea. Tour the hill's sights – ❿ **St Mary's Cathedral** (p59), ⓫ **Alexander Nevsky Cathedral** (p59), ⓬ **Toompea Castle** (p58) – then stop at the ⓭ **Patkuli viewing platform** (p59) for a break with a view. Head back down to the lower town via the curving stairs. Head along Nunne Street – notice the bas-relief dedicated to former Russian president Boris Yeltsin on the wall – and you'll arrive at ⓮ **Town Hall Square** (p52). From there, it's a short walk to Harju Street and historic ⓯ **St Nicholas' Church**, now a museum (p60).

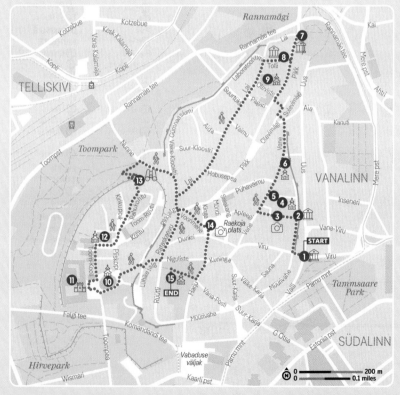

Continues from p53
festivals and exhibitions used to be held in the Middle Ages. The intricate tapestries currently on show are reproductions of Dutch originals commissioned in the 16th century, now displayed at Tallinn City Museum (p60). A separate ticket is required to climb the 115 steps of the **bell tower** (open June to October) topped by Tallinn's most notable icon, Old Thomas (Vana Toomas), the soldier-shaped weather vane that has guarded the city since 1530.

Hanseatic Wall Street

MAP P54

Where medieval merchants did business

As with many other northern European cities, in 15th-century Tallinn real estate taxes were calculated based on the width of a building's facade meaning the size of the **Great Guild Hall**, one of the most prominent buildings on Pikk Street (the city's main thoroughfare), testifies to the wealth and power of the merchant guilds that used to meet here. Behind the entry doors marked by two lion-head knockers – symbolising the power of the city's commercial elite – is a vaulted hall designed to hold public celebrations and meetings of major international traders. Completed in 1410, the Great Guild Hall continued to function as Tallinn's main business centre up until the 19th century, when stock market negotiations took place here. Since 1952, the building has housed one branch of the **Estonian History Museum**, whose permanent exhibition is dedicated to Estonia's 'Spirit of Survival': each thematic section recounts the country's history through objects ranging from coins to armoury, with a special focus on the golden era of the Great Guild Hall.

The Great Coastal Gate & Fat Margaret MAP P54

An entrance like no other

Tallinn's strategic position on the Baltic Sea's trade routes was a great source of wealth for the Hanseatic city in the Middle Ages, and it's no coincidence that the most important access point to the town in this period was the **Great Coastal Gate**, mentioned as early as 1359 as linking the port and Town Hall Square. The threat of enemy forces invading the city in an attempt to get a piece of the pie loomed over Tallinn for centuries, and in 1529, a defensive tower was added to the Great Coastal Gate's flank to protect this hugely important entrance point. Unprecedented in size, it measured 25m in diameter, with walls as thick as 5m. As defensive needs

Continues on p60

ST OLAF'S CHURCH

With a dark spire that reaches 124m in height, St Olaf's Church is the tallest building in Tallinn's Old Town. It used to be even taller, until in 1625 lightning led to a fire that burned much of it down and reduced the spire by 35m. The church, dedicated to King Olaf II of Norway, was originally constructed as a Roman Catholic place of worship, then passed to the Lutherans during the Reformation years before being ultimately changed into a Baptist place of worship in the 1950s. You can climb the 258 steps to a viewing platform for guaranteed awe-inspiring views of the city.

 WHERE TO EAT IN TALLINN

Peet Ruut
Organic cuisine at its best, Peer Ruut cares as much about flavours as the origins of each ingredient. €€

Pegasus
This restaurant has been cooking for half a century, but you wouldn't tell from the modern cuisine of its menu. €€

NOA
One of the top restaurants in Estonia, NOA's refined Nordic cuisine is worth the trip out of the city. €€

KAVALENKAVA/SHUTTERSTOCK ©, BOTTOM RIGHT: GEORGE TRUMPETER/SHUTTERSTOCK ©

PRACTICALITIES

Scan this QR code for more
history of Toompea Castle and
to book a tour.

TOP SIGHT

Toompea

Sitting above the lower part of Tallinn's Old Town, Toompea, or
Cathedral Hill, has long functioned as the city's centre of power.
Home of Estonia's Parliament, the fortified citadel presents itself
as a collection of stately palaces and towering churches, offering a
much quieter atmosphere than its lower counterpart. Enter via the
Short Leg Gate and seek out the viewing platforms for some of the
best panoramas over the capital.

DON'T MISS

Toompea
Castle

Tall Hermann
Tower

St Mary's
Cathedral

Alexander
Nevsky
Cathedral

Toompea's
viewing
platforms

Short Leg Gate

The only pedestrian gate connecting the lower and upper parts
of Tallinn's Old Town was purposely built to control the traffic of people heading up to exclusive Toompea. Completed in
1456 by the town council's official mason, Hans Kotke, this
steep, narrow, cobbled alley is now a charming street lined
with handicraft stores and cafes.

Toompea Castle

The Parliament of Estonia (Riigikogu) is the most recent gov-
erning body to operate from Toompea Castle, the centre of
power for eight centuries when Danish, Livonian, Swedish
and Russian elites ruled over the surrounding territory. The
complex has seen many transformations over the course of its
history, mixing different architectural styles: the pink classicist palace was added to the Livonian fortress by the Russians in the 18th century, while the Riigikogu Building – the

world's only expressionist structure to house a parliament – has been facing the castle's courtyard since 1922. Free guided tours are available for groups and individuals.

Tall Hermann Tower

Built in three stages between the mid-14th and early 16th centuries, Tall Hermann Tower (Pikk Hermann) is reached via the 1936 Governor's Garden, one of the earliest gardens in Tallinn, stretching from the southern flank of the castle. Estonia's blue, black and white national flag was first raised here in 1918 and returned in 1991 after the collapse of the USSR.

St Mary's Cathedral

Commonly known as the Dome Church, the Lutheran Cathedral of St Mary has its roots in the 13th century, when Danish rulers built it as a Catholic place of worship. Most of the northern gothic exterior dates to the 15th century, although a 1684 fire heavily damaged the structure, which was reconstructed with new baroque touches (such as the bell tower) in the 17th and 18th centuries, when it became a gathering spot for the Baltic German aristocracy living in Toompea. An impressive collection of over 100 hand-carved coats of arms still hangs from the church's bare walls. The tower was closed for renovation at the time of research, but it's normally possible to climb the 143 steps up for great views over the city.

Alexander Nevsky Cathedral

Brimming with sacred icons enclosed in golden frames and candles lit by Orthodox devotees, the onion-domed Alexander Nevsky Cathedral sits right in front of Toompea Castle and the neoclassical post office, well preserved despite its historically unpalatable presence. Named after the Prince of Novgorod, the cathedral was completed in 1900 during the final stage of the Russian Empire's control over Estonia and risked demolition as the country gained its independence two decades later. The Soviets initially planned to convert the church into a planetarium – it didn't happen. Instead, the cathedral was shut for 50 years, reopening to the public in 1991.

**Alexander Nevsky
Cathedral**

GREAT VIEWS
Toompea offers exceptional views over lower Tallinn from the hill's three viewing platforms. The Bishop's Garden (Piiskopiaia) platform faces the railway station and Kalamaja, while the Patkuli platform allows you to frame Old Town's red roofs with the Baltic Sea in the background. St Nicholas' Cathedral is best seen from the Kohtuotsa viewing platform. Another elevated spot is Harju Hill park, on the edge of Toompea.

TOP TIPS

● Tall Hermann Tower is open to the public only three times a year: Riigikogu Open House Day (23 April); National Flag Day (4 June); and the Day of Restoration of Independence (20 August).

● St Mary's Cathedral hosts organ concerts every Saturday at noon; tickets cost €4.

● Entering Alexander Nevsky Cathedral is free. Services are held at 8.30am on weekdays and at 9am on Saturdays and Sundays.

● The viewing platforms can be crowded in the late afternoons, but the sunset views over the city are hard to beat.

TALLINN CITY MUSEUM

The main branch of the Tallinn City Museum network, on Vene Street, covers Tallinn's history from its early days to the modern era. Housed inside a medieval merchant's house, the permanent exhibition explores how commercial dynamics have shaped the capital. Among the most precious exhibits are seven Renaissance tapestries originating from the Netherlands (commissioned by the city council in 1547), 31 original portraits of European rulers and a collection of rare, 16th-century handmade silverware once belonging to the local elite. The hall of paintings shows how Tallinn has changed over the centuries, with a miniature model of the city in its pre-industrial era. Entry is free the first Sunday of every month.

Continued from p57

declined under the rule of the Russian Empire, the tower became a storehouse for weapons and gunpowder, acquiring the name it is known as today, **Fat Margaret**. While the tower's bulky figure explains the first part of the name, Margaret's identity remains a mystery. Today, the structure houses the main branch of the **Estonian Maritime Museum**, where a collection of over 700 exhibits traces the history of navigation in the Baltic Sea. The unchallenged highlight is the wreckage of a *koge* (cog) ship, an 18m cargo vessel dating back to the 14th century. Inside the ship, unearthed in Tallinn's Kadriorg neighbourhood in 2015, archaeologists found kitchen utensils, footwear and clothing belonging to medieval sailors – an unprecedented discovery that offers a glimpse into the life of Hanseatic League traders.

A Stroll Through Pikk's Palaces

MAP P54

Where the one percent lived

Running directly from the Great Coastal Gate to the Great Guild Hall, **Pikk Street** has functioned as Tallinn's main artery since its early days, a coveted neighbourhood reserved for the city's trading elite. Here you'll find the former headquarters of medieval institutions such as **St Canute's Guild** (no 20), **St Olaf's Guild** (no 24), one of Tallinn's earliest guilds, and the **House of the Blackheads** (no 26), an association of shipmakers and artisans active for over five centuries. These buildings represent an important piece of Tallinn's history, but are only open to the public on special occasions. One of the most powerful names working in Tallinn was the Koch family, which had established its commercial enterprise in 1759 and by the turn of the 20th century owned all of the buildings on Pikk Street standing between Tolli Street and Fat Margaret. Things changed when the Soviets arrived – the **KGB Prison Cells** (five cells have been converted into a museum) were set up on the street and the neogothic villa at no 73, where the Koch family formerly lived, was turned into a branch of the Ministry of Culture. Today the villa houses the **Children's Literature Centre**.

Dancing with Death in St Nicholas' Church

MAP P54

Magnificent art in the Niguliste Museum

Not to be confused with the Orthodox church of the same name, **St Nicholas' Church** rises from the lower town and
Continues on p64

 WHERE TO STAY IN TALLINN

Nordic Hotel Forum
Contemporary rooms, a spa and a sauna steps from Old Town. €€

Hotel Viru
The KGB no longer spies on you in this (updated) monument of Soviet modernist architecture. €€€

Hotel Telegraaf
Historic building in Old Town location, with elegant rooms, a spa and fine dining at its restaurant. €€€

Pikk Street

PANDORA PICTURES/SHUTTERSTOCK ©

PRACTICALITIES

Scan this QR code to check what's on in Telliskivi.

Telliskivi Creative City

'Craft', 'artisanal', 'organic' and other trendy keywords recur often in graffiti-decorated Telliskivi, the area that resulted from the 2009 regeneration project of this industrial corner of Tallinn north of the railway station. Rundown warehouses and former factories located in the once-dodgy Kalamaja district are now home to an eclectic mix of cafes, bars, shops and galleries – plus a weekly flea market.

For Photography Lovers

The red building rising in the heart of Telliskivi houses the Estonian branch of the Swedish photography museum **Fotografiska**, a space where the work of emerging and established international artists is exhibited through changing shows. Three different events are typically held here every month. A fine dining restaurant serving seasonal tasting menus is found inside the glass-encased rooftop, offering great views over the city, and the cafe in the back spills onto an open courtyard. In front of Fotografiska sits **Dokfoto**, or the Juhan Kuus Documentary Photo Centre. Another space with rotating exhibitions, this museum dedicated to Estonian-South African photographer Juhan Kuus is focused on human-centred visual storytelling of the past and the present.

DON'T MISS

Fotografiska
The Flea Market
La Muu
Vaat
Sveta
Street Art

Second-Hand Everything

Every Saturday, Telliskivi hosts its **flea market** in the square next to the F-Hoone restaurant, one of the first to set up shop in the area. Visitors and local treasure hunters gather here in the morning searching for unique items in the second-hand clothing and antique stalls. But the market is not the only opportunity to look for vintage finds in Telliskivi. Behind the leopard-skin pattern covering its walls, **Kopli Couture** offers hand-selected branded fashion, with an emphasis on the 1960s and 1970s (and music to match). In the upper floor of the **Balti Jaam Market**, just outside Telliskivi proper, dozens of second-hand shops sell everything from furniture to fashion to Soviet memorabilia (including a giant Lenin head). **Sõbralt Sõbrale** sells clothing, homewares and books for just a few euros, with the sales funding social projects helping families in need. A variety of vendors gather at **Basaar**, while **Sveta Vintage** presents a more curated selection of well-known brands at higher price than its neighbours.

Street Bites, Fine Food & Hip Cafes

As you enter Telliskivi from Tallinn's railway station, you'll come across **DEPOO**, the 19th-century building formerly used for the maintenance of trains. The area has been converted into an open-air food market with something for every taste. Two carriages of the Soviet train that used to connect Tallinn with Moscow are now home to **Peatus**, where generous burgers are often accompanied by an electronic soundtrack played by DJs. Stop at restaurant-bookshop **Literaat** for an intellectually-inspiring brunch or take a break in the Scandinavian atmosphere of **Fika Cafè**, where speciality coffee comes with prized, freshly baked cinnamon rolls. Contemporary Indian food is served at **Lendav Taldrik**, while **Frenchy Bistro** prepares – you guessed it – authentic French cuisine, from snails to duck filet. **La Muu** is the unchallenged ice cream destination, serving organic flavours (vegan options available) from its seasonal shop in the heart of Telliskivi, competing with **Chocokoo** for the top dessert spot.

Craft Sips & Night Caps

If you like your cocktail served with a side of vinyl records, **Terminal** is the place to go – browse the shop's collection or listen to one of the frequent live gigs held at the store. The terrace of lively **Põhja Konn**, an extension of the nearby Põhjala brewery, fills up during warm summer evenings, while craft beer enthusiasts will appreciate the inventiveness of **Vaat**, whose minimalist taproom hosts weekly quiz and chess nights. Clothes stay on (usually) at **Nudist Winery**, where you can taste a wide selection of organic fruit wines in a funky atmosphere. The **Junimperium Distillery** is right next door; their award-winning gin is the basis for a wide selection of cocktails. Eyecatching (but slightly overpriced) **Tšungel** combines Mexican-inspired snacks and drinks with a tropical atmosphere and DJs playing on weekends. Partygoers make a beeline for **Sveta**, Telliskivi's favourite club.

TELLISKIVI'S STREET ART

Street art has long been one of Telliskivi's defining features and many large murals are easily spotted when walking around the neighbourhood.

French artist Alexandre Monteiro, better known as Hopare, painted the portrait of a woman visible near Fotografiska, while the giant eagle found on one of DEPOO's storehouses is the work of New Zealander Cinzah. Animals form a recurring theme – the blue deer by Estonian artist Sänk and the sphynx cat by Chilean artist Izak One have become two of Telliskivi's icons.

TOP TIPS

● Telliskivi is easily reached on foot in about 10 minutes from Old Town – cross the platforms of the railway station and turn left at the Balti Jaam market.

● Besides food, drinks and vintage shops, the area houses many design and artisan stores, including those of lamp makers Juheko, leather bag designer Stella Soomlais and the ceramicists of TEKE.

MORE CHURCHES IN TALLINN

Church of the Holy Spirit
If it wasn't for its hexagonal tower, this 14th-century Lutheran church could almost go unnoticed. A golden clock marks the hours outside, while timber furnishing inside recalls the Middle Ages.

St Nicholas' Orthodox Church
Younger than its medieval counterpart, a pale yellow, 19th-century exterior hides an altar richly adorned in typical Orthodox style.

Sts Peter and Paul's Cathedral
One of the few Roman Catholic churches in Tallinn, this blocky neoclassical structure built in 1844 overlooks a charming courtyard.

Ukrainian Greek Catholic Church
This small church functions as the gathering place for Ukrainian locals and holds many icons painted on wooden panels.

St Nicholas' Orthodox Church

Continued from p60

is topped by a notably pointy tower – it's best photographed from the Harju Street gardens. Founded in the 13th century by German traders, the church gained its current shape in the early 16th century, when the eye-catching spire was added. The building was badly damaged during WWII, together with most of Harju Street, when on 9 March 1944, a Red Army air raid killed 700 people and left 20,000 homeless. After reconstruction, it was converted into the **Niguliste Museum**, dedicated to medieval religious art. The collection's highlight is the *Danse Macabre* painting attributed to Bernt Notke, one of northern Europe's best-known artists at the time, and first mentioned in 1603. The 7.5m-long piece is the world's only surviving medieval 'dance of death' painted on canvas, and is actually only a fragment of a larger work believed to have measured 30m, displaying the macabre theme that developed in the late Middle Ages following the Black Death. Five people, including an emperor, a king and a cardinal, are seen holding hands and dancing with spectral figures – a reminder that everyone is equal before death. The church's main hall has a series of wooden altarpieces, while

 WHERE TO EAT IN TALLINN

Ill Draakon
Eel soup and sausages in a playful, medieval-inspired Town Hall Square tourist restaurant. €€

Peatus
Delicious burgers inside the carriages of a former Soviet train in Telliskivi's creative neighbourhood. €€

Tai Boh
Behind vine-covered walls, find excellent Thai food in a quirky, colourful space near Old Town gates. €€

the Silver Chamber houses precious silverware that once belonged to the city's guilds. The entrance ticket gives you access to the viewing platform on the top floor of the tower (accessible by stairs or lift), for Old Town views.

Strolling St Catherine's Passage   MAP P54
Old Town's most charming alley

Known as one of Tallinn's most photogenic streets, this cobbled lane running under a series of stone arches takes its name from St Catherine's Monastery, established by Dominican monks in the second half of the 13th century and believed to be the largest church in Tallinn when it was completed in the 15th century. Burned down by Lutherans in the 16th century, the monastery was abandoned for years before its partial restoration took place in the 1850s. Its western portals still show some of the symbols of Christianity carved in the stone frame by monks in the 14th century: a dog representing the Dominican Order; dragons and snakes illustrating the congregation's dedication to education. While the religious function of the monastery was never restored, the outer walls running along **St Catherine's Passage** – once known as the Monks' Alley – contain a series of 14th-century tombstones that were saved from ruin during restoration. Measuring over a metre in height and finely carved with inscriptions, the tombstones belonged to the city's ruling class: members of Tallinn's judiciary, of the Brotherhood of Blackheads and of the Great Guild. Today, the passage is dotted with a number of handicraft stores and an Italian restaurant whose tables spill out onto the charming street in good weather.

Secret Passages & Privileged Views   MAP P54
Kiek in de Kök's underground tunnels

One of Tallinn's most prominent medieval structures is the **Kiek in de Kök** tower, built between 1475 and 1483 to reinforce the city's southwestern defences. Standing at over 37m tall, the tower was nicknamed Kiek in de Kök, 'peek into the kitchen' in Low German, as guards working from its upper floors were said to be able to look into the homes of Tallinn's residents through their chimneys. A branch of the Tallinn City Museum, Kiek in de Kök consists of two main sections, the tower museum and bastion passages. The former offers a permanent, kid-friendly exhibition on the history of Tallinn's defences and military conflicts, with models of early fortifications that preceded the current walls surrounding Old Town

Continues on p70

THE BANNED BOOKS MUSEUM

The **Banned Books Museum** on Munga Street is one of the few free museums in the capital. It's run by a non-profit organisation dedicated to preserving and exhibiting publications that have been banned by various governments around the world, from volumes distributed as illegal *samizdat* (clandestine copies of censored literature) during the Soviet era to heretical texts challenging religious thought. A selection of the censored literature is available for sale, and if you're spending a longer time in Tallinn you could consider joining the Banned Books Club to explore in more depth the controversial ideas that have upset institutions in recent history.

MORE ART MUSEUMS AND GALLERIES IN TALLINN

Gallery Seek
Contemporary photography exhibitions around the ruins of the medieval St John the Baptist hospital.

Adamson-Eric Museum
See the work of 20th-century Tartu-born artist Erich Carl Hugo Adamson, better known as Adamson-Eric.

Contemporary Art Museum
Squatted in 2006 and turned into a semi-official gallery, this former office building hosts ever-changing installations.

VALERY BARETA/SHUTTERSTOCK ©

PRACTICALITIES

Scan this QR code for
tickets for the art museums.

TOP SIGHT

Kadriorg Park

Removed from the bustle of Tallinn's Old Town, Kadriorg Park is
the unchallenged art hub of Estonia's capital, housing museums
brimming with classical and contemporary works on the lush grounds
first commissioned by Russian tsar Peter the Great in the early 18th
century. Manicured gardens, mirror-like ponds and oak-shaded paths
add to the appeal of this 70-hectare park, east of the city centre.

DON'T MISS

Kadriorg Palace
and Gardens

Mikkel Museum

Swan Pond

Kumu Museum

House of Peter
the Great

Japanese Garden

Russalka
Memorial

Kadriorg Palace

The architectural focus of Kadriorg Park is its namesake palace, a baroque construction backed by a symmetrical French
garden Peter the Great had built as a gift to his wife, Empress
Catherine I, between 1718 and 1725. The seaside residence was
erected following Russia's victory against Sweden in the Great
Northern War (1700–1721), but the royal family never lived in
it: Catherine was apparently not too fond of the palace, and after Peter's death in 1725 she visited Kadriorg only sporadical-
ly. The building was refurbished in the mid-19th century, and
in 1934 it became the official, short-lived residence of Estonia's
president. Today, the palace is home to a branch of the Art Museum of Estonia. The main hall is one of northern Europe's
most impressive pieces of baroque architecture, created from a
design by Italian architect Nicola Michetti, with intricate stucco decorations symbolising the tsar's power and the initials of
Peter and Catherine nestled above the opposing fireplaces. The
ceiling fresco, inspired by Rembrant's interpretation of a scene

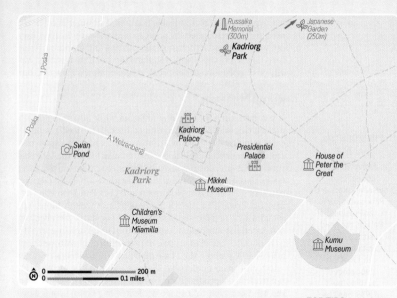

from Ovid's *Metamorphoses*, is an allegory for Russia's victory against Sweden. The other halls of the palace are dedicated to works by Russian, Dutch, Italian and German artists, ranging from the 16th to the 20th centuries. At the entrance you'll find an 1858 reproduction of the *Venus de Milo* by German sculptor Karl Voss. Upstairs, highlights include atmospheric paintings of 19th-century Tallinn by Russian landscape artist Alexey Bogoly-ubov, an 1899 bust of Tolstoy by Italian sculptor Paolo Troubetz-koy, a pair of moody 18th-century portraits by Swiss painter Angelica Kauffman, plus a set of Soviet ceramics adorned with hammers and sickles.

Mikkel Museum

The unassuming pink structure housing the Mikkel Museum, a smaller and often neglected part of the Art Museum of Estonia, used to function as the kitchen of the nearby Kadriorg Palace – yes, an entire building just for the kitchen. Converted into a residential complex during the Soviet era, the two-storey structure was restored after independence to welcome 600 artworks acquired by Estonian collector Johannes Mikkel over the course of his life. Mikkel purchased paintings and sculptures during the interwar period – many of the pieces were left behind by wealthy Baltic Germans who left as Estonia became independent – and later in life he became interested in porcelains from the Far East, making for an eclectic and intriguing collection.

Swan Pond

The round pavilion standing on the island that emerges from the centre of Swan Pond is the first thing you'll notice if you enter Kadriorg Park from the northwest. This tree-lined pool was first added to Kadriorg's grounds in 1741 and has since become one

TOP TIPS

● The Art Museum of Estonia network includes five museums, three in Kadriorg and two, the Adamson-Eric Museum (p65) and the Niguliste Museum (p60), in the city centre.

● A joint ticket for all five museums can be purchased online for €36 at kunstimuuseum. ekm.ee. Individual tickets range between €7 and €12.

● On the last Wednesday of every month individual tickets to the museums cost just €3.

● On the first Sunday of every month entrance to museums run by the city of Tallinn is free. Book at tallinn.ee/en/ museumsunday

of the park's most recognisable features. A number of cafes and restaurants surrounded the pond up until the early 20th century, but were removed in favour of the gardens and fountains found here now. Only the historic Katharinenthal Café remains, ideally positioned for a coffee break before or after a museum tour.

Kumu Museum

If you have time for only one museum while you're in Tallinn, make it this one. Kumu is contained inside a futuristic, semicircular building designed by Finnish architect Pekka Vapaavuori and showcases the evolution of Estonian art from the 18th century to the present day. Exhibitions are spread across three floors plus an outer courtyard and begin with Baltic German painters such as Oskar Hoffmann and Carl Timoleon von Neff, moving forward to the contemporary era through thousands of paintings, artefacts and sculptures. The early 20th century constructivist movement known as the Group of Estonian Artists contrasts the classic style of preceding eras with works by avant-garde painter Märt Laarman depicting society's entrance into tech-driven modernity. They are followed by increasingly political works produced during and after WWII, exhibited on the 4th floor next to a space dedicated to playful, ironic Soviet pop art and a selection of 1950s socialist realist paintings by People's Artist of the Estonian SSR Elmar Kits. Walk amid the speaking heads of prominent figures of Estonian history that form the *Seagull* installation, produced in 2006 by Villu Jaanisoo and featuring 83 busts of people who have left a mark on the country, then exit the museum to see Jass Kaselaan's *Square of Dolls* (2014) – 16 eerie concrete doll heads standing on pillars in the courtyard.

PRESIDENTIAL PALACE

Along with its collection of museums, Kadriorg Park is also home to the Presidential Palace, the head of state's official residence. The interior of this neobaroque building, built in 1938, can't be visited, but you are free to photograph the facade carrying the national coat of arms.

Kadriorg Palace (p66)

BORISB17/SHUTTERSTOCK ©

Russalka Memorial

House of Peter the Great

The little house found steps away from Kumu's cafe is a house-museum belonging to the Tallinn City Museum set up in the surprisingly unpretentious cottage where Peter and Catherine lived while Kadriorg was under construction. The house originally belonged to Baltic German aristocrat Hermann von Drenteln and was sold to the Russian tsar for 1400 roubles after the first owner's death. An introductory video shown in the underground room of the house explains the transformation of Tallinn in the 18th century. The rooms highlight objects and furniture that belonged to Peter the Great and his wife Catherine and which have been preserved for over three centuries – the museum is said to be the oldest in Estonia, founded by Alexander I in 1806.

Japanese Garden

The latest addition to the calming landscape of Kadriorg is the Japanese Garden that opened in 2011 as a relaxing oasis on the eastern edge of the park. This meditative space designed by Japanese landscape architect Masao Sone is built around a pond, with short bridges connecting a circular path that runs between boulders, small waterfalls and trees.

Russalka Memorial

Technically not inside Kadriorg Park, but best reached (and photographed) via the tree-lined Mere Alley that forms its natural frame, the 16m Russalka Memorial is one of Tallinn's oldest monuments still standing, produced in 1902 by Amandus Adamson. The sculpture, featuring an angel holding an Orthodox cross, was built to commemorate the Russian ship *Russalka* (Mermaid) which sank in the Baltic Sea on its way to Finland in 1893.

PARKS & GARDENS OF CENTRAL TALLINN

Lindamäe Park
Located near the top of Toompea, this patch of green covered by ancient linden trees gets its name from Linda, wife of the mythical Estonian leader Kalev.

Toompark
Built around Snell Pond, the city's only remaining 18th-century moat, Toompark (Dome Park) has the most diverse flora of all central Tallinn's green spaces.

Harju Hill
Easily reached via the Mayer's Staircase, adorned with cast iron vases, Harju Hill is a quiet oasis above bustling Freedom Square. Stop for a coffee break at the Harjumäe Kõlakoda cafe between sights.

Linnahall

Continued from p65

and life-size replicas of cannons used during wartime in the Middle Ages. The 17th-century bastion passages, stretching under Toompea hill, were built later than the fortifications above ground (they date to the Swedish era), and while originally meant as a safe link between the towers encircling the city, in recent times they've been used as WWII bomb shelters and gathering places for political activists and 1970s punks – as the unsettling mannequins in the darker corners of the passages show. Inside the tunnels you'll also find the Carved Stone Museum, displaying centuries-old stone decorations – columns, coats of arms, door frames – that used to adorn Tallinn's Old Town. Next to the Kiek in de Kök is the Maiden's (Neitsitorn) Tower, housing a pricey cafe and a forgettable museum about the history of the building (additional ticket required).

Dealing with a Troubled History   MAP P54
The Vabamu Museum of Occupations and Freedom

Outside the armoured door of the **Vabamu Museum of Occupations and Freedom** sits a collection of concrete suitcases, the starting point for the dark stories you'll hear inside. Marko Mäetamm's *21 Suitcases* commemorate the tens

 WHERE TO DRINK IN TALLINN

Valli Bar
Historic bar in front of the Sõprus cinema, attracting a local crowd with its cheap beer.

Winkel
Cave-like venue serving a wide selection of local beers, plus wine and cocktails.

Whisper Sister
A tiny plaque on Pärnu Street (no 12) marks this speakeasy-style cocktail bar – blink and you'll miss it.

of thousands of Estonians who fled during and after WWII as the country was occupied by Soviet and Nazi forces. Beyond is the glass-clad exhibition space where personal narratives follow the impact of half a century of foreign occupations. Divided into five sections, the museum begins and ends with videos of people who lived through the events that defined the nation from the 1940s on. Between are photographs telling the story of Jewish child Daisy, killed in 1941, a wooden fishing boat used to escape across the Baltic Sea, documents detailing the work of the 'Forest Brothers' anti-Soviet resistance movement, and a VR set which allows you to furnish your own Khrushchev-era apartment. The highlight, however, is not what you'll see, but what you'll hear – with the entrance ticket comes a pair of headphones which function less as a traditional audio guide and more as an immersive, documentary podcast, whose commentary shifts from chapter to chapter as you move between rooms. The exhibition ends with the aftermath of the Singing Revolution, the protests that started in the late 1980s and led to the restoration of independence, and Estonia's entry into the European Union. Near the exit, an art installation showing two people standing on the edges of a seesaw reminds visitors that freedom needs to be balanced with responsibility in order to function.

Soviet Giants

MAP P54

Architectural reminders of the USSR past

Talking about 'Soviet heritage' in Estonia might raise a few eyebrows, but some of the megabuildings erected in central Tallinn when the country was part of the USSR still form an impossible-to-overlook testament to the vision of communist urbanists. Those arriving by ship encounter the abandoned **Linnahall** on the way to Old Town, a concrete giant built as a sports complex for the 1980 Olympics and once known as the Lenin Palace of Culture and Sport. Inaccessible and covered in graffiti, Linnahall will eventually be restored and converted into an exhibition space – at the moment, it's only possible to climb to its rooftop to admire the Baltic from above. Even larger (and also under renovation) is the **Estonian National Library**, located near the Vabamu Museum. This monumental, avant-garde palace designed by Estonian architect Raine Karp in the late 1980s and completed only after independence, houses both the national book archive and the official parliamentary library. The current revamp will be completed in 2025. Built in the Stalinist neoclassical style of the 1950s is the **Sõprus Cinema** in Old Town, still one of
Continues on p74

THE FOREST BROTHERS

The Estonian resistance fighters known as the 'Forest Brothers' opposed the Soviet government from the early days of occupation and throughout the decade following WWII. Operating from the dense forests that cover much of Estonia, the group was made up of former soldiers and civilians who conducted sabotage operations and used guerrilla warfare tactics against the Red Army units. The Forest Brothers' struggle was overshadowed by the constant threat of death or deportation – thousands were executed or ended up in Siberia in the attempt to restore Estonia's independence. Despite their limited success, the Forest Brothers have become important figures in Estonia's collective memory.

WHERE TO DRINK IN TALLINN

Koht	Sessel	Chicago 1933
With a huge selection of craft beers you're sure to find something you haven't tried before.	Walk through a souvenir shop to get to Sessel, a cocktail bar overlooking Viru Street that also offers sushi.	Large bar in the Rotermann Quarter with live music every weekend and a summer terrace.

TOP SIGHT

Maarjamäe

Maarjamäe is where you'll find the pieces of the puzzle that is Estonia's 20th century. The seaside neighbourhood hosts the Estonian History Museum and two of Tallinn's most impressive monuments – the Soviet memorial to those who died defending the USSR and the more recent Memorial to Victims of Communism stand juxtaposed, epitomising Estonia's approach to its troubled past.

DON'T MISS

Maarjamäe Palace & Estonian History Museum

Maarjamäe Palace's Viewing Platform

Soviet Monuments Graveyard

Maarjamäe Soviet Memorial Complex

Memorial to Victims of Communism

Film Museum

Maarjamäe Palace

Overlooking Tallinn Bay from a privileged position, the restored Maarjamäe Palace is one of the few 19th-century manor houses still standing in the capital, built on a former sugar factory by Russian count Anatoly Orlov-Davydov in 1874. Today, it houses the rich collection of the Estonian History Museum – the best place to start your visit of Maarjamäe. The museum's permanent exhibition focuses on the events that have defined Estonia over the past century, starting in 1918, when it gained independence for the first time, to the present day. Try your hand at the playful 'Build your own Khrushchev-era apartment block' game, then climb to the top of the hexagonal tower for views over Tallinn and the sea. A smaller exhibition on Baltic currencies is found on the ground floor.

Soviet Monuments Graveyard

A small and freely accessible park behind the Maarjamäe Palace is the post-independence home of Soviet-era statues that once occupied public streets and squares around Estonia. Next to Joseph Stalin sits a collection of representations of Vladimir Lenin, including a giant head lying on the ground. Narva's Lenin Statue, the last to be standing in a public space in the country, is set to be relocated to the graveyard soon. The little publicity and secluded location of these monuments make clear that most Estonians would rather rid themselves of these figures – the 'graveyard' is more of an odd tourist attraction than a place to learn historical facts.

Film Museum

The long, rust-red building sitting between the Maarjamäe Palace and its stables houses the only museum dedicated to Estonian cinema, where you'll learn about both the history and the craft of filmmaking. The museum is set up to show what the process of making a movie looks like, from the script to pre-CGI effects that have appeared in famous moving images.

Maarjamäe Soviet Memorial Complex

The controversial memorial complex built as a tribute to the soldiers who perished fighting for the USSR is one of the largest Soviet monuments still standing in its original location in Estonia. Partly covered by a carpet of grass, the modernist complex was designed by Estonian architect Allan Murdmaa, who completed it in 1975. The memorial was built around Mart Port's 1960 pointy obelisk, which had been placed in Maarjamäe to honor the Bolshevik victims of the 1918 Estonian War of Independence – a need for commemoration not shared by Estonians who fought on the opposite side.

Memorial to Victims of Communism

Rather than demolishing the Soviet Memorial Complex after Estonia regained its independence in 1991, the country's Ministry of Justice chose to balance historical narratives by placing a new memorial in Maarjamäe. The Memorial to Victims of Communism, established in 2018, is composed of two sets of black walls running parallel towards the sea, carrying plaques with the 22,000 names of those who were killed or died in deportation under Soviet rule. The memorial is free to visit, but guided tours that help place it in context are available via the Estonian Institute of Historical Memory (memoriaal.ee).

THE MAARJAMÄE STABLES

The former stables of Maarjamäe were built as a shelter for the horses of the entrepreneurs running the sugar factory that preceded the palace. They have been converted into a branch of the Estonian History Museum. The museum was under renovation at the time of writing.

TOP TIPS

- The Estonian History Museum sells joint tickets (€10) which allow access to the palace and the Film Museum. The Soviet Monuments Graveyard is free.
- Both memorials are free and easily reached on public transport – buses run frequently along Pirita Road in both directions.
- At sunset, Maarjamäe offers beautiful views over Tallinn Bay and Old Town from the viewing platform on the palace's tower.
- Entrance to the palace is free on the birthday of the Estonian History Museum (19 February) and on International Museum Day (18 May).

Lembit submarine

THE MOLOTOV-RIBBENTROP PACT

In 1939, Stalin's Soviet Union and Hitler's Nazi Germany signed the Molotov-Ribbentrop Pact (named after the two powers' foreign ministers), an agreement of non-aggression which secretly divided Eastern Europe into spheres of influence, with Estonia falling into the Soviet sphere. In 1940, the USSR used this agreement as a pretext to set up military bases in Estonia, a move which led to its integration into the Soviet Union which would last until 1991. The secret protocol has left a lasting impact on Estonia's national consciousness – the Molotov-Ribbentrop Pact is perceived as a betrayal of the right of self-determination granted in 1918, when the country first gained its independent status.

Continued from p70

Tallinn's largest movie theatres, while just outside the medieval walls is the 1972 **Hotel Viru**, its white tower dominating Tammsaare Park. The lower floors house a shopping mall, while the top floor is home to the **KGB Museum**, where you'll learn how the Soviet secret police kept an eye on the hotel's international guests. Among other Soviet buildings around central Tallinn are the 1980 **Hotel Olümpia** and the **Kosmos Cinema** dating back to 1964.

Inside Seaplane Harbour's Submarine   MAP P54
A look at life at sea

Under the three concrete domes of the 1917 hangar known as **Seaplane Harbour** (Lennusadam) you find one of Europe's most intriguing maritime museums, opened in 2012. Originally commissioned by the Russian Empire as part of Tallinn's port, history turned Seaplane Harbour – a piece of cutting-edge architecture in its time – into the headquarters of the Estonian Air Force marine unit when the country gained independence in 1918. After decades of neglect, the hangar was restored to its former glory in 2009 and was awarded the European Union Prize for Cultural Heritage in 2013. Celebrating Estonia's long-standing relationship with the sea,

FESTIVALS IN TALLINN

Tallinn Craft Beer Weekend
For two days in June, local and international breweries provide visitors with the challenge of sampling hundreds of beers.

Estonian Song & Dance Festival
The biggest, held every five years, celebrates the country's history of choral singing.

Kalamaja Days
In mid-May Kalamaja turns into one big neighbourhood party, with markets, concerts and street food stalls.

the dimly-lit Seaplane Harbour is an extension of the Estonian Maritime Museum and exhibits historic vessels used to explore the Baltic – above and below the water. Occupying a large section of the hangar is the 59.5m **Lembit submarine**, built in the UK between 1935 and 1937 for the Estonian Navy. The submarine is the only Estonian vessel constructed before WWII to have reached the present day, and you can wander its claustrophobia-inducing interiors to get a feel for undersea life and walk through the vessel's eight sections, from engine rooms to sleeping quarters. Outside the hangar's perimeter but included in the ticket price, you can also board the **Suur Tõll icebreaker**, built in Germany in 1914 for the Imperial Russian Navy, the US-made Valvas ship, purchased by the Estonian government in 1997, and a series of smaller vessels.

An exciting addition to Seaplane Harbour's collection is a 24.5m medieval shipwreck, discovered in 2022 during excavations near Tallinn's Old Town and currently being restored under the giant white box to the right of the museum's entrance. Experts are still debating the ship's origin, although evidence seems to point to Scandinavian construction in the mid-14th century. At the time of writing conservation efforts are underway, but it's possible to take a sneak peek through the porthole windows of the protective cover. The remains of the ship, one of the largest of its kind to ever be found in Europe, will eventually be put on display in the museum.

Quirky Kalamaja, Above & Below Ground

MAP P54

Community museum and cemetery turned public park

From neglected industrial area to lively cultural hub, the capital's Kalamaja neighbourhood has undergone a radical transformation over the past two decades. The **Kalamaja Museum**, a recent addition to Tallinn's rich museum scene, opened in late 2021 and offers a glimpse into the life of a district that was considered 'best avoided' in the past. Rather than offering a linear, comprehensive overview of the local history, this community exhibition space occupies three stories of a 1930s house where donated everyday objects recount the personal stories of the area's former residents. The mismatched collection can be hard to navigate, but the friendly English-speaking staff is available to explain the concept behind this blend of art and local ethnography. Steps away from the museum is **Kalamaja Park**, the area's green lung, a calming space where tall trees shade ideal summer picnic spots and with no visible evidence of its previous life as Tallinn's oldest cemetery – thousands of people are buried under the park's surface.

PATAREI PRISON

The Patarei Sea Fortress, better known as the infamous Patarei Prison, was originally built under the orders of Tsar Nicholas I as a defensive structure for the Russian Empire, but was later turned into a prison used by the Estonian Republic, the Nazis and the Soviet Union. For years, the massive complex housed the eerie 'Communism is Prison' exhibition, but in 2023 tours of the interior stopped to allow for the complete overhaul of the fortress, which will be completed in 2026. Part of the former prison is currently being demolished to make space for restaurants, shops and office buildings, with only a section dedicated to the new International Museum for the Victims of Communism.

 FESTIVALS IN TALLINN

PÖFF Black Nights Film Festival
One of the Baltics' most important film festivals takes place in November.

Old Town Days
Old Town's largest cultural festival celebrates ancient traditions in early June.

Tallinn Street Food Festival
In early June, the Song Festival Grounds turn into a huge, open-air restaurant filled with food trucks.

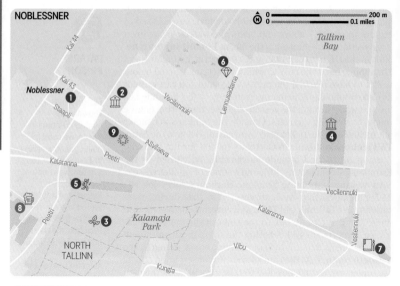

NOBLESSNER

Tallinn Bay

Noblessner

Kalamaja Park

NORTH TALLINN

From Tech to Techno in Noblessner MAP P76

Transformed Russian shipyard in upscale neighbourhood

The huge, golden ship propeller on the harbour's edge is the symbol of **Noblessner**, a former submarine shipyard of the Russian Empire, now an entertainment-centric neighbourhood with some highly-prized properties. Developed by a member of the Nobel family and his business partner in 1912, the shipyard produced eight submarines during WWI. Today, the buildings address more contemporary needs. One is home to the **Kai Art Centre**, where you can find changing contemporary exhibitions and a cinema. Another houses the **PROTO Invention Factory**, a museum-theme park hybrid loved by kids, where prototypes of famous historical inventions can be 'tried' first-hand thanks to VR headsets.

Adults may want to wait for the weekend to have their senses altered – the **Hall Techno Club** hosts local and international DJs year-round. International restaurants and bars overlook the marina, with outdoor tables and benches filling up on summer evenings. Look out for the **Iglupark**, a collection of saunas also overlooking the water. Available for rental, these saunas are designed by Iglucraft (iglucraft.com), a growing Estonian brand that has made steam rooms for the likes of Gordon Ramsay and David Beckham. For a sauna-drink

 WHERE TO GET COFFEE IN TALLINN

RUKIS
Enjoy coffee and freshly made cake under the huge chandeliers of this refined cafe.

Brick Coffee Roastery
Coffee is taken seriously in this roastery, as shown by the many coffee-related awards on the walls.

Kohvik Lummus
Inviting cafe in the heart of the city, where artists exhibit and workshops are held. Summer courtyard in the back.

combo, check out **Põhjala Brewery**, one of the largest independent beer makers in the Baltic. On the ground floor is the production area (tours available via pohjalabeer.com), while upstairs is the modern tap room – and a sauna. The 24 different beers available should be enough to warm you up, but you can increase the heat by booking a private sauna session.

Tallinn's Design Central
Internationally inspired Rotermann Quarter

Self-described as Tallinn's 'Bold Town', the **Rotermann Quarter** is definitely the result of some 'bold' architectural choices that have revamped the former industrial area where the roads leading to Tartu, Narva and Pärnu intersected. Today, refurbished warehouses and asymmetrical contemporary buildings combine to form a dynamic, walkable area of the city. The neighbourhood is, aptly, home to the **Estonian Museum of Architecture**, featuring models of many of the city's most iconic buildings, and the **PoCo Pop And Contemporary Art Museum**, displaying works by artists such as Keith Haring, Banksy and Andy Warhol. Most people, however, come here to either eat, drink or shop in the many restaurants, bars and designer stores that line the area's alleys. Squeezed amid big brands and modern hotels, **Tallinn Design House** sells an ever-changing selection of Estonian fashion, homeware, ceramics and furniture. And when it comes to food, try the artisanal pastries at **RØST Bakery** or a fancy dinner in one of the international restaurants (Belgian, Mexican, German, Spanish) found on Stalkeri käik.

Rural Estonia in an Open-Air Museum
A wander round rural Estonia

For a visit to rural Estonia without leaving the capital, head to the **Estonian Open Air Museum**, a centre for the preservation of traditional architecture located 7.5km west of Old Town in the Rocca al Mare district. Log houses typical of the Orthodox communities of **Lake Peipsi** (p112), temporary homes used by the semi-nomadic fishermen of Hiiumaa, wooden windmills and chapels dating as far back as the late 17th century form this 'little Estonia' exhibition that spreads over 70 hectares. The majority of the buildings here are not reproductions, but authentic structures that have been relocated to Tallinn for conservation purposes. In 2021, a 1960 apartment block that once housed families working on a southern Estonian *kolkhoz* (collective farm) during the Soviet era was transferred to the museum and is now open for visitors, standing in stark contrast with the wooden architecture that surrounds it. You can spend a whole day wan-

TALLINN ON FILM

Much has changed in the Rotermann Quarter since 1979, when Soviet director Andrei Tarkovsky used the neighbourhood as the backdrop for his sci-fi masterpiece *Stalker*. The area was yet to receive its 'design district' label, but that movie paved the way for others to be shot in Tallinn in the following decades, the most recent being Christopher Nolan's *Tenet* (2020), which was filmed in various locations including Linnahall, the Kumu Museum and Maarjamäe. This cinematic legacy and the Ministry of Culture's Film Estonia Cash Rebate initiative (a fund offering a reimbursement of up to 30 percent for filming expenses) have contributed to making Tallinn an attractive destination for international movie directors.

WHERE TO EAT AND DRINK IN NOBLESSNER

Wambola Surf
Cocktails and tacos on a pier and a docked ship, with frequent music events adding to the cool vibe. €€

Robert's Coffee
Breakfast, brunch and lunch are all reasons to visit Robert's, a Finnish franchise recently welcomed to Noblessner. €

Suvila
Suvila's urban garden is a hidden oasis where you can enjoy some of Tallinn's best pizzas. €€

dering the park's network of paths that connect 80 buildings representing different historical periods and different Estonian regions, but if you want to speed up your tour, rent a bicycle when you arrive. There are a few handicraft stores and cafes dotting the site, or bring your own food and picnic in one of the many idyllic spots between micro-villages. Many events take place in the museum in spring and summer, including folk music concerts, dance exhibitions and crafts workshops – check the full programme at evm.ee.

Beyond Tallinn's Favourite Beach   MAP P76

More than sand on the edge of the city

The district of Pirita, 6km east of central Tallinn, is best known for the sandy beach that attracts vitamin D-seeking city dwellers and windsurfers on sunny summer weekends. Its fame as a resort destination received a boost in the Soviet era, when the massive Olympic Yachting Centre was built to host the sailing events of the 1980 Moscow Olympics. Not far from the seaside are the **Pirita Convent** ruins, once the largest monastery in Old Livonia, dating to the early 15th century. The convent housed Bridgettine nuns until 1577, when Russian tsar Ivan the Terrible invaded and destroyed much of the structure. The roofless remains now stand on the edge of the Pirita River Valley Nature Reserve. A new convent dedicated to St Bridget was opened next to the ruins in 2001. Part of the forest that extends behind the convent is occupied by the **Tallinn Botanic Garden**, where more than 8000 species of plants coexist in protective greenhouses. Next to it is the **TV Tower**, also built for the 1980 Olympics but better known for the crucial role it played during the fight for independence. The story goes that on 21 August 1991 – the day after Estonia declared its independence from the USSR – a group of radio operators working in the TV Tower blocked access to Soviet troops attempting to gain control of communication infrastructure by hijacking the lift in order to protect the right of free speech the country had recently reacquired.

The Urban Experiment of Väike-Õismäe MAP P76

Soviet-era district on edge of the city

An experiment in socialist urban development took place in the mid-1970s, when the district of Väike-Õismäe appeared on the western side of Tallinn. Built around an artificial lake, the apartment buildings of the new neighbourhood formed a series of concrete rings that were meant to offer its residents easy access to the stores, schools and leisure centres found near the core of the district. This microdistrict still houses over 27,000.

WHAT'S IN A NAME?

Why does the Rocca al Mare district of Tallinn have such an Italian-sounding name? It's all down to a French aristocrat and businessman who in the 19th century had an estate created here – his summer residence was in the park that is now occupied by the Estonian Open Air Museum. After purchasing the land, Arthur Gerard de Sucanto decided to add a Mediterranean touch by giving the estate an Italian name, 'rock by the sea', that has since been applied to the whole neighbourhood. Besides the museum, Rocca al Mare features a promenade that links Kakumäe and Stroomi beaches, Tallinn Zoo and one of Estonia's largest shopping malls.

WHERE TO EAT AND DRINK IN NOBLESSNER

KaiF Agaveria
Creatively furnished tequila and mezcal bar, with tables spilling on the marina in summer. €€

Kampai
Modern, refined Japanese cuisine in a former storehouse, offering shareable small plates and hearty mains. €€€

180°
Michelin-starred Matthias Diether's tasting menus elevate Estonian flavours in a sophisticated atmosphere. €€€

Beyond Tallinn

Map labels: Lahemaa National Park, Viimsi, Maardu, Paldiski, Keila, **Tallinn**, Rakvere, **Rummu**, Kose, Tamsalu, Risti, **Rapla**, Järva-Jaani, Paide, Vändra, Türi, Põltsamaa, Viljandi

Estonia's northern coast stretches east and west from the capital, combining dense forests, rural fishing villages and Soviet relics.

The cosmopolitan character of Tallinn fades rapidly as you leave the capital behind. Travel east and you'll soon find yourself in the tall forests of the country's largest national park, Lahemaa, where hiking and cycling routes connect elegant manor houses once owned by the Baltic German aristocracy. Further east, past Lahemaa, are the ruins of Rakvere's 13th-century fortress. Go west, and you'll pass former prisons, mining operations and secretive military bases left behind by the Soviets on the road leading to Estonia's western coast. Inland from Tallinn are the agricultural plains of central Estonia, an area with few attractions besides a piece of 1970s avant-garde architecture between wheat fields.

Lahemaa National Park (p82)

Places

Viimsi p80

Rakvere p80

Rummu p81

Lahemaa National Park p82

Rapla p86

GETTING AROUND

Lahemaa National Park is best explored with your own vehicle, but bus 155 runs from central Tallinn to Loksa (the main town inside Lahemaa National Park) and the start of the Viru Trail. Viimsi and Rummu can also be reached by bus. The Baltic Express railway line once connected Tallinn with St Petersburg and Moscow in Russia. Today, the train ends before the border in Narva, stopping in Rakvere on the way. Trains also travel west to Paldiski and south to Rapla.

☑ TOP TIP

Frequent buses and trains run to and from the capital, so northern Estonia can be easily toured by public transport.

LEMANNA/SHUTTERSTOCK ©

ESTONIA'S NORTHERNMOST ISLAND

During summer months, the Vrangö ferry departs daily from the port of Leppneeme, on the Viimsi Peninsula, for the port of Kelnase, the main settlement on Estonia's northernmost island, Prangli. Fewer than 100 people live permanently on Prangli today, but the island – whose surface area measures less than 7 sq km – is believed to have been inhabited continuously for over 600 years. Day tours here departing from the capital, including a short hike through the nature reserve and a guided visit to the local fishing villages, can be organised via the Tallinn Tourist Information Centre on Niguliste Street between June and September.

Viimsi

TIME FROM TALLINN: **30 MINS**

Folk traditions on the outskirts of the capital

Despite its proximity to the capital, Viimsi Peninsula feels like a very different place. This sparsely populated district stretching north of popular Pirita Beach houses three museums, each representing a different facet of the local culture. **Viimsi Open Air Museum** echoes the concept of the more recent Estonian Open Air Museum in western Tallinn (p52), showcasing buildings and working equipment of the communities that lived on the shores of the Baltic Sea in the 19th century. While much smaller than its Rocca al Mare counterpart, it makes for a pleasant day out from the city, with beautiful views of Tallinn's harbour. Less than 1km away is the red building housing the **Museum of Coastal Folk**, where you can get more insight into the customs and traditions of the people living along the Gulf of Finland and on the northern Estonian islands. The most important cultural institution in Viimsi is the **Estonian War Museum**, which examines the conflicts that have defined the country's history. The exhibition space is found inside Viimsi Manor, originally founded by the nuns of the Pirita Convent in 1471 and rebuilt multiple times over the following centuries to become the residence of Swedish, Russian and Estonian generals. The Estonian Army's commander-in-chief Johan Laidoner, who lived in the villa until 1940, established the museum in 1919. His study has remained intact, although the most fascinating section of the museum is the military vehicle hangar, open only during weekends between May and October.

Rakvere

TIME FROM TALLINN: **1¼ HR**

Medieval family fun

Crumbling **Rakvere Castle**, dating back to the 13th century, marks the heart of this sleepy town located approximately halfway between Tallinn and Narva and easily reached by train from the capital. The dramatic ruins are part of a Danish fortress believed to have been built on the site of an ancient settlement known as Tarvapää, and later expanded by the Livonian Order to make room for a convent. Abandoned in the early 17th century after being heavily damaged by both Polish and Swedish armies, the castle is now a kid-friendly museum that comes to life in the summer, with medieval-inspired activities including archery and candle-making available to visitors.

Costumed actors often perform sword fights and cannon shooting shows for the public, while permanent exhibits include a torture chamber, the lab of a medieval alchemist and a reconstructed

WHERE TO EAT IN VIIMSI

Coccodrillo
Italian dishes served on an open terrace near the Estonian War Museum; ideal for a quick bite. €€

Reval Café
The Estonian chain Reval is a safe bet for good coffee, brunch or a snack. €

PAAT
This modern restaurant cooks up an international menu of generous dishes best enjoyed outside. €€

Rakvere Castle

KLOOGA CONCENTRATION CAMP MEMORIAL

Surrounded by woods near the village that bears the same name, the Klooga Concentration Camp Memorial commemorates the Holocaust victims who perished during the German occupation of Estonia. Nazi Germany set up the concentration camp in September 1943, and a year later, as the Red Army was approaching from the east, German soldiers exterminated the 2000 Jewish prisoners here. Klooga is remembered as one of the largest mass murders committed by German forces in Estonia. Today, two triangular stone sculptures resembling blades emerge from the ground, with text and images tracing the history of the concentration camp, next to a monument dedicated to all Jews killed in Estonia between 1941 and 1944.

refectory. You can combine a castle visit with a trip to the nearby **Aqva Waterpark & Sauna Centre** and the **Estonian Police Museum**, where children and adults can learn how to identify a murder weapon and photograph themselves in a police uniform. While you're in Rakvere, include a stop at the monumental **Tarvas Statue**, a 7m-long aurochs (an extinct ancestor of the modern bull) weighing over seven tonnes, placed near the castle in 2002 to celebrate the town's 700th anniversary. The animal is a reference to Rakvere's former name – in the 13th century, the *Livonian Chronicle of Henry*, one of the oldest written reports mentioning Estonia, described the settlement on which the town was founded as Tarvanpää, meaning 'head of an aurochs'.

Estonia has a growing population of 800–1000 brown bears, the majority of which live in the area of Alutaguse, southeast of Rakvere, together with deer, elk and a wide variety of birds. Outdoor tour company NatourEst (natourest.ee) has set up two wildlife watching hides in the middle of Alutaguse's forest where you can spend the night trying to spot the bears in their natural habitat. Late spring and early summer offer the highest chances of seeing the animals in the wild from the narrow windows of the hide, which can be reached by car or taxi from Rakvere.

Rummu

TIME FROM TALLINN: **1 HR 20 MINS**

Exploring an abandoned quarry

Partially submerged by the greenish waters of Lake Rummu, the derelict building that once stood in the middle of the **Rummu limestone quarry**, 45km west of Tallinn, adds a pleasant touch of eeriness to the calming scenery of this sandy corner of northern Estonia. Quarrying began in 1938

Continues on p84

 WHERE TO EAT IN RAKVERE

Schenkenberg Tavern
Medieval-inspired lunch inside Rakvere Castle; pricier than average, but the location is hard to beat. €€

Sarvik
Legendary burgers in a rustic yet sophisticated grill restaurant. €€

Berliini Trahter
A life-size brown bear statue welcomes you to this German restaurant serving pub dishes and beers. €€

PRACTICALITIES

Scan this QR code for info on hiking in Lahemaa.

TOP SIGHT

Lahemaa National Park

Covering 725 sq km, Lahemaa is Estonia's largest national park. Hiking, cycling, camping, kayaking and other activities are all great ways to explore the bogs, bays, lakes and forests of this rural landscape, easily reached from Tallinn. A number of villages and glamping facilities dot the area, allowing you to stay close to the action and away from the crowds.

DON'T MISS

Viru Bog Trail

Hara Submarine Base

The Baltics' Forest Trail

Palmse Manor

Sagadi Forest Museum

Käsmu village

Bog Walking on the Viru Trail

Nothing says Estonian landscapes like bogs. The spongy peat formations form cloud-like surfaces in wetland areas such as the southwestern corner of Lahemaa National Park, where the Viru Bog Trail extends for 3.5km. Many bogs formed in prehistoric times and are considered the oldest landscapes in Estonia. Due to their soft consistency, bogs are best walked on with footwear similar to snow shoes – bog-shoeing is a fun way to explore these unique areas – but in Viru you won't have to worry about such equipment. The trail here consists of a wooden boardwalk suspended over the bogs, wide enough to be wheelchair accessible, and leads to an observation tower found about 1.5km in. Although Lahemaa National Park is best explored with your own vehicle, the start of the trail can be reached in a little over an hour from Tallinn with buses that run to Loksa, a short walk from Viru. If you're visiting in summer, remember to bring mosquito repellent – bogs are a natural breeding ground for the merciless insects.

Hara Soviet Submarine Base

LAHEMAA'S FAUNA

The thick forests of Lahemaa are home to many mammals including moose, bears, elk, deer and elusive Eurasian lynxes – Estonia's only wild cats. These creatures are typically shy, and, given the size of the park, spotting them is unlikely unless you're with a guide. Binoculars are handy for observing over 200 bird species from watchtowers.

Hara Soviet Submarine Base

One of the many concrete reminders of the Soviet era, the Hara Submarine Base was once a military station for the USSR's navy whose existence was known to few outside the hundreds of workers employed here. Built between 1956 and 1958 on Hara Island, off the eastern coast of the Juminda Peninsula, this secret port was one of the few in the USSR equipped with the demagnetisation technology needed to make submarines undetectable by radar. After being decommissioned in 1991, the submarine base was abandoned and forgotten. Hara Island – whose residents were relocated elsewhere when the base's construction began – remains off limits, but it's possible to visit the derelict pier known as Hara Sadam that extends from the peninsula. Urban explorers and graffiti artists have been visiting the little known structure independently for years, but in 2018 an official ticket booth (tickets €10) was set up and Hara has become a fascinating historic site to add to your Lahemaa itinerary. Hara can technically be reached by public transport from Tallinn, although the trip is slow and schedules vary from day to day. If you don't have a car, your best option is to get to Loksa and either hike from there (2hr one way) or rent a bike at the tourism office (open noon–5pm). Hara Sadam (harasadam.ee) also features a few glamping cabins where you can spend the night, a sauna and a bicycle rental service.

Hiking the Baltics' Forest Trail

A section of the Baltics' Forest Trail, the long-distance hiking route stretching for 2141km across Lithuania, Latvia and Estonia, passes through Lahemaa, starting from the Oandu Visitor Centre and running all the way to Tsitre on the

TOP TIPS

- Lahemaa National Park can be visited year-round, but long summer days offer the best conditions for exploring nature.
- The Lahemaa Visitor Centre is found at Palmse Manor, in one of the former stables of the complex.
- Loksa is the main town within the park's borders, followed by Võsu. Both are small, but are connected to Tallinn via public transport, and have bike rental services and guesthouses.
- A tiny tourism office operates next to Loksa's bus station in summer, with bike rental available. In front of the office is a supermarket to stock up on supplies.

LAHEMAA'S RARE FLORA

Pine trees dominate the landscape of Lahemaa National Park, but many rare species of plants populate the forests, swamps and grasslands of this lush corner of the country. Sea sandplants form a green and yellow carpet on many of Lahemaa's beaches, while orchids, perennial honesty flowers and Arctic raspberries grow next to nearly 400 species of lichens.

opposite side of the park. Completing the itinerary will take about four days, and if you plan it correctly you'll be able to avoid pitching a tent by stopping at guesthouses along the way. Be aware that the Forest Trail is not a hiking trail that runs through a forest in its entirety – gravel and asphalt roads open to (minimal) car traffic compose much of the path, which can be viewed in the detailed maps and GPS tracks available at baltictrails.eu. Besides this multiday hike, it's possible to explore the park on shorter routes such as the 7km Majakivi-Pikanõmme Trail, starting near the Hara Submarine Base and running through bogs and boulders, or the 3km Altja Nature Trail, from the tiny coastal village of Altja, passing traditional log houses and rivers cutting through the trees.

Manors & Palaces

For centuries, the pristine nature of Lahemaa has made it a leisure destination for Estonia's aristocracy. The Baltic German nobility – a class of landowners and traders descending from the Christian missionaries that moved to the Baltics in the 13th century – built opulent villas in Lahemaa, some of which still stand today, converted into either museums or hotels. Palmse Manor, first built in 1720 and later reconstructed, is Lahemaa's prime historic building, housing the park's visitor centre, a museum with period furniture and clothing, and a restaurant. South of the beach town of Võsu is Sagadi Manor, a late baroque complex of 20 buildings built by a Baltic German family in the mid-18th century. Inside the pink buildings, now managed by Estonia's State Forest Management Centre, you can tour the interesting Forest Museum to learn about the flora and fauna of Lahemaa, the history of

Palmse Manor

Käsmu

Estonia's primary export – wood – and nature-oriented local folk traditions. In Sagadi you'll also find a hotel and one of the few hostels available within the park; book in advance if you plan to stay on a summer weekend. Those looking to upgrade can also sleep at the luxurious Vihula Manor, a 16th-century villa located in the eastern fringes of Lahemaa that has been converted into a country club with a spa.

Cycling to Käsmu

Nicknamed the 'captains' village' due to the maritime school that once operated from its harbour, charming Käsmu is a historic hamlet that has been watching over the Baltic Sea since at least the 15th century. A path ideal for cycling starts from the western edge of Lake Käsmu, easily reached through the road connecting Loksa and Võsu, and runs through the peninsula's forested grounds all the way to the village's rock beaches, where a few family-run guesthouses host guests during summer months. The Käsmu Sea Museum, housed inside a Russian-era border guard station, displays hundreds of sea-related objects that offer a glimpse into the settlement's long-standing relationship with the Gulf of Finland. It's possible to continue cycling past the village up to Cape Palganeem, the northernmost point on the Käsmu Peninsula, for expansive views over the Baltic. The complete loop stretches approximately 16km.

CAMPING IN LAHEMAA

Sleeping in close contact with nature is possible in Lahemaa. Besides a number of privately managed campgrounds and glamping cabins available in the park, the RMK, Estonia's State Forest Management Centre, has designated five campsites where you are allowed to pitch your tents, located in the areas of Oandu, Võsu, Purekkari, Juminda and Tsitre. Details available on loodusegakoos. ee.

Continued from p81

and intensified during the Soviet era, when forced labourers from the nearby Murru Prison altered the landscape forever, forming the lake with excess water from the mining operations. The atmosphere is especially ghostly (and photogenic) during foggy winter days, while in summer the 'beach' in Rummu comes to life with an open-air cafe, plus stand up paddleboards and pedal boats available to rent. Hike up the artificial hill overlooking the lake and the village of Vasalemma, but be careful as the sandy soil is shifting.

If you want to take a closer look at the abandoned structures of the former quarry and prison, head underwater – the local Rummu Adventure Centre (rummu.eu) organises scuba diving and snorkelling excursions to discover the hidden relics of the area. Entrance tickets (€5) to Rummu are available at rummu.ee. If you visit outside of summer you will need to call the number found on your ticket once you reach Rummu to have someone open the electric gate. Bus 146 regularly departs from central Tallinn and stops right outside the quarry.

ATOMIC PALDISKI

Besides the house-museum of Estonian sculptor and painter Amandus Adamson (1855-1929) and the Pakri Lighthouse standing on the edge of the eponymous peninsula, there is little to see in the small town of Paldiski, a 20-minute drive from Rummu. This is by design. During Soviet times the town was a secret and inaccessible nuclear submarine training centre, where mock up military vessels with nuclear reactors were built to train the navy. Military operations shut down in 1989, three years after the Chernobyl disaster, due to safety concerns. Today, most of the military infrastructure has been demolished.

Rapla

TIME FROM TALLINN: 1 HR 🚊

All things octagonal

Today it may sound odd to talk of central Estonia – an area mostly devoted to large-scale agricultural activities – as a hub of architectural experimentation, but things were different in the 1970s, when Estonian designer Toomas Rein picked the town of Rapla as the location of an extravagant new creation. The **Okta Centrum** was erected in 1977 as a multi-purpose building meant to house various commercial and administrative spaces, and it still stands, surrounded by apartment blocks, as a curious example of late 20th-century socialist modernism. Everything here has an octagonal shape, from the building itself which looks like a six-layer wedding cake, to the pool cut in the back garden and the concrete litter bins. The Okta Centrum didn't survive the privatisation of the 1990s, and after a brief stint as an office space the building was abandoned. In 2015 it was declared a cultural monument, although at the time of writing it can only be observed from the outside. A train runs directly to Rapla from Tallinn's railway station. From Rapla's station it takes approximately half an hour to reach the Okta Centrum on foot (with little to see along the way). A possible addition to your Rapla itinerary is the Maarja-Magdaleena Church, a short distance from Okta and designed by Baltic German architect Rudolf von Engelhardt in 1901. The church can hold more than half of Rapla's population at one time and hosts the yearly Rapla Church Music Festival in July (more information at raplafestival.ee).

OTHER SIGHTS AROUND RUMMU

Ämari Pilots' Cemetery
Cemetery commemorating Soviet pilots who fought in WWII, with airplane fins used as tombstones.

Keila Waterfall
A 3km hiking trail runs around Keila Waterfall, Estonia's third tallest with a 6m drop.

Treppoja Cascade
Treppoja waterfall is formed by six steps between one and two metres high, guiding the river toward the Baltic Sea.

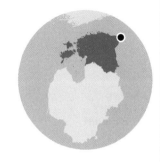

Narva

BORDERS | RELIGIOUS PAST | RIVER CRUISES

Running from the Gulf of Finland to Lake Peipsi, the Narva River forms a natural boundary separating Estonia from Russia. On its banks, in the easternmost part of the country, the city of Narva appears as a quintessential border town, facing its Russian counterpart Ivangorod across the water. The site of a major battle between Soviet and Nazi forces during WWII, the formerly baroque city Narva was razed to the ground in 1944, leaving little of its Swedish heritage left to see. According to estimates, only 2% of the buildings in the city were still standing following the conflict. Today, reconstructed Narva is a place inhabited by predominantly Russian-speaking residents, where Orthodox churches and Khrushchev-era apartment blocks shape much of the urban landscape surrounding its landmark castle. Standing in stark contrast with the tourist playground of Old Tallinn, Estonia's third largest centre is a post-war city standing as a vivid example of the complex historical and cultural layers that have defined this region in the 20th century.

GETTING AROUND

Narva is easily explored on foot. The city centre is a 15-minute walk from the railway station, and all the main attractions are within a short distance from one another. Buses 1, 2 and 4 run from Pushkin Street to Joala Park in 25 minutes, from where the Kreenholm Factory is steps away. A bike rental service is available at the Narva Joaoru Gym on Linnuse Street, with prices starting from €3/hour.

☑ **TOP TIP**

Multiple trains a day run from Tallinn to Narva in about 2½ hours. To reach Tartu from Narva you'll need to switch trains in Tapa, or take the (faster) bus. Narva's castle is walking distance from the railway station.

KRISTINE DOKANE/SHUTTERSTOCK ©

Narva River

NARVA'S AUTONOMY REFERENDUM

In 1993, the predominantly Russian populations of the cities of Narva, Kohtla-Järve and Sillamäe, in the eastern Ida-Viru district, set up a referendum to call for autonomous status within the Republic of Estonia, worrying that their rights could be limited in the newly independent nation. Despite the Estonian government's declaration of the referendum as unconstitutional, the vote proceeded in mid-July. In Narva, over half of the population participated, with an overwhelming 97% majority favoring autonomy. The effort was ultimately fruitless as the referendum's results were not recognised by the national government, but highlighted a division that continues to exist within Estonian society despite ongoing integration initiatives.

Narva Castle

Rival Castles

Narva's imposing fortress

The bulk of **Narva Castle**, also known as Hermann Castle, grabs all the attention as you look at the city from the river bank. Topped by the 51m-tall whitewashed Hermann Tower, the castle faces the equally intimidating Ivangorod Fortress, a stone's throw away across the water in Russia. At a time of geopolitical divisions, the scene is telling: the heavily policed Narva River running between the two structures marks the end of NATO territory and the beginning of the Russian Federation, as the white, blue and red flag flapping above Ivangorod makes clear. Built by the Danes in the mid-13th century and later expanded by Germans, Swedes and Russians, Narva's fortress was heavily damaged during WWII and its most recent renovation was completed in 2020. As you enter the castle, a large courtyard leads to the modern Narva Museum. The collections here extend across four floors and contain a series of interactive exhibitions on the history of the city from the Middle Ages to the 20th century, with many images of Narva before its destruction during WWII. On the top floor, a viewing platform provides 360-degree views: across the river towards Ivangorod and its 1492 fortress built by

 WHERE TO STAY IN NARVA

Narva Hotell
Centrally located, offering comfortable rooms with modern amenities. Worth the stay for the breakfast buffet alone. €€

Inger Hotel
Inger can feel a bit anonymous, but it's clean and has a wellness centre offering various treatments. €€

Central Hotel
The old-school rooms could do with an update, but they're well positioned for the city's landmarks. €€

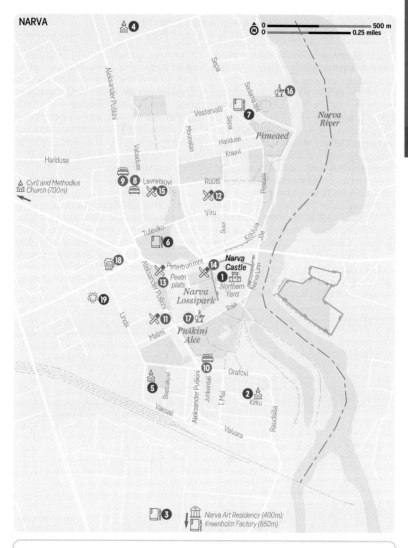

NARVA

0 — 500 m
0 — 0.25 miles

Narva River

Pimeaed

Narva Castle

Narva Lossipark

Puškini Alee

Narva Art Residency (400m);
Kreenholm Factory (850m)

TOP SIGHTS
1 Narva Castle

SIGHTS
2 Alexander's Cathedral
3 Cultural Palace of Vassili Gerassimov
4 Icon of Our Lady Church
5 Resurrection of Christ Cathedral
6 Veetorn
7 Victoria Bastion

SLEEPING
8 Central Hotel
9 Inger Hotel
10 Narva Hotell

EATING
11 Bublik Cafè
12 Kohvik Muna
see 10 M.Chagall
13 Old Trafford
14 Rondeel
15 Valge Kõrvits

DRINKING & NIGHTLIFE
16 Club RO RO
17 German Pub
18 Irish Embassy

ENTERTAINMENT
19 Vaba Lava Theatre

Start at ❶ **memorial to the victims of Soviet repression** which stands in Jaama Park, outside the train station. From there, you can easily visit Narva's main religious buildings: walk north to reach ❷ **Alexander's Cathedral** (p92) then then turn left along Grafovi Street to find the ❸ **Resurrection of Christ Cathedral** (p92). Continue along Linda Street beside the walls of the former Baltijets Soviet military factory until you see the big ❹ **mural depicting Estonian singer Jaak Joala** next to the Vaba Lava Theatre, then turn right on Kosmonaudi Street and walk to the bridge separating Estonia from Russia. South of the bridge is ❺ **Narva Castle** (p90). After a tour of the Narva Museum inside the castle pass below the ❻ **Veetorn Tower** and continue north to visit the ❼ **Town Hall**, one of the few buildings that survived the 1944 bombing, designed

in 1668 and recently restored. Next door is ❽ **University of Tartu Narva College** with its new oblique roof. Turn right on Kraavi Street to get to the ❾ **Dark Garden**, the city's oldest park. Steps away is the ❿ **Victoria Bastion**, while a little further on you'll reach ⓫ **Narva Art Gallery**, displaying a miniature version of the city before it was bombed and paintings ranging from Russian Empire-era portraits to Soviet industrial-inspired art. Continue north and then around the bastion along Sadama tee to get to ⓬ **Narva's port**, housed inside a former prison, from where the *Caroline* departs for Jõesuu in summer (p96). From here, return to the castle by walking along the promenade and continue on to the ⓭ **Narva Jõeoru Trail** for the best views of the two fortresses, eyeing each other across the river.

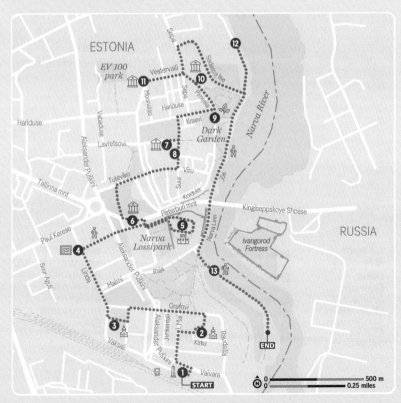

Russian ruler Ivan III in response to Narva's castle; and across Narva itself towards the brutalist Veetorn residential building and the metallic roof of Alexander's Cathedral reflecting the sky. In the summer a traditional crafts market is set up in the castle courtyard.

Inside the Victoria Bastion
A defensive structure protecting humans and bats

Coveted by empires east and west, strategically positioned Narva required a large defensive system to avoid enemy attacks. Walls were first built in the late 13th century, when the city was sold to the Livonian Order – together with all of northern Estonia – by the Danish Crown. The early fortifications did not stand the test of time, and the Swedes reconstructed and modernised the walls in the 17th century after conquering the city that had fallen under Russian control a century earlier. Military engineer Erik Jönsson Dahlbergh designed the new defences to include six bastions, but that was not enough to stop the Russians, who repossessed the city during the Great Northern War (1700-1721). Tsar Peter I would eventually complete Dahlbergh's project, although Narva lost its status of border city as it was absorbed into the Russian Empire, making the bastions unnecessary. Despite massive damage done during the Soviet bombings of WWII, some sections of the defences are still visible today, although a public park covers much of the former bastions along the river. The most impressive part is the 16m **Victoria Bastion**, at the northeastern corner of the city, which has been fully restored and converted into a museum. Enter for a guided tour of the dark tunnels that run through the casemates, which have long protected not only humans but also a large population of bats that inhabit the interior. Make sure to bring a jacket even if you're visiting in summer, as temperatures inside the tunnels are chilly year-round.

ESTONIA'S ALIEN PASSPORTS

Estonia's 'alien passports', also known as 'grey passports', were issued to non-citizens, primarily ethnic Russians, who continued to reside in Estonia after the dissolution of the Soviet Union in 1991, but didn't qualify as full citizens for lack of Estonian language and history knowledge. While provided with basic social services, holders of these passports cannot vote or move freely within the EU – Estonia has encouraged non-citizens to naturalise over the years, but tens of thousands of residents continue to maintain their 'alien' status to this day.

WHERE TO EAT IN NARVA

Rondeel	Old Trafford	M.Chagall
Come for the medieval feel and castle views, stay for the generous portions and beers. €€	A vast choice of Russian and international dishes served on the terrace (during summer). €	Named after artist Marc Chagall, the Narva Hotell restaurant offers a meat-centric menu in its art-filled hall. €€

TELIA/SHUTTERSTOCK ©

Resurrection of Christ Cathedral

A CRUISE ON THE NARVA RIVER

Between May and October, the *Caroline* ship departs from Narva's port (Narva sadam), located beneath the historic Victoria Bastion, taking up to 50 people on a cruise along the Russian border all the way to Narva-Jõesuu, the resort town at the mouth of the river. The two-storey boat departs twice a day and takes about 1½ hours to reach Narva-Jõesuu, where a number of spa hotels line up along the sandy beach. On board you'll enjoy live music and a small buffet. Make sure to have your ID with you, as you'll be traveling in a border zone. Tickets (€15 return) can be purchased on board; schedules available at narva-line.ee.

Narva's Religious Roots

City of churches

While broader Estonia is growing increasingly secular, Narva maintains a large population of Orthodox Christians and **Old Believers** (p119), as proven by the high concentration of churches found in its city centre. The most important religious building is the impressive **Resurrection of Christ Cathedral**, a late-19th-century neobyzantine structure that survived Soviet bombardments and still serves as Narva's gathering spot for its Orthodox community. The church, open daily to the public, holds services multiple times per week. Different in both use and aesthetics is **Alexander's Cathedral**, a neogothic church named after Tsar Alexander II that serves the city's Lutheran minority. The 19th-century building was heavily damaged during WWII and stopped operating in Soviet times. Only in the 2000s did it undergo major renovation work, including the installation of a lift in the bell tower, reopening as a barely used place of worship and a museum that includes a video detailing the history of the cathedral and a viewing platform. Other churches in Narva are the cubic **Cyril and Methodius Church** and the **Icon of Our Lady Church**, both topped by golden onion domes following the Eastern tradition.

 WHERE TO EAT IN NARVA

Bublik Cafè
Great lunch spot serving tasty *pelmeni* (dumplings), pasta, cakes and coffee. €

Kohvik Muna
Enjoy a slice of daily changing cakes or a vegetarian-friendly light lunch in this modern cafe in Town Hall Square. €

Valge Kõrvits
This homely, rustic cafe serves tasty Russian soups and salads, with a decent selection of wines and hot teas. €€

Industrial Heritage at the Kreenholm Factory

Once one of the world's largest cotton mills

The former **Kreenholm Factory** rises above the Narva River south of the city centre. Located on Kreenholm island, right on the border with Russia, the massive brick complex occupies much of the island and used to house the Kreenholm Manufacturing Company, a textile factory established in 1857 by a German industrialist who took advantage of the energy provided by the nearby Narva Waterfall to found what would later become the Russian Empire's largest cotton mill. With more than 10,000 workers producing over 10% of the whole empire's cotton output, the city became one of the world's most important textile centres. Such intense activity came at a human cost. Child labour, internal police control, poor hygienic conditions and endless shifts were the norm until 1872, when the first strike in Estonian history took place in the factory and the owners were forced to provide basic rights. Kreenholm declined in the 20th century. The factory was privatised after the collapse of the USSR, and closed in 2009. Plans to turn the area into an arts and nightlife hub were put on hold during the pandemic. Today, this former industrial heartland is a collection of monumental but abandoned buildings on the outskirts of the city. Visiting is possible on a guided walking tour organised by the Narva Museum. Starting at the Kreenholm gates opposite Joala Street, the 90-minute tours (Sundays from noon, April-October; book at narvamuuseum.ee) allow access to closed-off areas, with English speaking guides providing explanations on the life of Kreenholm.

Postwar Gloom

Understanding the reconstructed city

Travelling around Estonia, you'll struggle to meet anyone recommending a visit to Narva, a city often described as lacking historical heritage as a result of WWII destruction. But understanding modern Narva involves discovering its interesting post-war reconstruction. The majority of the centre is composed of the five-storey 'Khrushchevka' apartment buildings that shaped many Soviet cities in the early 1960s. A cheap solution to mass housing needs, these buildings were inhabited by the many families who moved to Narva from Russia and the countryside to work in its industrial sector. Such Khrushchevka flats surround the 12-storey **Veetorn residential building**, Narva's only skyscraper, in Peetri Square. The Veetorn (water tower) complex, completed in 1969, is topped

NART, NARVA'S ART RESIDENCY

Housed inside a red brick building that was once used by the director of the Kreenholm Factory, the Narva Art Residency is an exhibition space where creative experimentation takes diverse forms. Supported by the Estonian Academy of Arts and the Ministry of Culture, NART invites international artists from all walks of life to spend two months in the city, producing work ranging from sculpture to music to architecture. Since opening in 2015, NART has welcomed artists from all around Europe, the US, Japan, Canada and South Africa. Entrance to the temporary shows costs as little as €1, and you can check what's currently on show at nart.ee

 WHERE TO DRINK IN NARVA

Club RO RO
Summer-only bar at the port, with live music and cocktails served until the early hours.

Irish Embassy
Despite the name, a good selection of local beers (and pub food) is served in this Irish pub.

German Pub
There's nothing German about this place, but the pub grub and free-flowing beers make for a pleasant pit stop.

Cultural Palace of Vassili Gerassimov

ESTONIA'S PLACE NAMES ACT

The symbols of Narva's Soviet past are the source of a major ideological clash between the predominantly Russian residents of the city and the Estonian authorities, who have upped their efforts to get rid of monuments commemorating the USSR since the start of the war in Ukraine. In 2022, a T-34 Soviet tank that stood on a pedestal in central Narva as a WWII monument was relocated to the **Estonian War Museum** (p80). The central government has also asked the local council to change street names associated with Soviet figures, following the Place Names Act introduced in 2004, but Narva has done so only partially and continues to resist the request from Tallinn.

by a water reservoir that originally had a giant portrait of Lenin hanging from it. Close to the Resurrection of Christ Cathedral is the Baltijets plant. In Soviet times this gargantuan building did not appear on maps: the USSR's Ministry of Atomic Energy used it to develop secretive military technology, including nuclear weapons. Narva Museum organises regular tours of Baltijets, but at the time of writing they're only available in Estonian and Russian. The **Vaba Lava Theatre** operates in part of the building, and a 200-sq-metre mural depicting Estonian musician Jaak Joala covers one of the walls. The derelict, Stalinist-style **Cultural Palace of Vassili Gerassimov**, named after one of the organisers of the 1872 strike at the **Kreenholm Factory** (p93), stands south of the train station, near the **monument to Amalie Kreisberg**, another Kreenholm activist who died in prison after being arrested following a protest.

Beyond
Narva

An odd combination of secretive industrial towns and long sandy beaches with spa hotels characterises northeastern Estonia.

The Russian border stretches for about 70km along the Narva River from the Gulf of Finland to Lake Peipsi, forming a natural boundary between the two countries. Estonia and Russia continue to share a common history, culture, and language in the northeastern Ida-Viru County, where Russian speakers constitute 80% of the population. Heading north from Narva, you'll find the tranquil resort town of Narva-Jõesuu, where a 7km beach lined with pine trees functions as the main draw for summer holidaymakers. On the way back to Tallinn, you'll encounter the industrial towns of Sillamäe and Kohtla Järve, two urban centres that developed during the Soviet era and still carry traces of that former chapter in Estonia's history.

Narva-Jõesuu (p96)

Places

Narva-Jõesuu p96

Sillamäe & Kohtla Järve p97

GETTING AROUND

Narva-Jõesuu, Sillamäe and Kohtla Järve are all connected to Narva by public transport and can easily be explored on foot. Sillamäe's bus station is located a 20-minute walk from the centre of town, with comfortable Lux Express buses stopping on the way to/from Tallinn.

☑ TOP TIP

Comfortable Lux Express buses run along the northern coast connecting Narva to Tallinn via Sillamäe. Book tickets online (luxexpress.eu).

PÜHTITSA CONVENT

Located 60km southwest of Narva, Pühtitsa Convent, also known as Kuremäe Convent, is the last Russian Orthodox nunnery in Estonia to be still functioning. Founded in 1891 on the site of a previous 16th-century church, the convent has grown to house a largely self-sufficient community of approximately 100 nuns, who operate under the authority of the Patriarch of Moscow. The architectural design of the convent reflects traditional Russian Orthodox styles, featuring six buildings with ornate domes and beautifully decorated chapels, all surrounded by gardens. The main cathedral, dedicated to the Assumption of the Mother of God, houses particularly impressive frescoes and icons. Pühtitsa is open daily from 6am to 8pm, and is free to visit.

Narva-Jõesuu

Narva-Jõesuu

TIME FROM NARVA: **20 MINS** 🚌

A relaxing resort town

The sandy beach stretching for more than 7km along the Gulf of Finland is the main attraction of Narva-Jõesuu, the holiday resort located 13km north of Narva next to the mouth of the Narva River. The town has been a popular summer destination for Russian tourists for decades, and while crossborder traffic has recently slowed for obvious reasons, Narva-Jõesuu is still a place many visit to relax and recover. Among some elegant early-20th-century wooden houses scattered around, the Narva-Jõesuu Sanatorium stands out thanks to its functionalist architecture. Built in the 1960s, the spa hotel initially served the workers of Estonia's collective farms, and continued to provide various treatments after privatisation post-independence.

 WHERE TO STAY IN NARVA-JÕESUU

Noorus Spa Hotel
Family-friendly Noorus comes with a pool, wellness centre, small water park and beautiful views of the Gulf of Finland. €€

Narva-Jõesuu Sanatorium
Close to the harbour, this Soviet-era spa has kept true to its modernist roots, while updating its health treatments. €€

Hotel Veagles
About 1km from the beach, this frills-free, family-run hotel offers basic amenities. €

Sillamäe & Kohtla Järve   TIME FROM NARVA: **35 MINS** 🚗

Industrial cities revealing uncomfortable stories

Before WWII, **Sillamäe** was just a few houses overlooking the Baltic Sea, 27km west of Narva, but after 1944 this sleepy seaside town would rise to prominence. When Estonia became part of the USSR, Soviet geologists came to the coast here for its vast oil shale deposits, a type of rock that contains uranium – the essential ingredient of nuclear weapons. A processing plant was built and around it grew a closed town. Often omitted from maps and referred to by code names, Sillamäe played an important role in the USSR's nuclear programme and still stands as one of the best preserved examples of Stalinist urban planning in Estonia. With broad avenues, stately staircases, ornate window frames and some of the last hammers and sickles on display, it's as graceful as it is eerie. The **town hall** resembles a Lutheran church, while the stately **Cultural Centre** is adorned with a colonnade: enter for a tour and spot the portraits of Marx and Lenin. Nearby stands the **Peaceful Atom monument** and steps leading to the **Sea Boulevard** with a viewpoint over the Baltic, a small beach and a cafe. The plant stopped processing uranium in 1990, but by then over 12 million tonnes of hazardous waste had been deposited in an open 'pond', one of the most dangerous sites of its kind in Europe. It took Estonia nearly two decades to clean up the mess. After Sillamäe, if you're craving more industrial heritage, head to **Kohtla Järve**, 31km away, where the world's only museum dedicated to oil shale is open for visitors.

CAN THE HAMMER & SICKLE BE DISPLAYED IN ESTONIA?

Sillamäe and Kohtla Järve are among the few places in Estonia where you can still see the hammer and sickle publicly displayed. In 2007, the Estonian Parliament attempted to introduce a law to make the public use of Soviet and Nazi symbols a crime, but the bill didn't pass and the law never came into effect. In 2023, the topic was again discussed by the government, which passed an amendment in the Building Code preventing the construction of new buildings and monuments carrying icons that ideologically support or glorify the occupation. The amendment would also allow the removal of existing communist symbols, although heritage buildings will be discussed on a case by case basis.

Tartu

CULTURE | QUIRKY MUSEUMS | SCIENCE

GETTING AROUND

Despite being Estonia's second largest city, Tartu's centre is small and best visited on foot. Public transport runs frequently to sights outside of Old Town – take bus 7 to get to the Estonian National Museum and Raadi Park, and bus 1 or 2 to reach Aparaaditehas. Both sides of the Emajõgi River are lined with cycling paths, allowing you to easily explore the city on two wheels.

☑ **TOP TIP**

The Tartu Smart Bike Share has made 750 regular and electric bikes available to the public at 69 stations around the city. You can rent a bike (starting at €2 per hour) via the Tartu Smart Bike mobile app and drop it off at any station in town.

Nominated European Capital of Culture 2024, Estonia's second city has long been known as the country's cultural heartland. The arts and sciences have flourished here since 1632, when the *Academia Gustaviana* – the first and most prestigious university in the country – was founded by the Swedish Empire. Sitting on the banks of the Emajõgi River, Tartu gained prominence after entering the Hanseatic League in the 13th century, but a fire would destroy much of its urban core in 1775. The compact historic centre west of the river was rebuilt in the charming neoclassical style Tartu is known for today. The university was heavily damaged during WWII, but most of the city's core managed to survive both the conflict and the Soviet 'restyling' that shaped much of its eastern side. A quiet city of less than 100,000, Tartu is made vibrant by the student population that seasonally renews itself.

WALENCIENNE/SHUTTERSTOCK ©

University of Tartu (p105)

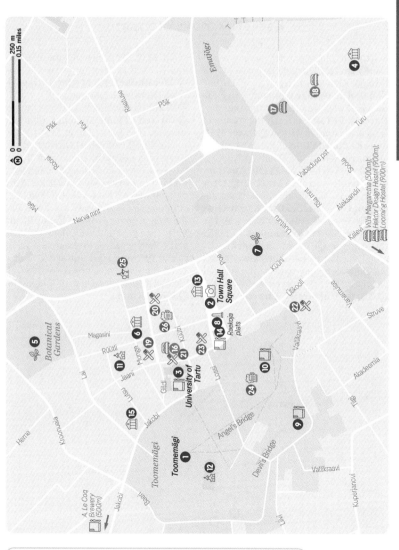

TOP SIGHTS

1 Toomemägi
2 Town Hall Square
3 University of Tartu

SIGHTS

4 AHHAA Science Centre
5 Botanical Garden
6 Estonian Sports and Olympic Museum
7 Kesk Park
8 Kissing Students
9 Old Anatomical Theatre
10 Old Observatory
11 St John's Church
12 Tartu Cathedral
13 Tartu Kunstimuuseum
14 Town Hall
15 Toy Museum

SLEEPING

16 Antonius Hotel
17 Dorpat Hotel
18 Hotel Tartu

EATING

19 Crepp
20 La Dolce Vita
21 Restaurant München
22 Vilde Ja Vine
23 Werner

DRINKING & NIGHTLIFE

24 Gunpowder Cellar
25 NAIIV
26 Pühaste Kelder

99

A STROLL AROUND OLD TARTU

Starting in front of the giant pig statue outside ❶ **Tartu's Market Hall**, take a stroll through Kesk Park to reach the ❷ **Father and Son sculpture** on Küüni. Cross the road and walk past the ❸ **Monument of Barclay de Tolly** to reach the statues of Irish and Estonian writers ❹ **Oscar Wilde and Eduard Vilde** sitting on a bench in an imagined meeting. Climb up Vallikravi and walk behind the ❺ **Old Anatomical Theatre** before a break at ❻ **ULA Baar**, under the shadow of the modernist ❼ **St Luke's Methodist Church**. Cross the ❽ **Devil's Bridge** and pass by the ❾ **Johan Skytte Monument** to reach the ruins of ❿ **Tartu Cathedral**. Descend via Lai Street then take a right. You'll notice a sign marking the original location of Tartu's University and then the ⓫ **Tartu University Church** found-ed in 1855. Walk around the block to find yourself in front of the neoclassical ⓬ **Headquarters of the University of Tartu** and continue all the way to ⓭ **St Johns Church** and, steps away, the ⓮ **Citizen's Home Museum**. Continue straight, then turn right at Lai Street to get to the ⓯ **Botanical Garden of the University of Tartu**. After a walk around the pond, take a quick tour of Supilinn, the working-class neighbourhood made of traditional wooden houses that extends east of the A. Le Coq Brewery. Once you find the giant wooden swing at ⓰ **Supilinna Kiik**, turn back and walk along the bank of the Emajõgi River to the arched bridges and ⓱ **Town Hall Square**. Continue along the river to complete the loop, after rewarding yourself with a mojito at ⓲ **Väike Kuuba**.

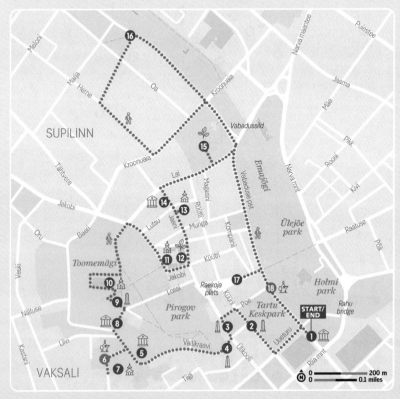

Tartu Town Hall

Musical Town Hall Square

Old Town's epicentre

The statue of the **Kissing Students** – a symbol of the city that was refurbished as part of the 2024 Capital of Culture programme – stands in Tartu's main square. This open space is framed by restaurant terraces that converge towards the 18th-century **Town Hall**, built by German architect Johann Heinrich Bartholomäus Walter following a fire that destroyed much of the city in 1775. Originally, the square hosted Tartu's main market (now moved to the Turuhoone hall near the bus station) but today stalls only appear in December, when the city lights up for Christmas. The Town Hall still serves as the local government's seat – only the Tartu Visitor Centre and the historic pharmacy found on the ground floor can be accessed. The baroque tower topping the Town Hall houses Estonia's biggest carillion, a system of 34 bells that play five times a day at 9am, noon, 3pm, 6pm and 9pm. The musical programme changes – while you're likely to hear songs by Estonian composers such as Ülo Vinter and Riho Päts,

Continues on p104

TARTU'S QUIRKY MUSEUMS

Tartu Kunstimuuseum

Situated in a slightly tilting historic building in the heart of Old Town, this art museum – the largest in southern Estonia – showcases Estonian and international art from the early 20th century to the present day.

Estonian Sports and Olympic Museum

Dedicated to the history of sports in Estonia, the museum features a wide range of memorabilia, exhibits on famous athletes and interactive displays that showcase the country's sporting achievements.

Toy Museum

A nostalgic journey through the history of playthings, Tartu's Toy Museum displays a charming assortment of toys from different eras, with interactive exhibits for children to learn about the evolution of toys over time.

WHERE TO STAY IN TARTU

Looming Hostel
Close to the railway station this funky hostel has been welcoming the backpacker crowd for years. €

Hektor Design Hostel
Matching the vibe of the surrounding Aparaaditehas, this 'smart' hostel comes with a sauna and a gym. €

Villa Margaretha
Elegant art nouveau villa in picturesque Karlova district, with an excellent restaurant. €€

SVETLANA MAHOVSKAYA/SHUTTERSTOCK ©. BOTTOM RIGHT: WALENCIENNE/SHUTTERSTOCK ©

PRACTICALITIES

Scan this QR code for information on exhibitions and events in Tartu Cathedral.

TOP SIGHT

Toomemägi

Crisscrossed by a network of paths, leafy Toomemägi hill is considered Tartu's birthplace. Early settlers built the first fortification here in the 7th century CE, but this was destroyed by crusaders in the 13th century and replaced with a bishop's castle in 1224. Forming the backdrop to Town Hall Square, 'Cathedral Hill' makes for a pleasant stroll among some of Tartu's most important cultural sites, with views of the city as a bonus.

DON'T MISS

Tartu Cathedral

University of Tartu Museum

The Old Observatory

The Gunpowder Cellar

Angels & Devils

Toomemägi is easily accessed from the city via the stately Angel's Bridge (Inglisild), built in the early 19th century and honouring the first rector of the University of Tartu. The 'Angel' name is believed to come not from the Bible, but from a mistranslation from German of *Englische Brücke* (English Bridge). The name stuck and a century later a second bridge built in Toomemägi, paying tribute to the Romanov tsars, acquired the nickname of Devil's Bridge (Kuradisild).

Tartu Cathedral

The gothic skeleton of Tartu Cathedral (pictured), the largest in the country, has stood on top of Toomemägi since the 13th century, when the knights of the Livonian Order conquered the city, driving the pagan natives out and introducing Christianity to Estonia. The cathedral took two centuries to complete before being largely destroyed during the Livonian War

(1558-83) and ceased to function as a place of worship, leaving Toomemägi with just its ruins ever since. In the early 19th century, the hill was acquired by the University of Tartu, which rebuilt parts of the cathedral and turned its main hall into a library. Today, the cathedral houses the University of Tartu Museum. Besides the historic library, you can visit the modern university treasury, which includes artefacts such as the death mask of Russian poet Alexander Pushkin and objects gifted by the Russian tsar Alexander I to the university's rector.

Prominent Scholars

Toomemägi has a number of statues that honour the scholars who left their mark on the history of the University of Tartu. Baltic German scientist Karl Ernst von Baer is considered the founding father of the field of embryology. The statue of Villem Reiman, designed by Amandus Adamson, celebrates the founder of the Estonian National Museum, while Friedrich Robert Faehlmann gained his spot in the park for being the first Estonian physician to obtain a doctoral degree.

The Old Observatory

The tower of Tartu's Old Observatory functioned as the city's prime stargazing spot for over 150 years, from 1810 to 1964. Originally run by German-Russian astronomer Friedrich Georg Wilhelm von Struve, the observatory was one of a network of measuring stations spread around the world built to calculate the exact circumference of Earth – the UNESCO-inscribed Struve Geodetic Arc. A concrete monument to Struve's efforts is located outside the observatory, which now operates as a museum dedicated to seismology.

The Gunpowder Cellar

If you enjoy your beer served with a side of historic architecture, there's no better place to go than the Gunpowder Cellar (Püssirohukelder) dug in Toomemägi in 1778 to house the Russian Empire's stock of gunpowder. After a brief stint as a university hall, the long gallery covered by 11m-tall arched brick ceilings was turned into a restaurant and pub spread across two floors, where live events are regularly held.

TARTU'S OLD ANATOMICAL THEATRE

The semicircular building standing on the southern end of Toomemägi used to be the city's main educational institution for doctors and surgeons. Its core dates back to 1805, but the neoclassical structure expanded over the course of the 19th century. The Old Anatomical Theatre is not accessible to the public, but the collection of preserved organs and body parts is exhibited at the AHHAA museum (p105).

TOP TIPS

- Multiple staircases lead up Toomemägi from different points in the city, but the main access point is via Lossi Street.
- The best views over the Town Hall and the red roofs of the historic centre of Tartu are found in front of the Old Observatory, near the Struve monument.
- For a coffee break between stops visit Toome Kohvik, by the cathedral; for a cocktail or beer, go to ULA Baar. Both offer outdoor seating in summer.

WALENCIENNE/SHUTTERSTOCK ©

St John's Lutheran Church

TARTU SYNAGOGUE

The earliest records of a Jewish settlement in Tartu date to the early 19th century, when migrants from Lithuania moved to the city. The Jewish community grew over the following decades, leading to the construction of a wooden synagogue in Turu Street in 1876, later expanded in 1901 to form a grand place of worship designed by architect Robert Pohlmann. As Nazi Germany invaded Estonia in 1941 the Tartu Synagogue stopped its activity. The Jewish population was decimated and Germany declared Estonia 'Judenfrei', free of Jews, in 1942. In 1944, the Tartu Synagogue burned down, ceasing to exist. A number of artefacts that survived the fire are now exhibited in the **Estonian National Museum** (p107).

Continued from p101
you might also notice some international classics (and all the expected Christmas tunes throughout December). Take a seat in one of the square's cafés and enjoy a drink with a musical accompaniment.

Climbing Gothic St John's

A Lutheran church rising above the city

One of the landmark buildings of central Tartu is the towering St John's Lutheran Church. Built as a Catholic place of worship in the first half of the 14th century, its current gothic form is the result of many transformations. Badly damaged during both the Great Northern War and WWII, the church lost the majority of the terracotta statues representing citizens of Tartu in the Middle Ages that once adorned its exterior – over 1000 were produced, but only about 200 have survived to the present day. Enter the building (tickets €3) to climb the 135 steps that lead to the steeple's viewing platform for a great view over the city's rooftops.

 WHERE TO STAY IN TARTU

Dorpat Hotel
Comfortable, upmarket rooms and a restaurant on the river, steps away from all the sights. €€

Hotel Tartu
A midrange choice that offers straightforward rooms near the bus station and Old Town. €€

Antonius Hotel
Old Town boutique hotel with elegant, antique furniture and top-notch service. €€€

Intellectual Pride

Estonia's first university

Named Dorpat by the Germans and Yuryev by the Russians, Tartu has shifted identities multiple times over the course of its history, growing from a medieval military outpost to the centre of Estonia's national revival in the late 19th century. Since the 17th century, the **University of Tartu** has functioned as the city's cultural pillar. Named *Academia Gustaviana* after Swedish King Gustavus Adolphus, historians tend to view the early days of the institution, Sweden's second university after Uppsala, as a colonial endeavour meant to educate future ruling classes of the conquered territories. The project was short-lived. The university operated in Tartu from just 1632 to 1699, when it was moved to Pärnu, only to be shut down a decade later. It was reopened in Tartu by Tsar Alexander I of Russia in 1802, growing to become Estonia's prime research centre at the turn of the 20th century. When the Soviet and German armies clashed in the 1944 Battle of Tartu, the university lost 15 of its buildings. But it survived, and continued to operate throughout the Soviet era. The **university's main building**, built during Alexander I's reign, is impossible to miss, with doric columns adorning its facade and ionic columns lining the auditorium. A section of the main building is dedicated to the **University of Tartu Art Museum**, Estonia's first art museum exhibiting a large collection of 19th-century plaster-cast copies of Greek sculptures obtained from all over Europe, and the **Mummy Chamber**, where two actual mummies from the university's Egyptian collection are available to view.

THE SNAIL TOWER

Rising high behind the AHHAA Science Centre, the cylindrical, residential Tigutorn tower – nicknamed the Snail Tower due to its vortex-shaped rooftop – has become one of Tartu's most notable modern landmarks, marking the skyline along the right bank of the Emajõgi River. Architects Vilen Künnapu and Ain Padrik completed the 23-storey structure in 2008 and it has since become one of the most highly prized pieces of real estate in the city, with unmatched views from the top floors.

Science City

A museum that makes you go 'AHHAA'

Tartu's dedication to scientific discoveries is not seen just inside its university halls. The city has many monuments and museums echoing the city's long-standing relationship with various scientific disciplines, from mathematics to botany. The **AHHAA Science Centre** is the most important of these. A model of an Ariane rocket welcomes visitors at the entrance of the museum, which exhibits hundreds of objects meant to demonstrate surprising physics principles. You can spend a full day playing with the interactive 'toys' of AHHAA (if you are with kids, you likely will). Besides riding the vertigo-inducing bicycle on the high-wire next to the world's largest Hoberman Sphere (a geometric structure that can expand and contract) hovering above the Hall of Technology, you can

WHERE TO EAT IN TARTU

Gunpowder Cellar	Werner	Crepp
Former military storehouse serving heartwarming dishes and a long list of local beers and ciders. €€	Always busy local favourite thanks to an array of freshly baked pastries. Sit in the hidden courtyard in summer. €	Sweet pancakes and big salad bowls are on the menu of this cosy lunch spot. €€

RAADI CEMETERY

Tartu's largest burial site is also its oldest. Raadi Cemetery was first established in the late 18th century, mainly serving the Baltic German population of the city and the university community – some of the most prominent scholars of the latter are buried here, including scientist and explorer Carl Ernst von Baer, whose statue stands by Tartu Cathedral. Monumental family chapels still dot the area, now a national monument. Some 900m away from the Raadi Cemetery, on Roosi Street, sits the Old Believers Cemetery, built in the 19th century for the sect's members and later expanded to serve Tartu's Jewish population.

YEGOROVNICK/SHUTTERSTOCK ©

Tartu Botanical Garden

visit the **Planetarium** and the gory medical collection of the University of Tartu, a display of preserved human skulls, organs and foetuses dating as far back as 1803 and once used for research purposes in the **Old Anatomical Theatre** (p103).

A Long Tradition of Botany

Explore a 150-year-old botanical garden

Established by the University of Tartu in 1870, the city's **Botanical Garden** houses over 1000 species of plants – both Estonian and imported, mostly perennial – in and around a triangular greenhouse on the edge of the historic centre. Tropical plants and desert flora grow enclosed inside the greenhouse that recreates their ideal climate, while the open-air collection showcases indigenous species of flowers and plants, split into 11 sections. The exterior is free to roam and partially covers the site where Tartu's defensive walls were once located. The city's medieval fortifications were built in the 13th century and protected the population until 1708, when the Russian Empire blew up most of the walls during the Great Northern War. A small section of the defences has remained intact, adding a touch of history to the tranquil, green oasis.

 WHERE TO EAT IN TARTU

Restaurant München
From schnitzels to pretzels, the menu here is a tasty dive into Bavarian cuisine. €€

La Dolce Vita
A checkered tablecloth kind of place serving authentic Italian dishes including excellent Neapolitan-style pizza. €€

Vilde Ja Vine
Opulent decor and a seasonal menu celebrating local flavours, plus an enviable wine list. €€

Raadi Park & Estonia's Cutting-Edge National Museum

Connecting the past and future

Designed in the mid-19th century as an extension of the **Raadi Manor** where the local Baltic German nobility resided, the green expanse northeast of the centre known as **Raadi Park** has undergone several transformations over its history. In 1914, the owner of the property, Reinhold Karl von Liphart, flattened part of it to allow Russian military airplanes coming from St Petersburg to land, and when the Estonian Government took control after independence, the area became the seat of the aviation regiment of the Estonian Defence Forces. Two hangars, built in 1926 and 1936, still stand as a testament to the early days of aviation. Most of the other structures were heavily damaged during WWII, including Raadi Manor itself, which had been converted into the country's first national museum in 1922. The park became a Soviet military air base after the war, but following the restoration of independence in 1991 a decision was taken to bring back the **Estonian National Museum**. The project committed to reflecting the park's history – the impressive glass-clad building was created as an extension of the asphalt airstrip – and has over 140,000 objects covering the history of Estonian customs and traditions. Especially intriguing is the 'Echo of the Urals' exhibition that explores the connections and roots of Finno-Ugric-speaking communities around the world. For something less intellectual, in front of the museum is the Instagram-friendly **Upside Down House** (exactly what the name suggests), while **Tartu Adventure Park** is less than 1km away.

From Widget Factory to Culture Centre

Exploring hip Aparaaditehas

Art galleries, handicrafts stores, speciality coffee shops, street art and vegan restaurants set against a backdrop of Soviet-era industrial architecture are what you'll find at **Aparaaditehas** (the Widget Factory), south of the city centre. Following in the footsteps of Tallinn's **Telliskivi** (p62), this place combines all the necessary ingredients to produce an attractive 'creative hub', with trendy dining and shopping options too. Group tours where you can learn about Aparaaditehas' history as an official umbrella production plant and non-official submarine parts factory are available upon request, although the contemporary elements of the neighbourhood are the main magnet for visitors. After biting into the fresh pastries

A STROLL THROUGH KARLOVA

Stretching south of the city centre, the neighbourhood of Karlova has managed to keep its historic character intact in rapidly modernising Tartu. The colourful wooden houses lining up along the leafy roads have maintained their 19th- and 20th-centuries appearance, contrasting with the more recent murals that are scattered in this charming corner of the city. During the Karlova Days festival, held each year in late spring (find dates at karlova.ee) historic houses open to visitors and markets and live music events draw the crowds.

 WHERE TO DRINK IN TARTU

Barlova	**NAIIV**	**Pühaste Kelder**
Karlova's neighbourhood pub has craft beers and ciders and regular live music.	Pink, two-storey boat docked on the Emajõgi River that gets especially busy in warm weather.	Below street level pub serving ever-changing artisanal beers from Estonia and the rest of the world.

of **Cruffin**, step into the **AG47 gallery** to check out innovative photography exhibitions or discover new artists at **Kogo**. A fun way to spend an afternoon is touring the **TYPA**, one of the earliest businesses to open in Aparaaditehas. Set in a former warehouse, the space collects antique but functioning letter presses that follow the evolution of printing technology in Europe. A guided tour is included in the entrance ticket (€10) on which besides learning how books and documents were produced in the past, you'll get to make a sheet of your own recycled paper and print one of Tartu's symbols on it to have a one-of-a-kind souvenir to take home with you.

The Oldest Beer in the World?

Touring a historic brewery

In 1820, Belgian merchant Albert Le Coq, descendant of a Protestant Huguenot family who had fled to Prussia in the 17th century, moved to London to expand his wine trading business. In England, Le Coq found the recipe for his success – exporting stout beer to the Russian imperial court. To avoid high customs duties, the brewery established by Albert ended up relocating to the Russian Empire at the turn of the 20th century, first to St Petersburg and later to Tartu, becoming Estonia's largest beverage producer. Known as Tartu Õlletehas during Soviet times, the brewery regained its original name, **A. Le Coq Brewery**, in 1999. The malt tower was converted into a museum, where interactive exhibits connect the brewery's history with the development of the beer-making process over various periods. The museum also holds a bottle of what is claimed to be the oldest beer in the world. In 1869, the *Oliva* ship was transporting a container of Imperial Extra Double Stout from London to Gdansk when a storm caused it to sink. A century later, the shipwreck was found and a number of bottles emerged intact from the sea, including the one on display here today. While cracking open the 150-year-old A. Le Coq stout is not possible, the ticket does include one glass of beer from the contemporary selection available at the bar.

KGB CELLS MUSEUM

The KGB Cells Museum in Tartu, located in the building that once served as the organisation's headquarters on Riia Street, offers a stark glimpse into Soviet-era history. The museum features a series of restored cells, designed to replicate the oppressive environment of a prison in the post-WWII era. While small in size (30 minutes is typically enough for a visit), the space is powerfully evocative, providing a compelling narrative of the experiences of political prisoners through personal objects that belonged to arrested members of the **Forest Brothers resistance movement** (p71) and tools used by Soviet police officers during investigations. The photographs and informative text panels provide context, with no grim details left out.

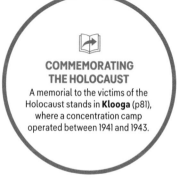

COMMEMORATING THE HOLOCAUST
A memorial to the victims of the Holocaust stands in **Klooga** (p81), where a concentration camp operated between 1941 and 1943.

Beyond
Tartu

Religious and linguistic minorities keep ancient traditions alive in the picturesque countryside.

Few of the thousands of visitors that come to Tallinn make it to southern Estonia, a region of rolling hills and rural settlements sparsely inhabited by Russian-speaking communities of Old Believers and musically gifted Setos. From the shores of Lake Peipsi to the twin city of Valga, the borderlands surrounding Tartu offer an intriguing blend of nature and culture, with much to discover for the curious traveller. Olympic skiers and snowboarders make use of the region's hilly surface to train for competition during snowy winter months, while in summer southern Estonia forms the backdrop to folk festivals and long forest hikes in the country's lesser-known parks.

Lake Peipsi (p112)

MPAULINE/SHUTTERSTOCK ©

GETTING AROUND

The fastest way to move around southern Estonia is by car, but many places are reachable by public transport – Go Bus services run from Tartu's bus station to most towns and since 2023, regional bus rides have been free. The long-distance Forest Trail, one of the two Baltic Trails (baltictrails.eu) that cross Estonia, Latvia and Lithuania, passes along the shore of Lake Peipsi and through Setomaa.

☑ TOP TIP

The Go Bus buses running from Tartu to the countryside are free. Foreign visitors are allowed on board without the public transport card locals use.

REGINA M ART/SHUTTERSTOCK ©

PRACTICALITIES

Scan this QR code for information on festivals and events in the city.

TOP SIGHT

Viljandi

Nestled between Tartu and Pärnu on the shore of the lake that carries the same name, charming Viljandi is celebrated for its cultural scene, which comes to life during summer through major open-air events such as the Viljandi Folk Music Festival. The historic centre surrounds the ruins of a medieval castle, forming a network of picturesque cobbled streets best explored on foot.

Viljandi Castle

DON'T MISS

Viljandi
Castle

Viljandi
Museum

St Paul's
Church

Kondas
Centre

Ugala
Theatre

Set on a hill overlooking Lake Viljandi, the crumbling remains of the town's castle are its most treasured landmark. German Knights of the Catholic Teutonic Order settled in Viljandi in the early 13th century, erecting the fortress in 1224 on the foundation of a former stronghold believed to have existed since at least the 9th century. The Polish-Swedish wars of the 1600s brought the castle to its ruinous state. Enter the leafy hill where the archaeological site is found via the path that runs next to the Kondas Centre or by crossing the 1879 suspension bridge running for 50m across the ditch on the southern side of the park.

Town Hall

At its inception, Viljandi's Town Hall looked nothing like it does today. Completed in 1774, the structure changed entirely in the 1930s, turning from baroque palace to functionalist administrative building, following the style in fashion at the time. The German-built clock embedded in the tower rising above the city was installed as part of the redevelopment project and is now listed as a national monument.

Viljandi Museum

The small museum covering the city's history is housed inside a historic building facing the old market square. Exhibits date as far back as the Stone Age, and include clothing and jewellery of past eras plus a model of the castle during its golden age.

Ancient Walls

The remains of the walls that once encircled Viljandi are found in two separate spots, with the longest section standing in the square between Tallina and Tartu streets. The defensive walls were completed in 1300, surrounding an area of approximately 10 hectares. As a result of 17th century conflicts, little is left to see today.

St Paul's Church

The earliest documents mentioning the parish of Viljandi go back to 1234, making historians believe that a church already existed on the site of the monumental St Paul's Church that now sits at the northern edge of the city centre. The church acquired its current neogothic form in 1866, when it was consecrated. It has been welcoming the Lutheran community continuously since then, and has been enriched over time by gifts including artworks, a precious organ and a set of chandeliers that once carried the image of Neptune, but had to be modified to remove the blasphemous figure to better align with their new Christian home.

Kondas Centre

You may notice a series of giant concrete strawberries scattered around Viljandi – they are a reference to the 1965 *Strawberry Eaters* painting by local artist Paul Kondas (1900–85), to whom the Kondas Centre is dedicated. The only gallery in Estonia exhibiting the work of self-taught 'outsider' artists, the red brick building facing St John's Church is a colourful addition to the city's collection of historic sites.

St John's Church

St John's has suffered from many conflicts since its first appearance in the 17th century, damaged by ongoing wars that have marked Estonia's history. During the Soviet era, the imposing church functioned as a warehouse, receiving its second consecration again only in 1992, allowing the public back inside to admire its stained glass windows and listen to the concerts that are performed on a regular basis.

VILJANDI FOLK MUSIC FESTIVAL

Every year during the last weekend of July the ruins of Viljandi's castle become the setting for the Folk Music Festival, the city's most important cultural event, drawing in over 20,000 spectators. Artists from all over Europe are invited to play in the city's historic heart. Check out the full programme at viljandifolk.ee.

TOP TIPS

- Viljandi can be easily visited as a day trip from Tartu or Pärnu. Lux Express (luxexpress. eu) buses from both cities take around 1½ hours.
- A sandy beach lined with restaurants, cafes, a playground and volleyball pitches is found on the shore of Lake Viljandi. A 12km hiking trail runs around the lake.
- One of Viljandi's most unusual icons is the 30m water tower in J. Laidoner's Square, built in 1911 and now housing art exhibitions.
- The modernist Ugala Theatre (ugala.ee) and the Estonian Traditional Music Centre (folk. ee) offer a rich programme of shows and concerts year-round.

A DRIVE ALONG LAKE PEIPSI'S SHORE

The shores of Lake Peipsi, Europe's fifth largest, are home to secluded fishing and farming villages, easily explored on a day-trip drive from Tartu. Heading north, you reach the town of ❶ **Varnja** from Tartu in a little over half an hour. Visit the ❷ **Old Believers Prayer House** here; in the centre of town, check out the nearby Russian market and stop for tea at the ❸ **Samovar House**, before continuing onwards in the direction of Kolkja. On the way, check out the ❹ **ambulARToorium gallery** in Kasepää, where photography exhibitions are regularly held (follow @ambulartoorium to check what's on). Once in Kolkja, the ❺ **Old Believers Museum** offers insights into the local customs, with traditional clothing and furniture on display. Continuing north, shortly after crossing tiny Lake Lahepera the road splits: take

the unpaved track on the right to get to charming ❻ **Nina**, where a white lighthouse overlooks Lake Peipsi's waters from behind the Church of the Protection of Our Lady and its adjoining cemetery. Nina has a number of guesthouses and modern glamping cabins, making for an ideal stop if you want to extend your visit. A short drive inland leads to the neogothic ❼ **Alatskivi Manor**. Built in the 19th century by Baron Arved von Nolcken as the centrepiece of his family's estate, it was inspired by Balmoral Castle in Scotland. A short detour south takes you to the ❽ **Liiv Museum**, dedicated to Estonian poet Juhan Liiv. The final stop is ❾ **Mustvee**, where five churches represent the different creeds coexisting in the largest town on Peipsi's coast.

ERIKS Z/SHUTTERSTOCK ©

Valga Town Hall

Valga

TIME FROM TARTU: 1¼ HR 🚆

Cross-border towns

Entering Estonia from the south, Valga is likely the first city you'll encounter, connected to both Latvian capital Rīga and Tartu by direct rail line. Until 1920 the city formed a whole with its Latvian counterpart, Valka, but when both countries gained independence a new border was established, splitting the once united community in half. Estonia got the railway station, an 1889 structure of strategic importance destroyed during WWII and rebuilt in 1949, making it one of few extant examples of Stalinist architecture in this part of the country. Outside the station you'll find a green 1949 Russian locomotive placed here as a monument in 1998 to celebrate the 110th anniversary of the now closed Pskov-Valga-Riga railway line. As you walk toward the city centre you'll see the **Issidor Cathedral**, finished in 1898, and **Valga Museum**, covering the history of the city. The heart of Valga is marked by the early 19th-century **Jaani Church**, which holds one of Estonia's most precious organs, built in 1867, and the red **Town Hall**, but the city's defining feature is the collection of checkpoints located along the border, made obsolete by the free

Continues on p118

WHERE ESTONIA FIRST RAISED ITS FLAG

The town of Otepää is one of Estonia's best-known skiing and snowboarding destinations, thanks to its Tehvandi Sports Centre which has functioned as the training ground for the Estonian Olympic team since 1978. Besides sports, Otepää is symbolically important as Estonia's blue, black and white flag was consecrated here on June 4, 1884. Each year on the same date the town celebrates the event with a parade that runs through its central square – fittingly home of Estonia's tallest flagpole – and a series of concerts held in St Mary's Lutheran Church and the local Culture Centre.

 WHERE TO EAT IN VALGA ───────────────

Lilli
A stately facade hides a welcoming space with old-school furnishings and Estonian flavours. €€

Puusepa Pizza
Good stone-baked pizza topped with seasonal Estonian ingredients, steps away from Jaani Church. €

Walk Café
Across the border in Latvia, Walk is a homely cafe preparing generous burgers and other pub classics. €€

AASTELS/SHUTTERSTOCK ©

PRACTICALITIES

Scan this QR code for information on sights and events in the region.

TOP SIGHTS

Setomaa

Stretching along the Russian border in the southeastern corner of Estonia, Setomaa covers only about 1% of the country's territory but its cultural heritage is as rich as it gets. The region, divided between Estonia and Russia, is home to the Seto minority, a group of Orthodox Christians whose Finno-Ugric language finds its best expression in the *leelo* polyphonic singing tradition, an art inscribed on UNESCO's Intangible Cultural Heritage list since 2009.

DID YOU KNOW?

The road from Värska to Saatse, where a Seto Museum is found, runs through Russian territory for a little over 1km. There are no checkpoints and you are free to drive through, but you are not allowed to stop and step out of your vehicle.

Värska

The historical capital of the region is the Russian city of Pechory, around which a territory of approximately 1700 sq km used to be home for the Seto community. Pechory Province was absorbed into Estonia in 1920, following the Treaty of Tartu signed with Soviet Russia, which recognised Estonia's right to self-determination two years after the country had declared its independence. The post-WWII Soviet takeover saw the region divided, and when the USSR collapsed only one quarter of the territory inhabited by the Setos remained within Estonian borders, the rest becoming part of Russia's Pskov Oblast. In contrast with Russia, Estonia implemented measures to keep Seto traditions alive and the community has been mostly concentrated on the western side of the border. Värska is the main settlement of the Setomaa region. St George's Orthodox Church, built with bricks and river stones in 1904, marks the town's core and it's the only church in the region holding services every Sunday – it's well worth taking a

St George's Orthodox Church

HOW MANY SETOS ARE THERE?

It's difficult to estimate how many people identify as Seto, as the Estonian census does not question the ethnicity of citizens. An estimate though comes from the number of speakers of Seto dialect: approximately 4000 people in Setomaa, and an additional 8500 people around the rest of Estonia can communicate in the Seto language.

peek to admire the combination of Orthodox and Seto symbols decorating the richly adorned interior. Steps away from the church is the boardwalk running along Värska Bay, where you can see some natural springs trickling through the sandstone banks.

Once the summer residence of General Nikolai Reek, the green building facing Lake Õrsava houses Värska's visitor centre, where you can gather information on the regional sights while you sip a coffee in the little café. The offices of the Seto Institute, the main organisation responsible for research into Seto culture, are found here, together with an exhibition on the former military training camp established here in the 1920s.

To get a glimpse of rural life in Setomaa visit Värska's Farm Museum, a complex of wooden houses and stables depicting living and working conditions of families in the pre-industrial era. The farm is still functioning and a number of animals can be seen roaming around the grassy fields surrounding it. Try to spot the large wooden statue of Pekko, the god of crops and fertile lands in Seto mythology, outside one of the storehouses. The museum has a large crafts shop – the best place to get souvenirs in the region – and the town's best restaurant, Café Tsäimaja, serving traditional dishes in clay bowls on its outdoor terrace.

Värska Sanatorium

Värska is best known for its mineral waters, sold everywhere in Estonia and beyond. The therapeutic qualities of the springs here have long been revered and the Soviet-era sanatorium, 4km north of town, is a prime rest and relaxation destination. Mineral water and mud bath treatments are available for guests staying in one of the 101 rooms overlooking Lake Lämmi, the southern section of Lake Peipsi, and a sunset cruise run by Seto Line (setoline. ee, tickets €10 with a glass of wine included) runs on summer

WHERE TO STAY IN SETOMAA

- **Kirsi Talo**
  Traditional Seto farm in Meremäe, restored to house guests in its log cabins and glamping tents.
- **Obinitsa Puhkemaja**
  Hostel-style accommodation mostly catering to groups, with a large shared kitchen and outdoor area.
- **Värska Sanatorium**
  Behind the yellow and white facade of the largest hotel in the area hide modern rooms and a spa with various mineral water treatments.
- **Pesa Hotell**
  Located in the town of Põlva, this family-friendly hotel makes a good base to reach Värska and Kiidjärve.

evenings from the sanatorium's quay to Lüübnitsa and back, along the Russian border. The lovely Pikalombi hiking trail stretches for approximately 4km inland from the sanatorium, leading to a wooden viewing tower and a narrow boardwalk hovering over fields of cotton grass and the Kurõsuu bog.

Podmotsa

Only a few houses compose the settlement of Podmotsa on the eastern edge of Setomaa. A green wooden chapel dating back to the mid-18th century stands in the middle of a medieval cemetery. Graveyards are not just for mourning in Setomaa; traditionally, Seto people bury their dead near the place where they lived, and during religious celebrations they hold picnics over the graves as a way to connect with their deceased relatives. Podmotsa is a borderland in the true sense of the term – only 100m separate the village from its Russian counterpart Kulje, on the other side of the river. The turquoise dome of Kulje Cathedral can be spotted from the riverbank.

Mikitamäe

Some of the oldest religious chapels in Setomaa are found in Mikitamäe, although the main reason to visit is to try the tasty *pelmeni* (dumplings) prepared by the politician-turned-chef Inara in the cafe that carries her name. Following a career as a parliamentarian in Tallinn, Inara returned to her native Setomaa and opened the seasonal Inara Vanavalgõ Kohvitarõ, where she hosts regular *pelmeni*-making workshops in a space brimming with vintage ceramic teapots, Seto fabrics and locally produced artworks. The cafe features a small stage where concerts are occasionally played during summer months – if you're lucky, you

SETO LEELO

The ancient polyphonic singing tradition known as *leelo* has long been one of the defining features of the Seto, and continues to be performed during events such as funerals and weddings to this day. Seto *leelo* is typically performed by a group of women led by a 'song mother' who guides the others, often improvising with verses created on the spot to form a hypnotic rhythm, somewhere between a lament and a lullaby.

View of a Russian orthodox church from Estonia

HEITI PAVES/ALAMY STOCK PHOTO ©

Härma Mountain Wall

might even get to listen to a traditional Seto waltz played with a *karmoshka* (a type of accordion).

Obinitsa

Thousands flock to the village of Obinitsa for the Feast of the Transfiguration on 19 August, the holiday that gives its name to the local church and which has long been one of the most celebrated events for Seto people. Surprisingly, the Obinitsa Church was built under Stalin in 1952, at a time when places of worship were rapidly declining as a result of the USSR's anti-religious policy, and still stands to this day as the settlement's focus, next to the medieval cemetery.

Obinitsa Museum offers a window into the region's history through an exhibition of handicrafts, clothing and photographs of important historical figures, with an emphasis on the role of women in Seto society. Women have been historically leading the preservation of the *leelo* singing tradition and 'song mothers' continue to be respected figures in the community. Not far from the museum is a monument to Seto song mothers sculpted by artist Elmar Rebane in 1995.

Härmä

Härmä is composed of no more than a handful of houses and farms where blackcurrant plantations cover the green plains. Here, you'll find the remote Härmä Chapel, rebuilt by the local community on the site of a destroyed 18th-century original. The place is believed to transmit positive energy and three former Estonian presidents planted trees here after they were elected to ensure successful terms in office. The chapel is closed outside of religious celebrations, but Härmä is worth a visit all the same as it leads to the hiking trail running along the Piusa River Valley over some of the highest sandstone outcrops in Estonia, including the Härma Mountain Wall (43m). The path is part of the long-distance Forest Trail – one of the Baltic Trails, the network of paths stretching for over 2000km through Estonia, Latvia and Lithuania.

**FESTIVALS &
CELEBRATIONS
IN SETOMAA**

- **Pop-up Café Day**
  On a Sunday in mid-August, local farms turn into cafes for a day and allow visitors to taste authentic Seto flavours.
- **Treski**
  Music and Inspiration Festival One of the biggest music events in the region hosts local and international acts on its wooden stage for three days in August.
- **Kingdom Day Food**
  Music and crafts are all essential elements of Kingdom Day, held in early August in Rõsna to elect the community's new representative.

Church of Sts Peter & Paul

KUKULINNA MANOR

Overlooking the deep blue waters of Lake Saadjärv, the ghostly Kukulinna Manor echoes the opulence of the past. As you explore southern Vooremaa your attention might be caught by this well preserved but completely abandoned estate, known to have existed since the 16th century. Formerly owned by the von Löwenwoldes, an aristocratic Baltic German family, the structure was restored in the 19th century, becoming one of the few standing examples of Tudor-style wooden architecture in Estonia. Kukulinna Manor turned into a school in the 1920s before being abandoned. At the time of writing entering the building is not possible and its future remains uncertain.

Continued from p113

movement allowed under the Schengen Agreement. The pedestrian border connecting Sõpruse tänav, in Valga, and Raiņa iela, in Valka, leads to the **Lugaži Evangelical Lutheran Church** on the Latvian side; since 2023 you can find a destroyed Russian T-72B tank donated by the Ukrainian Ministry of Defence sitting in the middle of the border square.

Vooremaa

TIME FROM NARVU: 1HR

Ancient remains of glaciers

A series of elongated lakes line up one after the other in **Vooremaa**, a protected area positioned across Tartu and Jõgeva counties. The lakes occupy the lowest points of the oval shaped hills, known as drumlins, that formed during the Ice Age from the movement of glacial sheets. The bicycle-friendly area stretches north of Äksi, on the shores of **Lake Saadjärv**, through mostly agricultural lands covered by yellow mustard flowers in springtime and isolated villages that see little to no traffic. Besides the calming landscapes, here you'll find Äksi's **Ice Age Centre**, a museum and theme park especially suited to kids where life-size prehistoric animals have been reproduced to detail the evolution of Estonia's wildlife. The Ice Age Centre runs daily raft trips on Lake Saadjärv,

CASTLES AND MANORS NORTH OF TARTU

Põltsamaa Castle
The residence of Livonian King Magnus in the 16th century, the castle reopened in 2023 after years of restoration.

Laiuse Castle
The 15th-century Laiuse Castle may be in ruins, but for 300 years it was coveted by Russian, Polish and Swedish forces.

Puurmani Manor
Established in the 1860s, this neoclassical villa has been perfectly preserved and now functions as a school.

one of Estonia's deepest lakes, every day between May and October (book ahead via jaaaeg.ee). For a more contemporary look into Estonia's fauna, you can visit the **Elistvere Animal Park**, founded in 1997 as a sanctuary to house injured and orphaned animals living in the surrounding forests, which now cares for a family of sleepy Eurasian bisons, plus elks, brown bears, wolves and many others. A wheelchair-accessible path runs along the fences enclosing the various species for 2km and a small museum dedicated to the geography of Vooremaa is found on the upper floor of the ticket office building.

Piirissaar

TIME FROM NARVU: 1HR

The islanders of Lake Peipsi

Piirissaar, the largest island on Lake Peipsi, measures under 8 sq km and has an official population of just 99 people. Connected to the mainland via a ferry that runs three times a day from Laaksaare, the island is home to the descendants of the **Old Believers** who settled here in the early 18th century to avoid conscription into the Russian Army during the Great Northern War. As you walk the path connecting Piirissaar's three villages – Piiri, Saare and Tooni – you'll notice that the dead outnumber the living by a large margin. Historic Orthodox cemeteries dot the island, which is eerily quiet on most days. Besides the traditional wooden homes and farms, Tooni is home to the abandoned **Church of Sts Peter & Paul**, whose silver onion dome rises from the thick vegetation not far from the community centre. The best place to learn about the island's history and culture is the **Piirissaar Museum**, located inside a traditional Old Believers' home in Saare. Knock on the door to get in and check out the old samovars, Russian icons and altars that used to adorn the private residences of this remote community. Money from the ticket sales goes toward the construction of a new chapel, which will replace a former prayer hall that accidentally burned down in 2016. The museum is also the only place where you can order a meal on the island, as there are no restaurants. The port of Laaksaare can be reached by bus (for free) from Tartu's bus station and links to the ferry schedule.

Piusa

TIME FROM NARVU: 2HRS

Caves, bats and ceramics

An unexpected sight in largely forested southeastern Estonia is the collection of golden sand dunes that rise from the valley of the **Piusa River**, near the village of the same name.
Continues on p122

WHO ARE THE OLD BELIEVERS?

The religious group known as the Old Believers emerged in 17th-century Russia as a result of a schism within the Russian Orthodox Church. Patriarch Nikon, supported by the government, introduced a series of liturgical and religious reforms which were rejected by the more conservative flank of the congregation, who formed a new group that later became known as the Old Believers. Repression followed the split and thousands of Old Believers fled their homes, finding a safe haven on the shores of Lake Peipsi, where they could maintain their traditions and erect new places of worship. Today, 11 Old Believers' parishes are registered in Estonia, with estimates for the number of members ranging from 2500 to 15,000.

 MUSEUMS OF SOUTHERN ESTONIA ────────

Estonian Aviation Museum	**Sangaste Manor**	**Palamuse Museum**
Estonia's only aviation museum, a short drive south of Tartu, has over 30 aircraft, plus hundreds of models.	Manor with an exhibition on ex-owner Georg Magnus von Berg, aka the Count of Rye after he developed a type of rye.	Estonian writer Oskar Luts set his 1947 novel *Kevade* (Spring) in Palamuse, which now has a museum dedicated to him.

Hiking in Kiidjärve's Forests

Running along the banks of the Ahja River, this looping trail stretching from the village of Kiidjärve to the Taevaskoja sandstone outcrops and back crosses ravines covered in thick pine forests and high cliffs. The route, identified by blue markers, officially runs for 11.8km starting from Kiidjärve's visitor centre, but can be extended further or cut short at different points along the way, making for an ideal hiking day trip from Tartu.

❶ Kiidjärve Visitors Centre

Begin at the green building housing Kiidjärve's visitor centre, near an old watermill on the shore of a mirror-like lake. Before heading into the forests, see if you can spot one of the common kingfishers populating the area – the only kind of kingfisher (out of 90 different species) to breed in Europe. From the visitor centre, walk east along the main road for about 600m and find the trailhead on your right.

The Hike: The Oosemägi outcrop is found approximately 3.5km from the starting point along the only path available.

❷ Oosemägi

About 30 minutes into the hike you'll pass the Talliorg Valley on the way to the Oosemägi outcrop. The remains of horses that were found in the area have shown that this patch of forest was used as a military station by Swedish troops during the Great Northern War, until they clashed with the Russians. From Talliorg an easy climb leads to the ridge of Oosemägi, a sandstone hill offering great views over the river.

The Hike: The narrow trail continues straight to Mõsumägi with some ups and downs amid tall pine trees – just follow the blue markers.

❸ Mõsumägi

On sunny days, kayakers can be seen navigating the waters of the Ahja River from the top of the outcrop. Continue along the river bank for another 30 minutes, until

REHO SAVISAAR/ALAMY STOCK PHOTO ©

Watermill, Kiidjärve

you reach Mõsumägi, another pink-hued sandstone outcrop rising above Kiidjärve. The name translates to 'wash hill', referring to the time over a century ago when people from the nearby Valgesoo village came here to do their laundry. A number of owls are known to be nesting in this area, although they tend to be too elusive to be spotted during the day.

The Hike: On the path to Taevaskoja, trees become more scarce until the path opens to the valley. A short bridge allows you to cross the river and get close to Neitsikoobas, the 'Virgin's Cave'.

➍ Taevaskoja

The Ahja River narrows down to a stream in the area of Taevaskoja, where a bridge allows you to turn back and return to your starting point. Taevaskoja, or Heaven's Hall, is a flat, grassy plain surrounded by the tall sandstone formation typical of the area. The caves you'll see around you have long been believed to be home to spiritual beings of Estonia's pagan folklore – according to the tradition, entering without permission may cause people to go insane.

The Hike: Add a few extra kilometres to your hike along the river by continuing to the village of Otteni before turning around to head back to Kiidjärve.

Kiidjärve Visitors Centre

From Taevaskoja you can continue hiking to tiny Otteni village before returning to the visitor centre on the opposite side of the river. This will add approximately 5km to the itinerary. Alternatively you can just cross the bridge and return to your starting point. A number of wooden staircases and platforms will guide you across the outcrops and back into the forest until you reach the main road in Kiidjärve. A train station linking to Tartu is found 1.6km from the visitor centre.

AIMUR KYTT/SHUTTERSTOCK ©

Piusa Caves

MAARJA KÜLA

The small settlement of Maarja Küla, on the edge of the Kiidjärve Park, is home to a project of social inclusion like no other. The village was created to help adults with learning disabilities gain professional training while living in an accepting environment where social skills can be developed. The village has a strong artistic drive, as you can see by going on a stroll along the forest boardwalk that runs from Maarja Küla's administrative office – paintings made by the residents hang on trees every few steps, forming a free, open-air museum embedded in nature.

Continued from p119

With some of the country's finest sand found in the area, Piusa has long been an important centre of glassmaking: between 1922 and 1966 the Järvakandi factory used the local sand as the raw material for its products, transporting it on the railway that connected the mine with the manufacturing plants. When sand extraction came to a halt, Piusa was left with a network of underground caves that turned into living quarters for a large population of bats. In winter, over 3000 can be found here, forming one of the largest hibernation areas in northern Europe. Since 1981, the area surrounding the **Piusa Caves** has been a nature reserve. It can be visited year-round, but entrance to the caves is only allowed mid-May to mid-September, when the bats are absent. The caves' viewing platform offers a glimpse into the intricate network of tunnels, with photographs tracing the history of mining operations. Above ground, a 1.4km hiking trail runs through the forest – look for craters formed by collapsed mines, now covered in vegetation. After exploring the caves and the little sand museum on site, pay a visit to **Piusa Savikoda** ceramics workshop nearby. Artists Signe and Meelis Krigul run this colourful shop housed inside a station building dating back to the Russian Empire days, producing unique pottery of every shape and size.

Pärnu

CHILLING | 18TH-CENTURY GRANDEUR | THE BEACH

As spring ends and the weather warms up, Pärnu comes to life with Estonians, Finns and Latvians heading to the Baltic Sea with fingers crossed for sunny weather. Doubling as a relaxing, wellness-oriented resort and party town, Pärnu attempts to cater to both families and hedonists, although the title of 'Baltic Ibiza' may disappoint those who have actually experienced the Balearic island's nightlife. Approximately mid-way between Riga and Tallinn on Estonia's western coast, Pärnu is moderately fun in a very Estonian fashion – you *can* stay up all night, but probably won't. The historic core boasts a collection of colourful palatial residences dating back centuries and a vibrant restaurant scene, while the shallow water lapping its sandy beach favours slow strolls over long swims. Much of Pärnu's coastline is occupied by a nature reserve stretching for miles and cut through by a cycling path, welcoming those who seek some quiet time away from the crowds.

Pärnu

GETTING AROUND

The pedestrian streets of Pärnu's centre make for pleasant walks amid the historic architecture, but if you want to venture out you'll need wheels – with cycle paths crisscrossing the city and its surroundings, greater Pärnu is best explored on two of them. The Baltreisen Bicycle Rental shop rents bikes for €10 per day from under the giant mural on Pühavaimu Street.

☑ **TOP TIP**

During summer months many concerts are held in Pärnu, both in old-school venues such as the Kuursaal, a former casino turned restaurant, and in parks such as Vallikäär and Munamäe.

YEGOROVNICK/SHUTTERSTOCK ©

Red Tower

THE CITY AT WATER LEVEL

Experience Pärnu from an unusual perspective by booking a kayaking session with the friendly people of Seikle Vabaks (seiklevabaks.ee), who organise bicep-propelled tours along the moat and the river that embrace the city, guided by kayaking pro Argo. If you'd rather leave the navigation to someone else, you can also jump on the 1963 MS *Kuha* wooden ship, departing four times a day from Tallinn Gate, for a relaxing cruise by Pärnu Cruises (parnucruises.ee).

Pärnu's 18th-Century Grandeur & More

Old Town magnificence

Pärnu's importance as a Baltic trading centre preceded its admission into the Hanseatic League in the 14th century, a move that allowed the city to flourish and attracted a large number of German merchants. **Pärnu Museum** is a good place to untangle these historical roots, and the pedestrian alleys that cross the old core connect remarkable buildings that reveal the grandeur of the past. The 15th-century **Red Tower**, once part of Pärnu's medieval fortress, is the only piece of architecture from the Hanseatic era to survive (reconstructed) and houses the municipality's archives. **Seegi Maja** (the Almshouse) on Hospidali Street is considered the city's oldest building, constructed in 1658 on the foundations of a 13th-century church, followed by the 1694 home of merchant Jürgen Vossbein on Kuninga 24. Hinting at the professional associations that united merchants and artisans in the Middle Ages, the **Mary Magdalene Guild**, around the corner from Seegi Maja, allows local artists to exhibit and sell their work. Nearby is the 1797 **Town Hall**, temporary residence of Tsar Alexander I, standing close to the 1768 **St Catherine's Orthodox Church**. For a glimpse into the living conditions of Pärnu's 18th-century upper-class inhabitants, you can

 ## WHERE TO STAY IN PÄRNU

Tiia Guesthouse
The cheapest rooms in town are in this basic but clean wooden home, close to the action. Shared bathrooms. €

Tervise Paradiis
Large family-oriented hotel, with an adjoining water park and beach views from the balconies. €€

Villa Ammende
Art nouveau villa successfully restored to become one of Pärnu's most refined boutique hotels. €€€

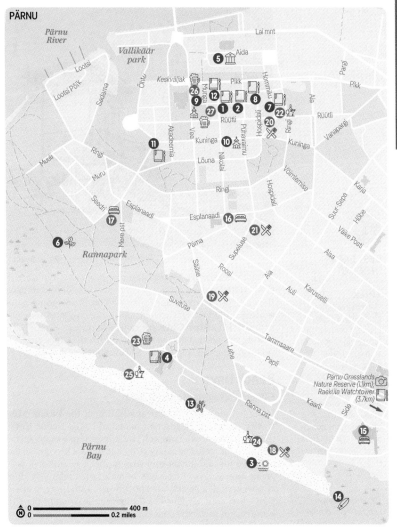

PÄRNU

SIGHTS
1. Citizen's House
2. Mary Magdalene Guild
3. Pärnu beach
4. Pärnu Mud Baths
5. Pärnu Museum
6. Pärnu Rannapark
7. Red Tower
8. Seegi Maja
9. St Catherine's Orthodox Church
10. St Elizabeth's Lutheran Church
11. Tallinn Gate
12. Town Hall

ACTIVITIES, COURSES & TOURS
13. Club Sunset

14. Pärnu Surf Centre

SLEEPING
15. Tervise Paradiis
16. Tiia Guesthouse
17. Villa Ammende

EATING
18. PÕKS Beach Bar
19. Villa Wesset
20. VoVa

21. Wrapimaja

DRINKING & NIGHTLIFE
22. APTEK
23. Kuursaal
24. OAAS
25. Que Pasa
26. Raasiku Õlletuba
27. Sweet Rosie

VALDIS SKUDRE/SHUTTERSTOCK ©

Pärnu beach

enter the **Citizen's House**, the oldest wooden building in town, dated at 1740, which now houses a small museum. As the city got richer, fortifications were built including gates leading into town. Of such entrances, the only surviving one is the pink **Tallinn Gate**, previously known as King's Gate, linking the promenade by the moat with the inner city surrounding the red spire of the **St Elizabeth's Church**.

Beach Days

Estonia's favourite stretch of sand

Lying behind the neoclassical building of the **Pärnu Mud Baths**, built in 1926 and now managed by the Hedon Hotel, the city's broad, sandy **beach** is the reason most people visit in the summer. The sandy stretch is lined with bars, cafes, playgrounds and hotels, and despite the large influx of people on sunny days, it manages to maintain a relatively calm atmosphere. The beach runs northwest all the way to a sea-wall – first commissioned by Catherine the Great in the 17th century and reconstructed two centuries later – that allows ships to enter the port, with the sculpture-laden **Pärnu Rannapark** expanding parallel to the sand to the bigger resorts that sit in the quieter part of town. On the southern edge of the beach you'll find the **Pärnu Surf Centre**, where you can rent kayaks and SUP boards or join a windsurfing course. Next to it, a short boardwalk forms the 'meadow trail', leading to the **Pärnu Grasslands Nature Reserve**, which runs for 3km along the coast to the **Raeküla Watchtower**. Between June and late August, the beach action continues after dark. **Que Pasa** and **OAAS** serve cocktails right on the sand, while **PÕKS Beach Bar** adds to the tropical feel with tacos to be enjoyed on the deckchairs by the water. When it comes to clubbing, the choice is limited to **Club Sunset** which hosts local and international DJs throughout the summer.

yond
Pärnu

Away from the glitz of the summer capital you'll find a national park and quiet beaches.

With so much to detain visitors in Pärnu itself, the resort's hinterland is often neglected, despite offering plenty of charm of its own. Fascinating Kihnu makes for a worthwhile island escape with cycling being the best way to explore it. Boggy Soomaa National Park, the only place in the world where floods seem to be welcomed, has canoeing, kayaking, bog walking or simply observing the scenery from a hammock as possible activities to draw you here. Or if you'd rather stick to the beach, consider biking up to wild Valgeranna, a place beloved by the Soviet elite where seaside bars, cafes and playgrounds have yet to take over the landscape.

Places
Valgeranna p128
Soomaa National Park p129
Kihnu Island p130

GETTING AROUND

While Pärnu itself is well connected by public transport, with buses regularly running to other major cities, the coast and countryside is best explored with your own vehicle. Organised tours to Soomaa National Park usually include transport, and a bicycle can get you far, given the low traffic on the flat roads of western Estonia.

Kihnu Island (p130)

SANDRIS VEVERIS/SHUTTERSTOCK ©

☑ TOP TIP
When heading to Soomaa National Park in the summer, pack insect repellent – the humid environment makes it a favourite spot for mosquitoes.

A BEACH FOR COSMONAUTS

The picture-perfect sunsets found along Estonia's shores west of Pärnu explain its 'romantic coastline' nickname. Besides Valgeranna, you can spend a few days in the resort town of Kabli, where Soviet cosmonauts would be sent to replenish their energy levels after space missions. According to a local myth cosmonaut Valentina Tereshkova, the first woman to go to space aboard the *Vostok 6* spacecraft in 1963, spent some time in Kabli following her mission, although she neved admitted to having done so. Another option is to head up to Matsi to hike a section of the Baltics' Coastal Trail and wild camp by the lagoon.

REGINA M ARTY/SHUTTERSTOCK ©

Valgeranna

Valgeranna

TIME FROM PÄRNU: **15 MINS**

A nomenklatura kind of stay

Far removed from the busy beach of central Pärnu, the stretch of white sand can barely be seen from across Valgeranna's thick forest, offering a secluded Baltic retreat from the crowds. The intimate atmosphere of this beach – and the distance from prying eyes – has been appreciated since at least the 1970s, when the ministers of the Estonian Soviet Socialist Republic built the resort known as **Villa Andropoff**, after the head of the KGB and General Secretary of the Soviet Union Yury Andropov. High-end, secretive meetings of the party's top members were held in the avant-garde, red-brick structure, considered one of Estonia's earliest examples of postmodernist architecture and declared a cultural monument by the National Heritage Board in 2020. Today, Villa Andropoff houses a hotel and a restaurant which have largely maintained their original style: a lectern carrying a hammer and sickle still stands on the ground floor near the entrance and a collection of black and white photographs recall Soviet leaders' holidays on the Baltic coast. The **Valgeranna Holiday Centre** also includes a series of cabins overlooking the beach and a campground where you can spend a few nights under the shadow of the towering pine trees.

FESTIVALS IN PÄRNU

Pärnu Music Festival
In July, Pärnu hosts this international classical music festival in its Concert Hall (parnumusicfestival.ee).

Pärnu Film Festival
Also in July, Pärnu's film festival is focused on science-related documentaries from all over the world (chaplin.ee).

Hanseatic Days
Spring is the occasion to celebrate traditions, with medieval-inspired markets in Munamägi and Vallikäär.

Soomaa National Park

Experience the 'fifth season'

In each season **Soomaa National Park** renews itself and transforms into a different place. Covering an area of some 36,000 hectares between Pärnu and Viljandi, this 'land of bogs' is especially well known for turning hikers into kayakers during the early months of spring, when the phenomenon known as the 'fifth season' usually occurs. As the winter snow melts away and rain starts falling on western Estonia, the rivers fill up and overflow. Soomaa gets flooded and the many narrow streams crossing the park join forces to form wide, navigable bodies of water covering the vegetation. Nearly half of the park's surface gets submerged and the only way of moving around is on the water. The fifth season usually happens from late March to early April, although it's hard to know exactly when the floods will occur and what level the water will reach as Estonia's weather is famously unpredictable. If rain comes, you'll have to be ready to hop into a canoe and go for a literal immersion into this temporary landscape unseen elsewhere. Two Pärnu-based companies specialise in kayaking and canoeing trips to the national park: Seikle Vabaks (seiklevabaks.ee) and Soomaa.com can organise day tours from the city with transportation. While early spring is the best time to visit, it's possible to enjoy the park's wilderness year-round. Snowshoeing expeditions are on offer during white winters; activities such as bog walking and swimming in Soomaa's ponds are available in summer, but be aware that mosquitoes are merciless during the warmer months.

TORI CIDERY

On the outskirts of Soomaa National Park, in the small settlement of Tori, you'll find the Tori Cidery, where a wide variety of award-winning organic fruit ciders have been produced for a decade. Tasting tours, available upon request, will allow you to compare dry and sweet ciders while learning how they are made. There's also a shop where you can buy beverages to take with you. Contact via siidritalu.ee.

VALDIS SKUDRE/SHUTTERSTOCK ©

Soomaa National Park

Kihnu Island Bike Ride

The cultural heritage of Kihnu reveals itself as you slowly cycle through the forests and beaches that cover much of this island located in the Gulf of Riga, easily reached from the port of Munalaiu north of Pärnu. Kihnu has long been described as one of Europe's last matriarchal societies: while men spend months at sea, women rule the island, keeping alive the long-standing crafts and traditions inscribed in UNESCO's Intangible Cultural Heritage of Humanity list. Coaches run from Pärnu's bus station to Munalaiu's ferry terminal and back four times a day, coinciding with the ferry schedule. The ferry ride takes just over one hour; tickets available at veeteed.com.

❶ Kihnu Port

Best visited between spring and autumn, Kihnu is connected to Estonia's mainland through the AS *Kihnu Veeteed* ferry that runs between Munalaiu, 40km from Pärnu, and Kihnu's port, Kihnu Sadam. Once you reach the island, a bike rental service

MARINA LESNITSKAYA/SHUTTERSTOCK ©

Ferry to Kihnu Island

(€10/day) is available at the harbour. The island has four villages and this 18km loop runs through all of them and will take under three hours to complete, with the possibility of extending the trip by taking some of the unpaved roads that cut through the forested interior.

The Ride: Find the sign pointing to Sääre at the first intersection on the road from the port. Take a right and ride north past the Njaputüe Pued souvenir shop.

❷ Lina

Cycle around the grassy field forming Kihnu's airfield. The bare, lightless landing strip was built in 1968 and operated until 2016, when the last regular Air Livonia flight landed in Kihnu. Since then, farm animals have taken over the field for grazing. The road runs parallel to the northern coast, with two secondary paths leading to the beaches of this corner of the island. Continue to the settlement of Lina, where a protected linden forest has been growing since the 19th century. Past the village spot the miniature lighthouse and the abandoned *Vana Ann* ship standing in the soccer field.

The Ride: Take a left after the *Vana Ann* and ride for less than 1km until you see the bell tower of the Church of St Nicholas.

❸ Kihnu Museum

Dedicated to the preservation of Kihnu's cultural heritage, the island's museum, divided between two wooden buildings, is

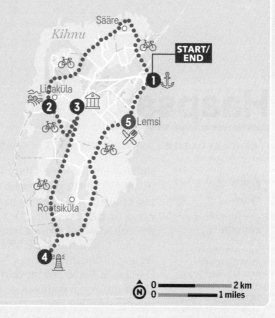

Baltic
Sea

Kihnu

Sääre

START/
END

Lipaküla

Lemsi

Rootsiküla

N 0 ————————— 2 km
   0 ————————— 1 miles

the best place to learn about local history and traditions. The first part of the exhibition pays tribute to the work of Theodor Saar, who dedicated much of his life to the study of Kihnu's customs, collecting thousands of pages of folk song lyrics, and to the translation of the local dialect into Estonian. The second structure, dedicated to life at sea, is where you'll find fishing nets and boats used to supply Kihnu with its primary food source. In front of the museum is the Church of St Nicholas, built in 1784 and belonging to the Estonian Apostolic Church. During holidays the local choir can still be heard singing inside.

The Ride: Cycle south on the only paved road from the museum, then take the dirt road to the lighthouse and surrounding rocky beaches.

4 Kihnu Lighthouse

Kihnu's white, 29m lighthouse marks the Pitkänä Peninsula, the southernmost tip of Kihnu, overlooking the Gulf of Riga.

Originally built in England and assembled in Kihnu in 1864, the lighthouse can be climbed (tickets €5) for one of the best views of the island. During summer months a small cafe is open too.

The Ride: To complete the loop, head back to the port of Kihnu via the road that runs along the eastern side of the island.

5 Rooslaiu Farm Shop

The itinerary stretches through the interior of Kihnu, returning to the coast in the surroundings of Lemsi, minutes away from the port. This area is largely empty, but you'll find a number of guesthouses turned into pop-up cafes selling coffee and small bites to day visitors. The only actual cafe on the way is the Rooslaiu Farm Shop, preparing soups with homemade bread and different kinds of smoked fish. Once back at the port, just drop the bike at the rental service and take the ferry back to Munalaiu, where a bus to Pärnu will be waiting.

Haapsalu

LEGENDARY CASTLE | HISTORIC BUILDINGS | COASTAL SWEDES

GETTING AROUND

Navigating slow-paced Haapsalu doesn't require much planning – the town is small and pedestrian-friendly. Bus 1 runs to the port of Rohuküla, stopping near the Ungru Castle ruins.

☑ TOP TIP

Haapsalu is easily walkable, but there are two bicycle rental stores in the centre of town – Rakser Sport and Rattad Vaba Aeg, both on Karja Street – should you decide to head out into the nearby countryside.

Built around the legendary castle that still marks its centre, alluring Haapsalu has grown into a calm resort town whose rustic charm invites a prolonged break on the way to the West Estonian archipelago, the collection of islands emerging from the Baltic Sea not far off the coast. The self-appointed title of 'Venice of Northern Europe' is a bit of a stretch, but the lagoon formed by the cold Baltic waters between Haapsalu's twin peninsulas will surely meet any romantic strolling needs. There are plenty of historic villas, spa hotels and guesthouses here, and the city and its surroundings have been welcoming wellness tourists for over a century – people from across Estonia come to Haapsalu to coat their bodies in curative mud. There are also lots of handicraft stores, comfy cafes and museums to keep you busy once the pampering is done.

Haapsalu's Crumbling Fortress
Home of the ghostly White Lady

Especially photogenic at sunset, the crumbling remains of **Haapsalu Castle** stand as a reminder of the city's glorious past. The foundation of the fortress dates back to the 13th century, when the local nobility commissioned a new castle and church to function as the seat of the Roman Catholic Bishopric of Ösel-Wiek, independent from the competing Livonian Order. The castle (and the city) grew over the course of the following three hundred years, but as Haapsalu's political role diminished in the late 17th century, the fortress' state gradually declined too. Despite the ruinous state of its outer walls, Haapsalu's castle is still one of the best-preserved medieval strongholds in Estonia. A large courtyard is accessible from

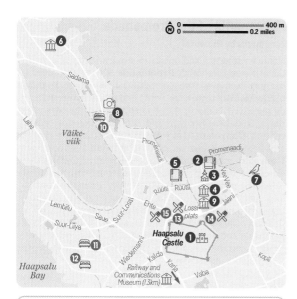

▲ N 0 ___ 400 m
0 ___ 0.2 miles

Sadama

Väike-viik

Lahe

Promenaadi

Ruutli

Lembitu

Ehte

Saue

Suur-Lossi

Suur-Liiva

Haapsalu Bay

Wiedemanni

Kalda

Karja

Vaba

Kopli

Haapsalu Castle

Railway and Communications Museum (1.3km)

TOP SIGHTS
1 Haapsalu Castle

SIGHTS
2 Allika Pavillion
3 Church of Mary Magdalene
4 Ilon's Wonderland
5 Kuursaal

6 Museum of Coastal Swedes
7 Tagalaht birdwatching tower
8 Tchaikovsky's Bench
9 Town Hall Museum

SLEEPING
10 Hestia Hotel & Spa
11 Old Hapsal Hotel
12 Päeva Villa

EATING
13 Herman's Bistro
14 Purtse Gastro
15 Talumehe Kõrts

BEST MUSEUMS IN HAAPSALU

Town Hall Museum
Close to the castle, a 1775 building formerly housing Haapsalu's town hall has been converted into a lovely museum detailing the history of the resort town through photographs of summer visitors.

Ilon's Wonderland
Dedicated to the work of Estonian-Swedish artist Ilon Wikland, illustrator of the globally known children's books featuring Pippi Longstocking, this child-friendly museum features low-hanging illustrations and exhibits about Wikland, who lived part of his life in Haapsalu.

Railway and Communications Museum
Historic steam and diesel trains are parked behind Haapsalu's monumental former railway station in a museum focused on rail transport and 20th-century communications.

Karja Street, and a viewing platform overlooking the town's rooftops is found on the eastern edge of the castle's perimeter. Purchase a ticket to enter the museum to learn about the medieval origins of the structure and visit St Nicholas' Cathedral. Once home to the local monastic community, the cathedral is also said to still be the home of the ghost of the mythical White Lady, a woman who in the Middle Ages was executed for entering the castle dressed as a male member of the choir to stay with a canon she had fallen in love with. Women were not allowed to enter the church back then and the bishop had no mercy on the couple, once he discovered the deception. Each year in late August, Haapsalu celebrates its White Lady Festival with markets and live music events in the streets surrounding the castle.

 WHERE TO STAY IN HAAPSALU

Päeva Villa
Pastel rooms, each with their own theme, in a family-run guesthouse with a peaceful atmosphere. €€

Old Hapsal Hotel
Surrounded by a garden, this charming boutique hotel combines modern amenities and old-school touches. €€

Hestia Hotel & Spa
This hotel is all about relaxation. Spa treatments are the main draw, but the views aren't bad either. €€€

UNGRU CASTLE RUINS

As you head from Haapsalu to Rohuküla to take the ferry to the islands, you'll notice the ruins of Ungru Castle on your left, about 5km west of town. This striking neobaroque structure, inspired by the Merseburg Castle in Germany, dates back to the late 19th century. Legend has it that the son of Ungru's owner fell in love with a princess living in Merseburg and attempted to recreate her castle to convince her to move to Estonia. He died in 1908 before completing the project and Ungru was left abandoned. The building has lost its roof but kept its facade intact, and now sits abandoned on the outskirts of town, offering some great opportunities for dramatic photos.

Monuments of the Promenade

Landmarks by the water

Historic buildings and quirky monuments line up one after the other on Haapsalu's **Promenade**, ideally positioned for summer evenings strolls along the bay. From the **Tagalaht birdwatching tower**, the white and red structure standing on the eastern edge of the city centre, cross the park where the Aafrika beach playground and the onion-domed 19th-century **Church of Mary Magdalene** stand. On the other side are the octagonal **Allika Pavillion** and the dreamy **Kuursaal**, a green and white wooden villa hovering above water that used to be a favourite holidaying destination for the Russian aristocracy in the 19th century. From the Kuursaal, look out over the sea to spot the floating polar bear sculpture, then continue to **Tchaikovsky's Bench** commemorating the Russian composer who visited Haapsalu in 1867. Cross the peninsula and as you return towards the city centre stop at **Wiigi Kohvik** for a seafood dinner with a view of the sun dropping behind the bay.

The Heritage of Coastal Swedes

A museum about a vanished minority

Estonian Swedes, often referred to as Coastal Swedes, are the ancestors of the tiny minority of Swedish-speakers that live in Estonia today, a population of just a few hundred people linked to the 13th- and 14th-century settlers of the region's islands and coastal areas. The Swedish population of Estonia reached its peak in the 16th century, when it surpassed 5000 people, but began dwindling following the Great Northern War (1700-21). Over time, most Estonian Swedes assimilated with native Estonians and then many of those still identifying as Swedish in the 20th century left the country to escape WWII. Their heritage, however, is still celebrated in Haapsalu's **Museum of Coastal Swedes**, housed inside a building inaugurated by none other than the king of Sweden himself in 1998. Besides the collection of scenes depicting the life of Estonian Swedes on the long, 20m rug in the main room, there are reproductions of wooden ships used by seafarers from Sweden to navigate the Baltic.

Beyond Haapsalu

Quiet and sparsely populated, the islands off the coast of Western Estonia welcome slow travellers for two-wheeled explorations.

From the port of Rohuküla, a 10-minute bus ride from Haapsalu, the islands of Vormsi and Hiiumaa are both a short ferry ride away, making for an inviting tour of isolated lighthouses, UNESCO-protected forests and sprawling countryside vistas. Further south are Saaremaa, the largest and most populous island in Estonia, and Muhu. Mostly flat and with little traffic, the islands are best explored on a bike during Estonia's long summer days. These are only four of the over 2000 islands that belong to Estonia, offering a glimpse into the life surrounded by water of communities that have long lived separate from the rest of the country.

Places

Hiiumaa p136
Vormsi p137
Saaremaa & Muhu p138

GETTING AROUND

Like in the rest of Estonia, public transport can get you almost everywhere. However, on the islands buses are few and far between – driving your own vehicle is the most efficient way of getting around in this part of the country.

☑ TOP TIP

Ferry tickets to Hiiumaa, Muhu and Saaremaa can be purchased online at praamid.ee; for Vormsi, they're available at veeteed.com.

Sõrve lighthouse (p140)

YEGOROVNICK/SHUTTERSTOCK ©

A BIKE RIDE AROUND HIIUMAA

Part of the West Estonian Archipelago Bio-sphere Reserve, Hiiumaa sees little visitor traffic despite its many natural and cultural sights. In ❶ **Kärdla**, the largest town, you can rent e-bikes at the tourist office in the town square or traditional bikes at the port – consider around three days to complete this loop. Following the 80 road around the is-land anti-clockwise, you'll reach the ❷ **Hill of Crosses**, a collection of hundreds of wood-en crucifixes built by 18th-century Swedes, and then the road leading to Takhuna, a pen-insula with ruined forts and bunkers show-ing the island's strategic role in WWII. Tanks, maps and Lenin busts are exhibited at the ❸ **Hiiumaa Military Museum**, near the ❹ **Tahkuna Lighthouse**, which you can climb. A 31m ❺ **wooden copy of the Eiffel Tower** (climb at your own risk) awaits in a small amuseument park of quirky wood-en structures in Reigi, while past Kõrgessaare

you'll find some of Hiiumaa's best beaches: ❻ **Luidja** on the north coast and the surf-ing spot of ❼ **Ristna**, on the Kõpu Peninsu-la, where the imposing ❽ **Kõpu Lighthouse** proudly stands, one of the oldest still-functioning lighthouses in the world, built by Hanseatic League merchants in the 16th cen-tury. Continue south to Käina, Hiiumaa's sec-ond town, where the modern ❾ **Windtower Experience** houses a five-floor, family-friendly museum dedicated to nature's role in shaping Hiiumaa's identity, plus a 20m climbing wall, the highest in all the Baltics. South of Käina is the ❿ **Kassari Reserve**, extending to the Sääretirp promontory, a wild, hikable strip of land emerging from the sea. ⓫ **Heltermaa** is Hiiumaa's port town, connecting the island with the outside world. There's not much to see besides the Handicraft House filled with quirky mementos.

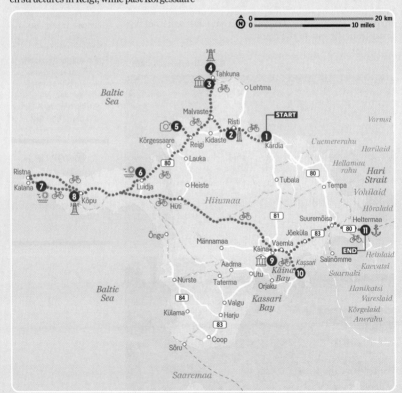

Matsalu National Park

Vormsi

TIME FROM HAAPSALU: **1 HR**

Riding through silent greenery

Departing from Rohuküla up to five times a day, the ferry takes 45 minutes to reach **Vormsi**, a green, sparsely populated island with a perfectly cyclable eight-shaped road. Locate the local bike rental shop at Sviby's harbour and start pedaling through the flat pasturelands that cover much of the sleepy island towards **Hullo**, Vormsi's main settlement. Marking the centre of the island is the white **Church of St Olaf**, dating to the 14th century and standing next to the wooded **Vormsi Cemetery** where over 300 stone sun crosses are partially buried in the mossy ground. These remarkable round gravestones – symbols of the island resembling Celtic crosses – were left behind by the Swedish population that once inhabited Vormsi and are not found in such numbers elsewhere in the country. The earliest sun crosses appeared on Vormsi in the mid-18th century and continued to be built up until the 1920s, before the entire Swedish population fled to escape WWII. The war also brought to an end the activity of the now-derelict Orthodox **Church of the Ascension of the Lord**, whose collapsing onion dome built in 1886 can be seen in Hullo. Two lighthouses stand at opposite ends of the island: **Norrby Lighthouse**, on the east coast, and the iron-built **Saxby Lighthouse** on the west. Hikers can tackle a 6.7km trail that runs through **Vormsi Landscape Reserve**, on the peninsula south of Rumpo village, where three observation towers make excellent birdwatching spots – bring binoculars. Cycling around the whole island will take about three hours, making it an ideal day trip from Haapsalu.

BIRDWATCHING IN MATSALU NATIONAL PARK

Some of the best birdwatching opportunities in Estonia are found in Matsalu National Park between April and May, when flocks of migratory birds – long-tailed ducks, swans and cranes – traverse the wetlands south of Haapsalu. Over 280 species have been counted in the national park, as explained in the visitor centre housed inside Penijõe Manor, where a small exhibition presenting the local fauna can be seen. On the northern side of the park the **Haeska Birdwatching Tower** and the **Piuse Peninsula** are optimal wildlife spotting locations. The Baltics' Coastal Trail runs through the national park, although cycling is probably more pleasant on the flat, often asphalted roads crisscrossing the area.

AIMUR KYTT/SHUTTERSTOCK ©

Kuressaare Episcopal Castle

TOP SIGHTS

Saaremaa & Muhu

Sea air blows through lush forests on Muhu, tempting those who visit to take their time along the largely empty roads that connect beaches, parks and historic sites. Saaremaa, meanwhile, might be far from Estonia's larger destinations, but many consider it a cultural heartland whose earliest settlements date back 5000 years. Tales of Saaremaa's Vikings still inform local mythology, stories of conquests and battles whose traces are visible today.

DON'T MISS

Kuressaare
Episcopal
Castle

Kaali
Crater

Kiipsaare
lighthouse

Muhu

The
Hoppet

Kuressaare

With a population of just over 13,000 people, the capital of Saaremaa is the obvious base to explore the island's cultural and historic sites, by car or by bike (available for rental at Bivarix, bivarix.ee).

The Episcopal Castle

In 1227, the Brothers of the Sword founded a bishopric in Kuressaare and a castle followed, first mentioned in 1381. One of the best-preserved fortresses in the country, the structure houses the Saaremaa Museum, covering local history from medieval times. The surrounding gardens – stretching above the castle's outer walls and freely accessible – were added in the 19th century, a time when turning fortifications into green spaces became common practice all around Europe. Stroll on the path that runs around the walls, then stop for a coffee at Õllekoda, in the castle's courtyard.

LON/SHUTTERSTOCK ©

Kuressaare

Museums & Galleries

Step away from medieval history for a glimpse into the lifestyle of the 1970s and 1980s at the new Saare Kek museum, north of Kuressaare's city centre. This collection of all things retro echoes the DDR museums of former East Germany, with every-day objects put on show to take visitors back to the Soviet era. Right in the heart of Kuressaare, in one of the rooms of the 17th-century Town Hall, is the Raegalerii, an art gallery showing works by contemporary Estonian artists. On Lossi Street, close to 18th-century St Nicholas' Orthodox Church, you'll also find the non-profit Saaremaa Kunstistuudio, offering workshops for adults and kids next to temporary visual arts exhibitions.

Shopping, Eating & Drinking

Crafts, secondhand and antique shops are scattered along and around Kuressare's main avenue, Lossi. Every weekend the Tallina Street market takes place – stop at Jaan Lember's wooden handicrafts stall for unique souvenirs – while places such as Saare Naise Näputöö, Arensburg Antiik and Lossi Antiik welcome treasure seekers every day. The scent of freshly baked cinnamon rolls coming out from BÖNS will entice you in whether you like it or not, while WAAG, housed inside a 1785 building where the governor of Livonia used to reside, offers sea-inspired dishes including a famous eel soup. For a glass of wine accompanied by oysters stop at Vinoteek, or make yourself comfortable on the sunny terrace of John Bull Pub, near the castle.

Kaali Crater

The circular lake known as the Kaali Crater might not look all that impressive to those unaware of its backstory. This 100m-wide pothole is the largest of nine craters found northeast of

---

TO ABRUKA ON BOARD THE *HOPPET*

Friendly Captain Pekka manages the *Hoppet*, the only preserved wooden ship made in Estonia before WWII to still be sailing. Built in 1926 and named 'hope' by its Swedish owners, the two-masted schooner takes groups (up to 50 people) to the island of Abruka, a small speck of land off Saaremaa whose core is covered by a protected broadleaf forest.

TOP TIPS

● Kuressare has the largest number of accommodation options, from budget-friendly guesthouses such as Laurits to high-end heritage hotels such as Ekesparre.

● A ferry runs from the Triigi village in Saaremaa to Sõru in Hiiumaa in summer, allowing you to visit both islands without returning to the mainland.

● East of Triigi, on the northern coast, are the impressive cliffs of Pranga, dropping into the sea from 21m.

● Kuressaare Airport links directly to Tallinn twice a day via a 40-minute flight operated by NyxAir (flynyx.com).

Kuressaare on the site of a meteoric collision which happened either 3500 or 7500 years ago. While scholars have yet to reach a consensus on the date, the Kaali Crater produced many legends now embedded in local legends, giving the 6m-deep lake sacred status in the past. A small museum and a cafe are close to the craters, and nearby you can check out the exterior of the abandoned Kõljala Mõis, a derelict neoclassical mansion dating back to the 17th century.

Sõrve Peninsula

A collection of tiny villages follow one another on the Sõrve Peninsula (Sõrvemaa), stretching for over 30km in the southwestern corner of Saaremaa. The geographical isolation of this slice of Estonia led the people living here to call for independence in 1992, when the USSR collapsed. Following a minor mistake in Estonia's constitution, Torgu Parish, one of the peninsula's settlements, declared itself the Kingdom of Torgu, an unrecognised micronation with its own currency, the Torgu Thaler, whose value is tied to the price of half a litre of local vodka. In 2022 the Kingdom of Torgu elected its second king. The dramatic Sõrve lighthouse is the region's main attraction, but the military museum and bunkers scattered along the peninsula, which experienced heavy fighting during WWII, are also worth visiting, together with the Soviet-era Monument to the Night Battle of Tehumardi.

Vilsandi

Stretching along the western coast of Saaremaa, Vilsandi National Park is more water than land, and has 160 islands contained within its mostly liquid borders. The visitor centre is located inland in the village of Rootsiküla, but to make the most

---

BEERS OF SAAREMAA

There's no shortage of good beer on Saaremaa, where hyper-local flavours have been bottled for decades in home breweries around the island. Besides the famous Saaremaa Tulik beer, no longer made in Saaremaa, look for the craft brews of Pöide, produced near Kuressaare. Pihtla, operating since 1990, claims to be the oldest microbrewery in Estonia and welcomes visitors to its tasting room every summer.

Sõrve lighthouse

CLOUDY DESIGN/SHUTTERSTOCK ©W

IMAGEBROKER.COM/SHUTTERSTOCK ©

Arctic tern, Vilsandi National Park

of the reserve's nature and prime birdwatching opportunities you'll need a private boat. Islander (islander.ee) runs tours to Vilsandi island during summer months. Alternatively, you can hike to the leaning Kiipsaare lighthouse, built in 1933 and now standing right in the water due to the shifting shoreline, on the Tagamõisa Peninsula via the 11km Harilaiu hiking trail.

Orissaare's Legendary Oak

The rural east of Saaremaa has little to offer in terms of attractions for visitors, but one oak tree in the town of Orissaare has gained iconic status after winning the prized title of European Tree of the Year in 2015. This is not the only title Orissaare's oak has gained. According to a local story, Soviet authorities tried to tear it down in the early 1950s to build a football pitch, but failed miserably as the tree wouldn't budge. At 150 years of age, the beloved oak is not the oldest nor the largest tree in the region, but has become a symbol of resistance for Orissaare's community.

Muhu

Relaxing fishing villages, traditional farm houses and a few wooden windmills standing in the picturesque countryside add charm to an island few take the time to explore. A ferry regularly departs from the mainland port of Virtsu and reaches Kuivastu, Muhu's main port, in under an hour. While there are buses that run around the island, Muhu is ideally explored with your own vehicle, either a car or a bicycle. Muhu Museum, in Koguva village, exhibits historical architecture of the island in its open-air grounds, with log barns and wooden homes preserved for visitors to see. On the island's northern coast you'll pass by the 300m Üügu Cliff, before continuing to Linnuse where you can cross into Saaremaa via the 2.5km Väinatamm causeway leading to the village of Põripõllu.

ANGLA HERITAGE CULTURE CENTRE

The family-friendly Angla Heritage Culture Centre, in the heart of Saaremaa, is a place where children can learn all about life in the island's rural interior and folk traditions rooted in local culture. Part museum, part amusement park, it also has handicraft workshops ranging from pottery to blacksmithing, plus a restaurant serving classic Estonian fare in its log hall.

FOTOHELIN/SHUTTERSTOCK ©

Arriving

Tallinn is the main point of entry for those who reach swEstonia by sea or air. Overland travellers can easily reach Estonia from Latvia – Riga is just a couple of hours away from the border. Estonia shares a 294km-long border with Russia, the majority of which runs through Lake Peipsi. Following Russia's invasion of Ukraine in 2022, Estonia closed its border to most Russian citizens.

By Air

Tallinn Airport is the main gateway, offering frequent connections to major European cities. Public transport and taxi services provide easy access to the city centre and facilities at the airport are modern and efficient. Tartu has Estonia's second international airport.

By Ferry

A dozen ships a day arrive from Helsinki, on the opposite side of the Gulf of Finland, docking at the capital's harbour near the city centre. From Tallinn's port, Old Town can be reached on foot in under 20 minutes.

Money

Currency: euro (€)

CASH
Cash seems to be disappearing from Estonian cities, although it's still commonly used for smaller transactions in markets. It's a good idea to keep some euros in your pocket, but it's likely that you won't end up using them. Currency exchange points are easy to find in cities, but ATMs generally offer better rates.

DEBIT & CREDIT CARDS
Credit and debit cards are accepted almost everywhere in Estonia, especially Visa and MasterCard. You won't have trouble using them in hotels, restaurants, larger shops and for online bookings. Occasionally, smaller establishments or shops in remote areas might only accept cash, but these are exceptions in this tech-driven country.

DIGITAL PAYMENTS
Digital payments, including mobile payment apps and contactless payments, are popular in Estonia, a country known for its advanced digital infrastructure. Services like Apple Pay and Google Pay are widely accepted. Digital transactions are the norm even for small amounts.

Getting Around

Driving your own vehicle guarantees maximum freedom, but with some planning, most of Estonia can be visited with public transport for a fraction of the cost.

JASON BUSA/SHUTTERSTOCK ©

ROAD CONDITIONS
Driving in Estonia is fairly easy, at least in summer. Outside of Tallinn, traffic is low to non-existent. In rural areas many roads are unpaved and might get muddy after heavy rains. Winter makes things trickier, as heavy snow can clog the roads: between December and March winter tyres are required when driving on public roads.

BUS & TRAIN
Public transport in Estonia is cheap and very reliable. Rural areas are served only once or twice per day, so make sure to check the schedules if you are planning a day trip. Intercity buses such as Lux Express or Flixbus are generally comfortable. Train tickets are slightly cheaper when bought online at elron.ee.

PARKING
Parking in Estonia is something one should worry about only when driving in larger cities. In Tallinn there are four parking zones, with prices ranging from €0.60 (in the outer neighborhoods) to €6 per hour (near Old Town). All parking rules can be found at parkimine.ee.

PLANE & FERRY
Regional airline NyxAir (flynyx. com) flies from Tallinn to Kuressaare and Pärnu, plus various destinations in Finland and Sweden. Ferries link to most of the inhabited islands with frequent scheduled trips during summer months. The Kihnu Veeteed (veeteed.com) and TS Laevad (praamid.ee) transport companies manage most routes.

HIRING A CAR
If you're flying into Estonia from abroad, you'll be landing in either Tallinn or Tartu. These two cities are where most car rental companies operate. Prices start at around €40/day, but you can find cheaper prices if booking ahead. Given the short distances between cities, a small car is usually enough.

DRIVING ESSENTIALS

Drive on the right side

---

50 **90**

Speed limit is 50km/h in cities and 90km/h on motorways

0.02

Blood alcohol limit is 0.02%

Helsinki

UNIQUE BY DESIGN

Juxtaposing Nordic tranquillity and European dynamism, Helsinki is a forward-looking city that manages to keep its Finnish character intact while growing increasingly international.

The Swedish crown founded Helsinki in the 16th century to create a commercial centre that would challenge Hanseatic Tallinn, lying across the Gulf of Finland, by breaking its monopoly on Russian trade. The attempt to strengthen Sweden's position on the Baltic Sea was far from successful, but such a strategic move meant that Helsinki was born as an experiment in urban planning, created from scratch rather than evolving over time like many other European capitals. Following the 1808–09 war between Sweden and Russia, Tsar Alexander I made Helsinki the capital of the newly created Grand Duchy of Finland, a semi-autonomous region controlled by Russia. During the 19th century the city modernised rapidly, acquiring its university, its first railway and many of its major public buildings, including Senate Square and Helsinki Cathedral, which continue to recall the neoclassical taste of the time. A new phase in the city's story began in 1917, when Finland became an independent nation after centuries of foreign rule. Despite two wars and the repeated bombings of 1944

halting Helsinki's development in the first half of the 20th century, the Finnish capital has managed to make up for the time lost – today, it regularly ranks among the happiest and smartest cities worldwide, thanks to its commitment to sustainability, digitalisation and transparency.

A city in perpetual reinvention, Helsinki may lack the medieval centre of Tallinn and other European cities, but to compensate it boasts a wonderful collection of quirky contemporary buildings and a thriving design culture. The capital is home to over a tenth of the country's population, yet it's hardly a bustling metropolis – with large parks, a long and fragmented shoreline and an archipelago of over 300 islands scattered along the coast, nature plays an integral role in the everyday life of its residents. Visit in winter and you'll find a snowy-white city lit by Christmas lights, where icy temperatures are forgotten between saunas and world-class museums. Come in summer and enjoy music festivals, open-air harbour markets and excursions to forests and beaches, making the most of the long, long days.

KENNY MCCARTNEY/GETTY IMAGES ©

THE MAIN AREAS

Senate Square	Kauppatori	Design district	Suomenlinna
Landmark square, home of Helsinki Cathedral. p149	Market square by the harbour. p149	Shopping and museums. p149	UNESCO-listed fortress islands. p153

Left: Senate Square (p149); Above: Uspenski Cathedral (p152)

Find your way

While Helsinki's metropolitan region is widespread, its centre is easily explored on foot, starting from Market Square by the harbour.

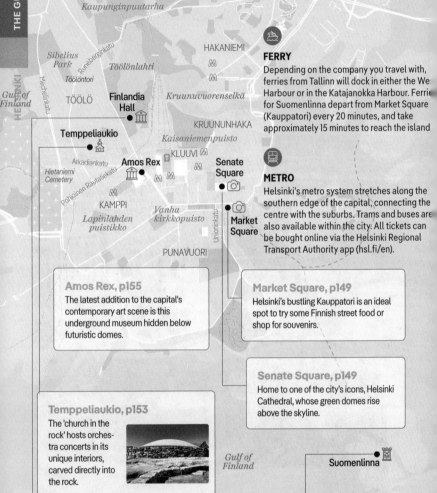

FERRY

Depending on the company you travel with, ferries from Tallinn will dock in either the We Harbour or in the Katajanokka Harbour. Ferrie for Suomenlinna depart from Market Square (Kauppatori) every 20 minutes, and take approximately 15 minutes to reach the island

METRO

Helsinki's metro system stretches along the southern edge of the capital, connecting the centre with the suburbs. Trams and buses are also available within the city. All tickets can be bought online via the Helsinki Regional Transport Authority app (hsl.fi/en).

Amos Rex, p155

The latest addition to the capital's contemporary art scene is this underground museum hidden below futuristic domes.

Market Square, p149

Helsinki's bustling Kauppatori is an ideal spot to try some Finnish street food or shop for souvenirs.

Senate Square, p149

Home to one of the city's icons, Helsinki Cathedral, whose green domes rise above the skyline.

Temppeliaukio, p153

The 'church in the rock' hosts orchestra concerts in its unique interiors, carved directly into the rock.

Finlandia Hall, p154

One of Alvar Aalto's masterpieces, this congress hall has long been a defining feature of design-centric Helsinki.

Suomenlinna, p153

The 18th-century island fortress is now a UNESCO World Heritage Site easily explored from central Helsinki.

0 ——————— 1 km
0 ——————— 0.5 miles

Islands near Helsinki

Plan Your Time

Helsinki will keep you busy whether you're here for a day or a full weekend, with inspiring museums, long sauna sessions and endless retail opportunities available in winter or summer.

A Helsinki Day Trip

● After docking, start your tour at **Uspenski Cathedral** (p152), then continue to **Senate Square** (p149) and **Kauppatori** (p149). Walk up Esplanadi to the **Design District** (p149), before catching a concert at the **Temppeliaukio** 'rock church' (p153). Continue to **Hakaniemi Market Hall** (p149) for food, then explore the Design Museum before heading back to Tallinn.

A Weekend to Explore

● Follow the day one itinerary above. On day two, take the ferry to **Suomenlinna** (p153) and wander the 18th-century fortress, then put things into context at the **National Museum of Finland** (p154) and admire nearby **Oodi Central Library** (p148). Visit **Hietalahti Flea Market** (p149), book a sauna and dinner at **Löyly** (p155), and check out the art at **Kiasma** (p155 and **Amos Rex** (p155).

You'll Also Want To

HOP GALLERIES AND BOUTIQUES	ADMIRE THE ARCHITECTURE	TASTE FINNISH CUISINE	DISCOVER FOLK TRADITIONS
From Marimekko to Iittala, roam the **Design District** (p149) in search of iconic items.	Seek the buildings by **Alvar Aalto** (p154) and art nouveau heritage of **Eliel Saarinen** (p154).	Choose **Kauppatori**'s street food (p149) or the upmarket **Ravintola Nokka** (p153).	Learn about the heritage of rural Finland at the **Seurasaari Open-Air Folk Museum** (p153).

As soon as you dock in Helsinki, head to ❶ **Market Square** (Kauppatori) to begin exploring the city. After a stroll through the market, cross the road and walk north to ❷ **Senate Square**, one block away. Here you'll find majestic ❸ **Helsinki Cathedral**, ❹ **Helsinki City Museum** – where you can get an overview of the Finnish capital's history – and the neoclassical ❺ **National Library of Finland**, which is well worth a peek. Head past the square to reach ❻ **Kaisaniemi Botanic Garden**, then over the bridge to get to ❼ **Hakaniemi Market Hall** where you can browse crafts and get some lunch in the food court. Continue by walking west along the water through ❽ **Tokoinranta Park**, admire the modernist architecture of the ❾ **Helsinki City Theatre**, then cross the rail tracks to reach Alvar Aalto's ❿ **Finlandia Hall**. Over the road, enter the ⓫ **National Museum of**

Finland to learn more about the country's roots, then go secondhand novel hunting at ⓬ **Arkadia International Bookshop**, on the corner of Dagmarinkatu and Nervanderinkatu. Steps away is the 'rock church' of ⓭ **Temppeliaukio**. After visiting the church, walk south on Fredrikinkatu to Pohjoinen Rautatiekatu. Turn left to get back to the city centre (along the way you'll find the ⓮ **Finnish Museum of Natural History**, and walk through the underpass to check out ⓯ **Oodi Central Library**. Head south on Mannerheimintie, cross the futuristic Lasipalatsi above ⓰ **Amos Rex Museum** and check out ⓱ **Kamppi Chapel** before ambling to the ⓲ **Hietalahti Flea Market**. Cross the Design District along ⓳ **Bulevardi** on your way back, and finally walk through ⓴ **Esplanadi Park** to return to your starting point.

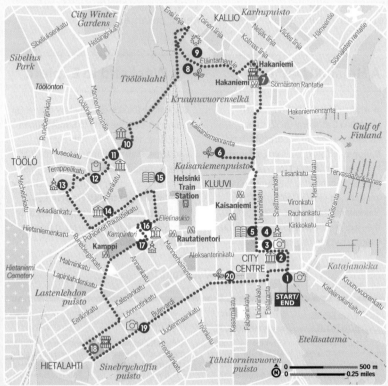

Design District

Design Central

Shopping in Helsinki's Design District

The Finnish capital was the first in Europe to establish a Chief Design Officer to make design an integral part of the city's development. Helsinki's dedication to design is visible on every corner, but for short-term visitors it's best appreciated in the great shopping opportunities of the city's **Design District**. Some 200 shops offer everything from fashion to home decor and lifestyle products, bringing together creatives, crafts makers and artists in Helsinki's central avenues. The boundaries of the district are fluid, but it's generally seen as lying between Senate Square, Kampii, Bulevardi and Korkeavuorenkatu. Iconic brand **Marimekko** is a symbol of Finnish style with its bright patterns and high-quality fabrics, but lesser-known gallery-style boutiques such as **Lokal**, focusing on handcrafted furniture and ceramics, are equally loved by locals. The **Artek** store funded by Alvar and Aino Aalto has become a defining brand of 20th-century Finnish design, while the **Kämp Garden**, on the upper floor of the Kämp shopping mall, is the place to discover up-and-coming fashion designers. Other evergreen brands to look out for are

Continues on p152

BEST MARKETS IN HELSINKI

Market Square (Kauppatori)
Helsinki's historic Market Square comes to life in summer, when stalls serving fresh peas and strawberries line up next to street food and souvenir stalls around the 1835 **Keisarinnankivi** (Tsarina's Stone) obelisk.

Hakaniemi Market Hall
Spread across the two floors of early-20th-century Hakaniemi Hall, this covered market (reopened in 2022 after renovations) houses both a food court and a space dedicated to crafts, textiles and flowers. Stop for a coffee or to find unique gifts.

Hietalahti Flea Market
A popular flea market at the western end of Bulevardi offering a large selection of secondhand clothing and unexpected surprises of all sorts. Most active on Saturday and Sunday.

 WHERE TO STAY IN HELSINKI ─────────────

CheapSleep
The name says it all. This hostel has long served the backpacker crowd with its huge dorms and inhouse bar. €

Hotel Helka
Unassuming building holding a characterful hotel with all the amenities. Great breakfast buffet. €€

GLO Hotel Art
A well-positioned hotel in a castle-like building, GLO stands out thanks to its quirky exterior and functional rooms. €€

HELSINKI

Sibelius
Park
27
Töölöntori

House Of
Culture (13km);
CheapSleep (2.2km);
littala & Arabia
Design Centre
(4.1km)

43

26 Eläintarhantie

Kruunuvuorenselkä

Gulf of
Finland

Töölönlahti

Pohjoinen Hesperiankatu

Hesperiankatu

TÖÖLÖ

Museokatu

Finlandia Hall
2

21

35

sisätöpan

Pitkänsilu

Kaisaniemenranta

14

Kaisaniemenpu

Temppelikatu

44

6
Temppeliaukio

Aurarankatu

23

Helsinki
Train
Station

KLUUVI

Kaisani

42

Arkadiankatu 10

16

Elielinaukio

7

Kaisaniemi

Kaisaniemiö

39

Hietaniemenkatu

31

Amos
1 Rex

15

Kampintori

Rautatientori
M

M

Kamppi M

Malminkatu

40

Kampintori

Lapinlahdenkatu

49

KAMPPI

41

37 47

9

Aleksanterinkatu

Lapinlahden
puistikko

Ruoholahdenkatu

Eerikinkatu

Kalevankatu

Albertinkatu

Fredrikinkatu

Annankatu

Vanha
kirkkopuisto

Ludviginkatu

Yrjönkatu

Porkkatankatu

34

30

38

Uudenmaankatu

48

Iso Roobertinkatu

8 19

Ruoholahti M

Lönnrotinkatu

46

Bulevardi

Sinebrychoffin
puisto

PUNAVUORI

Tarkk'ampujankatu

Jääkärinkatu

Vuorimiehenkatu

Punavuorenkatu

Merimiehenkatu

Pursimiehenkatu

Sepänkatu

Tehtaankatu

32

HIETALAHTI

EIRA

Merikatu

Ehrensvärdintie

Antoellintie

Laivurinkatu

Huvilakatu

Pietarinkatu

Merikatu

Gulf of
Finland

KALASATAMA

Eiranranta

Marisatamanranta

MUNKKISAARI

29

Gulf of
Finland

Sirpalesaar

Liuskasaar

TOP SIGHTS
1 Amos Rex
2 Finlandia Hall
3 Market Square
4 Senate Square
5 Suomenlinna
6 Temppeliaukio

SIGHTS
7 Central Station
8 Design Museum
9 Esplanadi Park
10 Finnish Museum of Natural History
11 Helsinki Cathedral
12 Helsinki City Museum
13 Jetty Barracks
14 Kaisaniemi Botanic Garden
15 Kamppi Chapel
16 Kiasma Museum
17 King's Gate
18 Military Museum of Manège
19 Museum of Finnish Architecture
20 National Library of Finland
21 National Museum of Finland
22 Nordic Arts Centre
23 Oodi Central Library
24 Suomenlinna Church

25 Suomenlinna Museum
26 Tokoinranta Park
27 Töölö Church
28 Uspenski Cathedral

ACTIVITIES, COURSES & TOURS
29 Löyly

SLEEPING
30 GLO Hotel Art
31 Hotel Helka

EATING
32 BasBas Kulma
33 Café Lov
34 Grön
35 Kahvila Rakastan
36 Ravintola Nokka

DRINKING & NIGHTLIFE
37 Café Aalto
38 Ekberg 1852
39 Juova Hanahuone
40 Kaffeecentralen
41 Pien
42 Sori Taproom

ENTER-TAINMENT
43 Helsinki City Theatre

SHOPPING
44 Arkadia International Bookshop
45 Hakaniemi Market Hall
46 Hietalahti Flea Market
47 Kämp Garden
48 Lokal
49 Marimekko

THE WOODEN HOUSES OF KÄPYLÄ

At the end of WWI, the capital of newly-independent Finland underwent major redevelopment to solve the housing shortage the conflict had created. Architect Martti Välikangas was commissioned to design a new residential area in the Käpylä part of Helsinki, to offer affordable homes to the working classes.

The neighbourhood, often referred to as 'wooden Käpylä', was completed in 1925 in the Nordic Classicism style, and now stands in sharp contrast with Helsinki's modern core with its collection of low-rise, colourful timber houses surrounded by greenery. Take in the picturesque villas with a stroll along tree-lined Pohjolankatu, the neighbourhood's main artery, or learn more about Finnish wooden architecture at the Museum of Finnish Architecture on Kasarmikatu.

Töölö Church

Continued from p149

Iittala, producing glassware since the late 19th century, and Fiskars, the oldest Finnish company still in operation, known for its orange-handle scissors. The **Iittala & Arabia Design Centre** in the Toukola area, containing a museum tracing the history of the brands and an outlet store, can be visited by booking a guided tour at designcentrehelsinki.com. To learn more about Finnish design, head to Helsinki's **Design Museum**, a collection of thousands of objects housed inside a red-brick, neogothic building in Korkeavuorenkatu street.

Helsinki's Churches, Orthodox & Unorthodox

Quirky and monumental religious monuments

As soon as you step onto Helsinki's harbour from Tallinn you're met by one of the city's most impressive pieces of architecture – beautiful **Uspenski Cathedral**. Completed in 1868 when Finland was a semi-autonomous Grand Duchy of the Russian Empire, it's made of bricks from Åland Bomarsund Fortress, destroyed during the Crimean War. This Eastern Orthodox church overlooks the dome of **Helsinki Cathedral**, the white neoclassical city symbol known as St

 WHERE TO EAT IN HELSINKI

Fat Ramen
Tasty, budget-friendly lunch spot, preparing ramen bowls and sides like kimchi. Locations across the city. €

Kahvila Rakastan
Comforting cafe focused on plant-based, traditional Karelian pies prepared following a family recipe. €

Café Lov
This welcoming little cafe specialises in *flammkuchen*, pizza-like bread with a variety of toppings. €€

Nicholas' Church in pre-independence days, standing tall in the middle of Senate Square just steps away. Besides these two major religious structures, the capital has a number of unusual churches. **Temppeliaukio Church** in the Töölö area is one of them. Carved into solid rock, this 1969 Lutheran church, designed by brothers Timo and Tuomo Suomalainen, regularly holds orchestra concerts in the circular hall due to its perfect acoustics (programme available at temppeli aukionkirkko.fi), and is a classic of Finnish minimalist, nature-inspired architecture. Climb to the roof to see the copper dome shyly emerging from the rock. Not far away is the blocky **Töölö Church**, a pink building that draws far fewer tourists, but which is worth seeing for an appreciation of the Nordic Classicism style that emerged in the early 20th century. Even more minimal is the **Kamppi Chapel**, a wooden, vase-like meditative space sitting next to the Amos Rex contemporary art museum. A showpiece completed in 2012 when Helsinki received the title of World Design Capital, Kamppi doesn't hold regular services but you can enjoy some silent contemplation inside by purchasing a €5 ticket.

Inside Suomenlinna's Fortress
An 18th-century island defensive structure

Today, the 800 or so inhabitants of Suomenlinna live a peaceful life, but in the past these six islands guarding Helsinki's main harbour functioned as an essential military outpost. The UNESCO-inscribed **Suomenlinna fortress**, first built by the Swedish rulers in the mid-18th century, is a fascinating window into the history of contested Finland. Visiting is easy: a public ferry departs multiple times a day from Kauppatori and reaches Suomenlinna in approximately 15 minutes. The best way to explore the site once there is by following the '**blue route**', a 1.5km marked trail starting from the Russian-era **Jetty Barracks** and ending at Suomenlinna's best-known landmark, the curved **King's Gate**, built in 1754 as the fortress' main entrance. Don't miss **Suomenlinna Cathedral**, completed in 1854 and converted into a Lutheran Church – to which most religious Finns belong today – when the country gained its independence in 1918. To learn more about the open-air museum formed by Suomenlinna's ruins, you can visit a number of museums on the islands. **Suomenlinna Museum** and the **Military Museum of Manège** are open year-round and recount the history of the fortress and Finland's defence forces. In summer, board the **Vesikko submarine**, which patrolled the Baltic Sea during WWII. Former barracks on Susisaari island, built to house 500 soldiers

THE SEURASAARI OPEN-AIR FOLK MUSEUM

Following a concept similar to that of the Estonian Open-Air Museum (p77) outside of Tallinn, the folk museum on the island of **Seurasaari**, west of Helsinki, features a collection of historic buildings that showcase the different lifestyles of rural Finland. Best explored during the summer, the forested grounds of Seurasaari are dotted with original wooden cottages and farmhouses, dating as far back as the 18th century, that have been relocated to the island to provide an insight into living conditions in all regions of the country. Bus 24 takes you from central Helsinki to the bridge leading into Seurasaari.

 WHERE TO EAT IN HELSINKI

BasBas Kulma
Book ahead for this popular, upmarket restaurant where a six-plate tasting menu explores Finnish cuisine. €€

Grön
Michelin-starred Grön elevates produce from local farms while keeping sustainability in mind. Vegan menu available. €€€

Ravintola Nokka
A ship propeller welcomes guests to one of Helsinki's top restaurants, serving Finnish cuisine with harbour views. €€€

153

THE WORK OF ELIEL SAARINEN

Though not as widely known outside of Finland as Alvar Aalto, architect Eliel Saarinen (1873–1950) also contributed to shaping modern Helsinki. Many visitors are introduced to his style as soon as they reach the city – the four massive male figures holding spherical lamps at the entrance of Helsinki's **Central Train Station** are an unmissable feature of the art nouveau building designed by Saarinen in 1919. Not far from the station is the church-like **National Museum of Finland**, which was completed in 1910, inspired by medieval rural architecture. The museum's building is considered one of the most important examples of the National Romantic style.

Jetty Barracks (p153)

of the Russian Empire in 1868, are home to the **Nordic Arts Centre**, offering rotating contemporary art exhibitions in a unique setting. Suomenlinna's four main islands, where most sights are located, are connected with bridges and can easily be explored on foot.

Alvar Aalto's Architectural Heritage

Discover the work of the best-known Finnish architect

Globally celebrated Finnish architect and designer Alvar Aalto (1898–1976) was much involved in Finland's 20th-century renaissance. Following the modernist principles in fashion at the time, Aalto spent much of his life working relentlessly to innovate every detail of a building, from the overall structure to individual pieces of furniture. The 1971 **Finlandia Hall** (set to reopen in 2024 after restoration work), in front of the National Museum of Finland, is one of Aalto's Helsinki landmarks, followed by the monolithic **House of Culture**, a lesser-known red-brick structure completed in 1958 for the Finnish Communist Party headquarters. Besides creating buildings all over his home country (and also in France, Denmark, Italy and Russia), Aalto also produced some of the objects that have become icons of Finnish design, first and foremost the Savoy Vase (also known as Aalto Vase), an ir-

 WHERE TO DRINK BEER IN HELSINKI

Pien
Colourful Pien has eight changing beers on tap – and hundreds of others from around the world in the fridges.

Juova Hanahuone
The beer selection is as mismatched as the furniture in this pub, which has 30 local and international options.

Sori Taproom
Showcasing Tallinn-based, Finnish-run Sori Brewing Company, with 24 taps to try and great bites.

regular glass container that continues to be produced and widely sold today. The success of Aalto's furniture led him to open, together with his wife Aino, the Artek brand, whose flagship store still operates in Helsinki's Design District inside a Keskuskatu street building designed by another great Finnish architect, Eliel Saarinen. Enter the store to find legendary minimalist pieces such as the Model 60 three-legged stool and the sinuous Paimio Chair. To learn more about Alvar Aalto's legacy, join a guided tour of the **Aalto House** and **Studio Aalto** (book via alvaraalto.fi) in the Munkkiniemi neighbourhood of the city. For a broader overview, the **Museum of Finnish Architecture** in central Helsinki makes for a few hours well spent.

Contemporary Art Wonders
World-class museums at the heart of Helsinki's art scene

The **Kiasma Museum** holds some of Helsinki's most valuable contemporary art. It owns over 8000 pieces by mostly Finnish artists and has a constantly changing series of shows, offering something new to residents and tourists on each and every visit. Facing the street behind the glass wall is the museum's cafe and well-stocked bookshop. Steps away from Kiasma is the more recent **Amos Rex** museum, opened in 2018 by the foundation created by late Finnish art collector Amos Anderson, which excavated Lasipalatsi – the 1930s square stretching behind the Bio Rex cinema – to make space for the 2200-sq-metre exhibition space. The latest addition to Helsinki's contemporary art scene now hides below Lasipalatsi's five white domes, each topped by an oculus that provides the hall with natural light. The main draw of Amos Rex is the temporary exhibitions of immersive, often tech-driven works that vary throughout the year (check what's on at amosrex.fi), ranging from audio-based experiences to light shows created with digital data. Avant-garde exhibitions contrast with the permanent **Sigurd Frosterus Collection**, neoimpressionist paintings dating back to the early 20th century collected by Finnish art critic Frosterus over the course of his life. Owned by the Sigurd Frosterus Foundation but held by Amos Rex, the pieces, which make up one of the most important private collections of modern art in Finland, include colourful scenes by the French father of pointillism Paul Signac and Finnish symbolist artist Magnus Enckell.

BEST SAUNAS IN HELSINKI

Löyly
A large, modern space for a sophisticated sauna experience followed by dinner in the elegant restaurant overlooking the sea.

Kotiharjun Sauna
The last traditional, wood-heated public sauna still standing in Helsinki has been operating for nearly a century and is going strong.

Uusi Sauna
Visitors and locals are welcome in this updated, neighbourhood sauna in the Jätkäsaari area, complete with inhouse restaurant.

 WHERE TO HAVE COFFEE IN HELSINKI

Ekberg 1852
Said to be Finland's oldest cafe, Ekberg sits on Bulevardi, giving off old-school elegance.

Café Aalto
Designed by the man himself, modernist Café Aalto sits on the Academic Library's upper floor.

Kaffeecentralen
A place for coffee nerds, with great drinks, coffee-making equipment and bags of house-roasted beans.

Above: Rīga (p162); Right: Turaida castle (p192)

THE MAIN AREAS

Rīga	Jūrmala	Vidzeme coast	Sigulda	Zemgale
National capital.	Latvia's main beach.	Stunning dunes.	Gateway to a magnificent national park.	Palaces and woods.
p162	p180	p186	p190	p200

Latvia

DUNES AND FORESTS

Explore stunning coastlines, an elegant capital city, charming
old towns and enigmatic lakes in mysterious woods.

Latvia is painted in blue and green – the blue of the sea and a multitude of lakes, the green of the forest canopy that covers much of the hinterland. However, that's only from afar. A closer look reveals more colours: the golden radiance of sand dunes and luxuriant beaches; the brownish hue of peat bogs sprinkled with cranberry red; the pastel tones of Rīga's art nouveau district; and the hardened black wood and the grey boulders in the walls of old barns that dot the countryside.

Latvia is defined by the juxtaposition of its only large cosmopolitan city, Rīga, accounting for 52% of the population, and the rest of the country. This is

one of the highest ratios in Europe. Rīga is a fantastically cosy and welcoming city that doesn't jump over its head in order to please but displays many quietly understated charms.

The country beyond Rīga is surprisingly diverse, with four historical regions presenting an intriguing interplay of distinct landscapes and idiosyncratic old towns: agricultural Kurzeme in the west, hilly and forested Vidzeme in the north, history-rich Zemgale in the south, and the lakelands of Latgale in the east.

But the main treasure is the coastline – 500km of stunning beaches and pine-covered dunes along the Gulf of Rīga and open sea in the west.

Find Your Way

Latvia can be crossed in a few hours, going in any direction, and it's easy to get around.

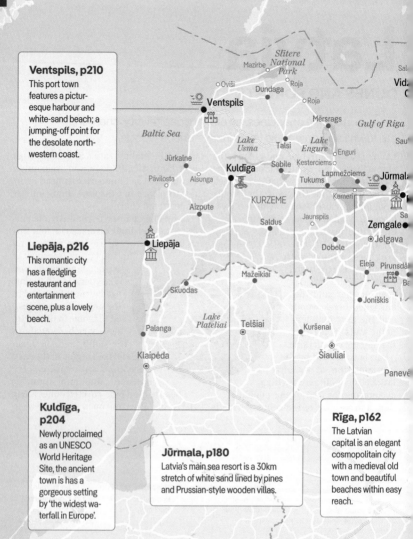

Ventspils, p210

This port town features a picturesque harbour and white-sand beach; a jumping-off point for the desolate northwestern coast.

Liepāja, p216

This romantic city has a fledgling restaurant and entertainment scene, plus a lovely beach.

Kuldīga, p204

Newly proclaimed as an UNESCO World Heritage Site, the ancient town is has a gorgeous setting by 'the widest waterfall in Europe'.

Jūrmala, p180

Latvia's main sea resort is a 30km stretch of white sand lined by pines and Prussian-style wooden villas.

Rīga, p162

The Latvian capital is an elegant cosmopolitain city with a medieval old town and beautiful beaches within easy reach.

Vidzeme Coast, p186

Enchanting dune landscapes in the Baltics await travellers on the northern side of the Gulf of Rīga.

BUS

Latvia has an extensive network of bus routes designed to cover most small villages and even stand-alone farmsteads. Buses are generally modern and comfortable, even on remote routes. Prices are very cheap by European standards.

CAR

Travelling by car around Latvia gives a lot flexibility and saves plenty of time. The road network is generally good, but there are no real highways. Unpaved roads are fairly common. Virtually all rental companies are located in Rīga.

TRAIN

The Latvian train network is limited to suburban destinations near Rīga and selected destinations around the country. Old Soviet trains serving these routes are due for replacement any time now. The high-speed Rail Baltica (p343) project won't be operational before 2028.

Zemgale, p200

The wooded historical region in southern Latvia is steeped in history and features two famous palaces.

Sigulda, p190

This Latvian hill station is the gateway to a wonderful national park offering every imaginable outdoor activity.

Daugavpils, p222

This is the gateway to Latvia's eastern lake district and the multicultural melting pot of Latgale.

0 50 km
0 25 miles

Plan Your Time

Latvia is a compact country with a lot to offer, so it's possible to pack many activities into a limited amount of time.

Pressed for Time

● If you only have a few days, base yourself in the capital, **Rīga** (p162), and take in as much of it as you can – the **Old Town** (p164) with its spired churches and museums, the Art Nouveau buildings of the **Jugendstil quarter** (p167), the impressive **Latvian National Museum of Art** (p173) and the **bar clusters** (p174) in the city centre.

● Make sure you allocate at least half a day for a trip to the seaside – **Jūrmala** (p180) if you like crowded, energetic places, or **Saulkrasti** (p187) if you are craving quiet and natural beauty.

Jūrmala (p180)

LIOX/SHUTTERSTOCK ©

Seasonal Highlights

Most people flock to Latvia in the summer, but the autumn, snowy Christmas and spring can be just as enchanting.

JANUARY

There's a good finally enough snow for cross-country **skiing** in Rīga; there always is for downhill skiing in Sigulda.

MARCH

It's still very chilly and forest trails are flooded, but there's already green grass in the parks. **Rīga Restaurant Week** kicks off.

MAY

Days suddenly become very long and the whole country is in bloom and awash with **storks** arriving from their African holiday.

Ten Days to Explore

● With more days to explore Latvia, follow the above itinerary but also that venture into **Kuldīga** (p204) to admire the quiet cobbled streets of its Old Town and the famous waterfall, then proceed to the lively port city of **Liepāja** (p216) for a healthy dose of seaside fun and to the surfer village of **Pāvilosta** (p221) for a chilled-out day on the beach by the Baltic.

● Next, head to **Ventspils** (p210) and take in its busy and colourful harbour and maritime park before returning to **Rīga** (p162).

Three Weeks to Travel Around

● Three weeks allow you to see a fair chunk of the country. Start with the 10-day itinerary, but also take a trip to the beautiful **Gauja National Park** (p195), visiting its gateway town, **Sigulda** (p190), as well as attractions around **Līgatne** (p195) and medieval **Cēsis** (p197).

● Proceed to lakeside **Alūksne** (p198) before venturing into the rural **Latgale** (p228) region. Admire the lakes around **Rēzekne** (p228), visit Latvia's holiest Catholic shrine in **Aglona** (p226) and the multiethnic community of **Krāslava** (p226) before ending your trip in **Daugavpils** (p222) wit its old fortress and a museum cluster.

JULY
The nation repairs to the **coastal dunes and lakes** or into the countryside.

OCTOBER
There's festivals galore in Rīga, from **Survival Kit** to **Rīga International Film Festival**. Crowds flock to Sigulda for autumn scenery.

NOVEMBER
It's very dark, but the **national holiday season** is in full swing and Rīga gets beautifully decorated with light installations.

DECEMBER
Drink Rīga Black Balsam with hot blackcurrant juice at **Christmas markets** and wait for the first snow to embark on **skiing** expeditions.

Rīga

ART MUSEUMS | URBAN VILLAGE | GREEN BELTS

GETTING AROUND

Rīga's airport is served by bus 22. To avoid taxi scams, it's safer to order on the Bolt app. The city centre is compact, but trams, buses or trolleybuses are essential if venturing further out. Fares are paid by e-talons. Buy and refill them at Narvessen convenience stores or vending machines aboard newer trams. The Mobillly app is handy if you're in Rīga for more than a few days. The Bolt app also rents scooters, a good option for travelling to Mežaparks or across the river. Carshare services are widespread.

☑ **TOP TIP**

There are no musts in Rīga – just go with the flow and do your thing: sip coffee on the pavement under art nouveau facades, enter Gothic churches, visit museums of your choosing, shop for fresh farm produce at markets and hop from one friendly bar to another in the evening.

Rīga is akin to an independent-minded and slightly mysterious lady who is always elegantly dressed despite modest income, keeps her house in good order, and has seen a lot but won't tell you everything. The city is composed of historical layers left by its former overlords. The tall spires and cobbled streets of Old Town (or Vecrīga) are the legacy of Baltic German and Swedish rulers. The art nouveau facades in the centre hark back to the Russian Empire. Gloomy apartment blocks on the outskirts are Soviet footprints. Having re-emerged as the capital of independent Latvia three decades ago, Rīga keeps filling up with tasteful, history-conscious new architecture and adopting a homey, user-friendly look. You also feel close to nature here. The border with the countryside and pristine woods is quite blurred, with furry visitors occasionally venturing into town and wild mushrooms prominently on sale at farmers markets.

BORIS STROUJKO/SHUTTERSTOCK ©

Old Town (p164)

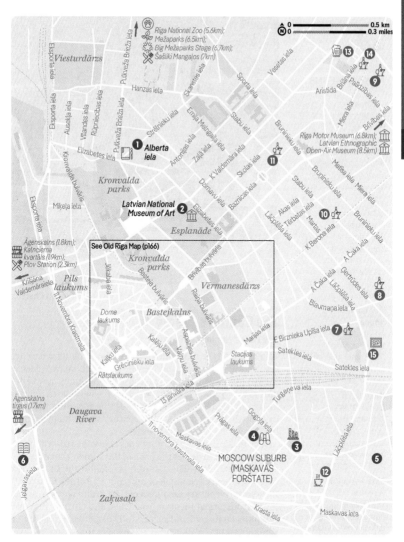

TOP SIGHTS
① Alberta iela
② Latvian National Museum of Art

SIGHTS
③ Choral Synagogue ruins
④ Latvian Academy of Science Observation Deck
⑤ Maskavas forštate

ACTIVITIES, COURSES & TOURS
⑥ National Library of Latvia

DRINKING & NIGHTLIFE
⑦ Aleponija
⑧ Bolderāja

⑨ Ezītis Miglā
⑩ Gauja
⑪ Gimlet
⑫ Katkevich
⑬ Labietis
⑭ Walters & Grapa
⑮ Zuzeum

BEST OLD TOWN MUSEUMS

Latvian Photography Museum
Early images of the Latvian capital as well as contemporary photography inside a house dating from 1500.

Latvian War Museum
Regional war history from medieval German knights to Latvia's NATO membership inside a medieval tower.

Mentzendorff's House
An insight into everyday life of a 17th-century German glazier at his Old Town residence.

Museum of Decorative Arts and Design
Impressive collection of furniture, tapestries and ceramics inside Rīga's oldest church.

Rīga Porcelain Museum
The story of Rīga's porcelain-making industry, which had its heyday at the turn of the 20th century, fusing German and Russian entrepreneurship.

NOMADKATE/SHUTTERSTOCK ©

St John's Church

The Capital's Cradle
See the beginnings of Rīga

When in 1201 the crusading bishop Albert von Buxhoeveden resolved to build a city on the site of an old marketplace at the mouth of the Daugava, he chose a spot that is now called **Jāņa sēta** (St John's courtyard). This is where the chronicled history of Rīga begins, which makes this enclosure, guarded by a partly reconstructed 13th-century wall, an apt point to begin your exploration of the city.

Once inside, note the curving lines above the red-brick gates – they are said to depict the back of the donkey that drove Jesus into Jerusalem. The gist of it is – follow the Christ. The courtyard bears the name of adjacent **St John's Church**, a 13th- to 19th-century amalgam of Gothic and baroque styles. It's first historical mention was when the citizens installed catapults on its roof and successfully dispersed attacking Livonian knights. Walk through Jāņa sēta into a square dominated by the needle-shaped **St Peter's Church**. The centrepiece of Rīga's skyline, this Gothic tower has been known since 1209, making it one of the oldest medieval buildings in the Baltics. Its soaring spire, added in the 17th century, is adorned with a golden-coloured weathercock, also a symbol

 WHERE TO STAY IN OLD TOWN (VECRĪGA)

Neiburgs
Occupying one of Rīga's finest art nouveau buildings, Neiburgs blends preserved details with contemporary touches. €€€

Hotel Justus
A tidy upper-floor hotel, with angled ceilings in the rooms following the roofline. €€

Naughty Squirrel
Backpackerdom star with homey dorms and a ritual shot of booze at check-in. €

Start by the rosarium at **❶ Vērmanes dārzs** (p172) and cross the gardens, exiting into Tērbatas iela. Here, make a short detour towards the **❷ Splendid Palace** cinema, an art nouveau masterpiece hidden within a modernist Soviet-era structure. Continue along Tērbatas iela, noting the brightly coloured art nouveau facades of **❸ School No 40** (Tērbatas iela 15–17) and the **❹ residential building** at Tērbatas iela 32–39. At Akas iela, look up at a controversial erotic **❺ mural** adorning a secondary school building. The inscription reads: 'We are like earthworms, we must hoe the earth.'

At the next crossing, you'll reach an important cluster of bars. If you're feeling thirsty, our choice here is **❻ Gauja**. Otherwise, turn into Stabu iela, one of Rīga's most elegant streets, and cross Brīvības iela near the **❼ Stūra Māja** (p169) museum. Turn into

Baznīcas iela near another notable cluster of bars, where you may be tempted to down a gimlet at a much-lauded venue called, well, **❽ Gimlet**.

Now you'll find yourself near central Rīga's top landmark, the **❾ St Gertrude Church,** which is located in a beautiful oval-shaped square. Note a knight's figure on the wall of the **❿ residential building** at Baznīcas iela 31. Continue to the next crossing and turn into Lāčplēša iela. At the following crossing, the famous **⓫ Kaņepes Kultūras Centrs** is a former music school turned beer garden-cum-concert venue that stays open during warm months. Continue along the Skolas iela, passing by the **⓬ Jewish Community Centre,** which contains a small museum, and finish at the **⓭ Latvian National Museum of Art** (p173) by the Esplanāde park.

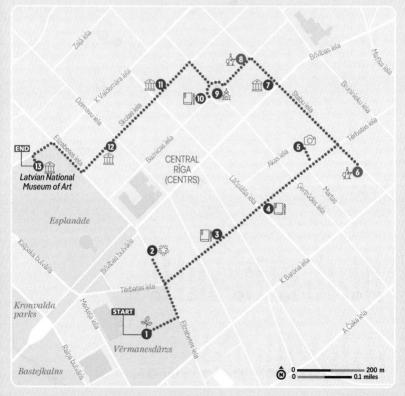

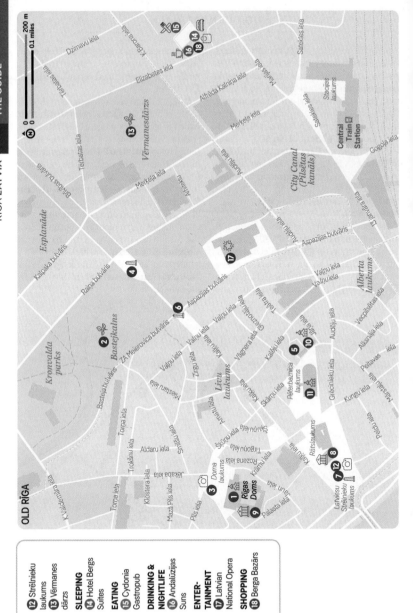

OLD RĪGA

TOP SIGHTS
1 Rīgas Doms

SIGHTS
2 Bastion Hill
3 Doma laukums
4 Freedom Monument
5 Jāņa sēta
6 Laima Clock
7 Latvian Riflemen Monument
8 Museum of the Occupation of Latvia
9 Rīga History and Navigation Museum
10 St John's Church
11 St Peter's Church
12 Strēlnieku laukums
13 Vērmanes dārzs

SLEEPING
14 Hotel Bergs Suites

EATING
15 Cydonia Gastropub

DRINKING & NIGHTLIFE
16 Andalūzijas Suns

ENTERTAINMENT
17 Latvian National Opera

SHOPPING
18 Berga Bazārs

of Rīga. In 1721 the spire was destroyed in a blaze caused by lightning, despite Russian Emperor Peter I personally rushing to the scene to extinguish the fire. It was destroyed once more in WWII and resurrected again in 1973, complete with a lift that whisks visitors to a viewing platform 72m up the copper-clad steeple.

Local History at Dome Square

Meet by the cathedral

In joy or grief, to celebrate or protest, or to stock up on Christmas gifts, the people of Rīga flock to Old Town's main square – a vast cobblestoned space in front of the enormous **Rīgas Doms**, the country's most prominent cathedral.

Founded in 1211 as the seat of the Rīga diocese, it's the largest medieval church in the Baltics. The architecture is a mixture of styles from the 13th to the 18th centuries – Romanesque, Gothic and baroque, with a trademark Hanseatic feature of glazed black bricks. During Soviet times services were forbidden, but the building, along with its huge 6768-pipe organ built in 1884, underwent a careful reconstruction in 1983. It was used as a classical-music venue, which it very much remains now, although services are held again and it's the home of the Lutheran archbishop of Latvia. At the back of the cathedral, the **Rīga History and Navigation Museum**, founded in 1773, presents a sweep of local history from the Bronze Age all the way to WWII. Artefacts, including lovely pre-Christian jewellery and clothing from the art nouveau period, help to tell the story. A highlight is the beautiful neoclassical **Column Hall**, built when Latvia was part of the Russian Empire. The square, **Doma laukums**, is relatively new – with the remainder of the old housing, which obstructed the view of the cathedral, cleared in 1936.

The best time to be here is before Christmas and Easter or during the November national holiday season when it becomes a venue for markets and various live events.

Architecture of the Imagination

Explore the Jugendstil quarter

Rīga entered the brave new 20th century (and the eighth century of its own history) as the sixth-largest city in the Russian Empire. It was also rapidly expanding under a new ambitious mayor George Armitstead, a native Rigan of British origin. In 1901 the city celebrated its 700th anniversary by inaugurating a new street, **Alberta iela**, built in the revolutionary

PAINTINGS & DWELLINGS

While you are at Dome Square, there are a few more must-sees. Rīga's lavishly restored 1852 stock exchange building, now **Art Museum Rīga Bourse**, is a worthy showcase for the city's art treasures. The Asian section features beautiful Chinese and Japanese ceramics and an Egyptian mummy, while the main halls are devoted to Western art, including a Monet painting and a scaled-down cast of Rodin's *The Kiss*.

A few hundred metres away, three old stone houses dubbed the **Three Brothers** conveniently line up in a photogenic row and exemplify Old Rīga's diverse collection of architectural styles. No 17 is over 600 years old, making it the oldest dwelling in town.

WHERE TO EAT IN OLD TOWN (VECRĪGA)

3 Pavaru
Stellar chefs run this jazzy gastro-show, with improvisation at the heart of the menu. €€€

Alaverdi/Locale
Clash of civilisations: idiosyncratic Georgian cuisine and wine list vs Italian and Middle Eastern. Who wins? €€

Milda
Dive into Baltic gastronomy: creatively reinvented Latvian and Lithuanian staples and a chatty chef. €€

CELEBRITY HOMES

Alberta iela is still a residential street, so generally you can't enter the houses unless you are invited by locals, but there are exceptions. Surmount the wonderfully lavish stairwell up to the 5th floor to find the **Janis Rozentāls and Rūdolfs Blaumanis Museum**, the former dwelling of a famous painter and his equally famous writer friend. Enter from Strēlnieku iela. Across the street, the **Rīga Art Nouveau Centre** is based inside a house architect Konstantīns Pēkšēns built for himself, incorporating images of plants and animals characteristic of Latvia into ornamental reliefs. Future British philosopher Isaiah Berlin was another local celebrity resident (as a child), as testified by a plaque at **Alberta iela 2a**, a lavishly decorated house guarded by sphinxes.

ELESI/SHUTTERSTOCK ©

Strēlnieku laukums (Riflemen Square)

Jugendstil (art nouveau) style and named after the founder of Rīga, Bishop Albert von Buxhoeveden.

Today, this street is in the heart of what is known as the **Jugendstil quarter**, a legendary collection of buildings erected in that style during a short epoch marked by rapid development and social optimism.

The style, a Germanic interpretation of art nouveau, allowed architects to unleash their imagination and display their passions, fears and hobbies on the richly decorated facades of what then looked like high-rise apartment blocks. Like a huge painting that you can spend hours staring at, as your eye detects more and more intriguing details, this must-see Rīga sight is in fact a rather functional street with residential houses, restaurants and shops. The architect responsible for many of the buildings was Mikhail Eisenstein, who happened to be the father of filmmaker Sergei Eisenstein (of *Battleship Potemkin* fame). Mikhail was a jolly man, and his bon-vivant personality comes through in his exuberant work. See the full range of his talents on display in five adjoining buildings he designed, from No 2a to No 8. Appreciate the fact that he was only 29 at the time, and an amateur architect who never made this craft his vocation.

 WHERE TO EAT IN JUGENDSTIL DISTRICT

Buberts
Away from the crowds, Buberts serves meat and fish dishes accompanied by craft beer. €

Zivju Lete
Cafe with bare-brick walls, wooden floors and date-friendly tables, offering fish and chips to towering seafood platters. €€

Space Falafel
Divine shakshuka in a convivial gastropub amid art nouveau treasures. €€

Age of Tyranny

History of totalitarianism at Strēlnieku laukums

The face of Rīga was shaped by foreign conquerors and political regimes that ruled Latvia for much of the last 800 years. The unforgiving 20th century left more scars than decorations. From 1940 to 1991, Latvia was occupied by the Soviets and Nazi Germans. The much longer Soviet period, accompanied by mass deportations to Siberia, left a far greater impact on the country's political psyche than the Holocaust and other atrocities committed by the Nazis and local collaborators.

Strēlnieku laukums (Riflemen Square) is a place to ponder the complexity and competing interpretations of what the nation has gone through. The black modernist slab in the middle is the **Museum of the Occupation of Latvia**, which contains a cutting-edge multimedia exhibition telling the gruelling story of Soviet and Nazi occupations in the didactic language of mainstream narratives about this period in Baltic countries. Outside stands a poignant **memorial**, a gigantic copy of a handkerchief with signatures of female Gulag inmates embroidered by Mērija Stakle, a survivor of Soviet terror. The original is exhibited inside the museum. The museum's Brezhnev-era structure originally housed the museum of Red Latvian Riflemen, the members of Latvian regiments glorified by the Soviet authorities for the crucial role they played in the success of the Bolshevik revolution in Russia. The Soviet-era **Latvian Riflemen Monument**, displaying three red-granite male figures dressed in WWI-style fatigues, stands in the middle of the square. Visible from here across the Daugava, the wave-shaped building of the **National Library of Latvia**, also known as the Castle of Light, symbolises the hope for the country's bright postimperial future.

Urban Village

The markets and gardens of Āgenskalns

The area across the river from Old Town, known as **Āgenskalns**, is almost central in terms of logistics, yet it displays strong countryside vibes thanks to the proliferation of wooden houses surrounded by lush gardens that bloom beautifully in spring. People from all over Rīga flock here during weekends for lunch and to stock up on fresh groceries at two famous markets. On any other day, it's just a pleasant area for long walks in quaint streets and vast parkland.

It's best to come here on a Saturday when **Kalnciema kvartāls**, a lovingly restored courtyard with several vintage wooden buildings now occupied by cafes and galleries,

OPPRESSION & RESISTANCE

In addition to the Museum of the Occupation of Latvia, two other museums in Rīga cover the history of totalitarianism and the fight against it. A real-life house of horrors, the fin-de-siècle building known as **Stūra Māja** (Corner House) is remembered by generations of Latvians as the headquarters of the Soviet secret police (NKVD, later KGB). Arbitrary arrests, torture, executions – it all happened here. It's now an exhibition dedicated to both victims and perpetrators of political repression. Latvia's independence came after enormous struggles. One of the most remarkable stories involves the barricades built by thousands of citizens around important public buildings in Rīga in January 1991. The excellent **Museum of the Barricades of 1991** is run by the organisation of barricade veterans.

THE GUIDE

LATVIA RĪGA

WHERE TO DRINK IN OLD TOWN (VECRĪGA)

Folkklubs Ala Pagrabs
Bubbling magma of relentless beer-infused joy, folk-punk music, dancing and Latvian nationalism.

Nosaints
Magic potions in dimly lit, cavernous premises. Cocktail masters are chatty and clued-up on alchemy.

Salons MyBeer
At 500 brands, a veritable encyclopaedia of Baltic and other European beer.

turns into a lively market that attracts some of the top food and produce vendors from across the region. Browse smoked meats, cheeses, vegetables, pastries and even spirits. The baked goods are extraordinary. If you're properly hungry, try authentic Uzbek *plov* at **Plov Station**. You'll get a good introduction to the quiet charms of Āgenskalns if you make your way here to the district's main market, **Āgenskalna tirgus**. The purpose-built red-brick structure was erected at the turn of the 20th century, its elegant shape complemented by the Eiffel-esque Āgenskalns TV tower in the background. The market building stood abandoned for a long time before being recently converted into a food court, with some stalls selling farm produce on the 1st floor and cafes on the 2nd. Outside it's still a pretty authentic farmers market, which turns into a flea market on some weekends.

RIGHTEOUS AMONG THE NATION

Clinging to Āgenskalns, **Ķīpsala** island is filled with wooden houses, ranging from modest cottages to fanciful villas. It is also the scene of Latvia's most celebrated Holocaust rescue story. A local resident, Žanis Lipke, saved more than 50 Jews from certain death during the Nazi occupation. A left-winger with an adventurist mindset, he found a job with the German air force, which allowed him to smuggle people out of the Rīga ghetto under the pretext of using them as labourers. He hid them in a bunker under the woodpile next to his house – now the site of the excellent modern **Žanis Lipke Museum**, which tells the story of the survivors and their saviour.

Ghostly Quarters

Decadent charm and old horrors in Maskačka

Behind the railway line that bisects central Rīga and the Central Market lies the vast **Maskavas forštate** (Moscow suburb) district, commonly known as Maskačka. Filled with decaying antiquated buildings and devoid of cafes, except for the venerable **Katkevich**, it feels both haunted and at the same time weirdly attractive. The atmosphere is partly due to the district's former criminal reputation, but there is also the burden of history. Once a vibrant multicultural district dominated by Russian Old Believers and Jews, it became the site of the Jewish ghetto established by the Nazis in October 1941. Almost all of its residents perished.

These memories are somewhat subdued. The underwhelming **Rīga Ghetto and Latvian Holocaust Museum** at the end of the gentrified Spīķeri warehouse quarter features a reconstructed flat like those that Jews had to move into in the badly crammed ghetto. More moving is the site of the large 1871 **Choral Synagogue**, which was burned to the ground by Latvian Nazi collaborators in 1941 with the entire congregation locked inside. No one survived and all that remains today are the haunting ruins. A concrete monument nearby is dedicated to the Latvians who risked their lives to help hide Jews during the war.

Maskačka is great for long walks, is photogenic and contains several nice parks. For a bird's-eye view of the area, take the lift to the viewing platform of the Stalinesque tower of the **Latvian Academy of Science** (a not-so-welcome Soviet-era present from Moscow), which looms incongruously above the city.

 WHERE TO EAT IN ĀGENSKALNS

Fazenda Bazārs	**Street Pizza**	**Gardā Pupa**
Pure culinary delight in a tiny terrace tucked between two old houses. Try the beef cheeks. €€	This tiny joint in a quiet street made it into Europe's 50 best pizzerias list. €	A terrific lunchtime vegetarian cafeteria where you pay per kilo. €

TANYA KEISHA/SHUTTERSTOCK ©

Bastion Hill

Rīga's Green Belt

Parks and monuments

A canal and a chain of parks that vaguely follow its course form a green semicircle around Old Town and separate it from the city centre. This is where Rīga gets especially romantic with canopies – green, red and yellow, or snow-covered – reflecting in the dark surface of the chilly water. It gets particularly picturesque near the bridge by the **Bastion Hill** (Bastejkalns), part of the old Swedish ramparts that was turned into a landscaped park during the Russian imperial period.

At the main entrance to Old Town, the park belt is interrupted by a vast square with a monumental female figure in the middle. Affectionately known as 'Milda' (after a match brand that had its picture on the cover), the **Freedom Monument** was designed by Kārlis Zāle and erected in 1935 on the spot where a statue of Russian Tsar Peter the Great once stood. Raising her hands to the skies, Milda is holding three stars that represent three main historical regions of Latvia – Kurzeme, Vidzeme and Latgale. Two soldiers stand guard at the monument throughout the day and perform a modest changing of the guards every hour on the hour from 9am to 6pm. Another major landmark nearby is the **Laima Clock**, a popular meeting place that carries the branding of a

MAKE TRADE NOT WAR

In what might be the world's most large-scale act of 'beating swords into ploughshares', several German-built WWI zeppelin hangars were brought into Rīga and converted into pavilions of the city's **Central Market** in the 1920s. Today, it's a major landmark and a place where friends bump into each other while shopping for smoked fish, forest mushrooms and berries, garden apples and red currants, homemade bread...you name it. Most of the action happens outside, while the hangars are gradually evolving into hipster-ish food courts. Come here to try fried herring with cottage cheese (Latvia's top delicacy) at **Siļķītes un Dillītes** or for freshly baked Uzbek flatbread at **Registan** bakery.

WHERE TO EAT IN CENTRAL RĪGA

Istaba	2Eat Falafel	Stockpot Borsch
An idiosyncratic celebrity-chef restaurant with no set menu – you are subject to the cook's fancy. €€	The Israeli owner of this intimate cafe indulges in recreating his Levantine childhood favourites. €	Ukrainian refugees run this tiny borscht and *varenyki* (dumplings) joint by St Gertrude Church. €

V. E/SHUTTERSTOCK ©

FATHERS OF CHRISTMAS

Who invented the Christmas tree? We did, Rigans say confidently. The story pertains to one of the city landmarks, known as the **Blackheads' House**. Facing the Town Hall, it was built in 1344 as a veritable fraternity house for the Blackheads guild of unmarried German merchants. It was here, on Christmas Eve in the year 1510, that a merrily intoxicated bunch of lads schlepped a great pine tree up to the clubhouse and decked it in flowers before setting it ablaze at the end of the night – and the tradition of the Christmas tree was born. The original house was ruined in 1941, but an exact replica of this fantastically ornate structure replaced it in 2001.

Vērmanes dārzs

popular chocolate manufacturer. Built in 1924, it was a gentle way to encourage Rīgans not to be late for work. Beyond, formal gardens lead to the neoclassical building of the **Latvian National Opera**, built in the 1860s.

Vērmanes Gardens Socialising

Get-together park

Vērmanes dārzs is a small park by Rīga standards, but it is universally beloved. It serves as an open-air social club, attracting more visitors per square metre than any other park in the city. During summer months, picnickers and sunbathers occupy the grassland, local bands perform in the outdoor amphitheatre, and artisans set up shop along the brick walkways, amid the chess matches, food stands and inviting benches. In the **rosarium** guarded by stone lions, a modest stone commemorates Anna Wörmann, the mother of the Prussian consul whose brainchild the gardens were and whose name they still bear (in Latvian transliteration).

WHERE TO EAT IN CENTRAL RĪGA

Cafe Osīris
A legendary stalwart with green faux-marble tabletops that haven't changed since the mid-1990s. €€

Karbonādes
The foundation stone of Latvian cuisine, *karbonāde* steak nears perfection in this Avotu iela venue. €€

Siļķītes un Dillītes
By the fish hall at the Central Market, this scallop-sized cafe makes superb seafood dishes. €

Picture the Nation

Browse Rīga's art galleries

What could be a royal palace in another European capital, the **Latvian National Museum of Art** is the country's main art treasury. The collection is a 'who's who' of Latvian art from the 18th to late 20th centuries. Baltic German artists from the 18th and 19th centuries might be yawn-invoking, but as you move into the Latvian revival era of the early 20th century, the collection proves truly captivating. You can trace the artistic thought growing more original, expressive, authentically Latvian and intertwined with politics in the age of world wars, revolutions and totalitarianism. The exhibition continues all the way to contemporary art via the Soviet occupation period.

If you still want more, head to the excellent **Zuzeum**, a privately owned art centre that stages top-notch exhibitions. Also take note of the annual **Survival Kit** festival, which fills Rīga's many crumbling and semi-abandoned buildings with intelligently curated art displays each September.

Rīga Deck Views

Cruising along the Daugava River

For much of Rīga's eight-century history, the initial perspective on the city for the new arrivals was from the water. You can reproduce that experience by exploring Rīga's waterways, which is possible by a variety of means. Small pleasure boats, some of them of historical value, take passengers aboard by the Bastion Hill (p171) and proceed along the Daugava River. Check rigabycanal.lv or rivercruises.lv for details and prices. They also rent out water bicycles. Kayaks and stand-up paddleboards are another option – see rigaslaivas.lv for a variety of circle routes that involve crossing the Daugava, exploring canals and islands on the other side and even entering Rīga's shipyard. Last but not least, large classical pleasure boats ply the Daugava, picking passengers at several moorings outside Old Town. In addition to short cruises within the city, they also enter Lake Kišezers, with the possibility of disembarking at Mežaparks (p175) and returning to the centre by tram. An ultimate boat experience is going to the mouth of the Daugava and then entering the adjoining Lielupe River with the final stop at Majori station in Jūrmala. For details, see rivercruises.lv.

EASTERN CROSSES

Russian-speakers make up almost half of Rīga's population, hence all the golden domes of Russian Orthodox churches popping up here and there. The largest of them looms over central Rīga near the expansive **Esplanāde** park. The **Nativity of Christ Cathedral** (1883) was designed in neo-Byzantine style by the local Baltic German architect Robert August Pflug. In their atheistic zeal, the Soviets turned it into a planetarium, but it was returned to the Orthodox church after Latvia regained its independence. A short walk away, the bright yellow structure of the neoclassical **St Alexander Nevsky Cathedral** looks quainter and more intimate. It was built in 1820–25 to celebrate the Russian victory over Napoleon.

 WHERE TO STAY IN CENTRAL RĪGA

Grand Poets	Edvards	Cinnamon Sally
It doesn't get any plusher than these park-facing rooms with fine retro touches. €€€	Room design matches the laconic no-nonsense elegance of this house, built in 1890. €€	This hostel displays a relentless effort to create a homey and sociable atmosphere. €

Village of Villages

Stroll the open-air folk museum

If you don't have time to visit the Latvian countryside, a stop at the **Latvian Ethnographic Open-Air Museum** is a must. Sitting along the shores of Lake Jugla just northeast of the city limits, this stretch of forest contains more than 100 wooden buildings (churches, windmills, farmhouses etc) from each of Latvia's four cultural regions. You can wander around, interact with resident craftspeople and sample traditional food.

Drinking Dens

Find your way to the next gimlet bar

Rigans have long conceded their Old Town to cruise-ship passengers and debauching stag parties, so the main bar clusters are located further away in the city centre. Don't expect anything wild and massive, this being the Baltics. A few good bars are located in the section of Stabu iela between Baznicas and Barona. Here you'll find the much-lauded cocktail bar **Gimlet** and the reincarnated legend, **Gauja**. The old-time haunt of Miera iela also has its share of drinking dens. The converted industrial space of Tallinas kvartāla is home to a particularly atmospheric branch of **Ezītis Miglā**, a popular chain of bars, and comes with a food court in a cosy courtyard. Spilling into the street, the homey **Walters & Grapa** precedes a dense cluster of bars at the intersection with Aristida Briāna iela. Here you'll find **Labietis**, the taproom of a famous craft-beer brand. Avotu iela and its surroundings make an up-and-coming entertainment area. Aim for **Aleponija**, based in an old wooden house; it doubles as a concert venue. **Bolderāja** is a haunt for moneyless bohemians.

Social Bazaar

Trading arcades' cafe cluster

If you are in Rīga for any length of time, it is very likely that you'll spend at least some of that time in the quaint courtyards of **Berga Bazārs**, the city's elegant fin-de-siècle trading arcades. Today they contain several popular restaurants-cum-bars as well as the fancy **Hotel Bergs Suites**. The larger courtyard, facing Elizabetes iela, features the long-time favourite, **Andalūzijas Suns**. The smaller courtyard, facing Dzirnavu iela, is home to **Cydonia Gastropub** as well as **Troubadour Gourmand**, part of a popular French-owned coffee-shop chain.

URBAN SKIING

Snow during winter is not really guaranteed in this Gulf Stream–affected city, but when it comes, people get the best of it, with cross-country skiing tracks and rentals opening across Rīga. Here are some of the best places to ski (you can rent skis and boots at each of them).

Biķernieku trase
An excellent track within the Biķernieku forest, with several loops to choose from.

Lucavsalas trase
A well-maintained track on an island in the Daugava River.

Uzvaras parks
Closest to the centre, a popular track in the largest of the Pārdaugava area's parks.

WHERE TO DRINK IN CENTRAL RĪGA ————

Čē	Gimlet	Kaņepes Kultūras Centrs
Scruffy and cavernous, with anarchic outdoor seating – an ultimate bohemian haunt.	Nordic-flavoured cocktails in an adorable setting at the intersection of two elegant streets.	A beer garden presided over by a giant green lion on the roof. An essential drinking and concert venue.

BITTER DELIGHT

What's your poison, Rīga? It's called **Rīga Black Balsam**. It's black, thick like oil and has an unforgettable, heart-wrenchingly bitter taste. How is that? Well, it was invented as a medicine and medicines are not supposed to be sweet. At least that was the case in 1752, when the recipe was drawn by pharmacist Abraham Kunze. So how to make it more palatable? The classical recipe involves mixing it with hot blackcurrant juice, a concoction you'll find in many bars in Rīga. Another way of consuming it is by adding it to coffee, tea or – an excellent combination – ice cream. That said, some have it on the rocks. Would you be one of them?

Rīga National Zoo

Rīga's Forest

Out and about in Mežaparks

Something most Rigans do once in a while is take tram 11 to **Mežaparks**. It's two in one: a district of huge and beautifully designed early-20th-century villas and the capital's largest park, part of which feels like a proper forest (indeed, its name translates as 'forest-park'). The park is filled with all kinds of activities, from rollerblading to disc golf. There's a beach and a few lakeside restaurants, but connoisseurs prefer to have their lunch at **Šašliki Mangaļos**, an extremely down-to-earth *shashlik* (Caucasian skewered meat) joint at the exit towards Mangaļi train station. Mežaparks is also home to **Rīga National Zoo**, which has a modest collection of animals including an assortment of tropical fauna as well as the usual cast of Noah's ark. An enormous stadium-like venue in the middle of the park, the **Big Mežaparks Stage**, is the place where every five years the country holds its main nation-building event, **Latvian Song Festival**. Each place in Latvia, down to the tiniest hamlet, delegates its choir to participate in the event. The next one is scheduled for 2028.

WHERE TO HAVE COFFEE IN RĪGA

Kalve	MiiT	Rocket Beans
For local connoisseurs, this tiny joint is *the* place to have their morning cup.	A sociable place that serves mean coffee as well as vegetarian desserts and lunches.	A large, comfortable space run by one of Rīga's most sophisticated roasters.

RĪGA'S BEST OBSCURE EATERIES

Rīga is famous for understated delights, especially on the culinary side. Local resident **Reinis Norkārkls** list his favourites.

Katkevich
A very unexpected place in the historical Moscow suburb, given its controversial reputation. I go there for the mackerel toast.

Trīs Viri Laivā
The best fish and chips in town and one of a few places that qualifies as a genuine local pub.

Belyashi Stand at Central Market
It's basic and admittedly unhealthy, but these are meat pies to die for.

Stop. Ēd
The Azeri owner makes *tantuni* kebabs, always with fresh meat he cooks in a large wrought-iron frying pan. He also bakes his own *lavash* flatbread.

TARTEZY/SHUTTERSTOCK ©

Rīga Motor Museum

Spot Stalin's Limo

Impressive Soviet-era car collection

The stars of the collection at the surprisingly well-funded and engrossing **Rīga Motor Museum**, hidden in the northern suburbs, are cars that once belonged to Soviet luminaries such as Gorky, Stalin, Khrushchev and Brezhnev, complete with irreverent life-sized figures of the men themselves. Stalin's armoured limousine drank a litre of petrol every 2.5km. Also worthwhile is the hall on the lives of Soviet citizens and their cars.

 WHERE TO SHOP IN RĪGA

Pienene
An exciting collection of Latvian-made clothes, souvenirs and fruit wines, complete with degustations.

Hobbywool
This magic universe of knitted products gives one the soothing that only wool provides.

Riija
A carefully selected collection of designer items that covers most aspects of domestic life.

Beyond Rīga

A plethora of suburban attractions are only a short train or taxi ride away from Rīga.

Latvia's serpentine Daugava River, known as the 'river of fate', winds its way through Latgale, Zemgale and Vidzeme before passing through Rīga and emptying out in the Gulf of Rīga. For centuries the river was Latvia's most important transport and trade corridor for clans and kingdoms further east. The modern E22 road follows the river's course, passing old towns known since the beginning of written history, from Ikšķile to Koknese, as well as two sights – the Rumbula and Salaspils memorials – pertaining to the horrors of the 20th century. Elsewhere, the suburbs of Rīga feature a few quirky attractions and solemn memorials. The exploration of Ķengarags district can be packed into the same day as the Moscow suburb if you don't mind strenuous walking.

Places

Ikšķile to Koknese p178
Ķengarags p179
Salaspils Memorial p179

GETTING AROUND

The railway line going towards eastern Latvia passes through the old towns in Daugava Valley.

☑ TOP TIP

If there is snow, definitely consider renting skis or sledges at Zilie Kalni nature park.

Rumbula memorial (p177)

A.STUDIO PHOTOGRAPHY/SHUTTERSTOCK ©

THE X-MAN OF INDEPENDENCE STRUGGLE

A man with bear's ears, the source of his superhuman strength, Lāčplēsis is the protagonist of the namesake epic, authored by 19th-century poet Andrejs Pumpurs. Aided by ancient Baltic gods, he leads Latvians in their struggle against the dark forces of German crusaders trying to Christianise the land. The story involves distinct Homerian motifs, with nods to both Achilles and Ulysses. Spoiler alert: the hero gets treacherously defeated when the enemy learns about his ear secret, but there is a promise of resurrection. The author, Pumpurs, lived an illustrious life volunteering into the Russian army to fight the Turks in Serbia, where he got inspired by romantic nationalism that influenced his writing.

REGINA M ART/SHUTTERSTOCK ©

Zilie Kalni (Blue Hills)

Ikšķile to Koknese

TIME FROM RĪGA: 1¼ HRS 🚗

Myths and ruins

A trip along the Daugauva takes you into the realm of nation-building mythology and riparian landscapes. The A6 road and a suburban railway connect a chain of small towns along the 'river of destiny', all of which can be explored in an easy day trip.

Sleepy **Ikšķile** is the unlikely precursor of Rīga. It was here that German crusaders initially based themselves in 1197 before relocating to what is now the Latvian capital. The ruins of the oldest stone building, **St Meynard's Church**, are located here on an island, which is inaccessible from May through September because it serves as a nesting ground for wild birds. The next town, wonderfully named **Ogre**, is the location of **Zilie Kalni** (Blue Hills) nature park – a forest-covered range with a tall observation tower at the very top, which offers sweeping views of the countryside and the Daugava. It is also a popular winter-sports area.

WHERE TO EAT IN DAUGAVA VALLEY

Dārzā
An upmarket fusion place in Ikšķile with floral elements and plants in the design. €€

Melnā Kamene
Head to this spot in Ogre for wok dishes and sumptuous salads. Large portions. €€

Rūdolfs
Occupying an atmospheric old barn, this place serves traditional Latvian fare. €

Next comes **Lielvārde**, home to **Andrejs Pumpurs Museum**, which is dedicated to the author of *Lāčplēsis,* an epic at the heart of Latvia's national consciousness. Finally, stop at **Koknese** to admire the ruins of the medieval **Kokenhausen** castle in a stunning location overlooking the confluence of the Daugava and Perse rivers. You can walk from here to the grandly named **Garden of Destiny**, a sprawling, unfinished project on an island in the river that celebrates Latvia as a nation. A 2.5km trail links areas with portentous names such as Alley of Destiny, House of Silence and Stream of Tears.

Ķengarags
TIME FROM RĪGA: 1¼ HRS 🚶

Scenic walk on the city's edge

Beyond the Moscow suburb, the riverside district of Ķengarags gradually blends into the countryside as you walk along the excellent 6km **Ķengarags promenade**. It begins by the Dienvidu (Southern) Bridge and runs past the Ķengarags beach, with splendid views of the opposite bank and Dole island. Soviet-era apartment blocks give way to a chaotic sprawl of cute summer cottages dotted with the green anthills of 1930s plane hangars, which are related to the **Rumbula airfield**, located near the end of the promenade. The route passes the historical **Mazjumpravas manor**, which was run by a succession of Baltic German aristocrats from 1259 till 1919. At end of the walk, you can cross the airfield – now used by extreme driving and drone enthusiasts – and catch a bus back to Rīga on the main highway.

Salaspils Memorial
TIME FROM RĪGA: 30 MINS 🚌

Brutal WWII history

The sound of a metronome, beating like a human heart, and a message on a reclining concrete shaft, which reads 'Beyond these gates, the earth is groaning' await you at the entrance to the striking Soviet-era **Salaspils Memorial**, 14km from Rīga. The green field beyond it is populated with brutalist human figures expressing the suffering endured by the inmates of a concentration camp that was set up here by the Nazis in 1941. The inmates were pro-Soviet locals, and Central European Jews, as well as Russian and Belarusian peasants arrested in anti-partisan reprisals, including many children. It was never a death camp or an extermination site like the nearby Rumbula forest, but it was a terrible place to be in and thousands perished here.

KILLING FIELDS

It took two days for the Nazis and their Latvian collaborators to exterminate 25,000 Jews who had to walk 12km from the Rīga ghetto to **Rumbula forest** before meeting their death. Two batches of victims were shot and buried using what the Nazis cynically referred to as 'the sardine method', 250m away from Rumbula station. Most were women, children, the elderly and the infirm, since able-bodied men were spared at the time to be used as workforce. Not everyone died instantly, so many people were buried while they were still alive. A poignant **memorial** in the shape of a menorah surrounded by rocks that resemble tombstones was erected here in 2022.

Jūrmala

BACKYARD BEACHES | NATURE PARK | SPA AND WATERPARK

GETTING AROUND

In addition to the railway line that runs through Jūrmala, there's a bus network that is useful for destinations near the mouth of the Lielupe River. You can rent bicycles at Velopark in Bulduri and cycle all the way from Rīga along a route that runs along the railway line.

Sitting on a massive sandbar formed by the Lielupe River, Jūrmala is Rīga's backyard beach and what passes for Latvia's golden mile, a playground for jet-setters and minigarchs from the east (Russian language still prevails here). This strip of wealthy suburbia squeezed between the river, the railway line and the sea stretches for 32km. Anywhere along this distance, you'll find perfect white sand and pine trees growing on low-lying dunes. When it comes to bathing, this beach is best for small children, with the water so shallow that an adult can seemingly walk all the way to Sweden before it gets deep. For anyone taller than a metre, this is more of a place to see and be seen – as carefully designed sunbed exhibits, muscular volleyball players or fashion-conscious beach strollers. Otherwise, Jūrmala is just a great place to breathe some fresh sea air and rest.

Do the Strand

Enjoy Latvia's main beach

The **beach** in Jūrmala doubles as Latvia's longest promenade. The white sand is hard-packed and ideal for walking – or packing into sand castles. Come here in any season and you'll see promenading urbanites, cyclists, and even skiers moving along the seafront if there is enough snow. In winter, you will still spot an occasional fitness desperado dipping into icy water. Few developments have encroached on the bluffs behind the sand, leaving the beach largely unspoiled, with only an odd beach cafe here and there.

Jūrmala's oldest area near Dzintari, Majori and Dubulti stations resembles Prussian Baltic resorts on the German Baltic coast, its skyline dominated by elegant timber-framed villas, some of which have intricate woodcarving decor. The heart of the action is the 1km-long pedestrian street, **Jomas iela**, which runs between Majori and Dzintari stations. This is the area where you'll find most restaurants and visitor-centric venues, including the well-funded **Jūrmala City Museum,**

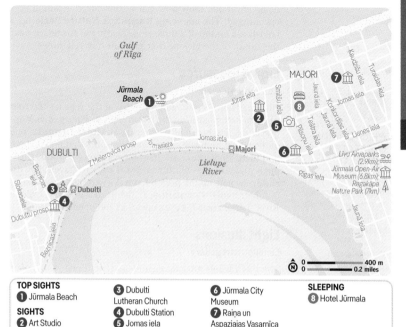

TOP SIGHTS
1. Jūrmala Beach

SIGHTS
2. Art Studio 'Inner Light'

3. Dubulti Lutheran Church
4. Dubulti Station
5. Jomas iela

6. Jūrmala City Museum
7. Raiņa un Aspazijas Vasarnīca

SLEEPING
8. Hotel Jūrmala

which features a cool permanent exhibition detailing Jūrmala's colourful history as the go-to resort town in the former USSR. Majori and Dubulti stations enjoy picture-perfect locations on the riverbank. The brave modernist structure of **Dubulti station** doubles as an art gallery that hosts intriguing exhibitions at any time of the year. Nearby, **Dubulti Lutheran Church** is a curious example of a religious building rendered in Jugendstil style. Away from the centre, Jūrmala turns into a quiet suburbia of wealthy residences, elegant parks and pine-covered dunes.

Jūrmala's Fishing Heritage

Open-air folk museum

Before the clothing of choice in Jūrmala was the bikini, the peninsula was home to fisherfolk who eked out a living through endless days of work. Get an insight into the lives of these hardy folk at the **Jūrmala Open-Air Museum**, which recreates a fishing village. On summer Thursdays,

---

☑ **TOP TIP**

Get off at Bulduri station and join the promenading crowds on the way towards Majori. The season is irrelevant as long as there is no strong wind or rain. Treat yourself to Latvia's trademark Vecrīga dessert at De Gusto on the main pedestrian drag after the walk.

 WHERE TO EAT AND STAY IN JŪRMALA

36.Line Food Truck
Jūrmala's legendary high-end restaurant runs a weekend-only food truck at its old location. €

De Gusto
Find all of Latvia's old-school sweet favourites in this little cafe in Majori. €

Parus Boutique Hotel
One of those Prussian-styled villas that define Jūrmala contains 12 traditionally decorated rooms. €€

demonstrations show how fish were smoked – sampling is encouraged! The adjoining **Ragakāpa Nature Park** has a boardwalk on top of a dune ridge leading to the beach near the mouth of the Lielupe over tall pine-covered dunes.

Liquid Pleasures
Spa and waterpark

Jūrmala is no Hawaii, and for much of the year it's too cold to swim or sunbathe on the beach. This is when you may appreciate a few hours of pampering at **Hotel Jurmala**, one of the Soviet high-rise recreation dinosaurs that pop up here and there along the coast. Its wellness centre contains three pools and six types of saunas. But if you are travelling with children, you might prefer **Līvu Akvaparks**, a massive, family-friendly waterpark near the bridge over the Lielupe River. Large areas here are enclosed and open year-round.

Light Illusions
Luminous art gallery

There is a whole alternative universe contained in one of of those villas in central Jūrmala, occupied by the **Art Studio 'Inner Light'**. It is the home of local artist Vitaliy Yermolayev, who dabbles with a secret recipe for glow-in-the-dark paint by creating paintings that morph when different amounts of light strike the artwork. You can linger over a glass of French wine in the tiny bar.

Titans on Holiday
Luminous art gallery

Poet Rainis (born Jānis Pliekšans) is the supreme deity of the Latvian cultural pantheon, iconographically indivisible from his spouse Aspazija (born Elza Rozenberga). Also a poet, she chose to be called after the independently minded wife of Pericles. Politically active throughout his whole life, Rainis is also one of the titans of independent Latvia's founding myth. Together, Rainis and Aspazija went through the tumultuous year of revolutionary struggle, exile in northern Russia, emigration and return to the newly independent Latvia. This is when they acquired a charming villa in Jūrmala where they spent some of their most productive summers. The newly restored house now contains the wonderful **Raiņa un Aspaziajas Vasarnīca** museum.

WHICH STATION TO GET OFF IN JŪRMALA?

If you arrive in Jūrmala by train from Rīga, you have options on where to start exploring.

Bulduri
A quieter part of Jūrmala, with restaurants and a short promenade leading to the sea.

Dzintari
Slightly removed from the sea, but close to a park and convenient for the namesake concert hall.

Majori
A station with a picture-perfect setting and in the centre of the action.

Dubulti
Has an art gallery inside the station, and glimpses of old Jūrmala nearby.

Asari
A beautiful station building, 10 minutes' walk from an unspoilt stretch of the beach.

Beyond
Jūrmala

Beyond Jūrmala's stretch of celebrity summer homes lies a verdant hinterland of drowsy fishing villages, quaking bogs and thick forests.

Much of the area beyond Jūrmala is covered by Ķemeri National Park, which offers great walks and vast expanses of untouched lakes, forests and bogs. The Great Ķemeri Bog Boardwalk, in particular, is a place of mesmerising beauty where one can spend hours meditating and savouring the view. The Kurzeme side of the Gulf of Rīga is a largely uninterrupted stretch of pristine sandy beach and pine-covered dunes. The well-marked Jūrtaka trail – Latvia's section of the trans-Baltic coastal trail – runs all along here, as does the coastal road leading up to Cape Kolka. On the way, you'll come across quaint fishing ports, a few lighthouses and many kiosks selling smoked fish.

Places
Ķemeri p184
Ķemeri National Park p185
Cape Kolka p185
Lake Engure p185
Mērsrags p185

Cape Kolka (p185)

BARGAIS/SHUTTERSTOCK ©

GETTING AROUND

Bus routes originating in Rīga ply the entire Kurzeme coast to Jūrmala. Tukums (at the end of the Jūrmala railway line) and Talsi (on the Rīga–Ventspils road) often serve as transfer hubs. The Great Ķemeri Bog Boardwalk is located near Ventspils road (A10). Alternatively, you can hike 4.5km from Ķemeri train station. Cinevilla Studio and Jaunmoku Pils lie further along the same road.

☑ TOP TIP
Walk the beautiful Ragaciems–Engure section of the Coastal Trail, or just the part between Apšuciems and Engure if 25km is too long.

183

SMOKY SHORES

Smoked fish is one of the top Latvian delicacies, and this side of the Gulf of Rīga is dotted with smoking sheds and little shops selling the produce, as fish smoking and canning remain traditional occupations in the villages. Just look out for *Kūpinātas zivis* (smoked fish) signs along the coastal road. The smallish market in **Ragaciems** village is one popular cluster of fish shops right by the P128. Several vendors sell myriad varieties of smoked fish – eel, sprat, salmon, tuna – while others specialise in tasty Latvian fare such as pickles, grilled meats and rye bread. Many smoking-shed owners run their business out of their own house, **Reinis-B** in Lapmežciems being a popular example.

Lake Slokas

Ķemeri

TIME FROM JŪRMALA: **30 MINS**

Spa in the woods

The town that gave the name to the national park, Ķemeri, came into being as a spa resort and at the end of the 19th century it was known across the Russian Empire for its curative mud and springwater. It is now being revived after decades of neglect. The vast park in the heart of the town has been nicely re-cultivated, although some of the old sanatorium buildings remain in semi-ruinous state.

Ķemeri is a station on the railway line that passes through Jūrmala and it also stands on the Mežtaka, or the trans-Baltic forest trail, which makes it a good starting point for forest walks. One option is walking from here towards the coast via **Lake Slokas**, a birdwatchers' haunt that has a nice boardwalk with a watchtower, as well as **Melnsezers** (Black Lake), famously devoid of usual lake life forms (which explains the name) but great for swimming. You'll eventually end up at the beach village of **Bigauņciems**, where you can down a plate of borscht at the Ukrainian restaurant **Sho** and catch a bus back to Jūrmala.

 WHERE TO STAY AND EAT ON KURZEME COAST

Sho	Noras	Roja Hotel
Best borscht on these boreal shores. An upmarket beachside restaurant run by Ukrainian refugees. €€	An exemplary campground in the shadow of a lighthouse, with comfortable, well-equipped cabins. €	A comfortable place with run-of-the-mill motel furnishings, located in the namesake fishing town. €

Ķemeri National Park
TIME FROM JŪRMALA: **20 MINS**

Marshland walks

Ķemeri National Park's main attraction might be the most meditative place in the whole of Latvia. The 3.4km **Great Ķemeri Bog Boardwalk**, to the southwest of Ķemeri train station, goes through an enormous bog where multicoloured vegetation is interspersed with round-shaped waterholes reflecting white clouds. There's an observation tower and plenty of benches along the way to sit and ponder life, universe and everything.

Cape Kolka
TIME FROM JŪRMALA: **2 HRS**

Journey along the coast

The coastal road from Jūrmala to Cape Kolka (and Jūrtaka, the coastal trail) initially goes through a virtually uninterrupted chain of holiday villages, but gradually pristine dune landscapes take over the scenery. The beach also becomes wider and more beautiful as your approach the villages of **Klapkalnciems** and **Apšuciems**, favoured by artistic intelligentsia types. The high dunes are Latvian classics, covered with light-filled coastal pine forest, silver-green moss and blueberry shrubs. Further along come quaint fishing harbours and wide, virtually human-free beaches. For a glimpse of the old life in fishing villages and Soviet collective farms, stop at the excellent little **Marine Fisheries Museum** in Roja.

Lake Engure
TIME FROM JŪRMALA: **1 HR**

Floodplain walks and birdwatching

The third-largest lake in Latvia, Engure is a haven for birds ,with almost 200 species calling it home. The vistas stretch far to the horizon across the shallow waters, and the only sound you'll hear other than bird calls is the breeze in your ears. The 5km-long **Orchid Trail** runs along the floodplain meadows on the lakeshore and through the damp conifer forest. A boardwalk extends into the lake to a viewing tower.

Mērsrags
TIME FROM JŪRMALA: **1 HR**

Boat trips on the gulf

The fishing port of Mērsrags is primarily known for is lighthouse. Built in 1875 out of cast iron, it looms over a popular beach that mixes gravel patches with white sand and dunes. It is also the mooring place of **Palsa**, a 70-year-old fishing boat, which takes people on a variety of coastal cruises including to the nearby Estonian island of Ruhnu. When moored, it serves as a hotel on water.

VENSTPILS HIGHWAY SIGHTS

If you're visiting the Great Ķemeri Bog Boardwalk by car, as most people do, two more attractions lie further down the road.

Cinevilla Studio
This village made of film decorations used by Latvian cinematographers includes a set depicting a rural hamlet, WWI-era train station and medieval Rīga. There's a collection of costumes you can try on, and a restaurant.

Jaunmoku Pils
Rīga's celebrated former mayor George Armitstead was British, so when planning a hunting lodge near the Ķemeri bogs, he wanted it themed on his father's native Yorkshire. This piece of England is now open to visitors, who can stay overnight.

Vidzeme Coast

WHITE SANDS | BEAUTY SPOT | FOREST WALKS

GETTING AROUND

The suburban railway from Rīga ends at Skulte, just beyond Saulkrasti. Buses from Rīga serve destinations all along the coast. Many of them take additional passengers at the Matīsa iela stop in central Rīga. The Jūrtaka trail runs along the coast parallel to a pan-Baltic cycling route.

It's just over 100km from Rīga to the Estonian border along the A1 highway to Tallinn, and this stretch of the coast is endowed with some of the most magical sand-dune landscapes in the whole of the Baltics. A suburban railway line covers half of this stretch, making attractions in this area an easy day trip from Rīga. You may still get a chance to ride a Soviet-era dinosaur train before they finally get phased out, but the best way to appreciate this part of Latvia is by walking the very well-marked Jūrtaka, the Latvian stretch of the pan-Baltic coastal trail, or cycling along the parallel EuroVelo 10 route. The centre of life here is Saulkrasti, a mellow-people version of Jūrmala. Other stretches feature fishing villages, beautiful boardwalk routes through the dunes and a theme park dedicated to a famous tall-tale inventor.

Pick Your Beach

Sea and dunes

While most visitors flock to Jūrmala, beaches north of Rīga are markedly quieter, wilder and more visually attractive – with pristine white sand and a faint whiff of raisin brought by the wind from the pine-covered dunes. The train line runs just slightly beyond the resort area of Saulkrasti, with stops every couple of kilometres, which makes it convenient not just for lazing by the sea but also for walking your chosen stretches of the Jūrtaka coastal trail, our personal favourite being Garciems to Carnikava.

Vecāķi is the first train station by the beach north of the Daugava River. It feels like a low-key Jūrmala with large old villas and a few cafes along the main promenade leading from the station to the beach. Beyond it, civilisation recedes while sand dunes grow taller. At **Kalngale** station, an atmospheric promenade runs through a darkly beautiful coniferous forest to a white-sand beach. In **Garciems**, you have the option of walking straight to the sea through the village or veering off towards the boardwalk that follows a beautiful little river seasonally dammed by beavers. **Carnikava** comes with its

☑ TOP TIP

Come to Baltā Kāpa a couple of hours before sunset, sit down on a bench and savour the mesmerising view for some minutes. Then walk along the Sunset Trail to the centre of Saulkrasti. Dip into the sea and watch the sun go down at the end of the route.

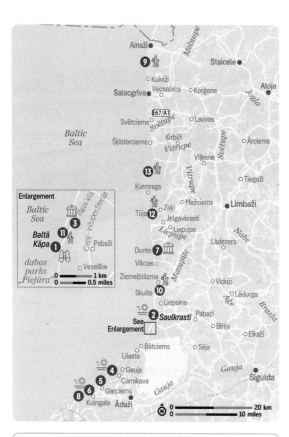

TOP SIGHTS
1 Baltā Kāpa
2 Saulkrasti

SIGHTS
3 Bicycle Museum
4 Carnikava
5 Garciems

6 Kalngale
7 Munchausen Manor
8 Vecāķi

ACTIVITIES, COURS-ES & TOURS

9 Randu Meadows Trail
10 Skulte
11 Sunset Trail
12 Tūja
13 Veczemju klintis

TASTY MONSTER

With its monstrous alien predator's mouth and snake-like features, the lamprey (*nēģis* in Latvian) is not exactly the cutest of fish, but it is a major delicacy in the Baltics, prominently represented at seafood shops and, of course, in the fish rows of Rīga's Central Market. It is typically sold pre-cooked – fried and marinated, grilled or smoked. Lamprey migrate between the sea and the rivers in a manner similar to salmon's. Vidzeme coast happens to be Latvia's lamprey central, with an annual **Lamprey Fest** held in Carnikava on 25 August. It involves folk concerts, a craft market and, of course, plenty of lamprey to consume on the spot.

own paved promenade that runs through a moisture-filled maritime forest to a wild, driftwood-covered, end-of-the-universe kind of beach that stretches to the mouth of the Gauja River. The shiny white dunes between north of the Gauja and **Saulkrasti** are the realm of backpackers, naturists and

WHERE TO EAT BETWEEN RĪGA AND SAULKRASTI

Šašliks un Reņģe
As advertised, Caucasus-styled *shashlik* (meat skewers) and smoked *reņģe* (Baltic herring) in Vecāķi. €€

Abra
A friendly family cafe in Saulkrasti, serving traditional Latvian and standard European fare. €

Cafe Terēza
This Saulkrasti old-timer makes delicious *shashlik*, as well as salads and pancakes. €

SERGEI25/SHUTTERSTOCK ©

Saulkrasti

**BAZAAR
MORNING**

Held on Saturday
mornings, the **Skulte
market** is one of
the most beloved
weekend markets in
the whole of Latvia.
It attracts an unusual
number of small farm
businesses from well
beyond Vidzeme
coast. Pretty much
everything on sale –
cheeses and cured
meat, smoked fish
and honey, pastries
and fruit wine – can
be counted as
homemade. There's
also freshly baked
bread and, of course,
many veggies. The
catch is that it kicks
off very early and
practically shuts
down by noon, so
consider that if you
are travelling here
from Rīga. Skulte is
the last stop on the
Saulkrasti railway
line, and the market is
1.6km from the station.

kitesurfers. People collect driftwood and build enclosures to protect themselves from chilly wind and unwanted looks, or simply out of architectural inspiration.

Saulkrasti's Dune of Perfection
Beauty spot and beach walks

Saulkrasti means the same in Latvian as Costa del Sol in Spanish, but unlike many 'sunny coasts' around the world, this one is about as laid-back as it gets, even during the height of the summer season. It is also very beautiful – with tall pine-covered dunes, glistening white sand and the amber-coloured sea. The lack of mass development provides a sylvan respite from the hubbub of the capital, and the streets are a quiet panoply of gentrified holiday homes. Get off at Pabaži station and walk 1.3km to **Baltā Kāpa** (White Dune), a viewpoint on top of a high cliff, with a forest river streaming its organic-rich brownish waters through the white sands on its last stretch before meeting the sea. This is one of the most enchanting places along the entire Latvian coast, and the wooden walkway along the 18m-high cliffs affords sweeping views of the Gulf of Rīga. The **Sunset Trail** runs to the centre of Saulkrasti, where you'll find an artfully designed organised

WHERE TO STAY AND EAT NORTH OF SAULKRASTI

Abinitio
A stylish pizzeria-cum-wine bar in a beautiful setting overlooking Salacgrīva's harbour. €€

Design Apartments Jūrmāja
This restored house in Ainaži fuses authentic fixtures with modern comforts, oozing loads of charm. €€€

Priedes Māja
Huge, beautifully designed rooms located by the bus station in Ainaži. €€

beach with a cluster of restaurants. An additional perk is proper depth near the seafront, allowing you to swim right away.

Cycling History in Saulkrasti
Two-wheeled antiques

A recommended stop on the way to Baltā Kāpa, the **Bicycle Museum** is a lovely collection of retro bicycles, including a 130-year-old specimen assembled in Latvia. Better yet, choose from a range of modern rental bicycles to explore the region, which is ideal for cycling. The owner is an excellent resource of local info. The museum is close to the Pabaži train station.

Hike the Boulder Coast
Explore the northern beaches

North of Saulkrasti, the beach narrows and granite boulders brought by the glacier become ubiquitous. The Jūrtaka coastal trail continues from the picturesque timber port of **Skulte** all the way to the Estonian border, with some seaside homes and an occasional campground along a largely human-free beach. Pine trees on the dunes get replaced with thicker boreal fir-tree forest. Arguably the best section to hike is between **Tūja**, a pretty town with a popular campground, and the mouth of the Virtupe River, where Tallinn highway comes close to the beach and it is easy to catch a bus back to Rīga. Here, the trail runs through a protected area known as the Vidzeme Rocky Seashore. The highlight is **Veczemju klintis**, a dramatic spot where waves have created picturesque grottoes in the jagged cliffs made of pressed sand that has a deep reddish hue. Closer to Estonia, the short **Randu Meadows Trail** runs through coastal meadows that attract many migratory birds.

Tall Tales at Munchausen Manor
Theme park with forest walks

A master of tall tales, Baron Munchausen is a literary character invented by Rudolph Eric Raspe. But his real-life prototype, Hieronymus Karl Friedrich von Münchhausen, was a German baron on the Russian service based in Rīga for much of his military career. The **Munchausen Manor** in Dunte is now a theme park largely dedicated to the literary character's imaginary exploits and geared towards children. It comes with a total of 4.3km of boardwalks leading through a boreal maritime forest and filled with woodcarved sculptures that are themed after the baron's adventures.

MUSEUMS BY THE BORDER

If you make it as far as **Ainaži**, on the A1 highway near the Estonian border, this small town has two cute museums worth visiting.

Museum of Ainaži Naval School
This museum contains ship models and navigation tools, and tells the stories of the school's graduates who went on to become brave captains conquering the seas.

Ainaži Firefighting Museum
A museum dedicated to the local firefighters' brigade, born in the aftermath of a major fire in 1925, adds a measure of feng shui balance to the maritime scene dominated by the water element.

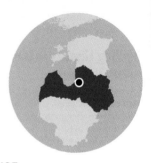

Sigulda

LONELY WALKS | CASTLES | BOBSLEIGH AND LUGE

GETTING AROUND

Sigulda attractions are quite spread out. The place is a cyclist's paradise, with several rentals around town, including Veloriba by the train station. Bus 3112 connects Sigulda and Turaida, with eight to nine services a day. Bolt taxi is widely available and useful.

☑ TOP TIP

Start your exploration of Sigulda with the excellent Tourist Information Office at the train/bus station. It's stocked with walking maps and other brochures; it's also a place to find out about events and tours on the day.

Sigulda serves as a veritable visualisation of what Latvians regard as ideal life and aesthetic perfection. The town is a sprawling area of large private homes surrounded by manicured grass and apple orchards, with plenty of space for lonely walks and bicycle rides through the magnificent valley of the Gauja River right nearby. Thousands of people flock here in autumn to savour what Latvians believe is a benchmark for a perfect *rudens* (Latvian autumn). Sigulda is Latvia's outdoors central with dozens of activities on offer, from the fairly straightforward, such as bungee jumps and downhill skiiing, to the rather exotic, like dashing down an Olympic-quality bobsleigh track or levitating on an artificial air stream. The main gateway to Latvia's most beloved nature area, the Gauja National Park, Sigulda sits on the pan-Baltic Meztaka forest trail as well as on a popular water-adventure route along the Gauja River.

A Tale of Two Castles
Medieval knights and a progressive prince

Sigulda has been known since the 13th century, when the Livonian Brothers of the Sword built a castle here. In the 19th century, Russian prince Nikolay Kropotkin, a nephew of anarchist thinker Pyotr Kropotkin, reinvented Sigulda (then Segewold) as a resort town – a Baltic answer to Switzerland. The **Livonian Order Castle**, constructed in 1207, and **Kropotkin's mansion house** stand next to each other, with the latter's neo-Gothic forms designed to match the former's medieval angularity. Both are perched on a hill above the forested Gauja Valley and form a single popular attraction. The medieval ruins are being restored and you can walk along the ramparts and ascend a tower with wonderful views over the Gauja. The freshly restored Kropotkin's manor house is a visual delight both inside and out. The interior is from 1937, when the mansion became the base of Latvia's journalists'

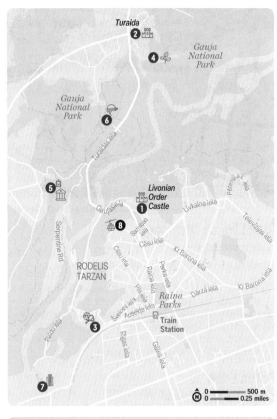

TOP SIGHTS
1 Livonian Order Castle
2 Turaida

SIGHTS
3 Bobsleigh and Luge Track

4 Folk Song Garden
5 Krimulda Manor

ACTIVITIES, COURSES & TOURS
6 Gutman's Cave
7 Kakīškalns

TRANSPORT
8 Sigulda Cable Car

union. Decorated by the best artists of the time, it is a gem of the national revival style. It comes with a marvellous terrace and a few elegant low-rise auxiliary buildings nearby, which now house artisan workshops and cafes.

MURDER AT THE CAVE

A 400-year-old story set in **Gutman's Cave** might serve as a reason to linger here and ponder the nature of human evil. In 1601, Maija Roze, a beautiful woman who resided in Turaida castle, received a letter from her fiancé asking to meet by the grotto. Tragically, it was a fake message sent by a Polish villain who wanted to force her into marriage. When Maija realised it was a trap, she challenged the man into axing her by falsely claiming that her scarf had magical powers that protected her from any bodily harm. The villain was caught and hanged, while the heroine became known as the Rose of Turaida. She's commemorated with a small stone memorial.

🛏 WHERE TO STAY IN AND AROUND SIGULDA

Mazais Līvkalns
No place is more romantically rustic than this idyllic retreat on the forest's edge. €€

Spa Hotel Ezeri
A luxurious spa complex offering fairly simple rooms with contemporary decor. €€€

Hotel Sigulda
The oldest hotel in Sigulda, built by Kropotkin. Charming facade, but rooms are fairly bland. €€

BARGAIS/SHUTTERSTOCK ©

Bobsleigh and Luge Track, Sigulda

Ride Like an Olympian

Test the bobsleigh track

Sigulda's 1420m **Bobsleigh and Luge Track** has a fine legacy as the Latvians punch above their weight in bobsleigh in Olympic Games. It is a serious professional facility, built in 1986 by Yugoslav experts responsible for the Sarajevo Olympics facilities, but it is open to ordinary folks from November till March. This is when you can fly down the 16-bend track at 80km/h in a five-person Vučko soft bob. Summer thrill-seekers can ride a wheeled summer bob.

Baltic Eden

Explore the Turaida castle

Turaida means 'God's Garden' in ancient Livonian, and this green knoll capped with a fairy-tale castle is an enchanting place. The red-brick castle with its tall cylindrical tower was built in 1214 on the site of a Liv stronghold. What you see now is a product of reconstruction undertaken in the 1980s. A museum inside the castle's 15th-century granary offers an interesting account of the Livonian state from 1319 to 1561; additional exhibitions can be viewed in the 42m-high Donjon Tower and the castle's western and southern towers. The rest of the site features a variety of buildings that have been transformed into small galleries and exhibits. It's worth stopping by the smith house, where you can try forging metal. There is a real blacksmith on hand who sells his crafts, and guests can try pounding Liv pagan symbols into small chunks of iron. The nearby **Folk Song Garden** is dotted with 26

 WHERE TO EAT IN SIGULDA

Jāņa Tirgus
This modern market hall is mostly a food court with a quality pizzeria in the middle. €€

Kaķu Māja
Load up your tray with cheap Latvian fare or get a coffee with a freshly baked tart. €

Doma Kafejnīca
Enjoy heavenly fruity deserts in an enchanted garden. €

sculptures dedicated to epic Latvian heroes immortalised in the *dainas,* poetic folk songs that are a major Latvian tradition.

Sigulda's Storied Cave
A picturesque grotto

One of Sigulda's top sights, **Gutman's Cave** is in fact more of a grotto. This 19m-deep fissure in the earth is most famous for its role in the tragic legend of the Rose of Turaida (p191). Most tourists visit to peruse the inordinate amount of graffiti spread along the walls – some of it dates back to the 16th century. Many legends are attached to the spring-fed water flowing out of the cave. There's a paid parking area and small information office (9am to 5pm) on the east side of Turaidas iela.

Gauja Valley Flight
Ride the cable car

A quintessential Sigulda experience is to cross the Gauja Valley, while enjoying terrific views in all directions, in a cute **cable car** that departs from a precipice in the centre of town. More adventurous can opt for a peculiar hybrid of zip line and hang glider that uses the same cable (check siguldaadventures.com for details). The cable-car ride is 1km in length and 43m above the river. It takes you to **Krimulda Manor** on the other side of the valley. The sprawling neoclassical structure, built in 1822, hosts a simple hotel and a hostel, in case you decide to call it a day right there and then. Otherwise, upon observing the tree-shaded ruins of a 14th-century medieval castle that was destroyed in 1601, you are presented with two options. You can walk 2.7km to the pedestrian bridge, covering several beauty spots in the valley on the way. The highlight on the route is the **Velnalas** sandstone cliff and **Velna ala** (Devil's Cave) at its bottom. Alternatively, walk down to the vehicle bridge, from where a path leads to Gutman's Cave and Turaida.

Hit the Slopes
Alpine skiing at Kaķīškalns

Alpine skiing feels special in a country that's flat as a pancake, but Sigulda takes its 'Latvian Switzerland' reputation seriously. The 320m-long and a whopping 80m-high **Kaķīškalns** slope has all the attributes of a serious alpine resort – a chairlift, instructors and après-ski mulled wine. In summer, this small adventure park maintains a ropes course with 77 obstacles split into six graded routes.

LEVITATION SPREE

So you tried the zip line and the bobsleigh track, but do you believe you can fly? Here is how you can prove this ability. The one-of-a-kind **Aerodium** is a giant wind tunnel that propels participants up into the sky as though they were flying. Instructors can get about 15m high, while first-timers usually rock out at about 3m. Even though you will only be airborne for a couple of minutes, there is a brief introductory course, so allow a full hour. Children over four are welcome; note that booking in advance is essential. To find the site, look for the sign along the A2 highway, 4km west of Sigulda.

A DISAPPEARED PEOPLE

Livonians (or Livs) are a virtually extinct ethnic group that once populated swathes of today's Latvia. Attempts at reviving their culture are taking place in **Cape Kolka** (p214) area in the country's west.

Beyond
Sigulda

Places

Amata Geological Trail
p196

Camel Park Rakši p197

Cēsis p197

Valmiera p198

Alūksne p198

GETTING AROUND

The most memorable way of traversing Guaja National Park is hiking or cycling the Mēžtaka trail. Otherwise, you'll need a combination of train and buses. Cēsis and Valmiera lie on the same train line as Sigulda and they are served by buses from Rīga via Sigulda. Līgatne's train station is located by the main road leading to Estonia and Russia, 8km from the town centre. There are a few direct buses daily to Cēsis. Otherwise, catch a local bus to Augšlīgatne on the main highway and proceed from there. Travelling to Alūksne, either take a Rīga bus on the highway or change buses at Smiltene.

Gauja National Park encompasses an enchanting landscape of forested hills that guard the white ribbon of the meandering Gauja River.

Providing vertical dimension to a lowland country, these hills serve as Latvia's miniature Alps, drawing hikers, downhill skiers and (not exactly white-water) rafters. But the main pull is the quiet, unpretentious beauty of this area – especially in autumn when the hills turn yellow and bright red. Gauja Valley is Latvia's number-one outdoors destination, but it also comprises Cēsis, a cute little medieval city, as well as various historical monuments, entertainment parks and old mansion houses converted into hotels. Most of these attractions are located along the Mežtaka (Forest Trail) route. Further away in the boreal woods of northern Vidzeme, Alūksne is a lakeside gem with a fledgling hospitality industry.

Gauja National Park

VIESTURS JUGS/SHUTTERSTOCK ©

SANTA BUSHUEVA/SHUTTERSTOCK ©

Bears, Līgatne

Līgatne

TIME FROM SIGULDA: **20 MINS**

Forest-trail pit stop

Away from the main road and deep inside Gauja National Park, Līgatne is a drowsy little town built around a defunct **paper mill**. It has a small cluster of cafes and shops next to a pretty pond and a rapid stream flanked by a sandstone cliff punctured with cavities. Some of the caves are being used as shops selling locally made fruit liquors. If you like dramatic postindustrial landscapes, the old paper mill perfectly fits the bill. Up the hill above it, on the way to Gauja, wooden houses built for the workers in the early 20th century are also worth a quick look. Most people stop at Līgatne on the way to or from the numerous attractions in its vicinity. It also serves as a stop between two of the most beautiful sections of the Mežtaka trail.

Līgatne Nature Trails, located 4km from Līgatne town, is an odd cross between a nature park and a zoo, where bear, elk, deer, bison and wild boar roam in open-air enclosures in the forest. From the parking area, a 4km trail links the main sights, which include several small cages holding some sad-eyed badgers and other critters. Along the way are observation stops and a 22m-high tower with good views of the birch and

☑ **TOP TIP**

Hike the Mežtaka trail during Latvia's gorgeous autumn or in spring when the forest is awash with snowdrops.

DESIGNATED SURVIVORS

The gentle hills of Gauja Valley is where, back in the times of the Cold War, Latvian communist leaders resolved to meet (and survive) in the case of a global nuclear apocalypse. What poses as a dreary rehabilitation centre is in fact a top-secret **Soviet bunker**, known by its code name, the Pension. Remarkably, almost all of the bunker's 2000 sq metres still look as they did when it was in operation, making it a scarily authentic USSR time capsule, if not for ridiculously inauthentic Soviet slogans added in recent years. English-language tours are available, although the guides tend to pepper their narrative with dubious anecdotes exoticising Soviet period for dramatic effect.

 WHERE TO STAY AND EAT IN LĪGATNE

Zeit
Elegant rooms inside a former helmet factory converted into an event centre. €€

Lāču Miga
A converted paper-mill workers' house, the 'Bear's Den' features rustic rooms and a gang of plush bears. €€

Vilhelmīnes Dzirnavas
Līgatne's most atmospheric restaurant serves traditional food and drinks. €€

CARRY ME, RIVER

Slow-motion downstream rafting and canoeing along the Gauja is one of the favourite pastimes in the national park, with several adventure outfitters combining with campgrounds to offer trips downstream from Cēsis towards Līgatne. Most activities are suitable for families and don't require any special training.

Žagarkalns
An attractive riverside campground (zagarkalns.lv), 3km west of Cēsis centre. In addition to rafts, it rents out canoes, kayaks and bikes.

Ozolkalns
Wooden bungalows and sites for tents, as well as rafts and inflatable boats for rent.

Apalkalns
Based at a lakeside campground near Cēsis and specialising in canoe trips.

VALDIS SKUDRE/SHUTTERSTOCK ©

River Amata

conifer forests and the Gauja River. Rihards, a local woodcarver, has filled the 10-hectare **Vienkoču Park** with his unique creations. Short trails snake past modern art installations, a classical garden, model houses and displays about wooden shipbuilding. Buy yourself a hand-crafted wooden bowl. The park is right off the A2, at the Līgatne turn.

Amata Geological Trail TIME FROM SIGULDA: 30 MINS 🚗
Hike past cliffs and rapids

South of the Gauja River, a rapid creek called Amata has carved out a valley with austere scenery reminiscent of Siberia. The **Amata Geological Trail**, which runs parallel to it, passes many picturesque white-water rapids as well as dramatic sandstone and dolomite formations – the reason for its moniker. The trail has two sections. The easy one runs for

 WHERE TO STAY IN AND AROUND CĒSIS

Glūdas Grava
Five studios with glassy front walls and individual entrances in a renovated brick garage. €€

Kārlamūiža
In the village of Kārļi, a former aristocratic manor is reborn as a gentrified country hotel. €€

Villa Santa Hotel
Three 19th-century wooden buildings have been transformed into a lovely hotel deep in the woods. €€

3km and forms part of the Mežtaka trail (Līgatne to Cēsis leg). That little section begins at **Veclauči** bridge and ends at **Zvārtes**, one of the particularly attractive cliffs. The other section runs for another 12km to the village of **Kārļi**, the location of the famed Ainavu cliff. The challenge is in getting to the starting and ending points. Kārļi is served by buses from Cēsis. Other entry/exit points can only be reached by car or on foot from Līgatne along the Mežtaka trail, via the Soviet nuclear bunker.

Camel Park Rakši
TIME FROM SIGULDA: **35 MINS**

Mežtaka trail's animal park

Gauja Valley hills aren't exactly the Andean Altiplano, but they are imbued with the same desolate melancholy, which is why the vision of grazing llamas and vicuñas doesn't feel entirely out of place. At **Camel Park Rakši** (llamas being distant relative of Eurasian camels), both are available for rides and friendly interaction. The park is primarily for children to learn about and make friends with domestic animals, including the ones that are more characteristic of Latvia. It stands on the Mežtaka trail between the Amata Geological Trail and Cēsis, and comes with a handy cafe.

Cēsis
TIME FROM SIGULDA: **45 MINS**

Explore a stunning castle town

Those of the Livonian knights who were responsible for founding Wenden (which became Cēsis seven centuries later) must have had a soft romantic spot. While its impregnability can be disputed, given a few successful sackings, the beauty of the hilltop castle town is universally acclaimed. The ambience of medieval Europe combines perfectly with the colourful palette of Gauja Valley hills.

Cēsis Castle is actually two castles in one that form a single museum. The moody dark-stone towers belong to the restored old castle. Founded by Livonian knights in 1214, it was sacked by Russian Tsar Ivan the Terrible in 1577. You'll be handed a candle lamp for your exploration of the dark ruins to be suitably atmospheric. The newer castle, a stolid 18th-century manor house, was once inhabited by the dynasty of German counts von Sievers and now houses a museum that features original fin-de-siècle interiors. The exhibition leads you all the way to the owners' library and study under the cupola at the very top. After visiting the castle, take a walk through the landscaped castle park.

FLAG OVER THE CASTLE

While you're perusing the exhibitions in the new castle in Cēsis, take a note of the section dedicated to the Latvian national flag. A banner with similar – carmine-red and white – colours was first mentioned in a 13th-century chronicle describing a battle that took place near Cēsis. In the late 19th century, these colours were taken over by a Latvian student corporation in what is now Tartu University. Finally, in 1917, the flag was officially adopted by the newly emerged independent Latvia. In 1988, not long before the country officially left the USSR, Cēsis Castle was the first place to start flying the nation's traditional flag once again.

 WHERE TO EAT IN CĒSIS

Kest
Famous chef Māris Janson works his magic inside a former fire department. Open only Fridays and Saturdays. €€

HE Vanadziņš
High-end Nordic cuisine in a charming courtyard setting in the heart of Cēsis. €€

Rūse
Enjoy sublime breakfasts and brunches at this centrally located coffee shop. €€

Nearby is the hilltop Russian Orthodox **Church of Transfiguration**, which the von Sievers built at their family cemetery (like many Germans on Russian service, they converted to Orthodoxy). Back in town, make sure you visit the 13th-century **St John's Church**, where armour-clad Livonian knights prayed and buried their dead in what was then a lonely island of Christianity surrounded by the lands of pagans. The church contains tombs of the order's grand masters and top bishops.

RIVER RACE

Valmiera often features as the starting point for boat trips on the Gauja River. A striking natural feature in town itself is the Gauja's **Kazu rapids**. These have been turned into a kayaking and canoeing slalom course of modest difficulty. Even if you're not into this kind of water sports, it's fun to watch the rowers go over obstacles and through the gates on the impetuous river. A short walk away, a cute little ferry-type raft, known as **Gauja Tram**, invites for a much calmer adventure on the river. You can rent a canoe or raft for your Gauja National Park adventure (such as the 45km float to Cēsis) from **Eži Veikals** in Valmiera.

Valmiera

TIME FROM SIGULDA: 1¼ HRS

History amid downtown woods

Thoroughly destroyed in WWII, Valmiera is not famous for outstanding architecture, but there is something magical about a forest and the bends of the Gauja River blending naturally into the town's centre. The forest is criss-crossed by hiking and cycling routes, including the pan-Baltic Mežtaka trail. If you've been on the trail for a whole day, it's also a tempting place to dip into the Gauja, but beware the strong current.

Valmiera has been around from medieval times. However, it was almost completely burned down during WWII, so uninspiring Soviet architecture prevails. The tiny historical core on the edge of the forest is quite pretty. The ruins of the 13th-century Livonian castle have been nicely fused with delicate modern architecture, including the airy structure that contains **De Woldemer** – an interactive exhibition explaining the town's history with an emphasis on its Hanseatic roots. A lovely **history museum** is housed in the same grounds. A short walk away, a Soviet **WWII memorial** occupies a patch of the forest, complemented by contextualising notes that reflect the fact that it was the Soviets who burned down Valmiera in that war.

Bittersweet with strong herbal undertones, **Valmiermuiža** beer is an essential taste of Latvia. True to its name, it hails from a *muiža* (manor) on the outskirts of Valmiera. Here you can see how Latvia's best-known beer brand is made; on an entertaining tour, expect friendly guides and plenty of samples. Enjoy hearty pints and Latvian favourites with a seasonal twist in the **Beer Kitchen**, a lively cafe.

Alūksne

TIME FROM SIGULDA: 2 HRS

Discover a lakeside town gem

Deep in the Vidzeme hinterland, and close to the Estonian and Russian borders, Alūksne rivals Kuldīga for Latvia's most beautiful setting. Its name pertains to both a lake and a town.

 WHERE TO STAY IN VALMIERA AND ALŪKSNE

Wolmar
A faultless, cutting-edge boutique hotel located in the heart of Valmiera. €€

Stadium
Comfortable and airy rooms are housed inside Valmiera's sports centre. €

Benevilla Hotel
This Alūksne boutique hotel features a soothing pale palette and wood-rich design. €€

Livonian castle ruins

The former is clearly the alpha party in this happy matrimony. For one, it looks bigger. The enchanting small town flanks part of the lakeshore and spills into an island, the location of Alūksne's **Livonian castle ruins** and the beach. Baron Alexander von Vietinghoff was responsible for the town's main charms – including his neo-Gothic palace, which now houses the **Alūksne Museum**, and a beautiful park on the lake's shores. The town remains the little paradise he had in the designs.

If you want to travel to or from Alūksne in appropriately old-world style, nothing beats the **Bānītis**. This narrow-gauge railway connects Alūksne to Gulbene, a town in Vidzeme's northern heartland. A preserved section of a longer line, built in 1903, it is operated by a shiny retro steam train. Once at the station, don't miss the interactive exhibition in the old baggage department that details the railway's history.

Renounce the perks of civilisation (such as a shower) and stay in an otherwise comfortable boathouse – complete with a boat, that's always at your disposal – on the shore of Lake Alūksne. At **Laivu māja** you get to sleep in a stylishly old-fashioned (if cramped) room on the 2nd floor. Below, there's only a washstand, a camping toilet, the boat and splashing waves. There's no electricity or running water. It's another unusual Latvian guesthouse, like many popping up across the country.

A PRIEST & THE EMPIRE

Pastor Johann Ernst Glück had an amazing life story, which you can dive into at his former Alūksne home, the **Ernst Glück Bible Museum**. Born in Germany, he spent much of his life in Alūksne (then Marienburg) surrounded by Latvians. His greatest feat was the translation of the Bible into Latvian, something he is revered for in Latvia today. Marienburg was part of Sweden, but in 1702 it was ravaged by Russians and Glück's foster daughter Maria Skowronska was forcibly taken to Moscow. There she became a lover and subsequently the wife of Peter the Great. For the last two years of her life she was known as Catherine I, the empress of Russia.

Zemgale

CASTLES | RIVERS | CULTS

GETTING AROUND

Most destinations in Zemgale can be easily reached by bus from Rīga, but you'll need to change in Dobele for Pokaiņi Forest. Additionally, Jelgava is served by numerous trains from the capital. The newly launched train to Rīga is also expected to call here. However, the most convenient and rewarding way of exploring Zemgale is definitely by car.

Milda, the Liberty statue in Rīga, holds in her hands the three stars symbolising three historical regions. But there is a fourth one that, as you might guess, is often underrated. Zemgale is a landlocked region spreading south of Rīga towards the Lithuanian border. Its name is derived from the ancient Baltic tribe called Semigallians. It is a thickly forested area that lacks strong identifiers, such as hills in Vidzeme or lakes in Latgale. However, it played a significant role in the country's history, so it is this rich legacy of past epochs – along with pristine nature and proximity to Rīga – that attracts visitors. Local history to a large extent pertains to one of the last dukes of Courland who built two palaces here, inviting an architect responsible for key landmarks in St Petersburg. Other attractions include a mystical forest, famous fruit gardens and a well-preserved medieval castle.

The Abode of an Adventurist

Admire a baroque palace

Built as a grand residence for the Duke of Courland, the magnificent **Rundāle Palace** is a monument to 18th-century aristocratic ostentation and is rural Latvia's architectural highlight. It was designed by Italian baroque genius Bartolomeo Rastrelli, who is best known for the Winter Palace in St Petersburg. About 40 of the palace's 138 rooms are open to visitors, as are the wonderful formal gardens, inspired by those at Versailles. There's a restaurant on the approach from the car park to the palace, and a kiosk selling artisan ice cream by the garden entrance.

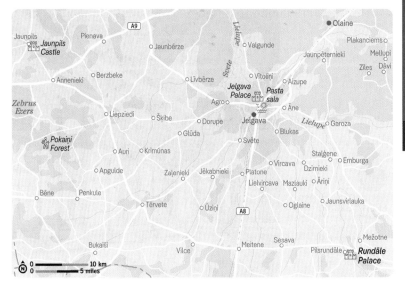

The owner, Ernst Johann Biron, was a lover of Anna Ioanovna, the Russian-born Duchess of Courland. She gave him the duchy when she became Russian empress, but he stayed with her in St Petersburg, becoming the most powerful political figure of the empire. In 1736 he commissioned the Italian architect Bartholomeo Rastrelli to construct his summer residence near Bauska. On her death bed, the empress proclaimed Biron the Regent of Russia, but two months later his rivals arrested him and sentenced him to death; the sentence was commuted to exile. The unfinished palace stood as an empty shell for another 22 years when, pardoned by Catherine II, Ernst Johann returned home. Rastrelli resumed the construction and in 1768 the palace was finished.

Detailed displays inside the palace offer fascinating insights into its design and restoration. The castle has two sections: the East Wing was devoted to formal occasions, while the West Wing was the private royal residence. The palace was badly damaged in the Franco-Russian War in 1812 and again during the Latvian War of Independence in 1919 – what you see now is the result of a painstaking restoration started by experts from Leningrad in 1972 and officially finished in 2015. The 'long' tour includes the duke's and duchess' private chambers, which is your chance to peek into the everyday life of 18th-century aristocrats and admire the opulent interior design.

☑ TOP TIP

You can cover all the main Zemgale attractions in one long day, starting either from Rīga or from Jelgava (where the CityBee car-sharing service is available).

 WHERE TO STAY IN ZEMGALE

Hotel Jelgava
Classically designed rooms in a perfect, super-central setting, overlooking the river in Jelgava. €€

Kārklu Muiža
This former manor house on the outskirts of Jelgava has large and comfortable rooms. €€

Zoltners Hotel
Utmost luxury in a seven-room top-end gem next to a fancy restaurant and craft brewery near Tērvete. €€€

Rundāle Palace (p200)

FRUITY ESCAPE

The massive gardens of the **Institute of Horticulture** near the town of Dobele draw throngs of visitors each spring when the scores of fruit trees are in bloom. There are apricot, cherry and plum orchards, as well as one of Europe's largest collections of lilacs. A museum tells the history of the gardens and a shop offers plants, seeds and shoots for sale. But the real reason to visit is the selection of house-made ice cream made with the farm's fruit. It's smooth, creamy and not to be missed. **Dobele**, centred on its ruined Livonian Order castle from the 1300s, is the gateway to a vast acreage of mystical forests and meandering rivers.

Jelgava's Forgotten Empire

Island palace, Soviet city

With 55,000 residents and dominated by Soviet-era architecture, Jelgava (known as Mitava for much of its history) is one of the most unlikely and obscure former imperial capitals in Europe. But back in the 16th century the Duchy of Courland, which was ruled from here, operated a fairly large commercial fleet and joined the scramble for overseas colonies by seizing the island of Tobago in the Caribbean and the delta of the Gambia River in Africa, which became two pieces of its mini-empire. Alas, it was soon swallowed by the expanding Russian empire and remains a historical oddity little known to the outside world. The devastation during WWII left precious little of the city's former glory, but the baroque **Jelgava Palace** still stands on an island in the Lielupe River. It belonged to Ernst Johann von Biron of Rundāle Palace fame. A former groom, he obtained Courland from its previous ruler and his lover, who went on to become Russian empress Anna Ioanovna. Both palaces were authored by the same architect, Francesco Bartolomeo Rastrelli. Not a museum, sadly, Jelgava Palace is being used as an agricultural university, so access is limited to the crypt that contains the tombs of

 WHERE TO EAT IN ZEMGALE

Cafe Elpa
Artfully prepared international food with cheap lunch options in an idyllic island setting in Jelgava. €

Kristīnes Picērija un Beķereja
When her Tērvete village shop is open (it varies), Kristīne makes delicious artisanal pizzas. €

Jaunpils Pils Krogs
Located inside a medieval castle, this is a progressive take on traditional Latvian staples. €€

UGIS RIBA/SHUTTERSTOCK ©

Courland's rulers. The nearby **Pasta sala** (in which *pasta* stands for 'post', not 'spaghetti') is an attractive leisure zone with sports facilities and a wonderful sandy beach, complete with changing rooms. In summer, the island hosts a large exhibition of **sand sculpture**, and in February it becomes one of the venues of the annual **Jelgava Ice Sculpture Festival**.

The Castle of Two Rivers
Go with the flow

The nearest town to the Rundāle Palace, Bauska was once an important seat in the Duchy of Courland. Today it's worth at least a brief stop to check out its most prominent attraction. **Bauska Castle** sits on a picturesque hillock squeezed between two rivers – the Mūsa and the Mēmele – that flow parallel to each other. It is actually two castles melded together. The older part is in ruins and dates back to the Livonian Order in the 15th century. The newer portion is a fortified manor house built by the Duke of Courland in the 16th century and is mostly intact. A museum covers the entire tangled history of the castle and the region.

Night Knight
Sleep in a medieval castle

The small but perfectly medieval **Jaunpils Castle** is unusual in the fact that it has largely retained its original look since 1301, when it was founded by the master of the Livonian Order, Gotfried von Roga. It also offers a chance to dine and sleep in the rooms that saw kings and knights do the same before your great-grandparents were born. For four centuries until the breakup of the Russian empire in 1917, it was the home of the German baron family von der Recke. Its walls witnessed a sword fight between Mathias von der Recke and Swedish king Charles IX. It was a friendly fight, apparently, for which the king awarded the baron a silver helmet and a sword. The castle hotel has four private rooms with brick floors, baldachin-covered beds and real fireplaces.

The Mystery Woods of Pokaiņi
Find traces of a prehistoric cult

It's one of Latvia's biggest unsolved mysteries: in the mid-1990s a local historian discovered stone cairns throughout the **Pokaiņi Forest** and realised that the rocks had been transported to the forest from faraway destinations. Historians have theorised that Pokaiņi was an ancient sacred ground used in proto-pagan rituals more than 2000 years ago. There are 15km of walking trails through the reserve, with themes including mystical healing, the seasons and the zodiac. The forest is 16km southwest of the town of Dobele.

MUSEUMS OF JELGAVA

There are a few museums in Jelgava where you can spend some hours. Here are the two flagships.

Jelgava History Museum
Located in a striking former school building known as Academia Petrina, this museum has a cramped history section, packed with paraphernalia from all epochs, including a wax figure of Duke Biron, on the 1st floor. The 2nd floor is a gallery, featuring colourful works by Jelgava's native son Ģederts Eliass.

Jelgavas Vecpilsētas māja
An interesting attempt at reviving the town's oldest preserved wooden house, with an interactive exhibition that might be too clever for someone with no deep interest in architecture.

Kūldiga

WATERFALLS | OLD TOWN | FOOD & DRINK

GETTING AROUND

The centre of Kuldīga can be crossed on foot in less than half an hour. But there are a few bicycle and moped rentals around town, including Rent Vespa Kuldiga and Ciskdrill, which rents out retro bikes.

A newcomer on the UNESCO heritage list (its old town was added in the autumn of 2023), charming Kuldīga – formerly known as Goldingen – has a striking setting above the supposedly widest waterfall in Europe and the vibes of Grimm brothers' fairytale-like Europe. Despite a short stint as the capital of the Duchy of Courland in the 17th century, it has always been simply a very pleasant and visually attractive town, which it very much remains today. Kuldīga's charm is infectious and people tend to get attached to it, many of them turning into regular visitors and eventually even residents. As the heart of Kurzeme's hinterland, Kuldīga is a jumping-off point for smaller towns, each with its own cute idiosyncrasies – especially Sabile, which displays a few. Also nearby, Lake Usma is surrounded by campgrounds and holiday houses, while the Abava river valley draws enthusiasts of slow, meditative rafting.

☑ TOP TIP

Try steamy meatballs or delicious curry, accompanied with a few cocktails, at Bārs Didro on Kuldīga's main pedestrian drag. If you can impress its philosopher owners with a deep knowledge of Hegel's early works, you might even get a freebie. Otherwise, just come and pamper your inner hedonist.

A Humble Niagara

Kuldīga's landmark waterfalls

Kuldīga's famous postcard feature, **Ventas Rumba**, is branded 'Europe's widest waterfall'. This description might be a tiny stretch, not in terms of width (249m) but in calling a human-sized threshold in the riverbed a waterfall. Still, it's a truly awe-inspiring sight when seen from above – a zigzagging ribbon of white water running across the Venta River, the banks drowning in lush greenery and a stunning 19th-century red-brick bridge a few hundred metres away. Come spring, this view is complemented by the *vimba* fish (a type of bream) jumping over the waterfall during its seasonal migration up the river. In summer, the waterfall turns into a natural hot tub, with people standing or sitting on the rocks under torrents of water. The deep lake-like lagoon above it is a favourite place for swimming and the location of the city beach.

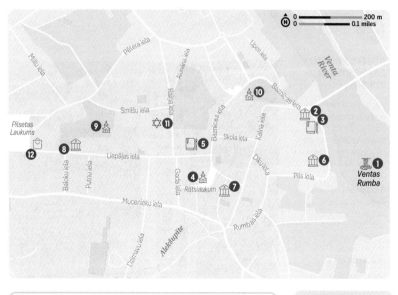

TOP SIGHTS
1 Ventas Rumba

SIGHTS
2 Art Residence
3 Castle Watchman's House

4 Church of the Holy Trinity
5 Duke Jakob's Pharmacy
6 History Museum
7 Kūldiga's Old Stories

8 Needle Tower
9 Russian Orthodox Church
10 St Katrīna's Church
11 Synagogue

SHOPPING
12 Liepajas iela

RIVERBED WALK

Disappointed by the modest height of Kuldīga's waterfall? Head over to what is – yes! – Latvia's tallest, at a whopping 4.2m: **Alekšupīte Waterfall**, at the confluence of the namesake stream and the Venta River. Sure, it's lined with concrete and was once used for a mill, but the cascade is one more tick on the town's checklist of charm. The tiny Alekšupīte runs through Kuldīga's Old Town, squeezed between ancient houses and barely visible. But the **tourist information office** runs fascinating tours along its riverbed, with participants issued long rubber boots. It's a very different perspective on the medieval city, as well as a lot of fun.

This entire idyll is best observed from the castle hill, which has only some stones left from the city's old castle. It is now home to a sculpture-filled park presided over by the stately 1735 **Castle Watchman's House**, a haunted place according to local legends. An elegant wooden villa nearby is the former Russian pavilion from the 1900 Exposition Universelle in Paris brought here by a sea captain who was implementing his idea of happy retirement. Today it houses a fine **History Museum** featuring recreated living rooms from the early 20th century. The **Art Residence** by the bridge combines a little gallery with a food court on a terrace with top-notch views of Ventas Rumba.

Cobbles & Spires

Walk around Kuldīga's Old Town

Kuldīga's Old Town is the realm of cobbled streets, German-style timber-framed houses, and fruit orchards enveloping more traditionally Baltic wooden cottages. A cursory exploration warrants no more than a few hours.

A short but delightful walking route from the waterfalls to the main square passes by **St Katrīna's Church** – the most important church in town dedicated to its patron saint, and

BEST PLACES TO EAT & DRINK IN KULDĪGA

Kuldīga's restaurant and bar scene is constantly improving, so you're likely to find new exciting places in addition to the ones below.

Bārs Didro
Fantastic travel-inspired food and cocktails in a bar run by real-life professional philosophers. €

Kuldīga Market
In attractive new premises, the town market brings together the best farm produce from the vicinity. €

Circus
Artisanal pizzas served in an attractive garden setting; in summer only. €

DUNA Brewery
An independent craft-beer outfit, complete with a shop and taproom for degustations.

Kviešu Šnaps Veikals
A hole-in-the-wall shop on Liepajas iela selling wheat-based schnapps-type liquors with fruity flavours.

BARGAIS/SHUTTERSTOCK ©

Needle Tower

also featuring its coat of arms. The church dates from 1252 and was rebuilt in the mid-1600s when the dukes of Courland and their families were the main guests at the Mass. Inside it's atmospherically musty; you can climb the tower for good views. Further along Baznīcas iela, you won't fail to notice **Duke Jakob's Pharmacy**, a half-timbered icon built in 1622. It serves as a private residence today. Near the Town Hall Square, drop by **Kuldīga's Old Stories** – a succession of dark-lit and theatrically decorated rooms, each telling its own (mostly spooky) tale from Kuldīga's tumultuous history. Originating in the main square, Kuldīga's pedestrian drag, **Liepajas iela**, is lined with shops and cafes. Side streets conceal the town's main religious buildings: the Catholic **Church of the Holy Trinity**, standing inside a crumbling courtyard, and Kuldīga's **synagogue**, now serving as a community centre. The Jews of Kuldīga perished in the Holocaust. At the far end of the same street, the ornate **Russian Orthodox Church** is barely in use but it's surrounded by a pretty sculpture-filled park. Nearby, the **Needle Tower** offers views of the town's rooftops and exhibits

 WHERE TO STAY IN KULDĪGA

Jēkaba Sēta
This typical Latvian inn, complete with a pub, has standard-looking rooms with wooden furniture. €

Hotel Metropole
Kuldīga's main full-service hotel features a modern pale palette and spacious rooms overlooking the Town Hall Square. €€

2 Baloži
Perched above a stream, this wooden house has rooms designed in the Scandinavian style. €

Beyond
Kuldīga

Venturing out of Kuldīga, you find yourself in Kurzeme's agricultural heartland that's filled with green pastures and idiosyncratic little towns.

When the glaciers receded at the end of the last Ice Age, the crescent-shaped Abava Valley was born. Gnarled oaks and idyllic villages dot the gushing stream, luring city slickers for a day of unhurried scenery. Branching off from the main road between Rīga and Ventspils, the road to Kuldīga follows the course of the Abava, passing a few small towns including the charismatic Sabile with its collection of unusual attractions. Outdoor artworks big and small plus some juice of the grape are but some of the highlights in this cobbled-street village. South of the road lies the large Lake Usma, surrounded by guesthouses and campgrounds, while the Abava itself is popular with water-adventure enthusiasts.

Abava River (p209)

Places

Sabile p208
Lake Usma p209
Riežupe Sand Caves p209
Abava River p209

GETTING AROUND

Sabile and other towns in the Abava Valley stand on the road that's served by buses connecting Kuldīga to Rīga and regional destinations.

☑ TOP TIP

All of the Abava Valley attractions can be visited on your way to Kuldīga – it's just a slightly longer route, if travelling by car.

RATIKOVA/SHUTTERSTOCK ©

LARA RA/SHUTTERSTOCK ©

Lake Usma

BARON'S ABODE

In the hamlet of Ēdole, 20km west of Kuldīga, you'll find a laudable and successful attempt to revive the medieval **Ēdoles Castle**. Part manor house, part castle, it was originally built in 1269 but thoroughly reconstructed by its Anglophile owner, Baron Adolf Werner Bär, in the 1830s. Today, this England-themed manor house with a park-like setting contains a museum section, with carefully preserved living quarters that provide insight into baronial life and feel like the residents have just gone out for a walk in their hunting grounds. But you can also stay here for the night in classically designed rooms and/or dine in the excellent **Pilskrogs** restaurant in the courtyard.

Sabile

TIME FROM KULDĪGA: **45 MINS** 🚌

Village of oddities and wine

There's hardly a place in Latvia that is more eccentric and artistic than Sabile, a little town 45km from Kuldīga. It begins right on the main road, where Latvia's answer to the Chinese terracotta army is lined up as if for a parade. The difference, though, is that the **Sabile doll garden** is entirely comprised of straw-filled unarmed civilians. Local folk artist Daina Kučera has filled a roadside garden with over 200 winsome straw dolls dressed as people of all ages and walks of life – from schoolchildren to policemen to village people. Kučera is around most of the time, chatting about her work and collecting donations.

Residents of Sabile, those made of straw and of flesh and blood alike, live in the shade of a hill occupied by another piece of local eccentricity – a vineyard. Once designated as the northernmost in Europe (climate change took care of that no longer being the case), **Vīna kalns** (Wine Hill) started operating during the 13th century and was resurrected in the 17th century by Duke Jakob of Courland. The duke's vineyard was never very productive and fell into disuse. Although operations resumed in 1936, the vineyard's focus lay in

WHERE TO EAT AND STAY BEYOND KULDĪGA

Plostkrogs
On the bank of the Abava River, this *krogs* (roadside pub) gentrifies traditional Baltic staples. €€

Abavas Pagrabiņš
A very down-to-earth little *krogs* serving simple Latvian food in a beautiful setting under the bridge. €

Kukšu Muiža
Unashamed luxury in a manor house restored to its former 19th-century splendour; near Kukšas village. €€€

researching hardy strains of vines rather than producing high-quality wines. The wine produced here is the stuff of legend – you're unlikely to find a way to try it. But you can try locally made cider as well as fruit wine at **Sabiles Sidra Nams** on the main square. The wines are made from an astonishing range of products, from gooseberry to birch-tree sap.

Lake Usma

TIME FROM KULDĪGA: **35 MINS**

Stay in a floating guesthouse

A large lake north of Kuldīga and immediately south of the Ventspils–Rīga road (A10), **Usma** is a popular holiday spot surrounded by campgrounds and guesthouses. If you are travelling between Kuldīga and Sabile, a turn near Renda will bring you to **Lejastiezumi**, a lakeside resort with an organised beach, a restaurant and a variety of accommodation. On the other side of the lake, near the village of Usma, a local artist built two floating houses with straw roofs, one shaped as a swan and another as a beaver's hut. The houses appear as separate accommodation under the names of **Gulbju māja** and **Bebru māja** on booking sites. Guests are served an enormous breakfast in a basket deposited on the lakeshore.

Riežupe Sand Caves

TIME FROM KULDĪGA: **10 MINS**

Explore a sandy labyrinth

Located 5km outside Kuldīga along the unpaved Krasta iela, **Riežupe Sand Caves** feature 2km of labyrinthine tunnels, of which 460m can be visited by candlelight. It's an aptly spooky place; the caves were originally formed by a spring but then enlarged by locals who used the sand for the production of glass. During the 1905 revolutionary unrest in the Russian empire, the labyrinth served as a hiding place for the revolutionaries. The temperature in the caves is a chilly 8°C (46°F), so bring a warm sweater.

Abava River

TIME FROM KULDĪGA: **20 MINS**

A kayaking adventure

More low-key than Gauja, the Abava is another popular river for relatively slow-motion, water-based adventures. Based in Renda, halfway between Kuldīga and Sabile, **Jūras Laivas** runs kayaking trips on the Abava, as well as the Venta and other waterways in Kurzeme.

CONTEMPORARY STONEHENGE

Occupying a hill on the other side of the river from Sabile, 1.5km south of the centre, is an open-air extravaganza founded by Latvian sculptor Ojars Feldbergs. The **Pedvāle Art Park** showcases over 100 thought-provoking installations scattered across 100 hectares of rolling hills. Every year the pieces rotate, reflecting the theme of the year. Standout works include *Chair,* an enormous seat made from bright blue oil drums; and the iconic *Petriflora Pedvalensis,* a bouquet of flowers whose petals have been replaced with spiral stones. The site is anchored by an old manor house. Brace for a long walk amid enchanting landscapes and watch storks fly over this modern-day Stonehenge.

Ventspils

ART | BEACH PARK | SCIENCE MUSEUM

GETTING AROUND

Ventspils can be easily negotiated on foot.

☑ **TOP TIP**

Pack your picnic of fresh raspberries, forest blueberries, artisanal cheese and bread at Ventspils market and head to the beach.

The colourful and photogenic port of Ventspils inspires wanderlust and curiosity about all those ships under exotic flags that load coal and other goods at the terminal across the harbour from Old Town. For most of its 760-year history, the city was dominated by Baltic Germans and known as Windau; in Soviet times, it was a vital ice-free port. Today, Ventspils is defined by its busy harbour, observed by visitors from an art-filled promenade or a pleasure boat. But most people come here for the marvellous white-sand beach flanked by lush maritime gardens, or use the city as a base for exploring the northern stretch of Kurzeme coast. That said, don't expect a lively food and cultural scene as in Liepājā down south. Ventspils is mostly geared towards holidaying families and its main attractions are kid-friendly, but perhaps a little tedious for adults roaming on their own.

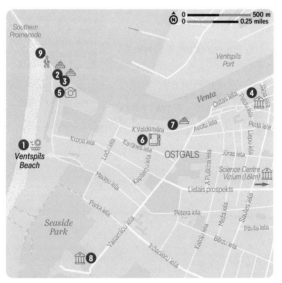

TOP SIGHTS
1 Ventspils Beach

SIGHTS
2 Azov
3 Grot
4 Livonian Order Castle
5 Observation Tower
6 Ostgals
7 Rota
8 Seaside Open-Air Museum

ACTIVITIES, COURSES & TOURS
9 Southern Pier

AIGARS REINHOLDS/SHUTTERSTOCK ©

Pilot ship Rota

Herd of Art

Stroll the harbour promenade

As if the view of the harbour wasn't colourful enough, the authorities in Ventspils have also turned the main waterfront promenade into an open-air art gallery with dozens of art forms and monuments along the route. It all begins with cows. Part of the international CowParade initiative, the whimsically shaped and decorated animal sculptures line the entire route (and dot the rest of the city). The *Black Cow* with industrial piping in the middle and the *Cow in the Swings*, a girlie one wearing a pink dress, will be your first encounters. Beyond the blocky **Livonian Order Castle**, which contains an entertaining interactive local history and art museum, there's also more serious art, such as the *Human Power* installation, made by Kirils Pantelejevs from a WWII ship propeller. This is in addition to a number of boats living an afterlife as artefacts displayed on the embankment. Pilot ship **Rota** worked in the harbour for decades before

DRINK & HAGGLE

The nicely renovated **Ventspils market** is right in the heart of Ventspils' Old Town, so it's more than likely that you'll find yourself here at some point, even if you don't need to stock up on fresh produce such as veggies, homemade cheeses, honey or forest mushrooms and berries. Open until 3pm, the market is best visited in the early morning, especially during weekends. The bell tower on the side of the market square plays popular Latvian tunes on the hour. Across the square, the **Courlander** pub makes its own beer and has a short menu largely based on Baltic fish. Nearby, **Windau Wines** sells fruity booze from its own winery.

 WHERE TO STAY AND EAT IN VENTSPILS

Raibie Logi
Cute simple rooms in the courtyard of a wooden house with colourful windows. €

Piejūras Kempings
A charming campus of grassy campsites and pine cottages in a park not far from the beach. €

Skroderkrogs
Enjoy Latvian comfort food in a leafy park setting. The fresh seafood is always good. €

becoming a monument in front of its former workplace. The promenade ends by a quay that you can walk around to reach an **observation tower** and two more ships, fishing vessels **Azov** and **Grot,** which can be entered and explored. Beyond them is the long **Southern Pier**, where you'll be greeted by the *Blue Cow*, dressed as a sailor. There's a modest lighthouse at the end of the pier, with thrilling views of huge freighters passing close by. You can access the beach from the pier and complete the walk with a dip in the sea.

Sand, Steam & Boats
Roam the beach park

For Ventspils, the wide stretch of dazzling white sand south of the Venta River is its main treasure. During the warmer months, beach bums of every ilk – from nudists to kiteboarders – line the pristine Blue Flag sands to absorb the sun's rays. The **beach** is backed by a belt of dunes and a lush manicured park. Walk from the centre to the beach through the **Ostgals** neighbourhood for a glimpse at Ventspils' days as a humble fishing village of wooden abodes.

For centuries, life in Kurzeme revolved around seafaring and fishing. Occupying a vast parkland territory, the **Seaside Open-Air Museum** features a collection of fishing crafts, anchors and traditional log houses, brought from nearby coastal villages. A large wooden mill presides over the entire idyll. A bonus attraction is a **narrow-gauge railway**, which recreates a line that connected coastal villages on the way from Ventspils to Cape Kolka. The route, operated by a cute little steamer made in Germany in 1916, runs for over 2km through the city's parks.

Life is an Experiment
Fun at a science museum

A new kid on the block, the **Science Centre Vizium** occupies a large futuristic building on the outskirts of the city and contains numerous gamified interactive exhibitions that strive to explain the laws of nature and the foundations of science to the younger generation. The older generation, in the meantime, can enjoy their Prosecco and city views at the cafeteria on the roof. That way, however, they will miss a lot of fun, such as watching an animated visualisation of their own skeleton, feeling the impact of an earthquake or playing virtual-reality football.

HARBOUR CRUISE

Another way of exploring the Ventspils harbour is by a boat called **Hercogs Jēkabs**, which departs regularly from the embankment and sails around the mouth of the Venta River. On a 45-minute trip, it will bring you close to the coal terminal and the loading ships, and take you to the end of the mall and the open sea. The caveat is that it only departs once there are five passengers, so it can be tricky getting on if you are alone on a working day outside the high season. Harbour views can be particularly enchanting and photogenic on a foggy (but not too foggy!) morning.

Beyond
Ventspils

The Baltic Sea meets the Gulf of Rīga at Cape Kolka, the tip of northern Kurzeme.

To the north of Ventspils, it's miles and miles of pristine beach and maritime forest, protected by Slītere National Park. The coastal road links a series of quiet, one-street villages like a string of pearls. These fishing hamlets preserve the memories of the Livs – the Finno-Ugric people who populated this coast for centuries but reached the point of full extinction in recent decades. During Soviet times the entire Kurzeme coast was zoned off as a heavily guarded border and out of bounds to civilians, which explains the lack development and rusty Soviet remnants occasionally dotting the landscape like abstract art installations. The west-facing beaches offer unforgettable sunsets over the churning sea and stark, sandy terrain.

Places

Cape Kolka p214

Alsunga & Jūrkalne p215

GETTING AROUND

Jūrkalne stands on the route connecting Ventspils and Liepāja. To get to Alsunga from Jūrkalne, you'll need to catch the infrequent Rīga bus or get a Bolt taxi. Travelling by car is a breeze. CityBee car-sharing service is available in Ventspils.

☑ TOP TIP

Arrange your beach picnic under the sandstone cliff in Jūrkalne by stocking up on *sklandrauši* cakes in Alsunga.

Slītere National Park

DACE KUNDRATE/SHUTTERSTOCK ©

Cape Kolka

SPY ON STARS

Once upon a time during the Cold War, **Irbene Radio Telescope** – hidden in the forest 24km north of Ventspils – was a Soviet facility used to spy on US satellites and intercept communications between the USA and Europe. These days, it's run by an academic institute and used for astronomical studies. The huge 600-tonne, 32m-dish mounted on a 25m-tall concrete base is open at certain times for tours. To visit, call or email at least three days in advance to book a spot on a tour. Just driving into Irbene is an adventure as you will pass by blocks of abandoned Soviet housing that are reminiscent of Chernobyl.

Cape Kolka

TIME FROM VENTSPILS: **55 MINS** 🚌

Where the seas meet

A journey to the enchantingly desolate and hauntingly beautiful **Cape Kolka** (Kolkasrags) feels like a trip to the end of the earth. It's here that the Dižjūra (the Great Sea, or Baltic Sea) meets Mazjūra (the Little Sea, or Gulf of Rīga) in a very dramatic fashion. Watching the blue swells of the former crash into the brownish swells of the latter is mesmerising. Find a spot away from the summertime crowds on the narrow beach; the 1km **Pine Trail** follows the beach southwest to the more serene environs, where there is uncrowded free parking and a watchtower to observe the coast. On the gulf side, the beach looks dramatic and a little spooky, with masses of driftwood, whitened by the sea salt, lying like

 WHERE TO STAY AND EAT BEYOND VENTSPILS

Ūši
Two holiday houses, stylishly modern and old-school, and a campground in Kolka. €

Pie Andra Pitragā
Learning about fish-smoking is part of the fun at this beachside guesthouse and campground in Pitrags. €

Tējnīca Sapņotava
A stylish teahouse-cum-cultural institution in Alsunga that also serves burritos and other snacks. €

carcasses of mythical sea monsters. A monument to those claimed by treacherous waters marks the entrance to the beach near the information centre. Locals claim the cape's waters are littered with more shipwrecks than anywhere else in the Baltics. For obvious reasons, Cape Kolka's beauty is best appreciated from the safety of the sand.

The village of **Kolka** features three churches that represent different confessions – Catholic, Lutheran and Orthodox – and are built in respective architectural styles, but all reflect the austere simplicity of fishermen's lives in their forms. Doubling as the visitors centre, the **Livonian Community House** has an exhibition dedicated to Livs and designed as a built-in closet with many departments, each containing an exhibit and a story related to Livonian culture and history.

Alsunga & Jūrkalne   TIME FROM VENTSPILS: 1 HR

Ethnic Suiti subculture

Two little towns south of Ventspils, **Alsunga** and **Jūrkalne**, form a peculiar pocket of Catholic population in the otherwise staunchly Lutheran Kurzeme. In 1623 the ruler of Alsunga, Johann Ulrich von Schwerin, wanted to marry a beautiful Polish woman so badly he converted into Catholicism with all of his peasants.

This group became known as Suiti after Polish-styled clothes they were required to wear. It developed its own distinct culture centred on a unique polyphonic singing style. Sang by large female collectives, these are improvisations in which women pass working instructions, tease each other as well as passing men, or even argue.

What remains of **Alsunga Castle**, von Schwerin's former residence, now contains a wonderful history exhibition built into the completely unrestored, decaying interiors. The resulting effect is haunting and dramatic. The **House of Crafts**, containing a modest exhibition about Suiti life, is the place to inquire about possibilities of diving deeper into Suiti culture. Alsunga is also also the best place to try *sklandrauši* – the round-shaped pie with a sweet carrot filling, typical of Kurzeme. You'll find a small cluster of *sklandrauši* stalls on the main road leading to **St Michael the Archangel Church**.

Alsunga is located 13km inland from Jūrkalne, another Suiti village on the coast famous for its tall sand cliffs, which makes it a popular beach spot. Within the village, definitely check out the **Museum of Storms**, a very entertaining venue dedicated to marine archeologist Rains Voldemārs. Nearby, the 19th-century Catholic **St Joseph Church** has a model of a sailing ship hanging from the ceiling.

PEOPLE OF THE SEA

Livs are (were?) Finno-Ugric people – that is, relatives of Estonians and Finns – who once populated the coast of the Gulf of Rīga and well beyond that. Their language remains in hundreds of place names all over Latvia, possibly even in that of the Latvian capital, but its last native speaker died in 2013. Villages between Ventspils and Kolka were the last Livonian cultural strongholds, lingering well into the 20th century. Mazirbe, home to the **Livonian People's House** (which can be visited in summer), remains at the centre of the effort to revive Livonian culture. In the best news so far, a baby whose mother tongue is Livonian was born in 2020.

Liepāja

PARTY TIME | JEWISH HERITAGE | MILITARY HISTORY

GETTING AROUND

Liepāja's only tram line cuts through the centre connecting it to the outlying bus and train stations. Karosta Prison can be reached by buses 3 and 4 from the centre.

☑ TOP TIP

Factor a musical performance at Lielais Dzintars or a rock concert at one of Fontaine venues into your Liepāja schedule. You are coming to Latvia's capital of music, after all!

Liepāja is a city where you'd want to hum an up-lifting tune while strolling around the harbour and Old Town. It has produced some of the country's best musicians and enjoys an overall reputation for flamboyance and good vibes. Deservedly, it will play the role of the EU's Capital of Culture in 2027. The stunning white-sand beach plays no small part in achieving that effect, but so does the colourful harbour that is the city's prime nightlife spot. For much of its history, Liepāja served as a navy base and the bulk of Latvia's modest navy is still proudly on display. Once populated by imperial Russian and later Soviet navy staff, the haunted district of Karosta is being resurrected as a tourist destination, with a grim prison aptly serving as its flagship sight. Liepāja presides over the southern Kurzeme coast, which features Latvia's top windsurfing spots.

Port of Fun

Ships, music and booze

Liepāja's lively harbour is in fact a canal that connects a lagoon-type lake with the sea. It features a colourful display of cargo ships, fishing boats and warships. The old and stout red-brick warehouses are being gradually converted into hotels, restaurants and bars. The effect is the whole area reinventing itself as the city's main get-together and party spot. The flagship of this newly arrived entertainment flotilla is the **Lielais Dzintars** (Great Amber) concert hall, a top-class venue that complements Liepāja's 'singing city' reputation and beautifies the skyline with amber-like forms and colour. A Danish entrepreneur and musician known as Louie

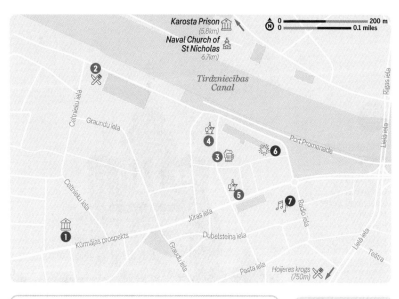

Karosta Prison
(5.8km)

Naval Church of
St Nicholas
(6.7km)

Tirdzniecības
Canal

0   200 m
0   0.1 miles

Caltnieku iela
Graudu iela
Cetnieku iela
Jūras iela
Dubelsteina iela
Kūrmājas prospekts
Graudu iela
Pasta iela
Hoijeres krogs
(750m)
Port Promenade
Rīgas iela
Lielā iela
Radio iela
Lielā iela
Teātra

SIGHTS
1 Liepāja History Museum

EATING
2 Spīķeris 53

DRINKING & NIGHTLIFE
3 Fontaine Gypsy Camp
4 Julianna's Courtyard

5 Valhalla Wine & Coffee

ENTERTAINMENT
6 Fontaine Palace Club
7 Lielais Dzintars

SAND & SEA

Liepāja's Blue Flag **beach** is a fabulous place for a dip. The white sand is over 50m in width and the shore stretches for 8km. In summer you'll find a few beach cafes and water-sports operators. Ancient trees, manicured flower beds, water features, walkways and cycling trails make the 3km-long **Seaside Park** the very definition of an urban oasis. To the east are the once-elegant 19th-century wooden holiday homes.

Festivals large and small are held here all summer long; during the two-day **Summer Sound** festival in August, rock, hip-hop and electronic music reverberate off the dunes near the beach.

Fontaine pioneered the development in the harbour with funky Berlin-esque projects, which these days look a bit like a set of nostalgic images from the 1990s. His entertainment empire is in permanent flux, but **Fontaine Palace Club**, complemented by a hotel and American-themed eateries, is still one of Latvia's prime rock-music venues. Around the corner, **Fontaine Gypsy Camp** is another concert venue-cum-beer garden, but its future was unclear at the time of writing. Set in a beautiful garden next to an artful boutique hotel, **Valhalla Wine & Coffee** is part of the same family. There are a couple of newcomers as well. A converted port building in **Julianna's Courtyard** contains four stylish bars. Further along the waterfront, an old red-brick warehouse now hosts an excellent fish restaurant, **Spīķeris 53**, which is fused with a craft brewery.

Celebrity Inn

Dine in a pub-museum

A *krogs* is a travellers' inn – typically a wooden building with guest rooms and a dining area. They were ubiquitous in the old times and Liepāja still has a few, now converted into restaurants and pubs. But **Hoijeres Kwrogs** is quite special – a carefully restored 17th-century inn that is a museum on the one hand, but also a place where you can eat food cooked

JURIJ KUZNECOV/SHUTTERSTOCK ©

Naval Church of St Nicholas

GOOSEBERRY SPREE

Vendors have touted their wares at Liepāja's **Peter's Market** since the mid-17th century. The market expanded in 1910, when an art nouveau pavilion was constructed adjacent to the square. Today you'll find stalls both inside and out at this bustling complex that sells everything from secondhand clothes and beautiful handicrafts to fresh, locally grown produce and baked goods. In summer, the stalls are awash with sweet cherries, black- and redcurrant, forest blueberries and garden gooseberries, as well as all kinds of wild mushrooms. Also venture into the underground floor, which contains picturesque fish rows. This is a northern European market, so there's no need to haggle, with all prices clearly displayed.

according to old recipes and using ingredients that were common a few centuries ago, but feel exotic now. Built by a Dutch immigrant in 1677, it hosted a burly Russian traveller 20 years later. The man introduced himself as Pyotr Mikhaylov, but in fact it was Russian tsar Peter the Great who was travelling incognito with his Great Embassy to Holland as he started 'cutting a window in Europe', as historians put it later.

Tycoon's Palace
Revisit Liepāja's Jewish heritage

On the way from the harbour to the beach, check out the elegant art nouveau building of the **Liepāja History Museum**, once the home of Jewish industrialist Nissan Katznelson who represented Liepāja in the Russian State Duma and

 WHERE TO STAY IN LIEPĀJA

Boutique Hotel Roze	Promenade Hotel	Fontaine Valhalla Hotel
Stylish and comfortable, this pale-blue wooden villa has spacious rooms, each uniquely decorated. €€	The poshest hotel in Kurzeme occupies an enormous grain warehouse facing the harbour. €€€	Cheap, brightly decorated rooms with shared bathrooms in a cosy wooden building near the harbour. €

helped many Jews move to Palestine (a life-saving feat given that almost everyone who stayed in Liepāja perished in the Holocaust). The museum features a variety of impressive displays, such as an interactive exhibit that brings to life the tough existence of people living in south Kurzeme in the 19th century. Another recalls the six months in 1918 and 1919 when Liepāja was the capital of Latvia as the nation fought for its independence.

Imperial Wreckage in Karosta

Discover Liepāja's military history

If haunted, ghost-ridden places are your thing, Karosta district – located across the canal from central Liepāja – is the place to go. The name translates as 'military port', and it came into being as the Russian empire's Baltic stronghold built in anticipation of WWI. It was used in the same capacity by a succession of political regimes before falling into decay after Latvia regained its independence. But local enthusiasts are painstakingly reinventing it as a tourist attraction.

Karosta's most striking landmark is the massive golden cupola of the magnificent Russian Orthodox **Naval Church of St Nicholas** rising above the drab grey Soviet-era *khruschevka* apartment blocks. Come inside to admire the ornate interior.

Aptly for its spooky image, the beating heart of the district's revival effort is **Karosta Prison**. Not exactly a Gulag camp and originally intended as an infirmary, it was used by all political regimes throughout its history as a detention centre for disobedient sailors. But conditions were torturous enough, as you will be able to attest after a guided tour of the dark prison cells covered in predominantly Russian-language graffiti, a legacy of its former inmates. If after that you still don't feel sufficiently thrilled (or depressed), you have the option of overnighting in one of the cells, with the choice of near-authentic accommodation experience (as well as treatment by the staff) or in the decadent luxury of gentrified premises. There's also a cafeteria designed as a Soviet-era garrison shop, which serves yummy lunch food.

KAROSTA HISTORIC SIGHTS

Karosta Prison doubles as a local **tourist information centre** that can point you to other attractions in the district. Among them, the **Karosta water tower** is now partly open for visitors with antiquated mechanisms on display, along with artists' residences occupying part of the building. An exhibition at **Redāns**, a piece of fortification, covers Liepāja's role in Latvia's struggle for independence, especially to the critical moment in history when, in 1918, the government-controlled territory of the newly independent country shrank to the size of the deck of the warship *Saratov*, which is moored in Liepāja's harbour. A walking route called **Freedom Trail** covers the main sites in Karosta, including its massive coastal fortifications. Inquire at the prison.

WHERE TO EAT IN LIEPĀJA

Spīķeris 53
Imaginative Baltic fish meals and craft beer inside and old warehouse right by the harbour. €€

Pavillion de Roze
Hinkali dumplings, *khachapuri* cheese pastry, *shkmeruli* chicken and other Georgian delicacies in a stylish villa. €€

Pastnieka Māja
This two-level restaurant occupies an old post office and serves traditional Latvian favourites. €€

Beyond
Liepāja

Southern Kurzeme coast is an uninterrupted stretch of picture-perfect dune landscapes, with sleepy old towns in the hinterland.

GETTING AROUND

Both Pāvilosta and Aizpute are served by frequent buses from Liepāja. It is also easy to get to Pāvilosta from Ventspils and to Aizpute from Kuldīga.

The white-sand beaches to the north and south of Liepāja are never too crowded, even though they are popular with holidaying Lithuanians who spill over into Latvia from their (not very long) stretch of the coast. Strong winds and frequent storms may not be too conducive to an ideal beach holiday, but they are a delight for surfers who have made the village of Pāvilosta their capital on the coast. This is a fast-changing, progressive destination with some of the best accommodation options in the country. Inland roads leading to Rīga and Kuldīga pass interesting historical towns such as Aizpute, which are striving to draw visitors with art projects and local booze.

Pāvilosta

SMILTENA/SHUTTERSTOCK ©

Windsurfing, Pāvilosta

Pāvilosta

TIME FROM VENTSPILS: **40 MINS** 🚌

Hit the Baltic surf

The beach town of **Pāvilosta** brings a chilled-out California surfer vibe to the chilly Baltic shores. Summer days are filled with windsurfing, kiteboarding, surfing, and sailing interspersed with beach naps and beers. It's a good place to learn basic surfing skills, with all equipment rental outfits offering beginners' and more advanced courses. Over recent years, Pāvilosta has started to resemble a growing new civilisation, as well-off startup types have been taking over an old fishing village and building *hygge*-rich eco-futuristic beach homes amid traditional wooden cottages. Apart from the cool little **history museum** and an **art residence** that stages an occasional exhibition, there is little else to do here but surf and mingle with other surfers in hipster-ish cafes and bars. It's worth walking to the other side of the harbour to climb a Soviet border-guard **observation tower** for the best views of brave souls conquering the waves behind the pier.

Aizpute

TIME FROM VENTSPILS: **35 MINS** 🚌

Pop art and booze

The prime reason for calling at Aizpute, a drowsy old town halfway between Liepāja and Kuldīga, is the **Art Park** – a garden filled with colourful, weird and ironic pop-art installations by the artist owner Ģirts Brumsons. Although the garden stays open, it's best to arrange a tour guided by the owner. And while you're here, you can also check out the interesting **history museum** and try some local booze. **Aizpute Winery** offers degustations of top-quality fruit wines, especially the one made of rhubarb and blackcurrant. Meanwhile, beer lovers can indulge in their sin at **Aizpute Manor Brewery**.

☑ **TOP TIP**

The no-frills summer-only Miezis un Kompānija is the go-to bar if you want to mingle with the surfer crowd.

BEST PLACES TO STAY IN PĀVILOSTA

Pāvilosta is blessed with some of the best accommodation options in Latvia, at least for a village.

Vēju Paradize
Simple yet nicely designed and distinctly beachy rooms plus a cosy on-site restaurant. €€

Šīfermāja
A wooden house of five beautifully designed apartments named after their former owners. €€

Das Crokodill
A funky outfit decked out in a delightful mishmash of ethnic styles, with a swimming pool. €€

OTTO Hotel & Sun
Pāvilosta's fanciest hotel, tastefully designed in Nordic style and in a prime location. €€€

Daugavpils

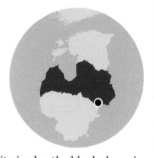

FORTRESS | SPIRES | DRINKING

GETTING AROUND

You can easily manage the centre of Daugavpils, where both the bus and the train stations are located, on foot. For Daugavpils Fortress, take buses 13 or 4 from the main square. Tram 3 brings you close to the fortress, but you'll need to walk to the next roundabout.

Latvia's second-largest city is also the black sheep in the happy Latvian family – once a provincial Russian imperial town, it's overwhelmingly Russian-speaking and chronically suspected of disloyalty. But it has grown much less alienated in recent years, with funds poured into the city making it more attractive for visitors and travellers alike. At the forefront of this change is an old imperial fortress, which has been turned into an impressive art and museum cluster themed on the most famous Daugavpils native, US artist Mark Rothko. Its assumed Russian-ness being quite superficial, Daugavpils has a fascinating multicultural history, in which Jews, Poles and Belarusians played a prominent role alongside Latvians. It is also the largest city in Latgale, a region of many beautiful lakes, ethically mixed population and its own dialect of Latvian, which some tend to regard as a language in its own right.

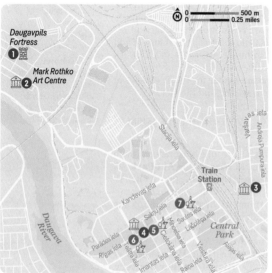

TOP SIGHTS
1 Daugavpils Fortress
2 Mark Rothko Art Centre

SIGHTS
3 Daugavpils Lead Shot Factory
4 Šmakovka Museum

DRINKING & NIGHTLIFE
5 Albrecht Art&Wine
6 Artilērijas Pagrabi
7 D.O.M.

PHOTO/DEOWORLD/SHUTTERSTOCK ©

Daugavpils Fortress

☑ TOP TIP

Watch the chase scene
from a Soviet film that
involves Latvian-made RAF
minibuses racing through
(and flying over) Rīga at
RetroGaraž-D, next to the
real-life protagonists.

WHAT ELSE TO SEE IN DAUGAVPILS FORTRESS

The profiles of newly
opened museums
within Daugavpils
Fortress may seem
random or eccentric,
but it plays into the
citadel's overall charm.

RetroGaraž-D
A massive exhibition
of old vehicles, in a
former arsenal.

Martisona Māja
A tribute to the local
ceramics artist Pēters
Martinson across the
square from the Mark
Rothko Art Centre.

Pie Komendanta
An interesting
collection of
WWI-related photos,
antiques and vehicles.
Call to book a visit.

Birth Control Collection
Everything you've
been afraid to ask –
medical-related retro
paraphernalia with
a special emphasis
on the evolution of
condoms. Call in
advance.

Arsenals of Art
The new life of Daugavpils Fortress

What was designed to project Russia's imperial military might
is now a cultural stronghold that's pulling Daugavpils out
of obscurity. Built on the orders of Tsar Alexander I on the
eve of the Napoleonic Wars, **Daugavpils Fortress** served
as an imperial stronghold during two Polish insurrections
in the 19th century and as a home away from home for tsars
exploring their realm. Although the architecture is rather
utilitarian, you can make out Gothic and Egyptian motifs
in the decor of its four gates – all named after Russian royals. A town within a city where sturdy imperial buildings
rub shoulders with generic Soviet apartment blocks, the fortress is being gradually re-cultivated after decades of near-
abandonment. As a result, it displays a curious and highly
photogenic mixture of carefully restored parts, complete with
imperial eagles and names of Russian royals on gate towers,
as well as the areas that still feel somewhat forlorn.

 WHERE TO EAT AND STAY IN DAUGAVPILS

SkovoroTka
A cosy place serving tasty
international foods. Try the
borscht and *lyulya* kebab. €€

Odesa Mama
Fried aubergines, *forshmak*
(salted herring), *barabulka* fish
– classic Odesa staples and
Black Sea coast vibes. €€

Biplan City
Right by the bus station,
with comfy and classically
designed rooms along with
passable breakfasts. €€

All Christian confessions in Daugavpils famously cling together in a show of ecumenical unity in the spot known as Church Hill, bisected by busy 18 Novembra iela about 2km east of the centre. Here is the full list.

Martin Luther Cathedral
The red-brick neo-Gothic abode of the Lutherans.

Holy Virgin Cathedral
The shiny pure-white temple of the Catholics.

Cathedral of Princes Boris & Gleb
White and sky-blue, with many golden domes; unmistakably Russian Orthodox.

Novostroyensky Church of Resurrection, Holy Virgin & St Nikola
Russian Old Believers populate this surprising piece of gold-domed art nouveau.

Like alien species, cultural institutions started re-populating abandoned arsenals and barracks during the last decade. The flagship of this development is the excellent **Mark Rothko Art Centre**. The famous artist and Daugavpils native left his home town for the USA at the age of nine and thus escaped the fate of local Jews who were the city's largest community at the time, but were exterminated in the Holocaust. At the heart of this contemporary art gallery is a small selection of Rothko's own works, coming to Daugavpils from the USA on rotation. The rest of the vast building is occupied by high-profile temporary exhibitions of Latvian and international artists.

Pouring Bullets
Retro war technology

As you will learn at the **Daugavpils Lead Shot Factory**, a tall brick tower built in 1886, creating ammunition used to require gravity. Molten lead was poured from the top of the tower, and by the time the drops reached the bottom, they solidified into perfectly round balls, ready to be used in guns. You won't see the actual process, but they will turn on century-old machines for you and let you climb the tower from which you can observe the city's bucolic environs. Check for English-language tour times. It's on a hill about 2km east of the centre.

Cocktails & Moonshine
Drinking dens

For all its reputation of Soviet-flavoured obscurity, Daugavpils now has a surprising lovely bar scene, with a few places opening in recent years. It was pioneered by **Artilērijas Pagrabi**, an easygoing subterranean place that sees itself as something of a Latvian cultural bastion in the east, its fire power generated by great local beer and regular live gigs featuring (mostly rock) bands from Latvia and lands beyond the frontier. The caveat is the owner's nationalist politics, which affects the service (no Russian in the bar), so make your own choices. Also very central, **Albrecht Art&Wine** is a new bohemian bar specialising in Portuguese wines. Another newcomer, **D.O.M.** bar is the place to go for cocktails. A folksier daytime drinking option is **Šmakovka Museum**, dedicated to the popular Latgalian moonshine. It goes through its history, demonstrates the distillery process and, of course, offers degustations.

Beyond
Daugavpils

Latvia's eastern frontier is the land of many mysterious lakes, dark forests and an exquisite multicultural mix.

Latgale region is very rural, with pristine mossy woods and flower-covered meadows, and is bisected by the mighty Daugava River. Scenic lakes are everywhere, often a few of them within walking distance from where you are. It's a border region with a fluid identity. More Russian is spoken here than elsewhere in rural Latvia, but many of the speakers have a remarkably rich multiethnic background. Latgale is the country's Catholic stronghold, with its holiest shrine located in Aglona. But it is also strongly influenced by Russian Old Believers who arrived here four centuries ago, fleeing the tsar. Jewish memories permeate the air in the absence of their protagonists who perished in the Holocaust.

Places

GETTING AROUND

Unless you are travelling by car, which will make your logistics much simpler, you'll be reliant on bus services that connect Daugavpils and Rēzekne with every place that matters, although frequency varies.

The international EuroVelo 11 cycling route runs from Daugavpils to Krāslava and onwards to Aglona, Dagda, Ludza and Rēzekne.

☑ TOP TIP

Ask to get the tourist information offices in Daugavpils or Rēzekne to book you an overnight stay at a farm, possibly with a steam-bath (*pirts*) experience.

Aglona Basilica (p226)

ANDREJS MARCENKO/SHUTTERSTOCK ©

225

Daugavas Loki

TIME FROM DAUGAVPILS: **30 MINS**

Journey along the 'river of destiny'

Latvia's 'river of destiny', the Daugava, originates in the Valdai Hills in Russia (next to the sources of the Volga and the Dnieper) and flows through Belarus before entering Latvia near Krāslava. It meanders between bucolic hills on the way to Daugavpils, forming gentle bends that are known as **Daugavas loki**. Secondary roads that run along the river are great for cycling. The **Vasargelišku observation tower**, 20km from Daugavpils, is possibly the best place from which to observe them. Further along the road, the village of **Slutišķi** stands on a beautiful stretch of the river; it was populated by Russian Old Believers who fled the tsar in the 17th century. One of the scattered farms has been transformed into the **Slutišķi Old Believers' Farmstead**. It's an introduction to traditional life dating back to the 1700s. Outside the fir-log building are exhibits about local farming and good signboards detailing local life. Nearby is a picnic area as well as riverside trails.

LORD'S TOTEMS

Christ the King Mount, a weird and captivating site just outside Aglona, is a hill dotted with dozens of ornately carved totem-like wooden poles. Seemingly Christian-themed, but looking profoundly primeval and pagan, they hark back to images of old Baltic gods. The church is not necessarily happy about this neighbour: its creator, woodcarver Ēriks Delpers, has been accused of heresy and sectarianism. A Soviet military pilot in his previous life, he has indeed evolved into a self-styled religious guru, but his artwork and his game of imagination don't fail to impress. One of the most provocative attractions in Latvia, it's a strange and meditative place worth the 3km hike from Aglona.

Krāslava

TIME FROM DAUGAVPILS: **45 MINS**

Meet a multiethnic community

Krāslava is a picturesque town of wooden houses set amid the green hills embracing the Daugava River. A former domain of the Polish Plater family, it has always been an intriguing multicultural melting pot. Its coat of arms displays five oars symbolising five local communities: Poles, Latvians, Belarusians, Russians and Jews. The latter used to be the largest group, but virtually all of them perished in the Holocaust. The story of the cohabitation is narrated in the small and retro **history museum** in the grounds of Platers' manor house overlooking the town from its highest hill. The imposing **Plater Palace**, sadly, stands abandoned.

Aglona

TIME FROM DAUGAVPILS: **45 MINS**

Latvia's Catholic pilgrimage

Even non-believers will find the setting of Latvia's version of Santiago de Compostela heavenly enough to spend some time here. Teeny Aglona sits on an isthmus between two large placid lakes, with the most beautiful spot taken by the twin-towered whitewashed **Aglona Basilica** – the holiest of all Catholic shrines in Latvia. More than 300 years ago, a group of wandering Dominican monks discovered a healing source hidden among a thicket of spruce trees ('Aglona' means 'spruce tree' in an old dialect). This turned it into a place of

 WHERE TO STAY AND EAT AROUND AGLONA

Terase Egle	**A, Kas Tja Byus?**	**Upenīte**
Perfect gourmet burgers and craft beer served on a rustic terrace. €	Gingerbread house refurbished as a fine boutique apartment, with an antiques collection in the shed. €	Lakeside guesthouse combined with a culinary adventure themed on Latgalian traditions and blackcurrants. €

POTOTSKIY/SHUTTERSTOCK ©

JEWS LIVED HERE...

What little remains of old Rēzekne can be observed at **Latgales iela**, the city's oldest street lined with dozens of charming brick facades constructed by wealthy Jewish merchants over a hundred years ago. The Jews used to make up a third of the town's population, but almost all of them perished in the Holocaust. Glimpses of old Jewish life are on display inside the **Green Synagogue**, built in 1845. Restored inside and out to its past wooden glory, it features the stolid wooden architecture popular in Latgale, as well as displays about local Jewish culture through the centuries. In a sad irony, it is open on Saturday (as well as Wednesday) but closed on Sunday.

Plater Palace

pilgrimage, but the beautiful edifice you see today was only created for Pope John Paul II's visit in 1993 to bestow the title of Basilica Minoris (Small Basilica) upon the holy grounds. On 15 August, thousands of Catholic pilgrims from all over Eastern Europe flock here to celebrate Assumption Day. At other times, Aglona is a quiet village notable – apart from its stunning lakeside setting – for its particularly lush vegetable and flower gardens.

Learn about the history and traditions surrounding traditional Latgalian dark rye bread, a local staple, and try your hand at milling grain and baking at the **Bread Museum** in Aglona. Little English is spoken, so call ahead to arrange a complimentary translator. Even if you don't have time for the one-hour presentation, be sure to buy a fresher-than-fresh loaf of gorgeous bread still warm from the large oven. Peek through the window into the kitchen to watch the bakers hard at work.

 WHERE TO STAY AROUND KRĀSLAVA

Dridži
Wooden cottages, volleyball nets and rafts on Lake Dridži, 25km north of Krāslava. €

Daugavas Loki
Tidy bungalows on the riverbank near Slutiški village, with boat rentals and a sauna. €

Klajumi Stables
Adorable gingerbread houses in a beautiful rural setting, attached to a horse-riding outfit. €

SEA OF LATGALE

Lying just south Rēzekne and surrounded by reed thickets and Russian Old Believers' villages is **Lake Rāzna**, Latvia's second-largest lake. The area was proclaimed a national park in 2007, but there's still no visitors centre or hiking trails, although there's a designated cycling route encircling the lake. The best thing you can do here is to join Captain Andris Strutskis for a lake voyage on his ocean-going sailing boat *Sea Esta*. It cost €200 for two hours for a group, so it makes sense to inquire in advance about the possibility of sharing. The business, branded as **Buru Guru**, also includes a guesthouse with sauna on the shore at Čornaja village. Check buruguru.lv for details.

DENISS IVENKOVS/SHUTTERSTOCK ©

Rēzekne

Rēzekne

TIME FROM DAUGAVPILS: 1¼ HRS

River walks and concerts

Latgale's second-largest city, Rēzekne furtively pokes its head up from a muddle of derelict factories and generic block housing. The town took a heavy beating during WWII, when most of its historic buildings were pulverised by artillery fire. More recently, it has been showing signs of gradual gentrification and it's worth a stop for a look around and a good meal. Frequent trains and buses also make it a convenient jumping-off point for exploring the quiet lakeland further south. A jaunt around town will be quick.

In the middle of the central roundabout stands **Māra**, a statue twice destroyed by the Soviet authorities in the 1940s and only re-erected in 1992. Its inscription 'Vienoti Latvijai' means 'United Latvia'. Nearby, the **Latgalian Museum of Cultural Heritage** displays a somewhat chaotic history and crafts collection, with an emphasis on locally made

WHERE TO EAT AND DRINK IN RĒZEKNE

Ausmeņa Kebabs
Turkish-styled kebab meets Latgalian nationalism. Water it down with a shot of *šmakovka* (Latgalian moonshine). €

IGGI
Classical Latvian *karbonāde* steaks, gourmet burgers and craft beer. €€

Pub Art Salon Mõls
This little rustic-style place, attached to a gallery, serves meaty, calorie-rich Latgalian fare. €

dark-coloured ceramics. Perhaps the most pleasant of Rēzekne experiences is walking along the newly constructed **riverside promenade**, which begins by the unimpressive **Rēzekne castle ruins** and passes quaint cottages on the way to the city's stadium. Another nicely re-cultivated area in the centre is **Lake Kovšu**; come here for a swim on a hot day. The pride of Rēzekne, **Gors** concert hall is one of the beautifully designed modern music venues that have popped up around the country in recent years. If you are overnighting, definitely check out the schedule.

Ludza

TIME FROM DAUGAVPILS: 1½ HR

Scenic ruins and Jewish memories

The lake views revealed through the gaping holes in the walls of **Livonian castle ruins**, perched on a grassy bluff next the soaring spires of the double-headed Catholic church, is the single most important reason to visit Ludza. The town was founded in 1177, making it the oldest in Latvia. Sitting at the junction of two lakes near the Russian border, Ludza feels like a frontier post. It has a modest **history museum** in the manor house of the Russian Napoleonic Wars hero Yakov Kulnev. The collection of rural wooden buildings brought into the grounds from all over the region is worth greater attention than the exhibition inside. Elsewhere in town, the recently restored **Ludza wooden synagogue** has a very limited exhibition but visitors get to see a fantastic 10-minute silent film by documentary director Herz Frank, who was born into a Jewish family in Ludza.

Lake Lubāns

TIME FROM DAUGAVPILS: 1¾ HR

Lakeside water sports

Latvia's largest lake, **Lubāns**, is very shallow, its shores covered in reeds and encircled by a fir-tree forest so dark and wild you could shoot films about Siberia here. Around 180 species of birds, including swans and eagles, nest here and there are several watchtowers in the area for spotting them. A way to experience the lake is to stay at **Baka Water Tourism Centre**. The striking three-storey building with a lighthouse motif anchors a range of activities that include stand-up paddleboarding, kayaks, waterskiing and more, or you can rent a bike and try the new waterside cycling route. It's a good overnight option if you are travelling from Latgale to Alūksne in northern Vidzeme.

BENDS OF DESTINY

The bucolic hamlet of Slutišķi served as an unlikely catalyst of Latvia's Third Atmoda (National Awakening). In the 1980s, the Soviet government decided to build a hydropower station, flooding Daugavas loki. But it was already the time of Gorbachev's *perestroika* reforms, so disagreement was tolerated. Journalist Dainis Ivans wrote a newspaper article criticising the project, using Slutišķi village as an example of historical heritage and natural beauty that would be lost. His article triggered a movement that encompassed many different causes until it crystallised around the cause of independence. This is how Dainis Ivans became the leader of Latvian Popular Front, which spearheaded the restoration of Latvia's independence in 1991.

KARLIS DAMBRANS/SHUTTERSTOCK ©

Arriving

With the exception of some people (mostly locals) arriving by ferries from Germany and Sweden to Liepāja awnd Ventspils, the vast majority of visitors enter Latvia either via Rīga International Airport or by bus from Estonia and Lithuania. Very few international travellers cross the border with Russia and Belarus today due to the war in Ukraine. A regular train service between Rīga and Vilnius launched in December 2023.

By Air
Rīga International Airport is a smooth operation. There is a cash machine and car rentals in the arrivals hall. Taxis await at the entrance, but it's better to use the Bolt app to avoid meter scams.

By Bus
Buses from Tallinn, Vilnius and Kaunas arrive at Rīga International Bus Station located in the heart of the city. Old Town is a short walk away. Main central streets can be reached by buses 3 and 21.

Getting Around

Latvia is very easy to get around, with bus services providing the bulk of public transport. The railway network is useful but limited to specific destinations. Taxi trips for a couple of dozen kilometres in the countryside won't blow your budget. The country is also fairly well set up for cycling.

GABRIELE DESSI/SHUTTERSTOCK ©

BUS
The bus network in the countryside is generally organised in such a way that you mostly find yourself within reasonable walking distance from the nearest bus stop. Check schedules and fares at 1188.lv, or install the Mobilly app.

TAXI
Taxi rides cost around €0.9/per kilometre during daytime, which makes them a reasonably convenient way for travelling to destinations 20km to 30km away, like the beaches near Rīga or Liepāja. Bolt is the most ubiquitous app service.

TRAIN
Train services are particularly useful for Jūrmala and the northern beaches all the way to the end of Saulkrasti. Other lines connect Rīga to destinations in the Gauja National Park as well as Latgale. There are also infrequent trains to Liepāja.

BICYCLE & WALKING
Latvia is criss-crossed by bicycle and hiking routes, which often overlap. It is also compact enough to be explored on foot, with the Latvian sections of the Baltic Coastal Trail (Jūrtaka) and Forest Trail (Mežtaka) best suited for it.

CAR & RIDESHARE
Car rental services are available at the airport and in the centre, but most locals use cheap and efficient rideshare services, which include Bolt and CityBee. The caveat is that there can be issues registering with a non-Latvian licencce.

DRIVING ESSENTIALS

Drive on the right side

 0.2 0.5

Blood alcohol level: 0.2% for drivers with under two years' experience, 0.5% for others.

All vehicle occupants must wear a seatbelt.

Lithuania

UNSPOILED NATURE MEETS MILLENNIAL HISTORY

Wandering coastal dunes, endless lake-dotted forests, rolling countryside, remarkable woodcarvings and vibrant cities: welcome to the most creative country in the Baltics.

A sliver of land flanked by pine forest and covered with giant sand dunes jutting into the Baltic Sea, the largest of the three Baltic states is also the most beguiling. Its ancient forests teem with its wildlife, hundreds of lakes and a coastline strung with white-sand beaches are irresistibly appealing to fresh-air fiends, while the tranquil country roads bisecting the rolling countryside, with its timeless villages and storks' nests, provide ideal terrain for touring cyclists and unhurried road-trippers.

Though Europe's last country to be Christianised has long traded paganism for Catholicism, pagan-style wooden grave markers dot its cemeteries, while other traces of its pagan past shine through in Lithuania's age-old craft of woodcarving and folk-metal mu-

sic. More agrarian than its neighbours, Lithuania is also more homogeneous, and became even more so when the majority of its Jewish population was wiped out during the Holocaust.

The multicultural exceptions, its two main cities are distinct in character: Vilnius beckons with its baroque finery, cobbled streets and multitude of churches, while creative Kaunas bristles with gorgeous interwar architecture and pays homage to basketball – the nation's passion. Lithuania's charms are many and varied: visit a nuclear power plant, explore genteel country manors, dine on exceptional seasonal cuisine and – above all – immerse yourself in the unspoiled nature of this land, to which Lithuania's national identity is so deeply tied.

LUKAS JONAITIS/SHUTTERSTOCK ©

THE MAIN AREAS

Left: Lake Plateliai (p302); Above: Vilnius (p238)

Šiauliai	**Aukštaitija National Park**	**Druskininkai**
Quirky museums and place of pilgrimage.	Land of lakes and forests.	Sedate spa town, Soviet sculpture park.
p295	p304	p312

233

Find Your Way

Lithuania is compact and easy to navigate using the network of comfortable buses and trains. Cars are only useful for reaching remoter countryside attractions. The country's flatness encourages cycling, while seasonal boats connect Curonian Lagoon villages.

Šiauliai, p295

Quirky museums and an appealing pedestrian drag make this industrial city worth exploring, but its biggest draw is the eerie pilgrimage site, the Hill of Crosses.

Curonian Spit, p278

Hiking up giant sand dunes, cycling along forest trails and feasting on smoked fish in fishing villages is all part of the appeal of this unique sliver of land.

Kaunas, p260

Lithuania's second city beckons with its castle and quirky museums of its handsome Old and New Towns, a lively craft-beer scene and a scenic riverside location.

Map labels: Zabar, Mažeikiai, Naujoji Akmenė, Jor, Skuodas, Seda, Salantai, Lake Plateliai, Telšiai, Kuršenai, Gr, Salantai, Palanga, Plungė, Šiauliai, Kretinga, Klaipėda, Rietavas, Varniai, Rad, Smiltynė, Laukuva, Lake Lūkstas, Kelmė, Priekule, Kvėdarna, Juodkrantė, Nemunas Delta, Sveksna, Šilalė, Kryžkalnis, Curonian Spit, Ventė, Šilutė, Skaudvilė, Rasei, Nida, Tauragė, Baltic Sea, Nemunas, Erzvilkas, Simkaiciai, Jurbakas, Nem, Sovetsk, Sakiai, Gulf of Gdańsk, Kaliningrad, RUSSIA (KALININGRAD REGION), Kudirkos Naumiestis, Pilviškiai, Vilkaviškis, Kybartai, Marijampo, Laz, POLAND

CAR

Lithuania has good-quality roads, but driving isn't necessary apart from visiting remote countryside destinations. Parking in labyrinthine Old Towns is tricky. Besides regular car-rental companies, in major cities Bolt and Spark offer rentals by the minute/hour. Winter tyres are compulsory from mid-November through March.

BUS & TRAIN

An extensive bus network links all major cities and smaller towns, with limited services to remoter villages. Buy tickets using the Autobusų Bilietai website or app. Modern double-decker trains (ltglink.lt) are cheaper than buses and useful for travel between Vilnius and Kaunas or Vilnius and Klaipėda.

BICYCLE, E-SCOOTER & HIKING

Lithuania's flat terrain is ideal for cycling. Major cities and Curonian Spit villages offer bicycle hire. Ferries transport bicycles for free; many buses have bike racks. Bolt e-scooters are found in all popular destinations. Hike between villages along the Baltic Coastal Trail and Forest Trail.

Aukštaitija National Park, p304

Canoeing and paddleboarding on myriad lakes, hiking or cycling through endless pine forest and visiting timeless villages are all on the menu here.

Vilnius, p238

Lithuania's historic capital comprises a cobbled Old Town, a breakaway artists' mini-republic, a converted prison, superb museums and countless bars, restaurants and cafes.

Druskininkai, p312

A tranquil pace of life, medicinal waters that heal all that ails you and a Soviet sculpture park draw visitors to this genteel spa town.

Plan Your Time

Hit Vilnius for sure, spare a couple of days for Kaunas, and spend several days hiking and biking the Curonian Spit and Aukštaitija National Park. Alternatively, explore the traditional villages around Druskininkai and the Baltic beaches around Palanga.

ASTA SABONYTE/SHUTTERSTOCK ©

Parnidis Dune (p281)

If You Only Do One Thing

● Focus your energy on **Vilnius** (p238), and allow at least a day to wander its cobbled **Old Town** (p238), summit **Gediminas Hill** (p241) and visit the **Museum of Occupations and Freedom Fights** (p244) to learn of Lithuania's sombre WWII history. For contemporary art, hit the **MO Museum** (p251) and the **National Art Gallery** (p251), and for Jewish culture and history, head to the **Samuel Bak Museum** (p249) and the **Holocaust Museum** (p249). Take in Vilnius' quirky side by visiting the breakaway mini-republic of **Užupis** (p246) and **Lukiškės Prison** (p254). Linger in speciality coffee shops and bars, and dine in Lithuania's most innovative restaurants.

Seasonal Highlights

Lithuania is loveliest in summer when days are long. Spring and autumn are good for hiking. Wintry cities can be magic.

FEBRUARY

Samogitia's exuberant, costumed **Shrove Tuesday** celebrations endeavour to chase away the winter darkness.

MARCH

St Casimir's Fair, Lithuania's biggest folk art festival, is held in Vilnius and Kaunas. Snow begins to melt as days lengthen.

JUNE

Midsummer's Eve is celebrated with gusto; days are long and warm, and numerous music and culture fests are held across Lithuania.

Four Days to Travel Around

● Bus it to **Klaipėda** (p289), and take a ferry to the **Curonian Spit** (p278) to cycle its trails, hike up giant sand dunes, sun yourself on white-sand beaches and explore its fishing villages.

● Alternatively, closer to Vilnius, visit **Trakai** (p257) for its island castle, then head to **Aukštaitija National Park** (p304) for a taste of Lithuania's forests and lakes with the help of LitWild.

● In summer, canoe and paddleboard on lakes or cycle between tiny villages.

● In winter, explore the snow-covered forest on skis. Visit **Kaunas** (p260) for its excellent museums, devoted to traditional music, Čiurlionis' art, devils and ethnographic treasures.

If You Have More Time

● On top of Lithuania's highlights, head south to **Druskininkai** (p312) to sample its healing mineral waters and marvel at Soviet statuary at **Grūtas Park** (p314).

● Explore the traditional villages of **Dzūkija** (p277), then proceed to the **Nemunas Delta** (p294) for birdwatching and kitesurfing. Cycle the forest trails and visit the Soviet nuclear bunker in **Žemaitija National Park** (p299).

● Spend a day at the beach resort of **Palanga** (p290) and admire 'Baltic gold' at the **Amber Museum** (p291).

● Pay your respects at Šiauliai's **Hill of Crosses** (p296), then head north to **Biržai** (p301) for a taste of Lithuania's farmhouse-style beer.

JULY
Ideal month for hitting the **beaches** and exploring Aukštaitija's forest trails and lakes. Klaipėda's **Sea Festival** celebrates its nautical heritage.

AUGUST
There's excellent **birding** opportunities in the Nemunas Delta. Lithuania celebrates its pagan roots with an **alternative music fest** near Zarasai.

SEPTEMBER
Autumn colours, cooler temperatures and fewer visitors make it ideal for **hiking** and **cycling** the Curonian Spit or Forest Trail.

DECEMBER
Vilnius and Kaunas are beautiful when snow-covered; their streets come alive with **Christmas markets** and other festive events.

Vilnius

CATHEDRAL | CRYPTS | HOT-AIR BALLOONS

GETTING AROUND

Much of Old Town, is closed to traffic. Hire bikes at CycloCity stations or from Velotakas (velotakas. lt). Use the Bolt app for scooters and the Baltics' version of Uber. Use official taxi companies, making sure the meter is turned on. Trains and minibuses run between the train/ bus station and Vilnius airport (30 minutes). Buy single-trip tickets (€1) from the driver. Getting a Vilniečio kortelė (electronic top-up card) from Rimi or Maxima supermarkets saves you money.

There is a dreamy quality to Vilnius, especially in the pearlescent glow of a long summer evening. Celebrating its 700th birthday in 2023, Lithuania's capital has a marvellously intact Old Town of rare authenticity where locals actually live, its cobbled streets lined with weather-worn period buildings that testify to centuries of turbulent history and burst forth with independent boutiques, restaurants and lively cafes and bars.

Vilnius doesn't hide its scars and imperfections. The former 'Jerusalem of the north' lost 150,000 of its Jewish community in WWII. The baroque, Gothic and Renaissance churches of the city's historic heart sit alongside Holocaust museums, former ghetto remnants, preserved KGB torture chambers, war cemeteries and buildings left derelict by decades of neglect.

Yet optimism perseveres. This compact, walkable city that feels like a big village seems to embrace everyone, from students and fashionistas to pilgrims and denizens of the breakaway artists' republic across the river.

☑ **TOP TIP**

It's easy to explore Vilnius on your own, but you may get more if you join a free Vilnius With Locals (vilniuswithlocals.com) tour, pedal around with VeloVilnius (velovilnius.lt) or opt for an active outing with feelZcity (feelzcity.com).

In the House of God

Lithuania's grandest cathedral and rulers' crypts

Built in the 13th century on the site of a pagan temple to Perkūnas, the Lithuanian thunder god, the columned neoclassical **Cathedral of St Stanislav and St Vladislav** on Cathedral Sq is a national symbol that marks Lithuania's transition from paganism to Catholicism. Look up above the Greek-temple-style portico of six Doric columns at the statues of Sts Helen, Stanislaus and Casimir, symbolising Russia, Poland and Lithuania, respectively. Inside, look for the 16th-century painting of the **Sapieha Madonna**, considered miraculous; the memorial plaque to Lithuania's exceptional military leader, Vytautas the Great, whose grave has never been found; and the intricate tabernacle door of the gold and silver high altar.

TOP SIGHTS
1. Cathedral of St Stanislav and St Vladislav
2. National Museum of Lithuania
3. Palace of the Grand Dukes of Lithuania

SIGHTS
4. Angel of Užupis
5. AP Galerija
6. Centre for Civil Education
7. Choral Synagogue
8. Contemporary Art Centre
9. Galera Gallery
10. Gates of Dawn
11. Gediminas Castle
12. Holocaust Museum
13. Kazys Varnelis Museum
14. Lukiškės Prison 2.0
15. Mermaid of Užupis
16. Mickiewicz Museum
17. MO Museum
18. Museum of Illusions
19. Museum of Occupations and Freedom Fights
20. National Art Gallery
21. Railway Museum
22. Samuel Bak Museum
23. St John's Church
24. Toy Museum
25. Tuskulėnai Manor
26. Užupis Cat
27. Užupis Constitution
28. Vilnius University

SHOPPING
29. Kolekcija

Gediminas Hill

WISH UPON A...STAR?

Not in Vilnius. Rather, a stone tile bearing the word *stebuklas* (miracle). It's a piece of inspirational history, a relic from a momentous, peaceful display of dissent against Soviet occupation that contributed to the Baltics' independence in 1991. On 23 August 1989, 2 million Lithuanians, Latvians and Estonians joined hands, forming the longest unbroken human chain in history, stretching from Tallinn and ending in Vilnius, on this very spot on Cathedral Sq. To make a wish, do a clockwise 360-degree turn on the tile. Unfortunately, superstition forbids us from revealing the location of this elusive-but-lucky spot, meaning you have to search for it yourself. Hint: we did tell you it was on Cathedral Sq...

Step through the magnificent marble portal beneath the coats of arms of the Grand Duchy of Lithuania and the Kingdom of Poland to enter the 17th-century baroque-style **Chapel of St Casimir**, the country's patron saint. This is where the grand dukes would have prayed; its magnificent stucco figures and frescoes of the saint's life are the works of Italian masters. Highlights include St Casimir's silver coffin, believed to cure disease even though he himself died of tuberculosis (spot the silver body parts left by the devout in hopes of having a particular ailment banished), and a wall painting of a three-handed image of the saint.

Inside the **crypt**, accessible by guided tour only, grand dukes, Polish kings and bishops are seeing out eternity, along with the heart of Vladislaus Vasa, while the wall fresco of the **Crucifixion**, dating from the turn of the 15th century, is Lithuania's oldest.

A Stampede Through Lithuania's History
Tour the National Museum of Lithuania

Housed inside the New Arsenal building, the 18th-century weapons storehouse and barracks around the corner from the cathedral, the **National Museum of Lithuania** is the

 WHERE TO STAY IN A HOSTEL

Jimmy Jumps House
Movie nights, pub crawls, tank-driving tours and free waffles on offer at this centrally located party hostel. €

Downtown Forest Hostel
Bright dorms, doubles, staff passionate about Vilnius, a BBQ area and ample camping in Užupis. €

25 Hours Hostel
Arty loft dorms, snug doubles, women-only digs, guest kitchen and a fantastic Gates of Dawn location. €

country's biggest museum and complements a visit to the Palace of the Grand Dukes (p242). It fleshes out Lithuania's rich history by shining a light on the lives of ordinary Lithuanians, rather than the country's rulers, up until 1945.

It's a merry stampede through the country's oldest archaeological finds, including 2nd-millennium-BCE arrowheads, 7th-century grave hauls and a pagan altar; the assortment of Iron Age weapons and tools; ample ethnographic displays with national costumes; floral-decorated furnishings, carved wooden crosses and recreated rural homestead interiors from different corners of the country; and farming tools and other everyday objects from various eras, such as perfume bottles and decorative boxes. Don't miss an executioner's sword, broken in half; Peter the Great's handprint in iron; an elaborately decorated, velvet-lined 18th-century sleigh; items unearthed in a mass grave of Napoleonic soldiers; or the pictorial history of the Grand Duchy, from the vanquishing of Knights of the Sword by pagan Samogitians in the 1236 Battle of the Sun to the partitioning of the Commonwealth between Prussia, Russia and Austria in the 18th century.

Mighty Fortifications & Lofty Views

Ascend to Gediminas Castle remains

The birthplace of the city, 48m-high **Gediminas Hill** stands sentinel over Vilnius, above the junction of the Neris and Vilnia Rivers, its surviving red-brick tower proudly flying the Lithuanian flag that became a symbol of the fight for independence. Its ideal strategic location led to the construction of early settlements and fortified buildings here since Neolithic times. The permanent stone fortification of **Gediminas Castle** that replaced the 11th-century wooden castle was mentioned in the Grand Duke Gediminas' letters in 1323 and rebuilt by Grand Duke Vytautas after a major fire in 1419.

Ascend to the viewing platform overlooking Old Town either by taking the historic **funicular** or via the steps behind the cathedral's southeastern side. It's worth visiting the engaging **museum** inside the tower (the only one left of the original three) for its displays elaborating on past centuries of warfare, medieval weaponry, and the Upper Castle's colourful history as a prison for disobedient nobles from the 16th century onwards, when it lost its defensive significance and its rulers migrated to the Lower Castle. For most visitors, the 360-degree views of Vilnius from the top alone are worth the visit.

VILNIUS' BEST CRAFT-BEER BARS

Alaus Biblioteka
Sip your lambic sour, surrounded by books at this friendly bar with numerous rotating craft beers on tap as well as bottled brews.

Būci Trečias
Split-level, wood-panelled microbrewery-pub serving cheap, sustaining Lithuanian lunches, alongside a dozen original brews including a superlative dark ale.

Špunka
This tiny, charismatic bar does a great line in craft ales from Lithuania and further afield, along with deep-fried beer snacks.

BeerHouse & Craft Kitchen
This labyrinth of medieval cellars stocks 300 globally sourced bottled beers, as well as 20 keg brews from local microbreweries.

 WHERE TO DRINK WINE IN VILNIUS

In Vino
Perch in the back garden and choose from a fantastic range of wines by the glass.

Amy Winehouse
Wines from the Old and New Worlds sit alongside on-tap Prosecco at this bohemian spot.

Somm
Come to this sleek bar and wine shop for tasting sessions and Lithuania's best wine selection.

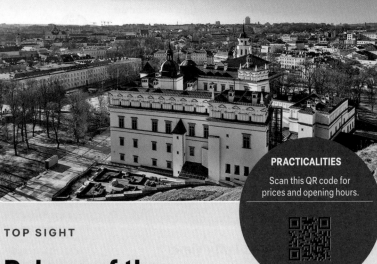

DANGEBUREI/SHUTTERSTOCK ©

PRACTICALITIES

Scan this QR code for
prices and opening hours.

TOP SIGHT

Palace of the
Grand Dukes of Lithuania

If you only see one museum in Vilnius, make it this one. On a site that has
been settled since the 4th century stands the latest in a procession of
fortified palaces of Lithuania's rulers, repeatedly remodelled, destroyed
and rebuilt. The baroque palace, built for the 17th-century grand dukes,
has been faithfully revamped with over 300,000 archaeological finds.

DON'T MISS

Key historic
characters (Route I)

The grand dukes'
treasury (Route II)

Recreated private
quarters of the grand
dukes (Route II)

Historic VR
experience (Route I)

Culinary traditions
(Route III)

Original palace walls
(Route I)

Weaponry (Route III)

History, Archaeology & Architecture (Route I)

Set amid surviving authentic walls from various historical periods, this extremely detailed exhibition deals with two main
themes. One is the construction of the castle, and the palace, and
the sacking of the palace. The other is Lithuania's transformation over the centuries from a pagan entity into the Christianised Duchy of Lithuania, centuries of uneasy coexistence with
Poland (occasionally under its rule), subjugation by tsarist Russia
and the Soviet Union, and bursts of independence between the
two world wars and following the collapse of the Soviet Union.

Notable Personalities

Over its millennium of history, Lithuania has been shaped by
larger-than-life characters. Look out for Mindaugas (1200–
63), Lithuania's only king who established the Lithuanian
state; Grand Duke Gediminas (1275–1341), Vilnius' founder; Vytautas the Great (1350–1430), an extraordinary military commander who defeated the Teutonic Order in the 1410
Battle of Grunwald; Bona Sforza (1494–1557), the queen of

Lithuania and Poland who imported Italian music, architecture and cuisine to Lithuania; Laurynas Gucevicius(1753–98), a Classicist architect responsible for the Cathedral and Town Hall; Emilia Plater(1806–31), Lithuania's Joan of Arc who fought in the 1831 uprising against tsarist Russia; Antanas Smetona (1874–1944), president of independent interwar Lithuania; and Vytautas Landsbergis (1932–), chair of Parliament when it declared Lithuania's independence in 1991.

Reconstructed Historical Interiors (Route II)

Walk through recreated private apartments of Lithuania's grand dukes, which reflect the fashions of their respective ages, from late Gothic and Renaissance to early baroque. Highlights include Sigismund the Old's Renaissance audience hall with a beautiful coffered ceiling, handsome Italian furniture in Sigismund Vasa's private quarters, and surprisingly modestly proportioned four-poster beds in the rulers' bedrooms.

The Grand Dukes' Treasury

Grand dukes brought their treasure hoards along when they travelled, but otherwise kept them in secure locations in Vilnius, Trakai and Hrodno. Though many items were plundered over the years, the remaining bejeweled caskets, goblets, delicate rings, replica crowns and burial insignia are worth your time.

Weaponry, Palace Life & Music (Route III)

Castle life from the Middle Ages onwards was fraught with peril, from infighting over the Lithuanian throne to external threats in the form of Teutonic Knights, Genoese crossbowmen, French soldiers and other foes. Displays bristle with pikes, halberds and two-handed bastard swords, as you learn about different types of armour and spot bullet-firing arbalests. Don't miss the *Battle of Orsha* painting reminiscent of *Where's Wally?* puzzles.

Medieval & Renaissance Culinary Traditions

Feasting was a serious business. In the Middle Ages, the ruler's table would groan under the weight of poultry, wild game, freshwater fish and spices from afar (nutmeg, saffron, and cloves), while a party thrown by Grand Duke Vytautas in 1429 involved 700 barrels of mead! During the Renaissance epoch, the wife of Sigismund the Old, Milanese princess Bona Sforza, introduced the Italian habit of eating more vegetables to the court. The descriptions of the provisions taken by grand dukes on their weeks-long hunting trips are particularly fascinating and involved prodigious amounts of cheese, cow intestines and beer.

Museum Exhibition Centre (Route IV)

Along Route IV, you'll encounter thought-provoking temporary exhibitions, such as Raymondas Paknys' 'Vestiges of Time': photographs of ruined Catholic churches across the former Polish-Lithuanian Commonwealth (present-day Belarus, Ukraine, Poland and Lithuania).

VR EXPERIENCES

The museum's two VR experiences are an entertaining high-tech stampede through the history of the Lower Castle and the Gediminas Tower. In the former, you're standing in the earliest hall, then soaring above the buildings as they change at great speed, with walls coming up or down, and a catastrophic fire. In the latter, you rise through the tower's floors.

TOP TIPS

● Visitors with plenty of time can opt for full admission, accessing the four 'routes' through Lithuanian history and saving €4.50 rather than buying individual tickets.

● If short on time, choose one or two routes that interest you the most. Route I requires the most time.

● The two VR sets (€3 each or €5 for both), available along Route I and Route III, are highly worthwhile. Buy tickets at the main ticket counter before entering either route.

● Visit valdovurumai. lt to check the calendar of special events, from film screenings in the courtyard to orchestra performances.

FAVOURITE VILNIUS HAUNTS

Vilnius local **Nomeda Navickė** shares her favourite places in the city.

Cozy
Its eclectic menu and good service has won it many regulars. It does hands-down the best Caesar salad in Vilnius.

Sparkling Ocean
This is where I go for girls' nights out; instead of house wine, they've got house champagne! It's near the excellent Maurizio's Italian Food pizzeria.

Bubbles Champagneria
If you love bubbly, dress nicely and come to this bar for its many champagnes, sparkling wines and oysters.

Augustin
An excellent spot for lunch if you want to treat yourself; beautifully presented dishes with a focus on vegetables.

PHOTODONATO/SHUTTERSTOCK ©

Hot air balloons, Vilnius

The Long Fight for Freedom

Learn about Lithuania's darker history

Inside the **Museum of Occupations and Freedom Fights** you're met with a blown-up image of human remains in a mass grave to your right, and mug shots of Lithuanian prisoners on the left. The gloves are off.

This former headquarters of the KGB (and before them, the Gestapo, Polish occupiers and tsarist judiciary) showcases a chronological progression of the horrors and privations experienced by Lithuanians, from the Molotov-Ribbentrop pact (1939) between Stalin's Russia and Hitler's Germany that decided Lithuania's fate, through Lithuania's forcible absorption into the USSR, to the country's independence in 1991.

This story is told using a mixture of grainy video footage, photographs, blown-up images on plexiglass and period artefacts. You learn about the decade-long, unequal fight of the 'Forest Brotherhood' (Lithuanian partisans) against the Soviets, their lives in permanent peril from informants; the mass deportations of Lithuanian intelligentsia and their families to the Urals and Siberia in late 1940s in cattle cars, with people plucked from their homes in the middle of the night and many perishing en route; former exiles returning after the 'thaw' of 1956; the constant surveillance of the Lithuanian

WHERE TO GO FOR COCKTAILS

Love Bar
Look for the neon pink heart before sampling concoctions made of seasonal, natural and locally sourced ingredients.

Nomads
Intimate bar with velvet bar stools, globe-roaming theme, and six original cocktails every few weeks.

Who Hit John?
Ponder the question while expert bartenders mix you any cocktail you can think of.

population by the KGB; the imprisonment and torture of dissidents in this very building; and the fight to keep Lithuanian culture alive in spite of repressions.

The use of period objects simultaneously humanises and horrifies: a brutal-looking truncheon, a rosary made of bread, a tiny bag with a pinch of Lithuanian soil inside, a letter written by a forced labour camp inmate on a piece of birch bark.

A descent into the KBG cellars reveals a punishment cell that was once partially filled with icy water, and another with padded walls to muffle the sounds. Messages of despair and defiance from those awaiting death remain etched into one of the walls, while an execution cell, where more than 1000 prisoners were killed between 1944 and 1960, is riddled with bullet holes.

There are contemporary touches: a back room features a direct accusation of Moscow in the genocide of the Ukrainian people, and an exhibit outside combines artwork commemorating Holodomor (the Great Ukrainian Famine of 1932–33) with photographs of a scorched Ukraine, c 2022–23.

Full of Hot Air

Ballooning over Vilnius

You're floating high above the city's rooftops, the dawn silence interrupted only by the occasional 'whoosh' of flame as the pilot fires up the burner of the hot-air balloon while you peer over the rim of the basket at the cityscape that slowly passes beneath you, bisected by the wide brown-grey ribbon of the Neris River. The Gothic spires of centuries-old churches and the dominant red-brick of Old Town compete for your attention with the gleaming skyscrapers north of the river. Your passage through the air is gentle and fluid, with none of the turbulence you encounter in an aeroplane. You barely notice the smooth descent as the city gives way to countryside. After the gentlest of touchdowns in the field, you toast your triumphant return with a glass of champagne.

Oreivystės Centras (ballooning.lt) and **Balloon** (balloon.lt) both offer shared hour-long flights above Vilnius, Trakai (p257) and Kaunas (p260), with dawn and sunset flights frequent between April and October, for groups of up to seven people (from €155 per person), and private flights for those wishing to soar above the Curonian Spit (p278). Book well in advance in summer.

VILNIUS' BEST FESTIVALS

Lithuanian Song & Dance Festival
This enormous festival of Lithuanian song, dance and folklore in July has been running in various forms since 1923.

Kaziukas Crafts Fair
Dating back to the 17th century, this epic festival of craft and culture comes to Old Town on St Casimir's Day (4 March), with stalls dotted about the medieval streets and squares.

Gastronomy Week
A food festival held at the beginning of November, with dozens of participating restaurants wowing diners with specially created dishes.

Gaida
The biggest and most important contemporary and experimental music festival in the Baltics, held in late October.

 WHERE TO GO FOR VEGETARIAN FOOD

Vegafe	**Rosehip Vegan Bistro**	**Pirmas Blynas**
Adhering to Ayurvedic principles (no garlic/onion), Vegafe delivers riotous plates of spring greens and momos. €	Colourful Buddha bowls, tempeh sandwiches, avocado toast and veggie burgers vie for your custom. €	At communal tables, fill your belly with crepes (with fresh berries, garlicky tomatoes, spinach and more). €

Among the Renegades
Step into the artists' republic of Užupis

Crossing the bridge that separates the artists' community of Užupis from central Vilnius on 1 April, show your passport to the border patrols. Appropriately, on April Fools' Day in 1997, this up-and-coming counterculture suburb that sits just outside Old Town's fortified walls declared its independence as a renegade republic, complete with its own constitution and holidays.

From the bridge, look to your left to spot the **Mermaid of Užupis**, gazing upwards from her stony perch and said to attract like-minded souls to Užupis forever. When musicians, woodcarvers, painters and ceramicists began to move here in the late '80s, electricity was scarce, buildings were mostly run-down hovels and sanitation facilities were few. There's still a charmingly dilapidated air to the brightly painted yet crumbling **Galera Gallery** by the river, reached via a mural-covered dead-end street. The main workshop and creative powerhouse of the Užupis Republic, it shows exciting temporary exhibitions by local talent, sells unique Užupis crafts and invites artists from around the world to engage in a dialogue about art.

The riverside path behind Galera takes you through an outdoor art gallery. There's a grand piano and stone cairns on the river, a giant rocking horse and stone sculpture along the path, a tree whimsically decorated with old vinyl, and Tibetan prayer flags strung from branches.

Head east along Užupio gatvė, passing the **Kolekcija** shop on your right with a pair of human-sized angel wings parked on the bench. The sign implores you to 'feel yourself like an angel'. Inside, €5 will buy you a certificate of genuine angelic authenticity. Proceed to the triangular Užupio square and the trumpet-blowing **Angel of Užupis**, the republic's protector. Around the square are several small art galleries and workshops. Two minutes' walk south along Paupio gatvė brings you to the engraved plaques of the tongue-in-cheek **Užupis Constitution** in English, French, Lithuanian and many other languages. It guarantees citizens, among other things, the right to hot water, to be free, to be happy (or unhappy), to love and to take care of a cat.

Back on Užupio gatvė, head further east, past the passageway with **AP Galerija** and Japanese-style teahouse, to the far side of the Užupio square, to meet the **Užupis Cat** on his fence perch and tickle him behind his metal ear for luck.

DISCOUNTED SIGHTSEEING

For travellers intent on visiting plenty of cultural attractions, the **Vilnius Pass** (govilnius. lt; €37/47/56 per 24/48/72 hours) grants free or discounted access to numerous museums and offers reduced rates at some other local businesses, such as restaurants, cafes and bike rental. Figure out which attractions you're interested in, and the website helps you calculate how much money you'll save with a Vilnius Pass. For a few more euros, you can get a card with unlimited rides on public transport; note that Old Town is quite walkable, so consult a map when deciding between the two cards. Download the app and decide on the duration of the Vilnius Pass, or else buy it at the tourist office or through the Vilnius Tourism website.

WHERE TO BUY JEWELLERY

Etelli Modern Amber
Eye-catching contemporary pendants, cufflinks, earrings, necklaces and other bold creations utilising 'Baltic gold'.

Terra Recognita
Striking, unusual, often symbolic jewellery crafted from Baltic stone by artist and designer Saulius Vaitiekūnas.

Amber Museum-Gallery
Peruse Neolithic amber amulets in the museum cellar, then buy modern pieces by leading amber masters.

Eastern Europe's largest Old Town is made for meandering – this walk takes in its highlights.

Begin at **❶ Cathedral Square**, spinning on its magical tile, climbing the bell tower, descending into the catacombs of Vilnius Cathedral, and devoting a couple of hours to a stampede through Lithuania's millennia-long history at the **❷ Grand Dukes' Palace** (p242).

Take the funicular up to **❸ Gediminas Castle** (p241) for 360-degree views of the city, then walk down the hill, grab a coffee at **❹ StrangeLove**, and walk past the red-brick arches of the flamboyant Gothic **❺ St Anne's Church**, which reportedly so charmed Napoleon that he wanted to relocate the church to Paris.

Follow Sv Mykolo gatvė to pedestrianised Pilies gatvė, and take Skapo gatvė to the 16th-century **❻ Vilnius University** (p252), then scale the bell tower at the late-baroque **❼ St John's Church** (p253). Stop by for some

19th-century noblemen's fare at **❽ Mykolo 4**, before proceeding south along Didžioji gatvė to admire the city's oldest baroque house of worship – **❾ St Casimir's Church** – off Rotušes aikštė. Continue south along Aušros Vartų towards the sacred **❿ Gates of Dawn** (p250), home to the 'Vilnius Madonna' that's been attracting pilgrims from all over Europe since the 17th century. Duck through the Gates of Dawn and turn west on Bazilijonų gatvė before heading north along Pylimo gatvė to discover the best of Vilnius' contemporary art at the **⓫ MO Museum** (p251). Afterwards, stop for an afternoon beer at **⓬ Alaus Biblioteka**. Continue east along Trakų gatvė, then cut through onto Stiklių gatvė for a pre-dinner flight of meads at **⓭ Leičiai**. Finish with a contemporary Lithuanian meal at **⓮ Nineteen18**, and find an outdoor terrace off Rotušes aikštė for evening people-watching.

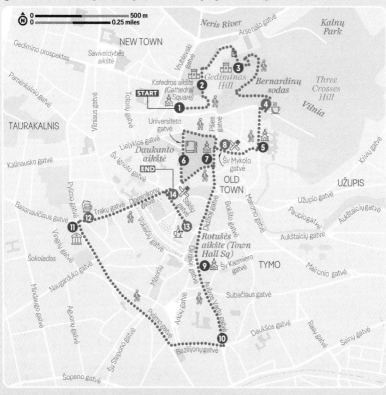

A WALK THROUGH JEWISH VILNIUS

This walk takes you through Vilnius' former Jewish quarter.

Begin on Gaono gatvė, near the square where five streets meet and where glass was sold before WWII. During Nazi occupation, it became the **❶ entrance to the Small Ghetto**; a memorial plaque outside Gaono gatvė 3 recalls the 11,000 Jews who were marched to their death from the ghetto between 6 September and 20 October 1941. Proceed along Žydų gatvė, where the 1572 Great Synagogue and its famous 1902 Strashun Library once stood. The synagogue was damaged in WWII, demolished by Soviet authorities in the 1950s and replaced by a school, with a **❷ small memorial** to mark the spot.

At Žydų gatvė 3, outside the House of Gaon Elijahu Ben Shlomo Zalman, is a **❸ memorial bust** of the spiritual leader who recited the entire Talmud by heart at the age of six. Cross Vokiečių gatvė – Vilnius' pre-war trading centre once lined with Jewish shops – to reach the former site of the Large Ghetto. A **❹ plaque** bearing a detailed map of the ghetto marks its entrance at Rūdininkų gatvė 18. The former **❺ Judenrat** (ghetto administration building) was at Rūdininkų gatvė 8; its courtyard shelters a commemorative plaque to 1200 Jews selected to be sent to Paneriai.

Nearby, at the junction of Mėsinių gatvė and Dysnos gatvė, there's a **❻ monument commemorating Vilnius Ghetto Martyrs and Fighters**. Diagonally across the street, a **❼ sculpture of Tzemach Shabad** (1864–1935) commemorates the doctor and humanist who helped disadvantaged children. A couple of blocks away, Arkliu gatvė 5 is where the **❽ Large Ghetto theatre** hosted concerts and plays directed by Israel Segal as some semblance of normal life in the shadow of genocide.

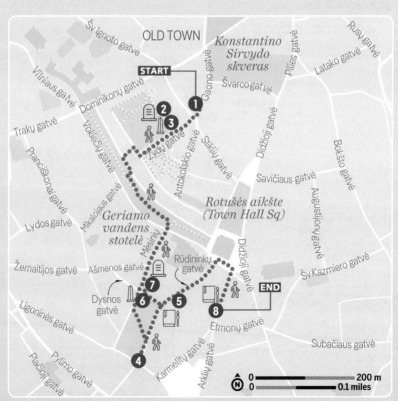

Holocaust Museum

Windows into the Litvak World

Seek out remnants of Jewish culture

On 28 March 1943, residents of the Large Ghetto who visited the art exhibition at the ghetto theatre were awed by the paintings of nine-year-old Samuel Bak, a young artist with extraordinary talent. The sketches and oils capturing ghetto life, as well as the surrealist images from his later repertoire, can be viewed at the **Samuel Bak Museum**. The artist survived the Holocaust and emigrated to Israel after the war; his paintings recall this experience with images of ruins, fruit symbolism and meditations on war, peace and retribution. Temporary exhibitions have included present-day photographs and life stories of Vilnius' Holocaust survivors.

Expect a rawer look at the Holocaust in Lithuania inside the **Holocaust Museum**, aka the 'Green House'. Many of the items on display were donated by survivors and victims' families and seek to tell the unvarnished truth behind the destruction of Lithuania's once-vibrant Jewish community, the Litvaks. Photographs and documents chart the 600-year history of Jews in Lithuania before WWII, while other photographic images and heart-wrenching eyewitness accounts (of life in the ghettos, the pogroms and the death marches)

BEST SHOPS FOR LITHUANIAN CRAFTS

Senųjų Amatų Dirbtuvės
A welcoming shop selling fine examples of a whole range of traditional crafts – weaving, papermaking, bookbinding, leather-working and metalworking.

Black Ceramics Centre
This workshop and retail outlet is dedicated to preserving and teaching the ancient Lithuanian art of black ceramics.

Jonas Bugailiškis
This Lithuanian master carver turns out all manner of weird and beautiful things from his woodwork workshop: sculptures of hands, ornate ironwork crosses and even musical instruments.

Vilniaus Puodžių Cechas
Learn the ancient art of making beautiful and useful items from clay or purchase an array of traditional ceramic items.

WHERE TO BUY LINEN

Lino Kopos
Linen collections by local master Giedrius Šarkauskas, along with accessories made from amber, wood and leather.

Lino Namai
High-quality tablecloths, bed linen and ready-to-wear pieces from Siūlas, the oldest flax mill in the country.

Linen Tales
Exit dressed stylishly in linen shirts, dresses, casual tops and smart trousers. Linen bedding also available.

TRABANTOS/SHUTTERSTOCK ©

Gates of Dawn

THE DEMISE OF VILNIUS' JEWRY

Before WWII, Vilnius was known as the 'Jerusalem of the North'. For centuries, it flourished as a centre for Jewish culture, with 60,000 Litvaks (Lithuanian Jews) making up almost half of the city. When the Germans invaded the Soviet Union in 1941, Vilnius fell within days. The **Small Ghetto** was established north of Vokiečių gatvė and destroyed 46 days later, its 11,000 inhabitants killed between 6 September and 20 October 1941 at Panerai (p259). The **Large Ghetto** was created in September 1941 south of Vokiečių gatvė to hold workers valuable to the German war effort, and liquidated in September 1943, with 26,000 more Jews perishing at Panerai, and 10,000 shipped to concentration camps. Only 6000 Vilnius Jews survived the war.

capture the demise of 90% of the country's 200,000 Jews at the hands of Nazis and their Lithuanian collaborators. Upstairs, watch a short video in a claustrophobic attic hideout that gives you an idea in what conditions Jewish families survived the Nazis. This profoundly disturbing chapter of history is essential to understanding Vilnius.

On Pylimo gatvė 39 stands the **Choral Synagogue**, built in 1903 – Vilnius' sole surviving Jewish temple out of 100 synagogues that served the Jewish community prior to WWII. Somewhat eclectic in its design, with elements of modernist architecture, it serves Vilnius' small congregation, with prayers in the Misnagdim (counter-Hasidic) tradition held daily. Ring the buzzer to attend a service or just to admire its sky-blue, vaulted interior and ornate Torah ark.

Mickiewicz & the Madonna
Pilgrimage site and renowned author

On a Sunday morning, you may find yourself at the **Gates of Dawn** – the only remaining 16th-century portal of the five that were once built into the city walls looking at the focal point above the gate. Beneath an all-seeing eye sits the chapel housing a venerated painting of the Virgin Mary by Flemish artist Martin de Vos, known as the *Madonna of the Gates*

WHERE TO EAT CHEAPLY

Halės Turgus
Traditional produce stalls mingle effortlessly with on-trend cafes at the pungent 1906 food market. €

Etno Dvaras
A temple to potato pancakes, pork roasts, dumplings and *cepelinai* (stuffed parcels of thick potato dough). €

Senoji Kibininė
Munch on *kibinai* (pasties filled with lamb, mushrooms, spinach or cheese), traditional to the Karaite minority. €

of Dawn. Dating from the early 17th century, she is depicted without Christ, with her arms crossed and her eyes half-closed. This Madonna is known to most Poles, thanks to the invocation of the Virgin from Polish poet Adam Mickiewicz's epic poem *Pan Tadeusz;* it is revered equally by the Catholic, Orthodox and Uniate (Greek Catholic) faiths and has evolved into one of Eastern Europe's leading pilgrimage destinations, attracting crowds of the devout from Poland and beyond.

Muse to Polish nationalists in the 19th century, Adam Mickiewicz (1798–1855) grew up near Vilnius and studied at the university (1815–19) before being exiled for anti-Russian activities in 1824. Visit the **Mickiewicz Museum** in Old Town – the apartment where he wrote the poem *Grażyna* – to peruse the displays dedicated to his life in Lithuania, his romantic entanglements and his membership of the secret Philomaths organisation.

For Art's Sake

Tour Vilnius' best art galleries

A pair of giant, hairy hands, one making the peace sign, greets you outside the **MO Museum**, Lithuania's first private art gallery, with around 5000 artworks dating from the 1960s onwards assembled within. All sharp angles, polished glass and white plaster, the ultramodern gallery was designed by visionary Daniel Libeskind, the architect behind Berlin's Jewish Museum. Even if you're a frequent visitor to Vilnius, it's always worth stopping by for the rotating exhibitions, which have included plaster casts of faces by Žilvinas Kempinas and a multi-sensory experience of Vilnius as a living, breathing entity, based on the cult Soviet-era *Vilnius Poker* novel by Ričardas Gavelis.

Nearby, the **Contemporary Art Centre** is the largest centre for contemporary art in the Baltics. Its changing contemporary exhibits include photography, video and installations by Lithuanian artists and visionaries from further afield. The only permanent exhibit consists of 100 or so works by the 1960s Fluxus Movement, with Yoko Ono being its best-known member. Just off Rotuses aikštė, the **Kazys Varnelis Museum** beautifully juxtaposes centuries-old antiques, the artist's personal collection of sculptures, maps and books, including works by Dürer, Goya and Matteo Di Giovanni, and his own three-dimensional paintings and eye-watering abstract patterns. Kazys Varnelis (1917–2010) fled to the USA in the 1940s and earned fame and fortune during his half-century there before returning to Lithuania in 1998.

VILNIUS' BEST BOUTIQUE HOTELS

Apia Hotel
Choose from courtyard, balcony or cobbled-street views in the heart of Old Town at this smart, friendly, 12-room hotel. €€

Dvaras Manor House
Eight atmospheric rooms with antique-style chairs await within easy walking distance of Old Town's sights at this heritage-listed 18th-century manor. €€€

Narutis
Sixteenth-century townhouse with vast beds, original 19th-century frescoes, opulent spa, and breakfast served in a vaulted Gothic cellar. €€€

The Joseph
Original brick walls and heavy wooden beams sit alongside contemporary art in seven individually styled rooms in this 19th-century building. €€

 WHERE TO DINE ON LITHUANIAN CUISINE

Lokys
Game roasts are the main event at this 'hunter's restaurant' inside vaulted 16th-century merchant's cellars. €€

Alinė Leičiai
Come here to sample flights of mead, flavoured with different herbs, plus Lithuanian cheese medleys. €€

Senoji Trobelė
Traditional stews, *cepelinai* and platters of cured meats and cheeses are served at this delightful hillside cottage. €€

Head across the river to the vast **National Art Gallery** to peruse the unparalleled collection of over 46,000 pieces of Lithuanian art from the 20th and 21st centuries. Arranged according to themes such as 'Crisis and rebellion', 'Women artists from interwar Vilnius' and 'At the crossroads of the epochs', it highlights particular styles from different eras, and tells the stories of art collectives such as Ars (1932) that comprised painters and graphic artists and held exhibitions considered particularly controversial at the time.

Take the riverside path east to the **Tuskulėnai Manor** to explore its 'Homo Sovieticus' and 'Hands can create and hands can destroy' art exhibitions inside the manor house and the former stables, the latter exhibition a commentary on the duality of human nature. In 1994, the bodies of over 700 victims executed by the NKVD were discovered and exhumed here, and reburied properly inside the mausoleum; the 'Secrets of Tuskulėnai Manor' exhibition details the horrors committed here.

Hallowed Seat of Learning
Visit Eastern Europe's oldest university

In the heart of Old Town, the red-roofed labyrinth of Gothic, baroque, Renaissance, classicist and eclectic-style buildings joined by 13 courtyards is Eastern Europe's oldest university, founded by Jesuits in 1579 and ran by them for almost 200 years, during which Vilnius became one of Europe's greatest centres of learning. **Vilnius University** (muziejus.vu.lt) survived being shut down by Tsar Nicolas I during the 19th century, as well as being rebranded under Soviet occupation. Its alumni includes poets Adam Mickiewicz and Juliusz Słowacki, writer and historian Simonas Daukantas and Nobel-winning author Czesław Miłosz; today, 20,000 students study at its 12 faculties.

Visit the university either by yourself or by joining a thematic tour (a good option for avoiding getting lost in the maze-like layout and for in-depth overviews of women in academia and the Observatory of Ideas). Orient yourself by using the map at Universiteto gatve 7. Highlights include the **library** with its 180,000 rare manuscripts from the 13th to 16th centuries, accessed from the Library Courtyard; the **White Hall** (Eastern Europe's first observatory), with panoramic views from the observatory tower; **S Daukantas Courtyard**, named after the author of the first history of Lithuania written in Lithuanian, and *The Seasons* frescoes in the adjacent **Philology Centre**; the splendid **Grand Courtyard** with its melange of baroque,

VILNIUS' BEST ASIAN RESTAURANTS

Kamikadze
Couldn't-swing-a-cat Japanese joint serving authentic ramen dishes, maguro don, sashimi and even natto. More extensive evening menu. €€

OISY Izakaya
Book ahead, then have yakitori and takoyaki assortments delivered to your barside seat, along with sake and local craft beverages. €

Blue Lotus
Two distinct cuisines (Thai and Indian) executed with aplomb. Expect fierce curries, stir-fries and plenty of vegetable extravaganzas. €

Sue's Indian Raja
Tandoori dishes, Goan fish curry, chana masala and biryanis are all present and correct at this white-linen-tablecloth joint next to the Indian embassy. €€

 WHERE TO STAY IN A GUESTHOUSE

Bernardinų
Baroque flourishes and original frescoes make each room unique at this B&B within an 18th-century townhouse. €€

Domus Maria
This austere guesthouse inside a 17th-century monastery features spacious rooms, some with Gates of Dawn views. €€

St Casimir Guesthouse
Choose between snug, exposed-brick-wall doubles and lofts, or more sizeable 'Comfort' rooms with desks. €€

Vilnius University

BEST SHOPS FOR LITHUANIAN DESIGN

House of Naïve
Organic, minimalist women's clothing line with a homespun vibe that puts an emphasis on handmade items and sustainable practices.

Lietuviški Drabužiai
Come here for streetwear with bold designs by Lithuania's up-and-coming young designers, statement backpacks and purses, and colourful socks.

Ramunė Piekautaitė
Bolero jackets, smart trousers, skirts, plus jumpsuits, loungewear and all manner of bags and accessories by the eponymous designer.

Moustache Boutique
Design workshop, specialising in hip streetwear for men and women by assorted Lithuanian designers. It has some unusual accessories, too.

classical and neoclassical architecture; the **Lelewel Hall** with its 18th-century rococo chapel arches; and the frescoed **Smuglevicius Hall**, its rare treasures including the first Lithuanian book, *Catechism* (1547) by M Mazvydas.

At the adjacent **St John's Church** (1387), look out for the magnificent great altar, the 18th-century baroque organ, and the fresco in the Chapel of St Stanislaus Kostka depicting university professors alongside Lithuanian and Polish nobles. Take the lift (or walk up 193 steps) to the 45m-high observation deck of the 60m-tall bell tower.

Vilnius Through Young Eyes

Best child-friendly museums

Inside the **Museum of Illusions**, the kids will find themselves dancing on the ceiling, solving riddles, drawing with a light, exploring the intersection between scientific inventions and illusions and participating in all manner of interactive entertainment. We shan't say any more so as not to ruin the surprise!

Less high-tech but equally interactive, the **Toy Museum** is a fun romp through the history of toys and games from the 12th century onwards. Start with the 14th-century whirligig (discovered during one of Vilnius' excavations), try to guess what Stone Age children would have played with, and compare your

 WHERE TO SEE UNUSUAL SCULPTURES

Tony Soprano
The 4.5m-tall mafia don, wearing a dressing gown and boxers, greets passengers at Vilnius' train station.

Frank Zappa
The rock'n'roll legend is immortalised as a pole-topping bronze bust off Kalinausko gatvė.

Sėkmės pilvas (Lucky Belly)
At 16 Gedimino prospektas, you'll find a brass male belly; rub it for good luck.

BEST COFFEE HOUSES IN VILNIUS

StrangeLove
An all-white interior, mellow jazz in the background and delectable cakes all make for excellent accompaniments to the coffee, sustainably sourced and roasted on-site.

Italala
Dangle in a window-side swing while consuming cannoli and superb speciality coffees, roasted in Italy.

Elska Coffee
Artfully mismatched furniture, excellent coffee, menu items such as avocado toast and chia-seed pudding, plus a small library and adjoining gallery of modern art.

Taste Map Coffee Roasters
This smart coffee shop is great for brunch and the favourite haven of the laptop-toting set; it also roasts its own beans.

VIKAU/SHUTTERSTOCK ©

Lukiškės Prison

childhood with that of children 100 years ago, discovering surprising similarities. OIder visitors may experience a wave of nostalgia during the 'Memories of the 20th century' – a parade of mostly Soviet-era dolls, wooden vehicles and retro games, while younger visitors will delight in playing with many of the exhibits.

At the **Railway Museum**, attached to Vilnius' train station, check out some of Lithuania's earliest railway equipment, ride a hand trolley, play with train models, marvel at Soviet-era locomotives and take part in augmented-reality experiences, including a train simulator and railway holograms.

Finally, the highly interactive **Centre for Civil Education** appeals to teenagers and adults alike by walking them through themed rooms that provide a balanced insight into Lithuania's history, and teaches visitors about the principles of a democratic state and how to participate in it. You find yourself contemplating your rights and duties as a citizen, and finding reasons to celebrate cherished freedoms that so many of us take for granted.

Inside a Soviet Prison

Fun penitentiary tour

If you've never visited a Soviet prison before, here's your chance! Surrounded by barbed wire, the pale-sandstone **Lukiškės**

WHERE TO GO FOR FUSION BITES

Telegrafas
Opt for affordable weekday business lunches consisting of smart, beautifully presented meat and fish dishes. €€

Selfish Bistro
Be shellfish and keep your dozen oysters, *vitello tonnato* and *otoro* with wasabi all to yourself. €€

Farmer & the Ocean
Octopus risotto, tuna tartare, grilled fish and French oysters served amid fishing nets within a wood-clad interior. €€

Prison actually predates Soviet times; it was built in 1904 and functioned as a penitentiary until 2019.

With red barrels doubling as benches and tables, the former exercise yard has been turned into an outdoor bar, concert venue and open-air cinema, while parts of the former prison complex are used by 250 musicians and artists. **Lukiškės Prison 2.0** has also appeared in *Stranger Things* (season four).

Entry to the prison's inner depths is by entertaining guided tour only, booked in advance due to high demand (lukiskiukalejimas. lt). Your guide takes you into the processing area with scuffed linoleum, liberally scrawled with Soviet-era graffiti in various languages, with phone numbers and offers of specific 'services' that allowed returning prisoners and first-timers alike to 'make friends' and useful connections. You visit the **prison chapel** – surprisingly egalitarian, since it allowed worship by Jewish, Russian Orthodox, Roman Catholic and prisoners of other faiths. The vaulted, tiled, multi-tiered reception area is particularly striking, with its green stained-glass windows and great acoustics; occasional DJ events take place here now.

As you proceed up the ramp to the second tier of the prison cells and peer into the spartan two-person cells in swamp green, with bunks and rudimentary toilet facilities, the guide explains how first-timers were separated from career criminals. 'This isn't so bad', you may think, peering into a multi-person cell with seemingly adequate ventilation in the building set aside for lifers and long-term sentences, until the guide reminds you that it would've been packed full of deodorant-averse men. Another dingy cell features an ominous promise in Russian: 'You're enjoying the sunshine now, but when I'm out, the only light you'll get is candlelight.' Don't miss **Cell 50**, aka the IKEA showroom of prison cells, and look out for a surprisingly familiar inmate!

Cemeteries of the Fallen
Final resting places of Lithuania's prominent people

Located in a leafy suburb and peppered with brutalist, art nouveau and modernist headstones, **Antakalnis Cemetery** feels like an open-air sculpture gallery. In the centre are the graves of those killed by Soviet special forces on 13 January 1991 beside Vilnius' TV Tower, memorialised by a sculpture of the Madonna. A mass grave holds the remains of Napoleonic soldiers who died of starvation and injuries in Vilnius while retreating from the Russian army. Southeast of the city, the 1801 **Rasos Cemetery** is the final resting place of Lithuania's prominent politicians, artists and academics, as well as the heart of Lithuanian-born Polish general Jósef Piłsudski. Look out for the mausoleums of MK Čiurlionis (p263) and renowned author Jonas Basanavičius.

VILNUS' BEST RESTAURANTS FOR ROMANTICS

Nineteen18
Tasting menus of reimagined Baltic cuisine by chef Matas Paulinas are paired with carefully chosen wines or original nonalcoholic beverages made in-house. €€€

14 Horses
Small organic Lithuanian farms provide the ingredients for nose-to-tail beef with squash, chicken with chanterelles and other smart creations. €€

Amandus
Expect creatively presented, monthly changing menus from the high priest of modern Lithuanian cuisine, Deivydas Praspaliauskas, and cloches trailing dry-ice smoke in a pop-art-adorned basement. €€€

Mykolo 4
This wooden-beamed, brick-walled bistro specialises in seasonal ingredient-forward dishes inspired by 19th-century 'bourgeois' recipes. €€

 WHERE TO STAY IN A DESIGN/LUXURY HOTEL

Artagonist
Individually styled, art-filled rooms, a giant wall mural and glass dome await at this 19th-century merchant house. €€€

Hotel Pacai
Slumber beneath timber beams and amid centuries-old statuary at this restored 17th-century palace. €€€

Stikliai
Luxurious French-style rooms in a 17th-century building; breakfasts use produce from the hotel's organic farm. €€€

Beyond
Vilnius

Places

Europos Parkas p258

Paneriai p259

GETTING AROUND

To get to Kernavė, take a minibus from Vilnius' bus station (one hour). Bus 66 runs from Zalgirio stop on Kalvarijų gatvė in Vilnius (35 minutes) to Europos Parkas. Reach Trakai from Vilnius by train (35 minutes) or bus (30 minutes). Trakai's main attractions are located within a few minutes' walk from one another. Daily trains (some terminating in Trakai) travel between Vilnius and Paneriai (10 minutes). To reach the museum, make a right down Agrastų gatvė and follow the signposted walk for 1km.

☑ **TOP TIP**

Kernavė comes to life during July's International Festival of Experimental Archaeology, while Trakai is liveliest during Summer of Trakai (early June).

A fairy-tale castle, a Holocaust site, a sculpture park at the geographical centre of Europe, and a UNESCO-protected site await outside Vilnius.

A short train ride from the capital, the peaceful forest surrounds of Paneriai belie the past horrors of the site where most of Vilnius' Jews met their untimely end in WWII. Another brief train hop gets you to Trakai, one of Lithuania's loveliest towns and home to the country's tiny Karaite community, along with an imposing castle on an island in Lake Galvė and numerous water-sports outlets. Take the beautiful road through Verkiai Regional Park to Europos Parkas, 21km north of Vilnius, and stroll the forest trails to discover sculptures created by dozens of international artists. Some 39km northwest of the capital, the Kernavė Cultural Reserve testifies to millennia of human settlement in Lithuania.

Trakai Castle

ASTA.SABONYTE/SHUTTERSTOCK ©

Kernavė

Lithuania's vital archaeological site

As you stand on one of the grassy mounds of the sprawling **Kernavė Cultural Reserve**, contemplating the rolling farmland and the slow-flowing Neris River, it dawns on you: you're at the site of Europe's oldest human settlements. The five strategically located hill-fort earthworks of this UNESCO World Heritage Site made it possible to repel invaders, and it's believed that the legendary Mindaugas (responsible for uniting Lithuania) made this now-soporific little town the first capital of the Grand Duchy of Lithuania. You don't have to try hard to imagine the bustling feudal town Kernavė once was, before being sacked by the Teutonic Order: head for the open-air museum with its reconstructed homesteads, animal sheds and artisans' workshops to get a taste of 14th-century life.

For a fun journey through Kernavė's 10,000 years of existence, visit the revamped **Archaeological Museum** nearby, where interactive multilingual displays guide you from prehistoric finds through the Stone Age and Iron Age to the town's medieval heyday at the crossroads between paganism and Christianity. Look out for a horse burial, gilded head decorations, a female buried with symbolic keys, dinars from Marcus Aurelius' rule that underline Kernavė's importance as a mercantile centre trading with the Roman Empire, cowrie shells from the Indian Ocean that indicate the breadth of trade routes, and a pagan swastika symbol.

Trakai

Fairy-tale castle and Karaite culture

An attractive little town 28km away from Vilnius that stretches along a 2km-long peninsula, **Trakai** is lapped at by the waters of the island-studded Lake Galvė and overlooked by Lithuania's most picturesque castle.

Trakai's pivotal role in Lithuania's history goes back many centuries – a fact underscored by the lakeside ruins of the 14th-century **Peninsula Castle** that you'll pass en route to the tip of the peninsula. Take the wooden bridge to **Trakai Castle**, noticing the discrepancy between the vibrant red-brick turrets of the imposing structure that looms in front of you, and the brown stone walls. Grand Duke Gediminas made Trakai his capital in the early 14th century; the castle was inherited by his son Kęstutis when the capital was moved to Vilnius in 1323.

Spread around the castle, the labyrinthine **museum** covers numerous subjects: in the far building, you learn that Trakai Castle was repeatedly sacked and plundered by the Teutonic Knights and other enemies, that it has served variously as a luxurious prison

---

THE KARAITES: TURKIC JEWS?

Lithuania's smallest ethnic minority (numbering 192 in 2023) are the Karaites. Great Duke Vytautas brought 383 Karaite families to Lithuania from Crimea in the late 14th century to serve as castle guards; they later branched out into horse-breeding and agriculture.

The Karaites, Turkic-speaking practitioners of Karaite Judaism (adhering to the Torah but rejecting the authority of rabbis and the Talmud), were initially settled in Trakai; some later migrated to Biržai, Panevėžys and other towns. In 1863, they were granted equal rights as Christians, legally differentiating them from Lithuania's ethnic Jews.

During WWII, the Karaites were spared the fate of Lithuania's Jews when Jewish historians, called upon by Nazis to weigh in on whether the Karaites were Jews, emphasised their Turkic origins.

 WHERE TO EAT AND STAY IN KERNAVĖ

Kernavės Slėnis	**Kerniaus Užeigėlė**	**Gallery Guest Rooms**
Kernavė's only proper restaurant (erratic opening hours) offers huge portions of barbecued ribs and chicken wings. €	Perch at the picnic tables and tuck into chicken *shashlik* and other grilled meats. €€	Art-filled guesthouse with cosy rooms and flower-filled garden that doubles as a steampunk sculpture gallery. €

KERNAVĖ'S MEDIEVAL FESTIVALS

Sleepy Kernavė explodes into medieval action in July, as 20,000 visitors arrive to partake in the **International Festival of Experimental Archaeology**. Clunky name aside, it really brings the ancient mounds to life, as artisans show off Viking age smithing, working with bone, leather and horn, plus ceramics production, and amber processing...A feast is cooked up according to centuries-old recipes, the crowds are serenaded by the Medgrinda folklore ensemble, and you can partake in ancient games and receive instruction in medieval combat in the 'Viking village'.

More medieval/pagan frolics take place during **Rasos** (Midsummer) celebrations on 23 June, when festive pyres burn all night, flower wreaths float down the river, and mead-making and axe-throwing are part of the hands-on fun.

for nobles and a noble residence as its strategic importance declined, and that it was finally restored to its 15th-century form in the 1950s. Proceed through miscellaneous displays of chain mail, medieval weaponry, 19th-century embroidery, glassware, intricately carved gunpowder flasks made of horn and antique pipes.

Your other major port of call should be the **Karaite Ethnographic Museum**, a short way down Trakai's main street. It traces the fascinating history of the Karaites (p257), a Judaic sect and Turkic minority originating in Baghdad. While the nearby **Kenessa** (Karaite prayer house) is no longer open to the public, here you can learn about their beliefs and peruse their traditional dress and everyday artefacts before grabbing some lunch at one of the lakeside restaurants that specialise in Karaite cuisine.

It would be a pity to leave Trakai without taking to **Lake Galvė** in one of the rowing boats, pedalos or stand-up paddleboards available for rent along the lakeshore, capturing the castle from unique angles and perhaps disembarking on some of its 21 islands. Linger overnight to experience Trakai's tranquillity without day-trippers, and rent a bicycle to explore the lakeside trails of **Trakai Historical National Park** that encompasses the town, its five main lakes and ample forest.

Towards the end of the 14th century, Grand Duke Vytautas invited Crimean Tatar Muslims (Lipka Tatars) to settle in pagan Lithuania, providing additional defence against the threat of the Christian Teutonic Knights.

The Lipka Tatars settled around Vilnius, Trakai and Kaunas. While today they number just over 3000, their heritage is still visible in the form of surviving mosques and monuments and their contribution to the country's cuisine (chebureki).

The historic village of **Nemėžis** near Vilnius is home to an attractive wooden mosque dating back to the early 20th century that survived Soviet occupation as a munitions store. Look for one of the most beautiful copies of the Quran near the mihrab, and for the ancient Tatar cemetery out the back.

Europos Parkas

TIME FROM VILNIUS: **35 MINS** 🚌

Discover artworks along forested trails

In a forest some 21km north of Vilnius, a small white pyramid marks the geographical centre of Europe, determined by scientists from the French Institute of Geography in 1989. Two metal acrobats soar above the main approach to **Europos Parkas**, the sculpture park that was the brainchild of Lithuanian sculptor Gintaras Karosas.

Footpaths branch off into the woodlands. Here, a maze made entirely of 3000 old TV sets leads to a shattered, headless statue of Lenin. There, the *Double Negative Pyramid* by Sol LeWitt

WHERE TO STAY IN TRAKAI

Apvalaus Stalo Klubas
Luxurious rooms with statement wallpaper, castle views, and sophisticated cooking on-site. €€

Viva Trakai Resort
Family-friendly hotel with lakefront views from retro-style rooms, basement sauna and terrace restaurant. €€

Panorama Hostel
Budget-friendly en suite rooms in cream tones, guest kitchen, and super-central location near the castle. €

is reflected in a small lake. Deeper in the forest stands a quartet of giant, almost ethereal leaves, and a giant copper head. East of the administration building and restaurant nestles a cluster of moss-covered dinosaur eggs. Nearby sits a giant armchair by Dennis Oppenheim. There are 150 artworks scattered amid the trees, by artists from as far afield as Japan, Mexico, Venezuela and Armenia, all of which can be touched (but not climbed). You can easily spend a day here, wandering the forest paths (bring mosquito repellent in summer). The park has introduced its eponymous app that shows each sculpture on a map, suggests routes according to your interests, distance and amount of time you have, and when you point your smartphone at the barcode by each work of art, you can see its process of creation in a video.

Paneriai
TIME FROM VILNIUS: **10 MINS** 🚗

Lithuania's biggest Holocaust site

Some 11km southwest of Vilnius, a trail leads you into the fragrant pine forest, arriving at a trio of memorials: a Soviet pillar topped with a star, dedicated to 'victims of fascist terror'; a squat trilingual slab that bluntly explains: 'Here, in the Ponary forest, from July 1941 to July 1944, German occupiers and their local collaborators murdered 100,000 people...including 70,000 Jews – men, women and children'; and a recent, monumental monolith with inscriptions in Hebrew and a Star of David.

Nearby, a small **museum** (jmuseum.lt) sheds light on the atrocities that took place at this forested site – chosen because of its distance from major inhabited places. It was here that the majority of Jews from Vilnius (p238) perished, along with Lithuanian and Polish soldiers and partisan fighters, Roma, Soviet prisoners of war, and clergy. Displays describe the practicalities of genocide, and how the killings began with the execution of 348 people on 11 July 1941. Alcohol was supplied to the shooters afterwards, and victims' belongings were sold to buy more vodka. Groups of victims were marched towards pits and gunned down, each successive massacre creating a layer of barely buried bodies. The museum's unflinching presentation includes testimonies from the Burners Brigade, prisoners of war forced to dispose of bodies.

As you follow further trails into the forest, leading to the pits where victims were shot, it's hard to reconcile the peacefulness of the location with it having been a place of such torment.

REHABILITATION OF LIUBAVAS MANOR

The Prussian-built **Liubavas Manor**, nestled in the Zalesa River valley near Europos Parkas, has endured a tumultuous history. Originally owned by Count Albertas Gostautas, a political player in the Grand Duchy of Lithuania, from 1542 onwards it passed through the hands of the royal family and the Golejevskis, Kirsensteinas, Tiskevicius and Slizenis noble families, among others, with the manor becoming a favourite residence for talented people in the arts. Languishing under Soviet occupation and then becoming the property of the Lithuanian government in a fairly derelict state, the manor has been restored to its former splendour at the initiative of Gintaras Karosas. Its superb **Watermill Museum** features the only fully restored early-20th-century mill in the country.

 WHERE TO EAT IN TRAKAI

Kybynlar
Excellent spot for traditional Karaite cuisine, from *kibinai* (Karaite pasties) to lamb and date stew. €

Senoji Kibininė
Antique-bedecked house serving superlative *kibinai* with multiple fillings, plus soups, salads and dumplings. €

Pirosmani
Georgian flavours, from *khinkali* (mutton-filled dumplings) to *khachapuri* (cheesy bread) and vegetable staples. €€

Kaunas

BASKETBALL | MEDICINE | THE NUCLEAR AGE

Old Town and New Town are very walkable and an easy walking distance from each other. Kaunas has numerous cycle lanes; bike rentals with multiple pickup points and Bolt e-scooters are dotted around town. Buses and trolleybuses (kvt. lt) run from 5am to 11pm and are handy for reaching outlying attractions and the airport, 10km north of the city centre; tickets from the driver cost €1. There are direct trains to/ from Vilnius. For Šiauliai and Klaipėda, it's quicker to take a bus; otherwise, change trains in Vilnius. Kaunas has numerous bus services to Birštonas, Druskininkai, Klaipėda, Palanga, Panevėžys, Šiauliai and Vilnius.

Sitting at the confluence of the Nemunas and Neris rivers, Lithuania's second city is no sleepy backwater. Transforming from a Russian garrison into a European city during its two-decade stint as Lithuania's capital in the interwar period, when Poland briefly annexed Vilnius, Kaunas became the centre of anti-Soviet dissent when Lithuania was forcibly incorporated into the USSR. Today, if Vilnius is the intellectual centre of Lithuania, Kaunas has its finger on the commercial pulse. Named European Capital of Culture in 2022 and brimming with innovations in the art and design fields, Kaunas is also the home of basketball, and its clutch of excellent museums rivals Vilnius' own. Kaunas is divided into two: the cobbled Old Town with its medieval castle, handsome square, numerous restaurants and churches; and New Town, bisected by the tree-lined Laisvės alėja and featuring the lion's share of museums, as well as attractive art deco architecture.

Hoopin' Heroes
Lithuania's basketball legacy

'They say that our kids are born with basketballs in their hands', reads the quote from Lithuanian basketball legend Modestas Paulaskas inside the striking **House of Basketball**. As well they might: tiny Lithuania has proved itself to be a nation of giant-killers at European Championships and Olympic Games alike.

Inside the soaring glass-and-chrome building, wrapped around a century-old oak, a 24-minute video inducts you into the history of basketball, pioneered by the likes of Senda Berenson Abott, a 19th-century Jewish Lithuanian emigrant to the USA. Vintage footage of adrenaline-fuelled basketball finals conveys the subjugation of a nation, when Lithuania's appeals to be allowed to compete as a country in its own right in the 1948 Olympics fell on deaf ears, due to its forced incorporation into the USSR. Then there's the story of a nation reborn: 'Who knew that the next time we'd be competing under our own flag!', exclaimed a Lithuanian player on the Soviet team in 1986, followed by footage of the Berlin

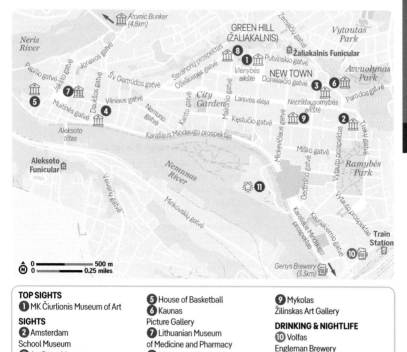

Wall coming down. The video deepens your appreciation of the exhibits, including the rule book from 1922 (the year basketball came to Lithuania), assorted trophies, signed basketballs from Olympic Games' finals, and photos of Lithuanian kids playing outside dilapidated farm buildings, using homemade, tin-bucket basketball hoops. Feeling inspired? Then catch a BC Žalgiris game along with crowds of exuberant local fans at the **Žalgirio Arena**.

Pagan Music Traditions?

Hands-on traditional music museum

A merry din of birch-bark trumpets, whistles and rattles sounds from upstairs at the **Folk Music Instruments Museum**, spread across two restored 16th-century formerly Jewish houses. As you head up the staircase to join other visitors acquainting themselves with traditional musical instruments with considerable mirth and gusto, it plays a *sutartinė* (polyphonic folk song) with every step you take.

With their millennia-old pagan roots and an agricultural lifestyle, Lithuanians have long been able to coax music out of the most unlikely raw materials. Spot a goose-feather pipe and a pig-bone roarer amid the lovingly put-together displays of reed panpipes, wooden flutes, cow-horn trumpets, clay

☑ **TOP TIP**

Kaunas has three private museums worth organising your trip around if you're interested in art deco architecture, Amsterdam School of architecture or Soviet memorabilia in a nuclear bunker. Visits are booked online in advance; the first two museums run English-language tours weekly. Basketball fans: catch a BC Žalgiris game.

KAUNAS' BEST CREATIVE RESTAURANTS

Uoksas
Book ahead for menus crafted from sustainable, seasonal ingredients from the Baltic Sea. Chef Artūras Naidenko never repeats the same dish. €€

Monte Pacis
A world-class wine list, Rokas Vasiliauskas' stellar, nostalgia-evoking dishes and 17th-century baroque splendor come together in one of Lithuania's top restaurants. €€€

Nüman
Paired-back Scandi decor and a succinct menu that's an essay on the finer points of Nordic cuisine. Book ahead. €€

DIA
The globe-spanning menu provides just the right edge of adventurousness; the tuna tataki, beef tartare and mushroom risotto stand out. €€

bird-shaped whistles, and instruments resembling alpine horns. In the room devoted to *kanklės* (zithers), try your hand at these multi-string wooden instruments, or slip on some headphones to hear Lithuanian musicians play 'I Was Riding Through the Pine Wood'. Downstairs, compose your own neo-folk or folk-metal tunes using the interactive DJ Folk podium, then head for the museum's answer to Dance Dance Revolution to learn traditional Lithuanian dance steps.

Mad, Macabre Medicine
Lithuanian pharmacies through the ages

If you had lived in the Middle Ages, your barber would have cut your hair as well as pulled your teeth and performed surgery on you without anaesthesia. Let that sink in as you peruse the displays on barber-surgeons and early medical practices in the subtly lit basement of the 16th-century edifice housing the **Lithuanian Museum of Medicine and Pharmacy**.

There's something matter-of-fact about the trepanned skulls, trepanation equipment, a 1540s print of a barber searing a leg wound, and the saw for limb amputation. That piece of felt next to the personal hygiene tools? Why, that's what happened if you were a Lithuanian peasant and didn't wash or cut your hair for fear of going blind. The healing wines in the vaulted cellar's barrels? That was to improve the quality of your blood.

Upstairs, there's an 1821 industrial pill-making machine alongside two authentic 19th-century apothecary shops with clay jars of herbs and copper distillation equipment. Ask Algis the curator to show you how it works, and look out for the ophthalmology mask in the attic.

Kaunas' Artistic Legacy
Explore the city's top art galleries

One of Lithuania's oldest and grandest galleries, the **MK Čiurlionis Museum of Art** is the place to acquaint yourself with the paintings of Mikalojus Konstantinas Čiurlionis (1875–1911), arguably the country's greatest modernist artist, composer and mystic. Begin with the glassed-in atrium, filled with carved wooden crosses – fine examples of the UNESCO-recognised folk art genre. The Čiurlionis galleries beguile with dreamlike landscapes: a thunderstorm above a sea, shadowy figures snaking their way up a mountain, a giant wave swamping fishing boats. Find yourself inside Čiurlionis' paintings using VR headsets, then explore contemporary sculpture and painting exhibitions, 16th- to 20th-century

 WHERE TO STAY ON A BUDGET

Monk's Bunk
Backpackers trade travel stories at Kaunas' original hostel, with spacious dorms and knowledgeable host. €

Hostel Lux
Great New Town location; spacious, spotless rooms with beds not bunks and shared bathroom facilities. €

Kaunas Archdiocese Guesthouse
Spartan, spacious rooms overlooking Old Town square; the guest kitchen is a boon. €

Lithuanian Museum of Medicine and Pharmacy

European works and Lithuanian landscapes and portraits from the 1900s to 1940s.

Several blocks away, the **Kaunas Picture Gallery** stages thought-provoking temporary exhibitions and has works by 20th-century Lithuanian artists, including a particularly poignant 'Lithuania In Exile' exhibition by émigré artists. Moody 1920s and '30s watercolours depicting bucolic countryside and fishing villages sit alongside such works as a vivid triptych by 20th-century painter Adomas Galdikas, while a 3rd-floor display honours the controversial Kaunas-born founder of the Fluxus movement, George Maciunas (1931–78).

Just south of St Michael's Cathedral, the **Mykolas Žilinskas Art Gallery**, fronted by the unclothed *Man* statue by Petras Mazuras, houses a private art collection particularly strong on European art from the 17th to 20th centuries, including Flemish tapestries, Lithuania's only Rubens (that might not, in fact, be a Rubens), alongside Dutch, Chinese and Japanese porcelain and Egyptian antiquities.

BEST CAFES IN KAUNAS

Green Café
Popular Laisvės alėja hangout, bedecked with coffee-related art and serving brews that span the globe, from Rwanda to Jamaica via Columbia.

Habits
Locals queue for fresh pastries at this popular brunch spot with excellent coffee, just off Laisvės alėja. Another branch is just north of St Michael's Cathedral.

Kavalierius
Friendly baristas, speciality coffees from around the world, roasted in Lithuania, expertly brewed espressos, flat whites and sticky buns await at this laptop-friendly cafe.

New York Café
People-watch from the two tiny tables outside this family-run, thimble-sized cafe that brews a variety of speciality coffees.

WHERE TO STAY IN A HOTEL

Moxy
Instagrammable bar and lounge, and sleek, minimalist rooms await at this trendy New Town spot. €€

Hotel Hof
Super-central yet quiet New Town location, helpful staff, business-style rooms and apartments with balconies. €€

Daugirdas Hotel
At this Old Town boutique hotel, 16th-century stonework and timber beams meet heated floors and hot tubs. €€

KAUNAS' BEST CULTURAL VENUES

Žalgirio Arena
Come to this 17,500-capacity arena for BC Žalgiris basketball games and major concerts by international performers.

Nemuno 7
This converted dredger on the Nemunas River is a May to September venue for concerts, artist residencies and exhibitions.

Kaunas Philarmonic
Housed in the former Palace of Justice, the city's main concert hall for classical music hosts Lithuanian and international talent.

Kaunas State Drama Theatre
One of the oldest dramatic venues in Lithuania stages classic drama productions and cutting-edge new material, some with English surtitles.

Kaunas State Musical Theatre
This handsome late-19th-century building hosts opera, operetta and other musical theatre from September to June.

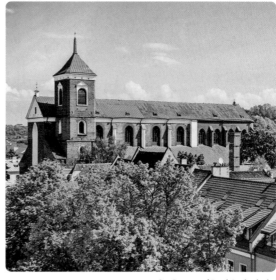

Sts Peter and Paul Cathedral

In the Shadow of Nuclear War
Nuclear-war-themed collection of Sovietica

Enter the former 1960s factory on the western outskirts of Kaunas that once produced harmonicas and torches, and you find yourself surrounded by busts of Lenin, communist banners, pre-WWII musical instruments, 1950s-style carbonated water, *kvas,* and Troinoy eau de cologne dispensers from the Soviet era. Your guide ushers you down into the **Atomic Bunker**, designed to protect factory workers from radiation in case of nuclear war, past graphic Russian-language posters depicting the effects of a nuclear blast, and you reach a vast, somewhat musty underground space with 7000 objects divided roughly into four thematic sections.

This private collection is a labour of love, and light-hearted moments during the tour (horsing around with gas masks, posing in a KGB officer's hat, handling an AK-47, cringing at the sight of a pedal-operated drill in a recreated Soviet dental surgery) are interspersed with themes of utmost seriousness.

You walk through pre-WWII Lithuania, with its vintage chocolate, coffee, cigarettes, Singer sewing machines, and a cigar-wrapping machine. Everyday objects (household tools, meat grinders) sit alongside Judaica: silver goblets marked with the Star of

WHERE TO EAT ON A BUDGET

Baking Mad
Burger joint with a *Breaking Bad* theme, mannequin in a hazard suit and excellent beef patties. €

A Andriukaitienė Firmos Valgykla
Canteen on Laisvės alėja with Soviet-era decor and helpings of Lithuanian standards. €

Peledinė
Pulled pork, chicken wings, sticky ribs and burgers clamour for your attention at this wallet-friendly gastropub. €

Start at the historic **❶ Aleksoto funicular** for great views of Old Town. Cross the bridge, passing the 15th-century **❷ Vytautas the Great Church** and the magnificent **❸ ouse of Perkūnas**, a 15th-century merchant's residence. Then walk to **❹ Rotušės aikštė**, Old Town's main square, lined with 15th- and 16th-century merchants' houses centred on the 17th-century former Town Hall. Its southwest corner is graced by an 18th-century **❺ mansion** dedicated to the literary endeavours of Lithuanian luminary Maironis. Take Jaksto gatvė and Papilio gatvė to the remains of the 14th-century **❻ Kaunas Castle**, a bastion against Teutonic attacks around which the town grew. Two blocks east and one block south bring you to the red-brick **❼ Sts Peter and Paul Cathedral**, Lithuania's largest Gothic building. Next to it, the **❽ tomb of Maironis** holds the remains of Lithuania's beloved patriot, priest and poet. Across the street, the **❾ Kaunas Photography Gallery** hosts temporary exhibitions.

Take the pedestrianised Vilniaus gatvė and the underpass to the handsome 19th-century building that was the **❿ Presidential Palace of Lithuania** between the two world wars. Reaching Laisvės alėja, New Town's pedestrian drag, turn right. Nearby, exhibits at the **⓫ Tadas Ivanauskas Museum**, founded by Lithuania's naturalist, span the animal kingdom along with mammoth remains. Pass the **⓬ Field of Sacrifice** (p270), then turn left along Maironio gatvė to the **⓭ Vytautas the Great War Museum** (p270), bristling with centuries' worth of weapons. Returning to Laisvės alėja, follow it to the blue-domed neo-Byzantine 0w**⓮ St Michael's Cathedral,** which houses the Museum for the Blind.

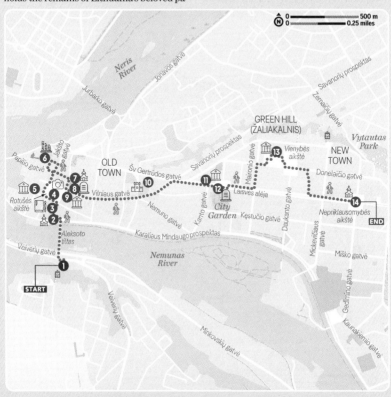

This walking tour takes in some of Kaunas' modernist architectural highlights.

Begin at the ❶ **Fire Station** at Kanto gatvė 1 – a curved 1932 building with a concave facade and twin towers. Proceed to Laisvės alėja 106, where the former art deco ❷ **Jewish Bank** (1925) is now part of the Tadas Ivanauskas Museum (p265). Head up to the former ❸ **Pasaka Cinema** (1940) at Savanoriu prospektas 124, the central plane of its art deco facade resembling a movie screen. Walk down to Zemaiciu gatvė 31a to the ❹ **Resurrection Church** (1933), the largest example of monumental architecture in the Baltics. Take the funicular down, then Putvinskio gatvė to Gedimino gatvė; at No 48, the 1929 house of Dr Pranas Gudavicius is now the ❺ **Art Deco Museum**, its art deco turret embellished with national symbols. One block south and one block east, at Vytauto prospektas 58, the ❻ **Amsterdam School**

Museum (p269) – the only example of this architectural style in the Baltics – is distinguished by its curved facade, segmented windows and sculptures. Take Parodas gatvė to Petrausko gatvė 31, where the ❼ **Petrauskas House** (1925) flaunts a wraparound balcony and floral braids accentuating the entrance in the national art deco style. Proceed south to ❽ **Villa Eglute** (1929) at Vaizganto gatvė 25, the Renaissance-style mansion built for Petras Klimas, signatory of Lithuania's Act of Independence. Descend the steps, cut across the park, then take Kestucio gatvė to Daukanto gatvė 14, a ❾ **residential building** with ancient Egypt motifs and narrow windows connected by relief ornaments in the northern modernist and art deco styles. Half a block north, the still-functioning ❿ **Romuva Cinema** (1940) was built in the historicism style, punctuated by a glass turret.

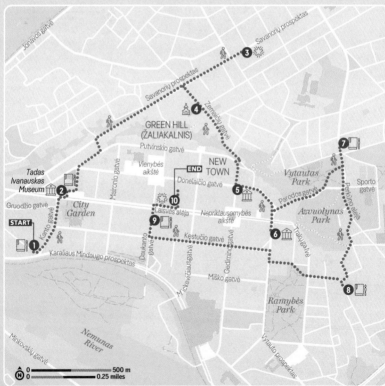

Resurrection Church

ARCHITECTURE OF OPTIMISM

In 2023, 44 buildings, constructed in Kaunas' Naujamiestis (New Town) and Žaliakalnis (Green Hill) gained European Heritage status as the city's architectural legacy was finally recognised by UNESCO. Between 1919, when the Polish annexation of Vilnius made Kaunas de facto capital of Lithuania, and 1939, when Vilnius was returned to Lithuania, Kaunas underwent enormous transformations. The rapid urbanisation of New Town in the interwar years saw the construction of over 1500 buildings in a variety of modernist styles, from art deco, neoclassicism and traditionalism to functionalism and even the Amsterdam School. Lithuania first submitted an application to UNESCO in 2013 to have its contribution to the modernist movement recognised globally, and that recognition has finally been granted.

David, a wooden chair with a menorah design, a candle-cutter, dreidels, figurines of Jewish musicians, and an original 'Jude' patch sewn onto a coat worn by a Kovno Ghetto (p268) inhabitant.

At the recreated KGB interrogation office, complete with a replica torture chair, the guide explains the repressions of ordinary Lithuanians under the Soviets, and how you may find your lost relatives in 'the Special Archive of Lithuania'. You are shown a copy of *Sovetskaya Litva* from the reported day of Stalin's death, along with Soviet spy paraphernalia: tiny F21 cameras secreted inside briefcases, covert listening devices, genuine KGB ID cards and ingenious murder weapons.

As the guide describes the tensions of growing up behind the Iron Curtain and school drills in preparation for nuclear war, you visit a room filled with scarily realistic mannequins depicting radiation burns, and a dramatic space full of gas masks, including some for children and horses (look out for a baby in a bag, and a scaled replica of 'Little Boy' that devastated Hiroshima). The visit finishes with you operating a hand-cranked siren, and hearing the real deal that's tested on Kaunas' rooftops twice a year at noon. Should you hear it outside that time, it means that Lithuania is once again under attack.

WHERE TO SHOP FOR LITHUANIAN DESIGN

kARTu	Livi Design	Kristi Andress
High-quality Italian leather transformed into exclusive bags and purses for women by Lithuanian designers.	Smart and sassy women's wear by Lithuanian designers, particularly Kaunas-born Lina Sliosoraitė-Janušauskė.	Kristina Kalinauskaitė's hound's-tooth jackets, cashmere coats and stylish tops, trousers and skirts sit alongside swimwear.

A SHORT HISTORY OF KOVNO (KAUNAS) JEWS

Known to be living in the Kaunas region since 1410, brought to Lithuania by the Grand Duke Vytautas as prisoners of war, Litvaks (Lithuanian Jews) settled in the present-day neighbourhood of Vilijampolė, on the western bank of the Neris across from Kaunas' Old Town. Many later became traders between Kaunas and Danzig (today's Gdansk in Poland). When rules regarding Jewish settlement were relaxed in 1858, around 29,000 of Kaunas' 35,000 Litvaks moved to Old Town to escape squalid living conditions. However, when Germany invaded Lithuania in 1941, the Nazis herded the entire Jewish population of Kaunas (37,000 people) back to Slobodka, across the river, where the Kovno Ghetto was established. Fewer than 3000 Kovno Jews survived WWII.

RADOWITZ/SHUTTERSTOCK ©

Art Deco Museum

A Tale of Two Apartments

Explore two unique private museums

In the interwar period, when Vilnius was appropriated by Poland, Kaunas took on the role of Lithuania's capital, and with the country (briefly) free from the Russian yoke, it channelled its national pride into the new architectural movement sweeping Europe.

The grey house at Gedimino gatvė 48 dates back to 1929, the height of the art deco movement in Kaunas. On the top floor, there's a flat, decked out with original art deco furniture sourced from all over Lithuania by its owners, young businessmen Petras and Karolis who came up with the idea of giving visitors a window into a flourishing, unique time in Lithuania's past in the shape of the **Art Deco Museum**.

The only way in is via an 'experiential visit'. Book a tour online in advance (in English, French or Lithuanian), and a guide takes you on a two-hour small-group tour of the flat that feels more like an intimate, time-travelling visit to a friend's home. You learn how the flat avoided the fate of so many abodes of the well-to-do, destined to become communal flats during Soviet occupation, and how thousands of these well-to-do lived in the interwar period: with maids cooking their meals

WHERE TO DINE ON CLASSIC LITHUANIAN CUISINE

Bernelių Užeiga
Munch on herring, meaty stews, beetroot soup and dumplings amid rustic decor. €

Višta Puodė
Local ingredients spun into Granny's chicken soup, curd dumplings with nettle sauce and duck breast with rhubarb. €€

Avilys
Wash down Lithuanian standards or beer snacks with pints of mead or unfiltered house beer. €€

and food delivered to their door. You'll sit on satin chairs, sip a glass of sparkling wine and watch the guide unveil secret compartments in the walnut-veneer furniture with a flourish, never interrupting the fluid storytelling. You'll learn the purposes of unusual furnishings and pieces of cutlery, use a vintage bread guillotine in the kitchen, stroke the polished wood of bedsteads, pad in socks across original tilework, and recline on a 100-year-old Swiss chair in the bedroom. Most of all, you'll gain an appreciation of a world that vanished with Soviet occupation, when living standards plummeted for everyone, and members of intelligentsia occupying apartments such as this one were imprisoned or exiled to Siberia.

A few blocks away, on Vytauto prospektas 58 stands a sinuous grey building that belongs to the same owners, its entrance flanked by four pillars and topped with fleet-footed Hermes figures. Built in the Amsterdam School style in 1928, it is the only such building in the Baltics, and one of the reasons why Kaunas is recognised by UNESCO for its wonderfully intact interwar architecture. Step inside the **Amsterdam School Museum**, or apartment No 6, and you find yourself treading on original parquet floors and admiring the walls, painted a vivid blue using lapis lazuli pigment. Like its sister apartment, the Amsterdam School Museum may only be visited as part of a small-group tour that allows you to handle the vintage furnishings and to thoroughly explore every corner of this restored piece of history.

But first, as you sit down in the lounge with its grand piano and cigar table embossed with Egyptian motifs (the height of 1930s fashion), the guide tells you the story of the apartment's original owner – a bon vivant Jewish entrepreneur – who would have entertained guests here, and dined with them in the adjacent dining room while pouring French sparkling wine into cut-crystal glasses.

Your questions are answered: why the building was built in this unique style, how and why this very apartment was recently used in the filming of the *Chernobyl* miniseries, why the owner chose a particular shade of paint for the master bedroom, and how the present owners have been able to procure rare period furnishings. While telling you these engaging stories during your migration from room to room, the guide demonstrates hidden compartments in cabinets, glass spice drawers in the kitchen and other hidden features, until you finally return to the lounge for the grand finale – learning of the fates of the owner and the other Jewish occupants of this building during the war, complete with a surprise twist.

KAUNAS' BEST CRAFT-BEER BARS

Nisha Craft Beershop & Taproom
Pint-sized bar packed with bottled brews from all over the world, from Belgian blonde to Icelandic Arctic pale ale.

Genys Taproom
A heavy-rock soundtrack, black walls, and 10 house brews on tap from the chocolate porter to interesting seasonal experiments.

Vingiu Dubingiu
Friendly bar inside an old blue wooden house, with an emphasis on farmhouse brews and the latest Lithuanian hop adventures.

Hop Doc Gastropub
Eight rotating craft beers on tap and five guests, paired with a supporting cast of seriously good burgers and oysters.

 WHERE TO CATCH A LIVE BAND

O Kodel Nė?
Rough-and-ready venue by the train station hosting DJ sets and local bands; hip bar attached.

Džem'pub
A craft-beer-savouring student crowd comes here for DJ sets, discos and great 5th-floor views.

Galera
Local rock and metal bands take to the small stage, and the beer is wallet-friendly.

Heroes of Kaunas
Immerse yourself in stories of valour

A star exhibit at the **Vytautas the Great War Museum** is the wreckage of a plane, *Lituanica*. Piloted by Lithuanian Americans aviators Steponas Darius and Stanislovas Girénas, it departed New York on 15 July 1933, bound for Kaunas. Two days after the duo set off, 25,000 people gathered at Kaunas airport for their triumphant arrival, but the plane had crashed in Germany, just 650km short of completing the longest nonstop transatlantic flight of the time, killing both pilots. After being embalmed, then hidden during Soviet occupation, the pilots' bodies came to rest at Aukštieji Šančiai Cemetery in 1964. Another local hero, 19-year-old student Romas Kalanta, doused himself in petrol and immolated himself in protest at communist rule on 14 May 1972, and is commemorated by the **Field of Sacrifice**.

Hopheads, Rejoice!
Tour two distinctive breweries

In the industrial eastern outskirts of Kaunas, you're welcomed to **Genys Brewery** by Jonas, the impressively bearded master brewer. The years 2015–16 saw an explosion in American-style craft-beer breweries across Lithuania, but few flourished. The expanding dominance of Genys' woodpecker logo all over Lithuania testifies to the quality of its brews. During the tour (book ahead!) of Lithuania's only brewery to run purely on renewable energy, after learning about the brewing process, you get to taste Genys' core beers: the complex, chocolatey Baltic porter, the pale ale infused with hemp and linden, the APA with pine notes, and the organic lager. Jonas' passion for his craft is palpable as he describes Genys' collaboration with breweries across Europe, Lithuania's burgeoning beer festivals, the difference between American-style craft beer and Lithuania's age-old farmhouse beer-brewing tradition (p303), and some of the challenges Genys has faced ('When we first introduced sours, some customers complained that the beer was off, since Lithuania has no tradition of brewing sour ales, Gose or Berliner Weisse-style beers'). As for the future, Genys aims at world domination, à la Brewdog.

By contrast, **Volfas Engleman Brewery** represents tradition and continuity. An amalgamation of Volfas and Engleman breweries that goes back to 1927, it's one of few businesses to have survived WWII and then been revived, post-Soviet collapse. The tour of this brewery is more streamlined: a straightforward walk through the production process, from milling, mashing and boiling to maturating, fermenting, and filtration, followed by degustation of a Baltic porter, IPA and Belgian-style ale.

KAUNAS' FESTIVALS NOT TO MISS

Kaunas Jazz Festival
Inaugurated in 1991, this lively festival brings world-class jazz musicians to Kaunas for two weeks every April.

Operetta
The Baltics' only open-air opera festival is staged in the ruins of Kaunas Castle over several nights in the first week of July.

Pažaislis Music Festival
Symphonic and chamber performances, choral work and folk ensembles enliven the splendid grounds of the 17th-century Pažaislis Monastery (p276) over the entire summer.

ConTempo
Unusual venues across the city become makeshift stages during this international performing-arts festival during the first week in August.

WHERE TO TAKE THE DISCERNING CARNIVORE

Mtevani
Stellar *shashlik* alongside superlative dolma, chicken tabaka, outstanding *khachapuri* and other Georgian classics. €

MOMO Grill Kaunas
This temple to steak is all exposed brick and chandeliers and prime cuts thrown on the grill. €€

Medžiotojų Užeiga
Roe deer, elk and wild boar grace the menu, alongside game pâtés and excellent wines. €€

Vytautas the Great War Museum

All the Devils Are Here

A unique collection of devil imagery

The Devil, Lucifer, Satan, the fallen angel, the seducer, the trickster, the cajoler...the Horned One has many names and appears in thousands of Lithuanian folk tales as man or animal, sometimes with evil intent, sometimes gullible or even pitiable. He resides in swamps and forests, is encountered on dark nights in inns, and has an irrational fear of flax, holy water, bread and wild ash.

The **Museum of Devils**, now containing over 3000 devil images, began with the singular obsession of landscape artist Antanas Žmuidzinavičius (1876–1966), who was presented with his first devil sculpture during an exhibition of folk art in 1906. Take time to explore three floors' worth of statuettes, masks and other images, starting with the intricate carvings and masks by Lithuanian folk masters, and proceeding to the top floor that showcases the breadth of devil imagery throughout European, American, Asian and African mythologies. Don't miss the exploration of celebrations held to drive away darkness and evil, from Walpurgis Night and Shrovetide to Halloween, and look out for Shrove Tuesday (p276) masks, and Hitler and Stalin dancing on the bones of Lithuania.

LITHUANIA'S BEST ALTERNATIVE MUSIC FESTS

MJR Alternative Music Festival (Mėnuo Juodaragis)
Head for Zarasai in August to celebrate Lithuania's pagan roots, attend historical reenactments and listen to alternative and experimental bands.

Sauletosios Naktys
Singing poetry, post-folk and experimental music shine at this non-commercial art and music festival that takes place in August on a historic farmstead in Gataučiai.

Kilkim Žaibu
Combining ancient traditions with heavy metal and hard rock, this festival is held during the summer solstice in Varniai.

Jotvos Vartai
Staged in late June, this living history fest in Alytus fuses medieval-style and folk music with battle reenactments.

✂ WHERE TO GO FOR VEGETARIAN AND VEGAN FOOD

Moksha
Dine on veggie (and fish) curries, sambals and chutneys at this thimble-sized Indian joint. €

Žalia Pupa
Vegetarian restaurant specialising in buckwheat patties, bean burgers and mushroom creations. €

Vilties Vaistinės Arbatinė
Two friendly women dish up borscht, mushroom dumplings, baked aubergine and soy cutlets. €

A STROLL AROUND JEWISH KAUNAS

Pre-WWII, Kaunas had one of Lithuania's largest Jewish communities. Begin at the ❶ **Lietūkis Garage Massacre Memorial** marking the spot where, on 27 June 1941, 'patriots' from the Lithuanian Activist Front murdered 70 or so Jewish men using crowbars and high-pressure hoses. Cut through Ramybes Park before ascending to ❷ **Sugihara House**, the modest former residence of Japanese diplomat Chiune Sugihara who, with the help of Dutch diplomat Jan Zwartendijk, saved 6000 Jewish lives between 1939 and 1940 by issuing transit visas to Polish Jewish refugees fleeing Nazi terror. 'Japan's Schindler' disobeyed orders from Tokyo for 29 days by signing 300 visas per day, and handed the stamp to a Jewish refugee when he left.

Cross Ramybes Park, then continue along Laisvės alėja, past the ❸ **art installation** that pays tribute to Jan Zwartendijk. Turn right, then right again for ❹ **Kiemo Galerija**, the ever-evolving courtyard project by artist Vytenis Jakas; one wall depicts Jewish families who had lived here but perished during WWII. A short walk west along Ozeskienes gatvė, the ❺ **Ohel Jacov Choral Synagogue** (1870) is Kaunas' only surviving house of worship. Call ahead to admire the dark-wood and gold bema or to attend a Sabbath service. A memorial commemorates 1600 children killed at the Ninth Fort (p275).

Follow Ozeskienes gatvė to Sv Gertrudos gatvė, continue to the giant roundabout, cross the river, then walk up A Krisciukaicio gatvė to the ❻ **granite memorial** at the junction of Ariogalos and Linuvos streets that marks the entrance to the Kovno Ghetto that existed in the area bounded by Jurbarko, Panerių and Demokratų streets.

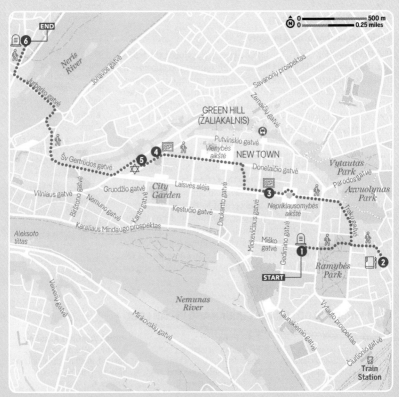

Beyond Kaunas

A superb ethnographic museum, a sedate spa town, a Holocaust memorial and one of Lithuania's oldest settlements are easily reached from Kaunas.

Just off the A1, 7km north of Kaunas, Ninth Fort was part of the city's historical fortification system, and a Nazi prison and execution site. Take the A1 for 20km east towards Vilnius, and you reach the wonderful Open-Air Museum of Lithuania in the village of Rumšiškės; besides being Lithuania's biggest and most complete ethnographic exhibition and collection of traditional dwellings, it hosts some of the country's most exuberant Shrove Tuesday and Midsummer's Eve celebrations. Some 55km north of Kaunas, compact Kėdainiai features an appealing cobbled Old Town and has interesting Scottish roots. Escape for a day of pampering to the spa town of Birštonas, 46km south of Kaunas, or catch Lithuania's biggest jazz fest there in March.

Birštonas (p277)

GETTING AROUND

From central Kaunas, Pažaislis Monastery is reachable by cycling the riverside path or taking a taxi/Bolt. To get to Ninth Fort, take bus 23 from Jonavos gatvė to the 9-ojo Forto Muziejus stop (25 minutes). From Kaunas' main bus station, Vilnius-bound buses stop in Rumšiškės once or twice hourly (30 minutes), and there are twice-hourly services to Birštonas (one hour) and hourly buses to Kėdainiai (one hour). Birštonas and Kėdainiai are walkable; there are also bicycles and electric scooters for rent.

☑ TOP TIP

Book spa accommodation in Birštonas weeks in advance if visiting on a weekend or during summer due to its perpetual popularity.

AUDRIUS VENCLOVA/SHUTTERSTOCK ©

Located some 55km north of Kaunas, Kė-dainiai was established along the Kaunas–Riga trading route c 1372.

Begin your stroll at the ❶**Great Market Square**, overlooked by 17th-century merchants' houses and the Renaissance Town Hall. At the square's heart, a massive chest symbolises the treasury of Grand Duchy of Lithuania. West along Radvilų gatvė is the ❷**Mausoleum of the Radvila Dukes**, where the hetmen and voivodes of the powerful Radvila family, responsible for 300 years of Kėdainiai's prosperity, are seeing out eternity in ornate sarcophagi. Across the street, the 17th-century ❸**Arnett House** was owned by the Scottish merchant John Arnett, back when Kėdainiai attracted a sizeable Scottish population as Lithuania's Protestantism centre. Displays focus on woodcarving, wicker- and cloth-weaving, and ceramics. One block north, dine on Lithuanian sta-ples at ❹**Beneto Karčema**. Head west to the ❺**Regional Museum** inside a former 18th-century Carmelite monastery. The displays – from Stone Age tools and Bronze Age weaponry to furniture, ceramics, and a multimedia presentation on Jewish Kėdainiai – are a fantastic introduction.

Have coffee at ❻**Kavamanija** across the street, then head west for two blocks to the ❼**Vytautas Ulevičius Museum**, home to oak carvings by the renowned artisan. Cross the Smilga River to reach the ❽**gallery** displaying the paintings by Janina Monkutė-Marks, as well as temporary exhibitions. Take Tiltų gatvė and Žydų gatvė to the 15th-century ❾**Old Market Square**, overlooked by a Holocaust memorial. Kėdainiai's Jewish community settled here in the 17th century. It features three former synagogues, with an exhibition dedicated to Kėdainiai's Jews in the ❿**Multicultural Centre**.

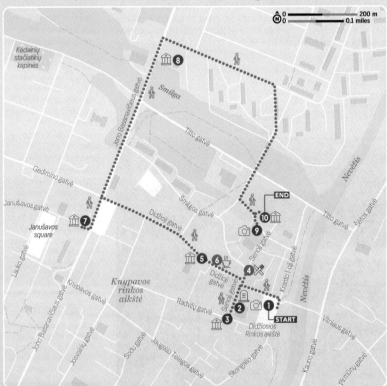

Ninth Fort

Ninth Fort

TIME FROM KAUNAS: **35 MINS** 🚌

Pay your respects at a Holocaust memorial

Seven kilometres north of Kaunas, a 32m-high, jagged stone memorial at **Ninth Fort** commemorates the killing of 50,000 people (30,000 of them Lithuanian Jews) alongside Jews from other parts of Europe, plus dissident Lithuanians and Russian prisoners of war.

Begin with the sombre **gallery** with striking stained glass that focuses on Lithuania's suffering under the Soviets and the Nazis. Continue uphill to the red-brick fort – part of Kaunas' late 19th-century outer town fortifications commissioned by Tsar Alexander II. A hard labour prison between the wars, then an NKVD (predecessor of the KGB) holding pen for political prisoners before they were deported to distant parts of the Soviet Union in 1940–41, it then became a Nazi prison and a final destination for Jews.

In the prison cells, displays pay tribute to individual victims of the Holocaust, detail the horrors of the Kaunas ghetto and honour the Righteous Among the Nations. Proceed along the **Way of Death**, marked by inscriptions in multiple languages and bas-relief works by Kaunas native Nehemia Arbitblat.

In 2023, the surrounding parkland was turned into an **outdoor gallery** featuring several art installations inspired by Soviet

FINAL RESTING PLACES OF KĖDAINIAI'S JEWS

For centuries prior to WWII, Kėdainiai had a large, thriving Jewish community. When the Nazis took control of Lithuania in July 1941, they forced the Jews of Kėdainiai, Šėta and Žeimiai communities to move into a closed ghetto. On 28 August 1941, the vast majority – 2076 Jews – were brutally murdered and dumped in a ravine, 15km northwest of town. Signposted off Rte 144, the **memorial** is marked by a metal board, imprinted with the names of the dead. Off Kanapinsko gatvė in Kėdainiai itself, the town's only surviving Jewish **graveyard** (of the two that existed before WWII) is well tended and features almost 600 mostly intact 19th-century gravestones with inscriptions in Hebrew.

🍴 WHERE TO EAT AND STAY IN KĖDAINIAI

Grey's House
Reside in an 18th-century Scottish mansion with simple rooms, a Turkish sauna and a vaulted-cellar restaurant. €€

Beneto Karčema
Lithuanian beers on tap accompany Lithuanian staples; the portions are large enough to get you through a siege. €

Ursulė
Devour beetroot carpaccio with herring, salads and meat- and fish-heavy mains beneath a stained-glass ceiling. €€

Birštonas

BEST FESTIVALS AROUND KAUNAS

Cucumber Festival
Kėdainiai's mid-July celebration of the town's favourite vegetable, gives you the opportunity to try a surprising variety of cucumber dishes.

Birštonas Jazz Festival
Going strong since 1980, this jazz fest held in March showcases Lithuania's greatest diversity of genres and styles, along with up-and-coming talent.

Shrove Tuesday
Join the exuberant costumed and masked processions at the Open-Air Museum of Lithuania, and scare away the February cold and darkness.

Midsummer's Eve
June sees more revelry at the Open-Air Museum of Lithuania in Rumšiškės village, along with bonfires and staff decked out in traditional dress.

repressions and Russia's war on Ukraine. A suitcase pays tribute to deportees, while the experiential **Walk As Freedom Walks** invites you to walk through a claustrophobic tunnel of barbed wire, with a glimpse of deliverance at the end.

Pažaislis Monastery
TIME FROM KAUNAS: **25 MINS**
Lithuania's greatest baroque monument

The 17th-century **Pažaislis Monastery** lies 9km east of central Kaunas, on a promontory jutting into the Kaunas Sea. Originally home to Camaldolese monks who came to Lithuania from Italy and took vows of silence, the monastery was turned into a German military hospital in WWI, then given to Catholic nuns of the St Casimir order. During the Soviet era, it served variously as a home for the elderly and a psychiatric hospital, before being returned to the St Casimir nuns in 1992.

The monastery complex, its orchards and gardens are a joy to wander. Highlights include the monumental church with its pink and black Polish marble interior, a hexagonal, 50m-high cupola with depictions of the glorification of the Virgin Mary painted by Giuseppe Rossi, plus stucco work by Battista Merli; the cloister, designed by Giambattista Frediani; and frescoes by Michaelangelo Palloni, who was also responsible for the Chapel of St Casimir in Vilnius. Book ahead for lunch at **Monte Pacis**, one of Lithuania's best fine-dining restaurants.

 WHERE TO EAT IN BIRŠTONAS

Namų Restoranas
Filled bao buns sit alongside globe-spanning, mostly pan-Asian dishes, with sauce splodges. €€

Old Town Grill
Dig into generous portions of ribs, salads and pasta at this waterside crowd-pleaser with summer gazebos. €

Kurhauzas
The pan-European repertoire at this smart bistro includes risotto with caramelised pear and steamed mussels. €€

The monastery is particularly atmospheric during the Pažaislis Music Festival (p277). To get here, cycle the riverside path or take a Bolt.

Rumšiškės

TIME FROM KAUNAS: **30 MINS** 🚌

Explore traditional Lithuanian farmsteads

Some 20km east of Kaunas, in the village of Rumšiškės off the A1, the 176-hectare **Open-Air Museum of Lithuania** has been expanding since its opening in 1974. You can easily spend half a day here, strolling the 7km of trails between 18th- and 19th-century villages, hamlets, farmsteads and windmills transferred from Lithuania's main regions (Dzūkija, Aukštaitija, Suvalkija, Žemaitija and Lithuania Minor), their recreated interiors showing off typical furniture, kitchen and farm implements.

Beginning in the cobbled **Rumskės** township, don't miss the exhibits inside the residential buildings, barns, school, wholesale trader's house and wooden chapel, which range from contemporary art by Laima Dzigaite to 19th-century wooden sculptures.

Heading east to **Žemaitija**, peruse the sledge collection at the typical roadside inn, Shrove Tuesday masks in the **Gintaliskes** farmstead, and accoutrements of wealthy landowner life in the **Darbenai** farmstead. Detour to **Lithuania Minor** for lunch, then continue past a huge windmill to **Suvalkija**, with its own rich collection of granaries, peasant dwellings and an apiary with hollow tree-trunk hives. Tailors and weavers demonstrate traditional crafts in the handsome **Aukštaitija** village, while a detour to the north brings you to the isolated manor house, decked out with ornately carved furniture. Check out an affluent **Dzūkija** farmstead, then look for an overgrown example of a Forest Brotherhood (p71) hideout near the exit.

Birštonas

TIME FROM KAUNAS: **1 HR** 🚌

Enjoy a spa getaway

Some 46km south of Kaunas, riverside **Birštonas** has long been known in Lithuania for its spa treatments, built around the region's mineral springs. In 2021, Birštonas opened Lithuania's first ever spa complex for those over 21 years only.

Your pampering options are numerous. **Vytautas Ego Spa** specialises in hyperbaric oxygen therapy, signature couples' massages ('feed your Ego'), facials and wellness and beauty packages. Not to be confused with the above, **Vytautas Mineral Spa** sits on a source of mineral-rich spring water and offers rejuvenating soaks, as well as massages, salt treatments and a full pool and sauna complex. There's a medical angle to **Egles Sanatorium** and its vast array of therapeutic mud, physiotherapy and kinesitherapy treatments. Meanwhile, **Royal Spa Residence** adheres to the wellness principles of Sebastian Kneipp, a 19th-century German priest whose health philosophy revolved around water, plants, exercise, nutrition and balance for a healthy life.

BEST SPA HOTELS IN BIRŠTONAS

Vytautas Ego Spa
Canoodle with your sweetie at this adults-only retreat, complete with sea-green or passion-pink room decor and oxygen spa. €€€

Medical Spa Eglės Sanatorija
Carpeted rooms in brown shades won't make your Instagram posts, but the swimming pool and sauna complex is a massive boon. €€

Sofijos Rezidencija
Expect pseudo-Renaissance splendour and four-poster beds in rooms themed after great figures of Lithuanian history, along with a small wellness centre. €€

Vytautas Mineral Spa
On-trend, minimalist rooms with balconies and stylish suites with leather couches make for wonderful post-treatment relaxation spaces. €€€

MORE SPAS

For more pampering, mineral water and healing mud treatments and various off-the-wall offerings, head for **Druskininkai** (p312).

Curonian Spit

AMBER | WIND | SEAFARING

GETTING AROUND

A ferry for foot passengers and cyclists connects Klaipėda's Old Ferry Port and Smiltynė. Car ferries from Klaipėda's New Ferry Port dock further south.

A 50km bicycle trail runs between Nida and Smiltynė. Rent bikes in Nida, Juodkrantė and Smiltynė during summer.

Buses travel between Smiltynė and Nida via Juodkrantė; some stop in Preila and Pervalka. Buses from Nida to Kaunas and Vilnius via Klaipėda stop in all villages.

From early June to September daily boat services connect Curonian Spit villages with the opposite side of the Curonian Lagoon: Nida and Ventės Ragas; Nida and Mingė; and Juodkrantė and Dreverna.

According to legend, sea goddess Neringa created this long sliver of land that juts out into the Baltic Sea by carrying sand in her apron to form a protected harbour for the local fisherfolk. The non-legend origins are no less enchanting. The youngest part of Lithuania – a mile across, 98km-long, and split almost evenly between Lithuania and Russia – the Curonian Spit (Kuršių Nerija) was formed around 5000 years ago. Its dense cover of birch and pine forest, criss-crossed by cycling trails and home to part of the long-distance Baltic Trail, shelters elk, wild boars and roe deer, while its extraordinary, wind-sculpted giant sand dunes have earned the Spit the nickname 'Lithuania's Sahara'.

Over the centuries, the Spit has been occupied by Curonians, Germans and the Soviet army. Since 1992, its four picturesque fishing villages – Nida, Juod-krantė, Pervalka and Preila (known collectively as 'Neringa') – have reverted to a largely tranquil existence (outside the summer season).

Nida's Baltic Gold

High-tech, sensory exploration of amber

As you enter the atmospherically lit interior of Nida's state-of-the-art **Mizgiris Amber Museum**, the undulating screen above you comes alive. A black-and-white documentary reconstruction depicts a misty forest of primeval pines, with the yet-to-be amber – sap from the trees' wounds – pouring down their trunks like molten lava. 'They're in pain', intones the narrator, 'and so they weep'.

As you slowly move around the exhibits, from raw chunks of amber to the hands-on space where you may touch the Perkūnas (Thunder) Stone – the world's largest single piece of marine amber, weighing 3.8kg – the same resonant voice talks you through the formation of the gems: how young amber fell into seawater, got buried under layers of sediment

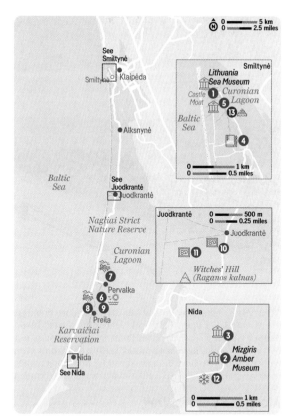

TOP SIGHTS
1 Lithuania Sea Museum
2 Mizgiris Amber Museum

SIGHTS
3 Amber Gallery
4 Dune keeper's house
5 Ethnographic fisherman's farmstead
6 Karvaiciu Bay
7 Pervalka
8 Preila
9 Preilos Bay
10 Waterfront sculpture trail
11 Witches' Hill

ACTIVITIES, COURSES & TOURS
12 Irklakojis

TRANSPORT
13 Fishing vessels

☑ TOP TIP

The Spit is particularly buzzy during the summer season (mid-June to end of August); accommodation prices are high, particularly in Nida. Outside this time, most restaurants and bars shut down. To experience its forest, dunes and villages in tranquillity, plan a spring or autumn visit or stay in Preila or Pervalka.

and become fossilised under intense pressure over millions of years, and how these droplets of ancient tree sap, ranging in colour from white and pale yellow to golden, blood-red, the very rare black and blue, and even a spangled blue-green, are witnesses to a world long gone.

Magnifying displays allow you to peer at insects, suspended within golden depths, only a third of them still around today. Through interactive displays, you learn about the extraction process, how amber became a valuable commodity traded with the Roman Empire, and how the legendary Amber Hoard was dug up in Amber Bay near Juodkrantė in the 1860s. You view amber offerings to the pagan gods, millennia-old amber figurines and amber amulets from ancient graves, and watch the Curonian Spit's 5000 years of existence flash by in seconds.

Finally, you get to touch and smell chunks of amber, discover how to distinguish the real thing from plastic if buying amber from street stalls, then venture upstairs to view amber transformed into delicate jewellery and other creations by 50 artists from all over the world.

MORE AMBER
While not as high-tech at Nida's museum, Palanga's **Amber Museum** (p291) complements your amber journey with some fantastic rare pieces and creations by Lithuanian designers, available for purchase.

BEST PLACES TO STAY IN NIDA

Hotel Jūratė
Super-central
Soviet hotel
featuring spacious,
comfortable rooms
in soothing creams,
with blond-wood
furnishings and TVs.
€€

Spa Nida
Thoroughly
contemporary
apartments, suites
and doubles,
innovative restaurant,
and pool, sauna and
spa access. €€€

Miško Namas
Nab a room with a
balcony or kitchenette
at this immaculately
maintained
guesthouse with a
library and garden. €€

Gerda
This traditional
fisherman's cottage, a
stone's throw from the
lagoon, has two fully
equipped apartments
for rent. €€

Nidos Kempingas
An assortment of tent
sites, spartan doubles
and self-catering
apartments, with
bikes for hire and
tennis and basketball
courts. €

OLEZZO/SHUTTERSTOCK ©

Nida

Entry is by hour-long guided tour only; advance bookings are essential. For more 'Baltic gold', check out the old-school **Amber Gallery** – a fisher's hut housing a collection of amber pieces, including chessboards, sailing ships and some truly unusual jewellery. Inquire ahead for hour-long amber-processing classes, and explore the amber-ornamented garden.

Along the Coastal Trail
Curonian Spit's most scenic day walk

Spanning the coastlines of Lithuania, Latvia and Estonia, the **Baltic Coastal Trail** runs for 1322km from Lithuania's Nida to Tallinn, Estonia. Lithuania's coastal section straddles both sides of the Curonian Lagoon, taking in both the Nemunas Delta (p294) and the Curonian Spit.

The most scenic 20km-long day hike along the Curonian Spit takes you from the waterfront in **Nida**, along the airstrip, and around **Bulvikis Cape**, with the trail running through pine forest and past coastal reeds, teeming with birdlife. As you round Great Preila Cape and find yourself in **Preilos Bay** with its small sandy beach, you'll pass an unmarked dirt path that allows you to detour to Vecekrugas Dune (p284). Alternatively, as the coastal footpath brings you to **Preila**, take the

 WHERE TO STAY IN JUODKRANTĖ

Villa Flora
Centrally located, 19th-century timber villa offering split-level rooms with lounges and bedrooms. Open year-round. €€

Už Jūrų Marių
Self-catering apartments opposite the sculpture park; spacious, modern flats in creams and blues. €€

Villa Riviera
These serviced apartments come with thoughtful extras (mushrooming knives, walking sticks). €€

steep steps up Preilos Hill (57m) for spectacular, unobstructed views of the Curonian Lagoon. The trail briefly follows Preila's main street/cycling path before veering off towards **Ozku ragas** (Goat Cape), where you may spot sunbathing cormorants. Passing another small sandy beach in **Karvaiciu Bay**, you skirt Pervalkos Cape before finding yourself in one-street **Pervalka**. It's well worth pressing on for another 1.1km through pine woods to **Zirgu ragas** (Horse Cape), partly to check out the small lighthouse (1900), and partly for the sandy beach just beyond the cape, from which you get fantastic views of the huge Dead Dunes in the distance.

Harnessing the Wind & the Waves

Boat trips, paddling and ice-sailing

Besides scheduled boat services, there are other ways of getting out on the lagoon from Nida. Watercraft running pleasure cruises include the classic yacht *Matsya* and classic speedboat *Hanuman* (laivu-nuoma.lt) that sail past Parnidis Dune at sunset and also whisk you off on day trips to Mingė and Rusnė, combined with fresh fish lunches at Šturmų Švyturys in Ventė (p293). Alternatively, hop aboard the wooden yacht *Lana*, which flies the Jolly Roger for hour-long cruises past Parnidis Dune; longer trips include the five- to six-hour Nemunas Delta jaunt, stopping in Mingė and Uostadvaris. Charter it for yourself and 20 of your closest friends if you'd like to arrive in Šventoji (p288) in style after sailing past the Dead Dunes, Klaipėda and Palanga.

During the January to March season, when the Curonian Lagoon typically freezes over, take to the ice in an ice-blokart (a cross between go-karting and windsurfing, using skates) in -15C temperatures with local operator **Irklakojis**. In summer, it rents SUPs, offers stand-up paddleboarding tours and can arrange blokarting (windsurfing on land) on Nida's airstrip.

Juodkrantė's Art of Wood & Stone

Explore two sculpture trails

Stretched along the lagoon shore 28km north of Nida, the fishing village of **Juodkrantė** (Black Shore), founded in the 15th century, morphed into a luxurious Lithuanian resort in the 1920s. Besides its 1860s amber fame, it's known for its celebration of Lithuania's pagan and folkloric roots.

Follow the Raganų Kalnas sign into the old-growth forest to a coven of wooden sculptures that has taken shape along a woodland trail up **Witches' Hill** since 1979; this is appropriate, since the 42m hill was a focus of pagan ritual before

CURONIAN SPIT VISITOR RULES

● Neringa entrance fee (pay on arrival or in advance via unipark.lt): motorbike/car June to mid-September €5/30, mid-September to November €5/10; rest of year €5/5.

● Speed limit is 50km/h in villages, 70km/h on open roads.

● Don't walk on the dunes, pick flowers or stray off designated footpaths.

● Some beaches are women-only; others are men-only.

● Don't damage flora or fauna, disturb bird nests or light campfires.

● Don't pitch a tent or park a camper overnight in the park.

● Don't fish without a permit; purchase them at tourist offices.

● Beware of elk and wild boar crossing the road; don't go near them.

● On-the-spot fines for rule-breaking are up to €150.

● In case of forest fire, call 01 or 112 (general emergency).

WHERE TO EAT IN JUODKRANTĖ

Žvejonė	Pizza di Mare	Flora
Chow down on grilled halibut, eel soup and other fish specialities at this waterfront restaurant. €€	Wood-fired pizzas served inside a glassed-in space. Summer weekdays; year-round weekends. €	Expect hefty portions of Lithuanian staples and refined pan-European fare. Summer daily; weekends year-round. €

Bustling with holiday-makers during the summer months, Nida is the Curonian Spit's most popular village.

This walk begins at the **❶ Neringa History Museum**, which focuses on the Curonian Spit's defining traditional crafts: fishing, crow-catching and amber collecting. Look out for photos of a fisherman biting a crow's neck to kill it, then taking a shot of vodka to dull the taste. Proceed along Pamario gatvė to the **❷ Ethnographic Cemetery** featuring some fine examples of *krikštai* (wooden grave markers) that hark back to Lithuania's pagan roots. Follow Pamario gatvė to the **❸ open-air exhibition** with scenes from traditional Curonian Spit life in the 19th century: a fisherman transporting his weeping bride to the other side of the lagoon, villagers drying fish on lines and escaping the encroaching sands. Proceed to the **❹ Ethnographic Museum**, with original

weather vanes decorating the garden, and rooms inside arranged as they were two centuries ago.

The waterfront path through pine forest brings you to the base of the 52m-tall **❺ Parnidis Dune**, a landscape of mountain pines, meadows and blond sand speckled with purple sea-rocket flowers. A 1700m-long boardwalk path picks its way to a grand panorama at the height of the dune, where you'll find a sundial with a granite obelisk.

A 1km-long footpath near the parking area cuts through the woods to **❻ Nida public beach**, an expanse of white sand battered by Baltic waves and divided into a nude beach, a women's beach and a family section. From Taikos gatvė, a trail leads to the 27m-high **❼ Urbas Hill Lighthouse** (originally built in 1874, then rebuilt in 1945). Climb the 132 steps to the top for all-encompassing views.

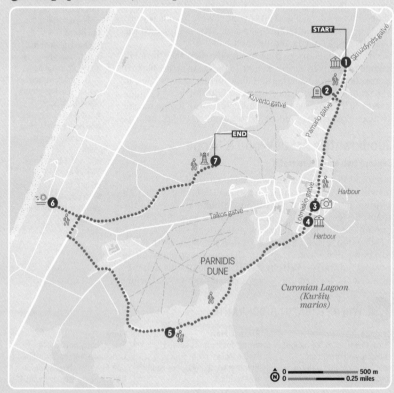

Lithuania adopted Christianity. The figures represent various characters from regional folklore, from witches and devils to dwarves, as well as Neringa, the legendary giantess said to have protected Ventės Ragas (p293) from the year-long storm brought by the sea god Bangputys. Besides Neringa, spot a dragon-slaying knight, a witch with a lopsided bosom and owl on her head, a devil and a witch playing cards, and the particularly intricately carved Lucifer peering through the Gates of Hell, its pillars alive with faces: some twisted in anguish, others in rage. There's an interactive element to some of the carvings: slide down a giant devil tongue or sit on a carved throne.

Once you emerge on the waterfront, follow the 2.4km-long **pedestrian and cycling trail** along the bay, admiring the 31 stone and metal compositions erected here in 1999 as part of the international 'Earth and Water' symposium.

Smiltynė's Seafaring Heritage
Boats and sea creatures galore

The 500m-long trip on the passenger ferry from Klaipėda gets you to **Smiltynė** (population 50), one of the oldest Curonian Spit villages. You'll disembark near the **dune keeper's house** (1870), whose job it was to contain the rampaging sands.

Smiltynė's fortunes have been shaped by its relationship with the sea since it was founded in the 15th century, and were invariably linked to Klaipėda's. When the latter got sacked by Sweden during the Seven Years' War in the late 16th century, Smiltynė saw its only inn burned down. Later, an essential stop en route from Prussia to the Livonian lands, Smiltynė became part of Konigsbeg–Memel (later Klaipėda)–Courland postal route, and then a popular summer resort for Klaipėda's residents.

Discover all this when you step inside the **Lithuania Sea Museum** inside the late-19th-century fort at the north tip of the seafront promenade – Kopgalis, the youngest part of the Curonian Spit that formed in the mid-19th century. Engaging displays in the casemates and the former gunpowder depositories showcase Lithuania's early-20th-century transition from a nation of farmers and fishermen to a seafaring country. There are scale models of key vessels, such as the *Sovereign of the Sea* that carried Lithuanian emigrants to a new life in America, the steamship *Kaunas* and icebreaker *Perkunas,* while the ramparts display a unique anchor collection. Attached to the museum is the **aquarium** that shows off the denizens of the North and Baltic Seas and Lithuania's lakes and rivers, as well as Baltic seals and, randomly, penguins.

Continues on p286

WEATHERVANES

Travelling around the Curonian Lagoon, you'll notice that each village sports unique, elaborate weathervanes. A ruling in 1844 decreed that each *kurėnas* (Neringa fishing vessel) be identifiable by the weather vane specific to its village, so that they stuck to their designated fishing grounds. Originally made from tin and later from wood, the weathervanes from the Spit side were 60cm x 30cm, while those from the Nemunas side were twice as large. Each settlement had its unique symbol – a black-and-white (Spit villages), red-and-white (Nemunas) or blue-and-yellow (southern coast) geometrical design, embellished with animal and bird figures and mythical cutouts. The Neringa History Museum has a handsome collection of weathervanes; buy one at Juodkrantė's **Weathervane Gallery**.

 WHERE TO STAY AND EAT IN PERVALKA

Vila Artvė
Steam in your private sauna after a day's hiking or biking in this light-filled family-sized cottage. €€€

Vila Junda
Classically decorated lagoon-side apartments, all with balconies, terraces and barbecue facilities. €€

Garden
Menu of grilled fish, meat, dumplings with mushroom sauce and imaginative, filling breakfasts. €

Nida to Juodkrantė

This scenic 30km-long bike ride takes in some of the biggest highlights of Lithuania's Curonian Spit, starting in Nida, 6km from the border with Russia, and finishing in Juodkrantė. En route you visit two other appealing fishing villages, climb ancient dunes that once buried entire settlements, and meander through pine forests and along the Baltic coast. Coming back, either retrace your steps or catch a bus with a bicycle rack.

❶ Nida

Begin in Nida (p280), the most popular of the Spit's villages due to its scenic location, abundance of summer restaurants and attractions such as the Parnidis Dune and Mizgiris Amber Museum.
The Ride: Take the cycle path along the spread-out waterfront, past the pier, and follow it into the pine forest (20 minutes).

❷ Vecekrugas Dune

Around 5km north of Nida, detour to the base of the highest dune (67.2m) on the Curonian Spit. Climb the steps to its pine-topped summit for panoramic views of the Curonian Lagoon, Bulvikis Cape (at 3.6km, the widest part of the Spit), and the Great Preila Cape, adorned with birch groves.
The Ride: Continue through pine forest for 3km to the village of Preila (10 minutes).

❸ Preila

A fishing village of around 200 people, Preila was established in 1843, and attracted many German artists in the pre-Soviet period. Gaining in popularity with summer visitors today, it has several guesthouses, a couple of cafes, and a 19th-century ethnographic cemetery, complete with *krikštai* (wooden grave markers).

Vecekrugas Dune

WIRESTOCK CREATORS/SHUTTERSTOCK ©

CURONIAN SPIT LITHUANIA

THE GUIDE

The Ride: The trail continues for 6km along the east coast of the Spit, alternating between forest and waterfront views of two bays (30 minutes).

④ Pervalka

The smallest of Neringa's settlements, the one-street village of Pervalka was founded in 1844 by 11 families whose prior village, Negeln, was buried by the sand of drifting dunes. Clumsy, imitational buildings hint at its past as a Soviet resort, while today it attracts mushroomers with particularly rich crops of *Boletus* in September and October.

The Ride: The trail veers west through woodland until it meets the main road, then runs alongside it to the car park at the base of Nagliu Dune (10 minutes).

⑤ Nagliu Dune

From the parking area, a 1.1km-long, sandy trail (entry €5) runs to the summit of Nagliu Dune (53.1m), with a viewpoint over-looking the Dead Dunes that stretch for 9km between Pervalka and Juodkrantė. Their expanse hides three villages, claimed by the sands. From the summit, you get glimpses of dune-buried, centuries-old forest.

The Ride: The trail shadows the road before peeling away to the west and running along the Baltic Sea. Turn right past the pungent cormorant colony to reach Juodkrantė (30 minutes).

⑥ Juodkrantė

Stretching for 2km along the waterfront, and connected to the Spit's Baltic side by paths through old-growth forest, the large, appealing village of Juodkrantė (p281) has existed as Schwarzort from 1429 and has been receiving holiday-makers by steam-ship from Klaipėda since 1858, expanding as it absorbed the exiles from nearby sand-buried villages. Swing by Witches' Hill, its biggest attraction.

Neringa

BEST RESTAURANTS & BARS IN NIDA

Pas Joną
Select mackerel, carp or eel from the traditional smoking rack, then wash it down with kvas or beer while watching the sunset. €

Kavinė Kuršis
This year-round all-rounder serves omelettes and scrambled eggs for breakfast, then soups, salads, *cepelinai* (stuffed parcels of thick potato dough), pasta and more the rest of the day. €

Malkinė
Seriously good wood-fired pizzas (including vegetarian and vegan options), consumed on picnic tables by the sea. €

Purvynė
Rub shoulders with yachties while slurping oysters served by Lithuania's shucking champion and sipping bubbly. €€

Continued from p283

On the waterfront near the museum, you can admire venerable **fishing vessels**, including three Baltic Sea fishing trawlers built in the late 1940s (climb aboard the *Kolyma*), *Lituanika-01* (Lithuania's first submarine), and a 1935 *kurėnas* (a traditional flat-bottomed Curonian fishing boat), before taking the short footpath to the small **ethnographic fisherman's farmstead**. Peering inside a granary, dwelling house, cellar, smokehouse and cattle shed, you get an appreciation for 19th-century fishing life.

Neringa's Shifting Sands
Visit the UNESCO site – but stick to the trails

Neringa's distinctive landscape and unique marine, archaeological and cultural heritage that have earned it UNESCO recognition are under threat both from human impact and natural forces (wind and tide). Intensive logging and resulting deforestation in the 17th and 18th centuries destabilised the sand dunes, which began to move towards the Curonian Lagoon, burying the oldest villages – some relocated several times, trying to outpace the shifting sands. In 1768 an international commission set about replanting the forests in a bid to anchor the dunes, and there are constant efforts to prevent erosion today using brushwood hedges. But the sands are still moving – at least 1m a year, so it's more important than ever to stick to designated trails.

 WHERE TO STAY AND EAT IN PREILA

Preilos Perliukas	**Vila Preiloja**	**Kęsto Rūkyta Žuvis**
Three bright, well-equipped duplex apartments overlooking the shore, each with a double and two single beds. €€	Choose between the fisher's cottages or spacious, luxurious VIP options, complete with wood-burning stoves. €€	Platefuls of golden-skinned, freshly smoked mackerel, eel and perch at unthreatening prices. €

Beyond
Curonian Spit

A former German port, a quintessential beach town, traditional Nemunas Delta villages and spectacular white-sand beaches lie beyond the Curonian Spit.

A short ferry hop from the Curonian Spit's Smiltynė, the appealing port city of Klaipėda – the gateway to the Spit – proudly flaunts the Germanic-style, half-timbered buildings that line the cobbled streets of its compact Old Town. North of Klaipėda, Lithuania's Baltic coast is lined with pine forest and white-sand beaches, with the busiest ones in the buzzy beach resort of Palanga, Lithuania's answer to Blackpool (only much prettier). Superb birdwatching, kitesurfing and villages steeped in tradition await in the Nemunas Delta, on the opposite side of the Curonian Lagoon. Orvydas Garden and Kretinga Museum, both northeast of the Spit, welcome visitors with an enchanting statue garden compiled by political dissidents and a vast tropical plant collection, respectively.

Places

Klaipėda p289

Palanga p290

Svencelė p291

Nemunas Delta p294

GETTING AROUND

Klaipėda is connected to Šiauliai and Vilnius by train via Kretinga. There are buses from Klaipėda to Palanga, Kaunas, Nida via Juodkrantė, Šiauliai and Vilnius. Getting around Klaipėda is easy on foot, by Bolt taxi or by bicycle; rent a bike from Du Ratai. In Palanga, there are bicycle rental outlets, plus pedal-powered taxis and Bolt taxis. Driving or cycling is the easiest way to explore the Nemunas Delta. There are buses from Klaipėda to Šilutė. Boats are another way of exploring the delta. Hire boats through Šilutė's tourist office.

Klaipėda (p288)

☑ TOP TIP

The Baltic coast shuts down in winter. Birdwatching in the Nemunas Delta is best during autumn and spring.

The flat, signposted, 50km-long Seaside Cycle Route (bicycle.lt/seasideroute) runs from Klaipėda to the Latvian border. It' easily done in a day, but two or three days are better.

From **❶ Klaipėda**, take Manto gatvė past Klaipėda University, across the crossroads, past the concert stage and through Giruliai Forest to **❷ Giruliai**, where Vasarotojų gatvė leads you to the railway crossing. Proceed along Stoties gatvė to the beginning of the Seacoast Regional Park (protected area between Giruliai and Palanga).

Detour to the **❸ Girulai Džotai**, impressive WWII defensive fortifications, then press on to the spectacular, pine- and oak-covered **❹ Dutchmen's Cap Hill**, overlooking the crashing waves. Continue to **❺ Karklė**, a 16th-century village famous for its roadside inns (a good lunch spot) and well-preserved farmsteads. A short way north, pause by **❻ Plazė**, a small lake of glacial origin from 10,000 years ago, home to plentiful waterfowl, with a picnic spot and birdwatching tower.

Further along, detour briefly from the village of Saipai to spot nature's engineer from the beaver-watching house overlooking Saipai marsh, then take the coastal trail to **❼ Nemirseta**, a 13th-century village turned sea-vessel rescue centre. The cycle path skirts Palanga's **❽ Botanic Park** before following the seashore to **❾ Hill** (15m), allegedly the grave of the giant Naglis.

The 14km-long Ozupis Path between Palanga and **❿ Šventoji**, a 16th-century fishing settlement, later major port and now a smaller resort version of Palanga, runs through pine forest, following the shore. In Šventoji, check out the Fisherman's Daughters sculpture and **⓫ Žemaičių Alkos**, the recreated ancient paleo-astronomical observatory, before shadowing the Palanga–Liepaja road towards Latvia.

Teatro aikštė

Klaipėda

TIME FROM NIDA: 1½ HRS

The seaport's Hanseatic heritage

There's a distinctly German flavour to the compact, cobble-stoned Old Town of the seaport of **Klaipėda**, the gateway to the Curonian Spit. Founded in 1252 as the Memelburg fortress by the Livonian Order, Lithuania's third-largest city spent most of its existence as the Prussian port Memel, before joining Lithuania in 1923.

In the centre of Old Town's **Teatro aikštė** (Theatre Sq), there's a fountain dedicated to Simon Dach, a Klaipėda-born German poet (1605–59). On a pedestal in the middle of the water stands **Ännchen von Tharau** (1912), a replica statue of the one originally sculpted by Berlin artist Alfred Kune and inspired by Dach's poem, written in 1637 in the East Prussian dialect.

Nearby, inside one of the attractive buildings constructed in the German Fachwerk style (with distinctive half-timbered facades), the **Lithuania Minor Museum** provides insight into the lives of German and Lithuanian speakers who inhabited this coastal region (aka East Prussia) prior to WWII. Prussian maps, coins, artefacts of the Teutonic Order, wooden furnishings, displays of folk art and traditional weaving machines

BEST RESTAURANTS IN KLAIPĖDA

Monai
Romance your sweetie with on-trend modern European dishes that change with the seasons. Legendary Sunday brunches. €€

Stora Antis
This atmospheric 19th-century cellar elevates classic Lithuanian fare (baked duck, bean soup, pan-fried plaice) to haute-cuisine heights. €€

DOCK Craft Beer & Burgers
Sometimes all you want is a beautifully stacked burger oozing all over your hands, washed down with Genys on-tap craft beer. €

Katpėdėlė
Potato pancakes, grilled pork neck, and soups in hollowed-out bread bowls are served with a flourish inside a former merchant's building. €

 ## WHERE TO STAY IN KLAIPĖDA

Michaelson Boutique Hotel
An 18th-century warehouse with wood-beamed rooms in sleek greys and creams overlooking the Danė River. €€€

Preludija Guesthouse
Minimalist, modern rooms await at this handsome mid-19th-century guesthouse in the heart of Old Town. €€

Ararat
Business-style apartments with on-site Armenian restaurant serving grilled meats and herb-filled vegetarian dishes. €€

**BEST
RESTAURANTS
IN PALANGA**

Žuvinė
Dine on zander with
beetroot cream,
smoked eel or halibut
with black lentils in
an interior straight
out of *Architectural
Digest*. €€

Ukrainetiska Virtuvė
Borsch, chicken Kiev,
assorted dumplings
and other Ukrainian
meat-heavy mains
brought to the garden
terrace by costumed
waiters. €

Onorė
Palanga's most
creative culinary
offerings (such as
tuna tartare with
avocado or octopus
with lemon-peel
confit) served with a
side of river views. €€

Restauranas 1925
Profoundly committed
to dairy fats and
filling, stodgy
dumplings, this
handsome timbered
tavern has been
catering to hungry
crowds since 1925. €

Basanavičiaus gatvė, Palanga

abound. Nearby, the **Baroti Gallery,** partly housed in a converted fish warehouse (1819), features contemporary art and photography exhibitions. Around the corner, ornate forged-iron works such as 19th-century stove doors compete for your attention with elaborate crosses salvaged from the town's former cemetery at the **Blacksmith's Museum**.

Founded by the Teutonic Order in the 13th century, the moat-protected **Klaipėda Castle** was razed and rebuilt on multiple occasions; the museum inside its atmospherically lit tunnels traces the history of Klaipėda as a port. The terrific, high-tech **Museum 39/45** charts Klaipėda's fate during WWII, from its occupation by the Nazis and locals waving swastikas with a smile, to the city lying in ruins, while explosions sound in the background.

Palanga

TIME FROM NIDA: 1¾ HRS

Amber, tactile sculpture and beachside walks

Palanga's pedestrianised **Basanavičiaus gatvė** is a full-on sensory assault consisting of arcade machines, bungee-jump simulators, merry-go-rounds, electric cars, portrait artists,

 WHERE TO STAY IN PALANGA

Palanga Spa Hotel
Award-winning spa and floor-to-ceiling windows are perks at this glass-and-chrome stunner wrapped in a pine grove. €€€

Vila Ramybė
Individually styled, pine-clad, pastel-hued rooms (some with terraces) on a quiet street near Basanavičiaus gatvė action. €

Žuvėdra Hotel
Unmemorable room decor is trumped by the beach-end location on Basanavičiaus gatvė and a spa complex. €€

buskers, bars playing thumping music, and stalls selling candy floss, popcorn, ice cream and hot dogs. But in spite of the town's reputation as Lithuania's wildest beach resort, much of Palanga is incredibly tranquil, its tree-lined streets redolent of pine. An important trade centre since the 13th century and later Lithuania's biggest port until it was destroyed by the Swedes in 1701, Palanga was transformed into a genteel seaside resort and spa town in the 19th century largely through the efforts of the Tyszkiewicz family, much of whose legacy remains intact.

Take some of the 18km of footpaths in the **Botanical Park**, with its rose garden, over 500 plant species and pine copses. Ascend the chapel-topped **Birutės kalnas**, Palanga's highest point and formerly a pagan shrine. According to legend, it was tended by vestal virgins, one of whom, Birutė, was kidnapped and married by Grand Duke Kęstutis.

Linger at the **Amber Museum**, housed in a neoclassical palace built by Count Feliksas Tyszkiewicz in 1897, and showcasing over 15,000 examples of Baltic gold, ranging from the formation of amber and its early use in Neolithic times to the large collection of striking, contemporary jewellery by amber masters. Magnifying glasses help you zoom in on ancient insect life in golden stasis; don't miss one of the world's rarest amber pieces with a lizard trapped inside, or the Sun Stone – an amber chunk weighing 3.52kg.

If you want to try fashioning your own amber jewellery, head for the **Amber Processing Gallery**, run by the Palanga Guild of Amber Masters. Nearby, visit the **Antanas Mončys Museum**, and run your hands over the abstract wooden sculptures, collages and masks by Lithuanian émigré artist Antanas Mončys (1921–93), very tactile himself and insistent that his wooden pieces be handled.

Grab lunch off Basanavičiaus gatvė, then perambulate along the coastal path that winds its way north and south through pine forest from the pier end of Basanavičiaus, detouring to the beach for sunbathing and swimming. After sunset-watching off the pier, and dinner, listen to live music at the **Palanga Concert Hall**, which has wonderful acoustics.

Svencelė

TIME FROM NIDA: **2 HRS**

Lithuania's top kitesurfing destination

Lithuania's veteran kitesurfers remember the village of **Svencelė** as a quiet little place where you just turned up with your car and your kiting gear for DIY kitesurfing holidays. Kitesurfing conditions here are the best in the country:

Continues on p294

KLAIPĖDA'S SCULPTURES

Klaipėda is studded with sculptures, including 120-odd abstract pieces from the late 1970s in **Klaipėda Sculpture Park**. Nearby is a monumental granite sculpture of Martynas Mažvydas, author of the first book published in Lithuanian in 1547. The red granite pillar propping up a huge, broken arch on Manto gatvė engraved with the quote, 'We are one nation, one land, one Lithuania', by poet Ieva Simonaitytė (1897–1978), celebrates Klaipėda joining Lithuania in 1923. Outside the train station stands *Farewell,* a statue of a mother with a suitcase, holding the hand of a small boy. It was given to Klaipėda by Germany to remember Germans who said goodbye to their homeland after the city joined Lithuania in 1923.

 WHERE TO EAT IN THE NEMUNAS DELTA

Šturmų Švytyrus, Ventė
The menu at this nautically themed restaurant consists solely of wild-caught fish fresh from the Curonian Lagoon. €€

Mėlynasis Karpis, Kintai
Devour superlative carp and other fish dishes at this countryside hotel-restaurant overlooking fishing ponds. €

Meat Lovers, Svencelė
Unapologetically carnivorous pub grub (burgers, German sausages, smoked ribs) entices voracious kitesurfer types. €€

Nemunas Delta on Two Wheels

South of Klaipėda, where the Nemunas River spills into the Curonian Lagoon, splitting into four tributaries, the land dissolves into a wetland delta of considerable beauty, teeming with birdlife and dotted with islands, bird hides and flooded meadows. It's a slow-paced land of fishing villages, ethnographic farmsteads, polder systems and water-pumping stations, ideal for two-wheeled exploration. Allow three days for this loop that takes in the main highlights.

❶ Šilutė

Named after a 16th-century tavern, the Nemunas Delta's main town was under German rule until its integration into Lithuania in 1923. Peruse the area's history, plus ethnic costume and weaponry at the **Hugo Scheu Museum** (silutesmuziejus.lt). **The Ride:** Take Rte 165 east out of town, head north along Rte 141 and turn off at the Macikai signpost (15 minutes).

❷ Macikai

Arranging the visit in advance at Šilutė's tourist office (inside the Hugo Scheu Museum), visit the WWII prisoner of war camp and former KGB prison for Lithuanian dissidents. The journals, drawings and personal effects of the prisoners are sobering. **The Ride:** Retrace your steps to Šilutė and follow Rte 206 through the fields and across the Atmata River bridge (30 minutes).

❸ Rusnė

A mere 1.5m above sea level, the Rusnė Island fishing community (population 3000) features an ethnographic fisherman's farmstead that gives you a glimpse into ye olde life in Lithuania Minor. Rusnė residents can see Russia from their houses: the Skirvytė River marks the border between the two countries.

Rusnė

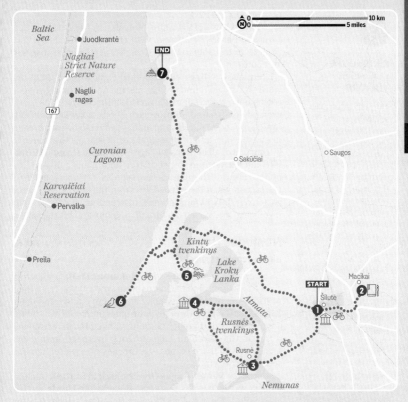

The Ride: Take Rte 4205 northwest to the village of Uostadvarsis via Pakalnė, then take the riverside path west for another 1km (20 minutes).

4 Uostadvaris

Housed in the region's first water-pumping station (1907) on the Vilkinė, the **Polder Museum** is home to the fascinating technology that Nemunas farmers use for land reclamation and to keep floodwaters at bay.

The Ride: Follow the path along the Atmata River back to Rusnė, return to Šilutė, take Rte 4217 west, then head south along unpaved Rte 4228 to Mingė (1½ hours).

5 Mingė

Straddling both sides of the Minija River (connected by boat rather than bridge), the 'Venice of Lithuania' is the most atmospheric place to stay in the Delta. It has existed since the 16th century, growing affluent thanks to centuries-long trade along the Nemunas channels and rich fishing grounds.

The Ride: Return to Rte 4217, head west, then south to Ventės Ragas (25 minutes).

6 Ventės Ragas

Extending far into the Curonian Lagoon, Ventės Cape is tipped with a 19th-century red-brick lighthouse. The nearby ornithological station is Lithuania's top spot for bird-watching (p294).

The Ride: Head north, then take the minor road west of Kintai, past the kitesurfing capital of Svencelė (p291), to Dreverna (one hour).

7 Dreverna

The 13th-century fishing village of Drawohnen has morphed into a popular summer escape from Klaipėda, complete with a yachting marina, waterfront promenade, nature trails, an observation tower and boat rides through the wetlands. Don't miss the **homestead of Johann Giszas** (klaipedos rajonas.lt), the most famous of Curonian shipbuilders.

Continued from p291

it's a natural area of flat water, protected by the Curonian Spit from the Baltic Sea's waves, with consistent winds varying from 12 to 15 knots to much stronger, particularly in spring and autumn.

The mellow village vibe changed rapidly from 2020 onwards. Now you'll find a yacht marina and gleaming condos with mooring docks for well-heeled sailing aficionados. However, you'll also find multiple gear shops, a **wakeboarding** (wakescout.com) playground for days when the winds are not in your favour, and professional kiting schools that cater to kitesurfers of all abilities and ages: **Svencele Dunes**, **Wind-iGo** and **Kaitavimo**. Between April and October, 60% to 70% of days are rideable, with kiting schools ferrying you across the lagoon when the winds blow from the east. Full courses cost around €390 for six hours' instruction, or €75 per hour if you need a refresher. So turn up, sign up, and hit the waves.

Nemunas Delta

TIME FROM NIDA: **1 HR** ⛴

Birdwatchers, rejoice!

Birdwatching in the 240-sq-km **Nemunas Delta** is absurdly easy. Storks patrol the fields, or stare down at you from their nests on top of electricity poles as you cycle down to Ventės Ragas (p294). Peer through your binoculars and you might spot great crested grebes or white-winged black terns, paddling on the Curonian Lagoon. Look overhead in late August, and you'll see cranes, tits, finches and geese, heading south for the winter.

Stop by the **Ventės Ragas Ornithological Station** (zoomuz iejus.lt). With an exhibition room full of stuffed birds, a staircase gallery decorated with superb close-ups of terns feeding their young, and an observation deck encouraging visitors to spot species firsthand. The office can put you in contact with local English-speaking ornithological guides (€25 per hour).

Further north, Dreverna (p293) is the starting point for a 7km-long, signposted nature trail that shadows the western bank of the **King Wilhelm Canal** – part of the Baltic Trail – through ancient woodlands, before cutting west across the Tyrai bog and waterlogged meadows to the coast. En route, scan QR codes for more information on yellowhammers, meadow pipits, great reed warblers, black-headed gulls and other feathered denizens, and download the **Merlin Bird ID** app beforehand to identify the birds by the calls.

RINGING THE FEATHERED VISITORS

The first bird-ringing station was established at the Ventės Ragas Ornithological Station in 1929, but it wasn't until 1959–60 that large bird traps were installed. The station is on the path of one of the world's busiest bird migration routes, stretching from the Arctic to Eastern Africa, with 270 of the 294 bird species found in Lithuania frequenting the **Nemunas Delta Regional Park** (nemunodelta.lt), and 170 species stopping here to breed. Many rare birds nest in the marshes around Rusnė, including black storks, white-tailed eagles, black-tailed godwits, endemic pintails, dunlins, ruffs and great snipes. Today around 100,000 birds pass through the station each migratory period; zigzag, snipe, cobweb and duck traps ensnare up to 5000 birds daily to be ringed.

Šiauliai

PILGRIMAGE | MUSEUMS | PHOTOGRAPHY

Lithuania's fourth-largest city doesn't overwhelm you with beauty at first sight. It first appears in historical sources in 1236, coinciding with the Battle of the Sun, when the local pagan Samogitian tribes decisively defeated the Germanic Knights of the Sword (hence the multiplicity of sun symbols all over the city). Its appeal is understated: a compact, cobbled historic centre, juxtaposed with communist-era architecture that replaced WWII ruins; and quirky, niche museums dedicated to bicycles, photographic equipment, radio and TV – a reflection of Šiauliai's importance as a major industrial centre.

But Šiauliai's biggest draw by far lies north of town. Every day, visitors from far and wide descend on the Hill of Crosses – a mound covered in giant crucifixes and tiny crosses alike. The first were erected here in 1831, following the violent suppression of an uprising against the tsarist Russian rule, and thousands more have been added since.

GETTING AROUND

Central Šiauliai is compact and easily explored on foot. Rent a bicycle from the tourist office to cycle to the Hill of Crosses. Frequent buses from Šiauliai serve Kaunas, Klaipėda, Palanga, Panevėžys and Vilnius. Trains from Šiauliai service Klaipėda (1¾ to three hours), Panevėžys (1½ hours) and Vilnius (2½ to 2¾ hours).

☑ **TOP TIP**

Allow ample time for your visit to the Hill of Crosses. It rewards multiple visits, so even if you've been before, you'll end up discovering new things during your perambulations by peering closely at what other visitors have left behind. It is particularly atmospheric on misty autumn mornings.

Contemplation on the Hill of Crosses

Unique memorial and pilgrimage site

A disquieting sight greets you 10km north of Šiauliai: a small hill covered in thousand upon thousand crosses. Many are strung with rosary beads, or hung with dozens of smaller crosses that rattle softly in the breeze. Some are simple and unadorned, while others are fine examples of ironwork, or finely carved wooden folk-art masterpieces, accompanied by mournful statues of the Virgin Mary. They symbolise devotion and defiance, hope and compassion.

Come here early in the morning for some quiet contemplation, and take your time wandering past the rows of crosses and around the hill's base, drinking in the details: traditional Lithuanian *koplytstulpis* (wooden sculptures of a figure topped with a little roof), magnificent sculptures of the Sorrowful Christ (Rūpintojėlis), and elaborately carved scenes from the Passion of the Christ. There's some unusual offerings, too: crocheted crosses, Lego crosses, a cross made up of bicycle gears, a lone Star of David and a papal cross commemorating the 1993 Mass held here by Pope John Paul II.

The devout come from far and wide; you may spot a memorial to 9/11 victims, recent tributes to COVID dead, blue-and-yellow ribbons in memory of Ukrainian civilians who have perished in Russia's war on Ukraine, and Ukrainian poems, commemorating Ukrainian and Lithuanian fighters from the Azov, Donbas and other battalions.

Plant your own cross, lose yourself in your thoughts, perhaps stumble across a group of elderly Lithuanian ladies quietly singing something soothing, or contemplate the hill from the floor-to-ceiling window of a chapel nearby, designed by Italian architect Angelo Polesello.

Šiauliai's Quirky Museums

Bicycles, radios and photography

Of Šiauliai's clutch of niche museums, some reflect the city's industrial heritage, while others are a passionate expression of a single-minded hobby.

To date, Šiauliai is the only place in the Baltics that continues to manufacture bicycles, and the **Bicycle Museum** traces the history of Baltik Varas from 1948 to the present day and showcases some remarkable Lithuanian cycling achievements. Start by testing your own pedal power on one of the interactive exhibits, then marvel at the single-gear rattlebanger that carried 73-year-old Liudas Alseika partway from Klaipėda to Vladivostok in 1960; when an accident took his life en route,

THE FRENKEL LEGACY

If Chaim Frenkel (1851–1920) had listened to his parents and become a rabbi, Lithuania would have been deprived of one of its most successful entrepreneurs. Instead, learning the craft of leatherwork, by the age of 25 he had bought leather-tanning workshops in Šiauliai and built a factory that employed over 1000 workers by WWI. After WWI, his son Jacob took over production, but WWII ended the Frenkel leather empire, and Jacob barely escaped with his life. The family's legacy remains in the form of the art nouveau 1908 **Frenkelis Villa** (ausrosmuziejus.lt), its sumptuous dark-wood interior a backdrop for exhibits on the family and interwar life in Šiauliai. The synagogue built by Chaim for his Jewish factory workers is due to be revived as a cultural centre.

WHERE TO STAY IN ŠIAULIAI

Šaulys Hotel
Šiauliai's swankiest choice with plush rooms in understated greys, a 1950s-style restaurant and English-speaking staff. €€

Juro Guesthouse
Spotless guesthouse a short stroll away from most museums, with balcony and super-helpful owner. €

Hotel Šiauliai
Soviet-style monolith with great views from higher floors, unremarkable rooms and decent breakfast buffet. €€

ANDRIUS MACIUNAS/SHUTTERSTOCK ©

Hill of Crosses

HISTORY OF THE HILL OF CROSSES

Some claim it was created by the bereaved families of warriors killed in battle. Pagan traditions tell of sacred fires being lit here, long before the first crosses appeared (allegedly in the 14th century), multiplying after every uprising against the Russian tsars. Although during Soviet times planting a cross was an arrestable offence, pilgrims kept coming to commemorate those killed or deported to Siberia. In 1961, the Red Army destroyed the 2000-odd crosses on the mound and dug ditches at the hill's base, but overnight more crosses appeared. In 1972 they were destroyed after the immolation of a Kaunas student. Yet by the time Lithuania regained its independence in 1991, the hill comprised over 40,000 crosses, which have multiplied tenfold since.

his companions completed the journey after 162 days. Check out the steed that took part in the Great Millenium Peace Ride across five continents from 1998 to 2000, and ponder bicycles through the ages, from penny farthings and hugely uncomfortable-looking 19th-century contraptions to sporty Soviet designs and a vintage Imperial Triumph.

At the **Photography Museum**, borrow an iPad with detailed info on the exhibits and check out the permanent collection, from the oldest pinhole cameras and vintage Welta, Cnopm and Rollercord cameras to mid-20th-century photos of Lithuanian partisans, and a hollow-cheeked young pioneer looking like one of the *Children of the Corn*. Temporary exhibitions shine a spotlight on Lithuania's contemporary photography talent.

At the tiny, time-warped **Radio & TV Museum** down the street, delve into the wonderfully nerdy world of ham radio, radio receivers produced by amateur radio operators between 1922 and 1980, reel-to-reel tape machines and other then-marvels produced in Šiauliai during the Soviet era. The retro TV sets are works of art in their own right.

MORE QUIRKY MUSEUMS
If single-minded focus on a niche subject thrills you, check out Kaunas' **Museum of Devils** (p271) – an extensive collection of Lucifer images from Lithuania's mythology and beyond.

Beyond
Šiauliai

Places

GETTING AROUND

Žemaitija's villages and towns are walkable, but it helps to have your own wheels to get between them. You can reach Biržai by buses from Šiauliai, Kaunas, Vilnius and other major centres. Kretinga is served by buses from Palanga. Three buses between Kretinga and Skuodas stop in Salantai and Mosėdis. For Orvydas Garden, get off at the last stop before Salantai and walk. Buses from Šiauliai to Palanga stop in Plungė; there are also buses from Klaipėda and Kaunas. Plungė is on the train line from Klaipėda to Vilnius. From Plungė, there are buses to Plateliai in summer.

☑ TOP TIP

The Cold War Museum is accessed by guided tour only; book online.

Sample farmhouse-style beer, hike the Forest Trail, attend a Mardi Gras celebration or visit the Soviet Union's first nuclear bunker.

Ninety-eight kilometres west of Šiauliai along the A11, the town of Plungė is the gateway to the 200-sq-km Žemaitija National Park, home to a nuclear bunker turned Cold War museum, spruce forests and myriad lakes, the most attractive and accessible being Lake Plateliai. Cycling trails abound; Plateliai village hosts one of the most exuberant Shrove Tuesday (Mardi Gras) celebrations in Lithuania; and the long-distance Forest Trail passes through it. Take the country lanes for 101km northeast of Šiauliai to Biržai, Lithuania's northernmost town at the heart of the country's age-old farmhouse beer-brewing tradition that's making a post-Soviet comeback, or go road-tripping around Žemaitija to discover its offbeat attractions, from exceptional woodcarving and sculpture parks to winter gardens.

Lake Plateliai (p301)

VAIDOTAS GRYBAUSKAS/SHUTTERSTOCK ©

Dominated by the bewitching lakes and forests of 200-sq-km Žemaitija National Park, mysterious Žemaitija, dotted with once-sacred oaks, was the last part of Europe to convert to Christianity.

Begin in **❶ Rainiai**, where the Chapel of Suffering, marked by a large granite cross, is the site of one of the worst Soviet massacres of locals, which took place on 24 and 25 June 1941. The A11 and countryside lanes bring you to **❷ Reitavas** and the 19th-century Oginski Manor, once an autonomous noble domain with its own laws and currency, and the first residential property in the country to get electricity.

Take Rte 164 to **❸ Plungė**, where the Žemaitija Art Museum inside the 19th-century neo-Renaissance Oginski Palace displays ironwork crosses by Vytautas Jarutis and elaborate wooden carvings of mythological figures by Vytautas Ulevicius, as well as amber jewellery and contemporary art by Lithuanian artists. Continue up Rte 164 to **❹ Žemaicių Kalvarija**, known for its route of the Stations of the Cross, studded with 13 wood and six brick chapels.

Minor roads lead you past Lake Plateliai to **❺ Plateliai**, the region's best base for cycling (p302) and hiking in Žemaitija National Park. Head west to **❻ Orvidas Sodyba**, a vast, overgrown farmstead displaying the works of stonemason Kazys Orvydas (1905–89) and his son Vilius (1952–92). As you stroll the footpaths and tunnels of greenery and moss-covered stone, you'll discover numerous stone and wrought-iron crosses, mythological figures bursting forth from wood or stone, and rusty missiles.

Further west, **❼ Kretinga** is best known for the Kretinga Estate that once belonged to the Tyszkiewicz family of Polish nobles. The winter garden houses a tropical mirage of 850 species of exotic plants.

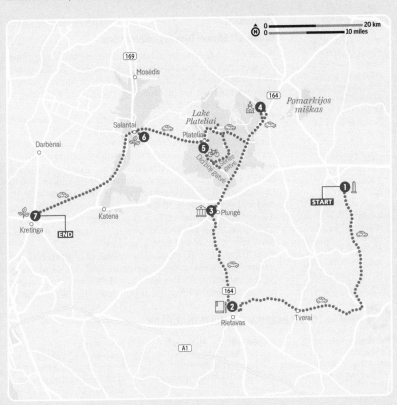

HIKE THE FOREST TRAIL

Connecting the forests, ethnographic regions and national parks of Lithuania, Latvia and Estonia, the long-distance **Forest Trail** (baltictrails.eu) stretches for 747km in Lithuania, divided into 36 day sections of around 20km each. Starting in the Dzūkija region, it proceeds along the Nemunas River, passes by Kaunas and along the banks of the Dubysa River before entering Žemaitija. Here, Lithuania's longest trail section (276km) loops through Žemaitija National Park and around Lake Plateliai; Zemaiciu Kalvarija and Plateliai make excellent overnight stops. Detailed trail section info is available online; much of the time you'll have the forest footpaths largely to yourself, even in summer months, with designated camping spots en route letting you immerse yourself fully in nature.

MARIUS SUTKUS/SHUTTERSTOCK ©

Celebrating Jonines, Plateliai

Plateliai

TIME FROM ŠIAULIAI: **1½ HRS**

Exuberant Shrove Tuesday celebrations

A bewitching landscape of lake, forest and small, traditional villages that has spawned countless fables of devils, ghosts and buried treasure, Samogitia celebrates Shrove Tuesday (Mardi Gras), aka **Uzgavenes** (Fat Tuesday) in a big way, 'to drive the winter out the yard'.

In the small lakeside town of Plateliai, deep in Žemaitija National Park, villagers wake up early and fortify themselves with a fatty breakfast of buttery porridge, made with pigtail and pig feet, then don masks and costumes before venturing out into the surrounding villages, accompanied by musicians, banging on people's doors and getting them to join in with the noisy, joyful celebration that's supposed to chase away the cold and the darkness. In the evenings, there is music, dancing and feasting, and visitors are welcome to observe or join the celebrations, ideally first procuring a *lycyna* (mask), the most important Mardi Gras accessory.

Come the summer solstice, the villagers of **Plateliai** (and all over Lithuania) come together to celebrate **Jonines** (St John's Festival, or the shortest night of the year); it was known as Rasos (Dew Holiday) in pagan times. In Plateliai, wom-

WHERE TO EAT IN ŽEMAITIJA NATIONAL PARK

Pakalnutė, Salantai
Bring a friend to share your slab of ribs, chicken escalope or hearty soup. €

Giria Bistro, Plateliai
Opt for a Supersonic or Mamma Mia burger at Plateliai's most popular cafe. €

Flow, Plungė
Chow down on globally inspired dishes in a chic setting at Oginski Hotel; non-guests welcome. €€

en dress up in traditional costumes – the textiles specific to this regions are still woven in the village – and crown themselves with wreaths of wildflowers and branches of greenery. A bonfire is lit on the banks of Lake Plateliai and everyone stays up till the wee hours, telling stories, singing songs and jumping over the bonfire. At midnight, young people look for a particular flower that tells them whether they'll be lucky in love that year.

Cold War Museum

TIME FROM ŠIAULIAI: 1½ HRS

Explore a Soviet nuclear bunker

Built in the 1960s in secret from the Lithuanian people, deep in the heart of the Žemaitija National Park, the only Soviet nuclear missile base in the region packed enough firepower to flatten all of Europe. Between 1963 and 1978, this site, consisting of four low-lying silos behind a chain-link fence, housed four medium-range ballistic SS-4 missiles, armed with 2Mt thermonuclear warheads.

The highlight here is the opportunity to descend into one of the **underground bunkers**, complete with multimedia displays, ominous music and displays of weaponry and mannequins in military attire. In the former missile control room, peruse the history of the Cold War and the nuclear arms race, then proceed to the armament exhibition to learn about the internal structure of the missile silo.

In the next room, you can see an actual replica of the SS-4 missile, as well as the reconstructed headquarters of the bunker commander, the man with his finger on the nuclear button. There's an exhibition on Soviet propaganda – which was perhaps as effective in the Soviet Union as beyond, since adjacent to it are displays on how Soviet leadership tried to prepare civil society for nuclear conflict.

Once you've taken the narrow, claustrophobic corridor inside the silo, to see where the combat missile was kept, and emerged above ground afterwards, you're likely to inhale the fresh forest air and marvel at how close the world came to nuclear Armageddon.

Biržai

TIME FROM ŠIAULIAI: 1½ HRS

Sample old-school farmhouse-style beers

Northern Lithuania is the land of barley-malt beer, with ale-makers keeping to ancient recipes and rituals practised by their ancestors 1000 years ago. People here drink 160L of beer a year, say proud locals. The quiet town of **Biržai** – Lithuania's northernmost, and one of its oldest – sits along the

THE CONTROVERSIAL ART OF MASK-MAKING

The Plateliai region has a long tradition of carving Shrove Tuesday masks out of wood, adorning them with fur trim, goat horns, horse tails and other accessories, and painting them. The highlight at the **Plateliai Manor** is the old stable, housing a fascinating exhibition of local Shrove Tuesday customs, with around 250 elaborately carved masks of devils, witches, horses, bears and other characters gazing and leering down at you from the walls. The folksy caricatures of Jews and Roma with exaggerated features are the less savoury part of traditional mask-making. Plateliai's helpful, multilingual **Žemaitija National Park Visitor Centre** (zemaitijosnp.lt) can direct you towards the homes of master mask-carvers, though you'll need to speak some Lithuanian or Russian.

WHERE TO STAY IN ŽEMAITIJA NATIONAL PARK

Vila Runa
Choose between doubles or bright family-sized apartments on this farmstead near Plateliai, ideal for outdoor pursuits. €€

Oginski Hotel
Neutral shades and river views dominate at this sleek spot next to the Oginski Palace. €€

Soprano Forest Spa
Soak in the hot tub outside your private villa, a stone's throw from Lake Plateliai. €€€

This 24km-long cycling route takes you around the largest lake in the park. Begin in **❶Plateliai**, and go anticlockwise past the **❷Siberia Telmological Reserve**, a marshland that can be observed from above if you climb the 15m-high tower. A short stretch past the pike-rich Lake Beržoras and Lake Ilgis brings you to **❸Prokšciai**. It's worth detouring in the Plungė direction for 1.6km to visit a **❹19th-century water mill** housing the artworks of L Černiauskas, before retracing your steps and pedalling past the forested, off-limits **❺Plokštine Strict Natural Reserve** to the **❻Cold War Museum** (p301). After visiting the nuclear silos, stretch your legs along the adjacent 3km-long **❼Plokštine Educational Walking Trail** that meanders along forested hills and past the Pilelis spring. Back on your bike, head for the **❽ Lake Plateliai viewing platform** for panoramic views from its eastern shore.

Nearby, the 2.3km-long **❾Paplatelė Educational Walking Trail** shows off local flora and fauna along the shores of Sultekis pond. Some 4.3km further north along the lakeshore, detour for 400m to the **❿Pakaštuva Telmological Reserve** to spot swans, marsh harriers, grebes, cranes and other birdlife.

Passing the millennia-old **⓫Užpelkiai Mound**, detour for 3km to the village of **⓬Dovainiai** to check out the folksy woodcarvings of Kazys Striaupa inside a granary turned museum. Heading towards Plateliai, part of the cycling trail coincides with the **⓭Seirė Educational Walking Trail** that points out rare plants and fungi. Finish with a visit to the **⓮Plateliai Manor**, erusing its incredible collection of Shrove Tuesdays masks (p276) and displays on Samogitia's nature and archaeological findings from Sventrokalnis and Pilies islands on the lake.

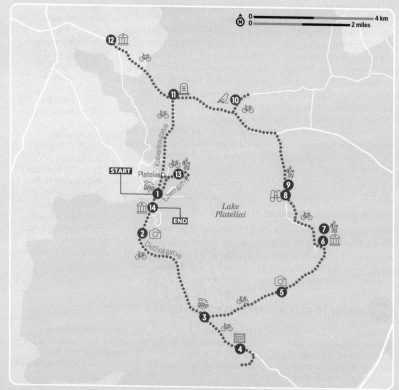

Plateliai

LITHUANIA'S FARMHOUSE ALE-BREWING TRADITION

It's hard to think of a more 'local' beverage than Lithuania's farmhouse-style ales, known locally as *kaimiškas alus* (village beer). Brewed in the countryside for a millennium, using locally grown hops (or peas, if hops were in short supply), these vary vastly in style and flavour: some are *šviesus* (pale), others are *tamsus* (dark) or even *juodas* (black); most are unpasteurised and unfiltered and taste very different from filtered, 'dead' beer. During Soviet times, the farmhouse brewing tradition was all but wiped out, but is now making a resurgence, particularly in and around Biržai. A number of these farmhouse-style ales are bottled and sold commercially, but sampling them fresh at the source makes a huge difference to their flavour.

shores of two beautiful lakes and the confluence of two rivers. Its handsome 16th-century castle aside, the biggest draw is its fantastic brewery which is at the heart of the revived farmhouse brewing tradition. The two-day **Biržai Town Festival** in August – a madcap fiesta where the town's breweries sell their wares on the street – is a particularly exciting time to be here, but if you're a hophead, you can book a tour ahead of time, year-round, at the **Rinkuškiai Brewery**.

Tours start with standard 90-minute walk-throughs of the brewing facilities, where you get to witness the process from malting, milling and mashing up through to fermentation, bottling and the finished product. In the attached museum, the guide will initiate you into the secrets of centuries-old farmhouse brewing tradition. At the end you get to try six types of unfiltered beer, from the black ale and temptingly sweet porter with a bitter kick to the Witbier, a cold-filtered Hops & Cannabis and the pale lager. The Gourmet tour (2½ hours) is even more beer-focused, and concludes with pairing gourmet snacks and eight different beers from the Rinkuškiai repertoire that comprises over two dozen beers, including the Port of Discovery and Microhistory series, along with a smoky house *gira* (kvas). Get you hop-heavy souvenirs from the shop next to the brewery.

Aukštaitija National Park

DENSE FOREST | LEISURE TIME | CYCLING

GETTING AROUND

Ignalina is well connected to Vilnius by a dozen daily buses (two hours) as well as trains (eight daily, 1½ to 1¾ hours). Rent bicycles and watercraft in nearby Palūšė.

☑ TOP TIP

The main jumping-off point for the park is Ignalina, with the greatest concentration of accommodation, and excellent cross-country skiing in winter.

Encompassing dense pine, spruce and decidious forest, and dotted with 126 lakes, the 406-sq-km Aukštaitija National Park is Lithuania's oldest protected area. Wandering the myriad woodland trails that criss-cross it, berrying in the summer, mushrooming in the autumn, and summiting Ladakalnis Hill – a sacred pagan site in centuries past – you truly come to appreciate the ancient beliefs that tie Lithuanians to their land and their love for nature. You can enjoy a quintessential Lithuanian summer here, foraging for bilberries and wild strawberries, swimming wild in the lakes (including the 60.5m-deep Lake Tauragnas, the country's deepest), playing volleyball on lakeside beaches, fishing for eel, and canoeing or paddleboarding the streams and channels that connect the main bodies of water. Besides ample wildlife, including wild boars, elk and rare amphibians, the park is home to 116 tiny settlements, many of them mere hamlets – some of them well worth exploring for their ethnographic heritage.

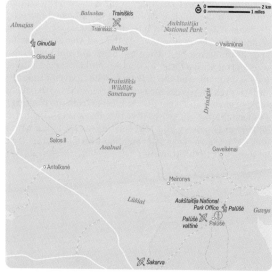

Aukštaitija National Park

Getting Active in Aukštaitija National Park
Enjoy an idyllic Lithuanian summer

Few places in Lithuania do active leisure as well as Aukštaitija National Park. For many Lithuanians, idyllic summers are spent swimming in lakes, playing volleyball on sandy lake beaches, hiking or cycling through pine forest, and taking to Aukštaitija's many bodies of water by kayak, canoe or paddleboard. Located in Palūšė, the **Aukštaitija National Park Office** (aparkai.lt) is handy for park maps and information about the main self-guided walking, cycling and water routes, and can arrange treks and backpacking trips by boat, with English-speaking guides.

While the numerous footpaths and forest trails in the national park can be combined into countless different outings on foot or by bike, there are five main signposted hiking trails, ranging from the educational, family-friendly 3.7km trail from **Palūšė** to a 15km hike from **Ginučiai** (five hours). There are also seven designated cycling routes, ranging from half-day 25km jaunts to a 110km overnighter.

Some of the park's lakes are interconnected and superb paddling opportunities abound, whether you're paddling from Palūšė to Vaišniūnai (15km, four hours), or tackling the two-day, 33km paddling challenge from Rūgšteliškis on **Lake Utenas** to Vaidžiuškės on **Lake Baluošas** via the Būka River, and then onwards to Palūšė via multiple lakes, camping by **Lake Almajas** overnight. In Palūšė, rent fibreglass two-person canoes (€5/20 per hour/day) and stand-up paddleboards (SUPS; €10/30 per hour/day) from **Palūšė valtinė**. Based in Trainiškis on Lake Baluošas, **Trainiškis** rents fibreglass canoes, SUPs and mobile saunas, offers campsite bookings, and has put together numerous self-guided paddling routes. **Šakarva**, near Palūšė, offers similar services.

BEST PLACES TO STAY IN AUKŠTAITIJA NATIONAL PARK

Lake & Library Hotel, Ignalina
Aukštaitija's lovely boutique hotel, with individually styled rooms overlooking Gavys Lake, a beach and a volleyball court. Excellent breakfast. €€

Ginučiai Watermill, Ginučiai
Relax by the fire, use the guest kitchen, then retire to your wood-clad room inside this 19th-century watermill. Open April to October. €

Miškiniškės Sodyba, Miškiniškė
Beautifully appointed logwood rooms and apartments in a woodland setting, with a sauna, wood-fire burners and good hiking nearby. €€

Tiki Inn, Palūšė
Polynesia-themed lakeside inn, with a terrace for sunset-watching, hot tubs, sauna, free water-sports equipment for guests, and spartan rooms. €

FREEWHEELING IN AUKŠTAITIJA NATIONAL PARK

This 110km-long cycling loop along forest trails and country lanes through Aukštaitija's lakelands hits the national park's diverse natural and cultural highlights.

Beginning in ❶ **Ignalina**, head west to ❷ **Palūšė**, the park's water-sports base, before skirting Lake Asalnai and crossing the bridge to ❸ **Salos**, an ethnographic village with a cluster of well-preserved homesteads you can peer into. Continue along a narrow isthmus and summit ❹ **Ladakalnis**, the 155m-tall hill named after the pagan goddess Lada, for an unfolding panorama of seven lakes. Descend to the road leading to the village of ❺ **Ginučiai**, where you can visit a 19th-century watermill in full working order, then take a minor road through pine forest to the entertaining ❻ **Ancient Beekeeping Museum** near Stripeikiai, complete with interactive exhibits for kids, hollow log and straw hives used by local beekeepers

for centuries, and honey for purchase. Join Rte 4902 in the village of Sėlė and press on towards Tauragnai, detouring to ❼ **Taurapilis**, one of several ancient hill-forts overlooking Lake Tauragnas – Lithuania's deepest lake. Follow Rte 4930 along the north shore, past more hill-forts and picnic areas, to the island-studded Lake Baluošas, pausing to admire traditional architecture in the villages of ❽ **Strazdai** and ❾ **Šuminai**.

Once you reach Rte 1423, detour briefly to ❿ **Trainiškis** to be awed by its mighty 800-year-old tree and former pagan sacrificial site. Head east, then take Rte 1410 south towards Ignalina, detouring to the ⓫ **Gaveikėnai watermill** (1800). Returning to Palūšė, pedal south along Rte 114 to ⓬ **Kaltanėnai**, the park's largest settlement, then head back to Ignalina along the east side of Lake Kretuonas, the park's largest, passing more burial mounds and ancient hill-fort sites en route.

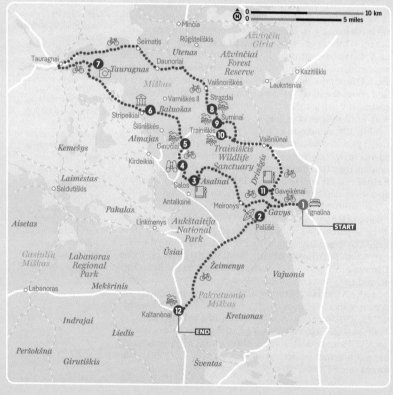

Beyond
Aukštaitija
National Park

Go stargazing, visit an equine-themed museum and a defunct nuclear power station, peruse wooden sculpture and ride a narrow-gauge railway.

Some 40km northeast of Ignalina in Aukštaitija National Park, the Soviet-built, Russian-speaking town of Visaginas is the gateway to the decommissioned Ignalina Nuclear Power plant, where much of the HBO series *Chernobyl* was shot, and which can be visited on a group tour. Head to the Molėtai Astronomical Observatory, 58km west of Ignalina for nighttime stargazing, visit Anykščiai for a ride on Lithuania's last functioning narrow-gauge railway, and swing by the village of Niūronys to delve deep into Lithuania's long-standing love affair with the horse. Rokiškis is well worth the 113km drive north for its 15th-century estate and manor house, where you can admire the exceptional collection of intricate wooden sculptures by local 'godmaker' Lionginas Šepka.

Places
Visaginas p309

GETTING AROUND

All towns in Aukštaitija are walkable; all are connected to Vilnius and some to each other via public transport. Out-of-the-way attractions such as the Niūronys Horse Museum, Labanoras protected area and the Molėtai observatory are best reached by car.

☑ TOP TIP

Arrange tours of Ignalina Nuclear Power Plant (iae.lt) well ahead of time. Molėtai Astronomical Observatory (mao.tfai.vu.lt) also requires advance bookings.

Molėtai Astronomical Observatory

LUKAS JONAITIS/SHUTTERSTOCK ©

307

This 261km-long drive through largely agricultural and lake-blotched Aukštaitija can be done in a couple of days.

Some 31km from ❶ **Ignalina**, the 528-sq-km Labanoras Regional Park is dotted with 285 lakes. ❷ **Labanoras**, the largest village within the park, is the jumping-off point for exploring the forests and raised bogs on foot or by bicycle. Continue along Rte 114 for 27km to ❸ **Molėtai**, a dark-sky destination, to visit the Astronomical Observatory on Kaldiniai Hill (193m) where two telescopes provide outstanding views of the surrounding lakeland (arrange night tours in advance).

Some 45km north along Rte 119, ❹ **Anykščiai** is home to Lithuania's sole narrow-gauge railway, with 68km of track still in use today. The fun Railway Museum offers rides on manual rail cars and railway bicycles, while the warehouse is full of beautifully restored vintage cars and motorcycles.

Continue for 6km north along Rte 1209 to ❺ **Niūronys**, where the Horse Museum welcomes hippophiles with its smithy, farmer's residence, a fine collection of horse-drawn fire engines, carriages and taxis, and horse and carriage rides during warmer months.

Retracing your steps to Rte 120, drive for 62km north to ❻ **Rokiškis**, whose star attraction is the 19th-century, baroque-style Manor House. Besides the neo-Romantic interior, the museum is particularly worthwhile, due to 3000 wooden sculptures of local 'godmaker' Lionginas Sepka (1907–85). Rte 122, then Rte 117 bring you to lake-fringed ❼ **Zarasai**, a jumping-off spot for rural tourism in the surrounding countryside. In town, drink in lakeside panoramas from the Observation Wheel, then drive southeast for 25km to ❽ **Visaginas**, a Soviet-built town and gateway to nuclear tourism at the Ignalina Nuclear Power Plant.

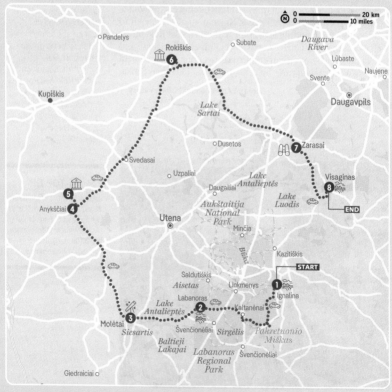

Observation tower, Labanoras

PULLING THE PLUG ON IGNALINA

The Ignalina Nuclear Power Plant (INPP) was originally designed to have four 1500MW nuclear reactors, which would have made it the Soviet Union's biggest producer of nuclear energy. But only two of the reactors were completed when the Soviet Union collapsed. Since the design of the reactors at the INPP is similar to the one used at Chernobyl in Ukraine, after Lithuania joined the EU in 2004, it came under pressure to shut them down. Though electricity is no longer produced here and the reactors are due to be fully dismantled by 2038, controversy abounds, from the prohibitive decommissioning costs and the lack of blueprints for dismantling Ignalina to the long-term problem of disposing of redundant radioactive material.

Visaginas TIME FROM AUKŠTAITIJA NATIONAL PARK: **35 MINS** 🚗

Exploring Lithuania's nuclear power plant

Russian-speaking Visaginas, built in 1975 to accommodate employees of the nearby **Ignalina Nuclear Power Plant** (INPP), is not your typical tourism hot spot. And yet, its unpretty Soviet blocks of flats belie its recent popularity as an epicentre of nuclear tourism. The massive rise in public interest is largely thanks to the 2019 HBO miniseries, *Chernobyl,* shot partly at the INPP, and partly in a simulator control room that replicates the one near Visaginas.

There are two ways to visit the INPP. For an in-depth three-hour guided visit of the inner territory in English, Russian or Lithuanian (over-18-year-olds only; Wednesdays, Thursdays and Fridays at 10.30am) that allows you to witness the live operation of the nuclear power plant, including the turbine hall, the RBMK reactor hall and unit control room, complete the online application form weeks or months in advance.

It's easier to attend an hour-long Information Centre tour (Monday to Friday, 10am and 1pm), though you still have to apply ahead of time. Absorbing videos explain the INPP's history, operation stages and decommission process, with the guide pointing out the nuclear reactor and explaining

 WHERE TO STAY IN VISAGINAS ──────────

Private apartments	**Idile B&B**	**Hotel Kornealita**
Visaginas' most abundant sleeping options are private apartment rentals inside the Soviet residential buildings. €	Friendly B&B near Lake Visaginas; buffet breakfast is included and owners can arrange bicycle rental. €	Snug, carpeted, beige rooms have access to the gym, pool and billiard room at Visaginas' only hotel. €€

BEST PLACES TO EAT & DRINK IN VISAGINAS

INPP Canteen
Join workers on their lunch break for hearty soups, dumplings and meat dishes (11.30am to 1pm Monday to Friday). €

Café Banga
Borscht, beef stew with buckwheat and lamb plov lunches served inside the lakeside community centre. €

Ikura
Visaginas' branch of the reliable Lithuania-wide sushi chain serving a melange of well-executed sushi rolls, sashimi and noodle dishes. €

Bear & Boar Brewery
Tour Visaginas' craft brewery and sample its nature-inspired Atomic Blonde, Silence of the Lambs and Visa-Ginnes.

SAVÀ Coffee Bar
Lakeside cafe responsible for excellent espresso, consumed to a soundtrack of chill beats.

its workings using a scale model. You learn about the significant challenges facing the INPP and view scale models of radioactive waste depositories yet to be constructed that will make it someone else's problem 50 to 300 years from now, before donning a VR headset and viewing the nuclear waste disposal process close up.

Averting a nuclear disaster

Imagine: you're in the INPP control room, in charge of the nuclear reactor. The dials in front of you indicate the reactor is overheating. What do you do? Press the red button to perform an emergency shutdown? Behind you, examiners are watching you through the window of the observation room. Get this wrong, and you'll live. Get this wrong twice, and you'll never work in a nuclear power plant again.

Following the Chernobyl disaster in 1986, it was decreed that all nuclear power stations worldwide needed to have simulator control rooms in which staff received mandatory training on handling emergencies. **LitWild** runs entertaining tours of the Visaginas simulator control room, which involve detailed explanations, a fun video, a dressing-up session and a chance to poke at buttons.

Fatbike adventuring and nuclear power plant

Follow Anton out of Visaginas along hidden forest trails, with your fatbike navigating the uneven, occasionally swampy ground with ease. Your multilingual guide regales you with stories of Visaginas life, points out edible berries and mushrooms, and takes you to a scenic viewpoint overlooking Lithuania's biggest lake. You pass through a quirky *dacha* settlement, drink water from a mineral spring, or graze on apples at Anton's friend's *dacha*. After a dramatic final approach, you arrive at the Ignalina Nuclear Power Plant just in time for lunch, then take a different route back to Visaginas.

Visaginas has become a hub for fresh-air fiends, largely thanks to the efforts of the young, dynamic **LitWild** operators who love exploring the surrounding wilderness on fatbikes, by kayak, or paddleboard, or on foot. Contact them a few days in advance to arrange an outdoor adventure, from romantic sunset paddleboarding and full-day treks through Aukštaitija National Park to exhilarating fatbike rides.

Ignalina Nuclear Power Plant (p309)

Druskininkai

MINERAL-RICH WATERS | SPAS | SOVIET SCULPTURE

GETTING AROUND

Druskininkai is compact and walkable. Bolt electric scooters are scattered about town, and there are bicycles for rent during the warmer months. Bolt also provides a taxi service. Take bus 2 via Viečiūnai (two to four daily) from Druskininkai directly to Grūtas Park, or ask one of many Vilnius-bound buses to drop you at the Grūtas stop and walk for 20 minutes. From the bus station, there are daily direct buses to/from Vilnius (two hours), Kaunas (2½ to 3½ hours), Klaipėda (five hours) and Palanga (5½ to 7¼ hours).

☑ TOP TIP

Druskininkai's spa hotels (particularly those with waterparks) are extremely popular with families. Book rooms and health procedures a couple of months ahead for the summer months and weeks ahead for weekends, year-round. Midweek outside the summer season, hotel prices drop by as much as 30%.

Fringed with pine forest at the confluence of the Nemunas and Ratnycia Rivers, the genteel spa town of Druskininkai with its wide, tree-lined boulevards is renowned for the healing properties of its mineral waters. In centuries past, locals noticed that sores on their bodies healed faster if they bathed in particular springs, and Druskininkai was declared a centre for healing in 1794. The first spa opened in 1832, attracting Polish and Lithuanian nobility and Russian officials with its salty mineral water (Druskininkai takes its name from *druska*, or 'salt'), and during the days of the USSR, the old and ailing sought miracle cures at the famous health resort. Today, you can join Lithuanian and Polish visitors queueing up at the Health Resort Druskininkai to drink this healing elixir, stroll past attractive timber houses with carved gables, along the riverside, or indulge in a more extreme kind of water therapy at Lithuania's biggest aqua park.

City of Healing Waters

Immerse yourself in aquatic fun

To experience Druskininkai's aqua-centric delights, commence with drinking its mineral-rich waters, either at the pump room of the **Grand Spa Lietuva** health centre or the riverside **Mineralinio Vandens Biuvetė** with stained-glass windows; look out for a 1960s image of Eglė, Queen of Serpents. Perhaps you'd prefer to preserve your youthful looks by washing your face in the nearby riverfront **Beauty Spring** – the saltiest and most mineral-rich of Druskininkai's springs, with the water pumping from a depth of 327m.

Immersing yourself in the mineral waters is supposed to help with joint pains, digestive issues and respiratory ailments. Of Druskininkai's numerous spas, the ones offering healing soaks include Grand Spa Lietuva, **Spa Vilnius SANA** and **Mineral Spa Draugyste**.

Since you're here, why not sample other available treatments? Spa Vilnius SANA specialises in amber baths, deep-tissue massages and mineral-rich mud immersions. Besides facials, massages, mud baths and water treatments,

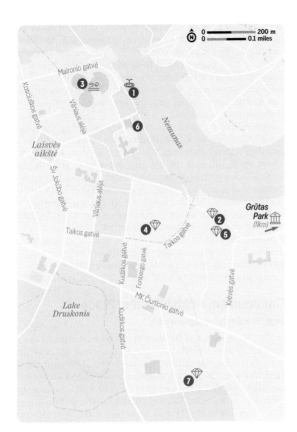

SIGHTS
1 Beauty Spring

**ACTIVITIES,
COURSES & TOURS**
2 Amberton
Green Spa
3 Aqua Park
4 Grand
Spa Lietuva
5 Mineral
Spa Draugyste
6 Mineralinio
Vandems Biuvetė
7 Spa
Vilnius SANA

Amberton Green Spa offers relaxing Somnarium sessions, paired with oxygen therapy, while Grand Spa Lietuva's wellness menu includes wraps, volcanic stone treatments, salt-room sessions for asthmatics, Charcot's showers and the ominously titled 'rectal mud tampon'.

Curative properties aside, Druskininkai is Lithuania's waterpark central. At the vast **Aqua Park**, attached to Druskininkai's year-round indoor skiing arena, you can plummet down the Extreme and Adrenaline water slides, float in the whirlpool and steam in infra-red, dry and log saunas, plus a hammam. Grand Spa Lietuva has its own waterpark with two water slides, wave pool, saunas, steam room and ice room.

If you're staying at any of the spa hotels, decide on treatments, book them in advance, then go to the designated room

 WHERE TO EAT IN DRUSKININKAI

Etno Dvaras
Lakeside restaurant serving *cepelinai* (stuffed parcels of potato dough), pork with sauerkraut and other staples. €

House
Pleasant summer terrace and menu that covers most bases (burgers, pasta, risottos, salads, grilled meats). €€

Sicilia
Druskininkai's top spot delivers wood-fired pizza and vaguely Italian-style fish and seafood with aplomb. €€

in your hotel bathrobe and flip-flops (the latter a boon for waterparks as well). Otherwise, casual wear will do. Some treatments (healing mud bath, Charcot's shower etc) require you to disrobe completely in front of the healthcare practitioner. If getting a full body massage, you'll get disposable single-use underwear. Swimwear is mandatory in waterpark saunas and steam rooms; bracelet-operated lockers are provided for your valuables.

Approaching Druskininkai from the east, along Čiurlionio gatvė, look out for **Girios Aidas**, 2km east of town. You'll spot the architectural brainchild of Algirdas Valavičius by the 'forest inside': literally an oak tree bursting forth from the large wooden cottage with gabled eaves, looking like something out of a folk tale. Inside, a museum explains humanity's place within the natural world, with engaging displays of stuffed local fauna, woodcarvings and an exhibition dedicated to Lithuania's most famous naturalist, Tadas Ivanauskas. However, the real highlight is out the back: a trail through the woods acts as an outdoor sculpture gallery, showing off intricate pagan- and nature-themed woodcarvings – fine examples of artisanship that Lithuania is rightfully famous for.

Communism's Final Resting Place
Explore a Soviet sculpture park

In the small village of **Grūtas**, 8km east of Druskininkai, a locomotive with a cattle car – identical to those that carried deported Lithuanians to Siberia – greets you at the entrance of **Grūtas Park**. This Soviet sculpture park's collection of communist monuments, rescued from the post-1991 scrapheap by enterprising collector Viliumas Malinauskas, and displayed along forested trails flanked by barbed wire, watchtowers and a moat (for greater prison-camp resemblance) pays black-humoured homage to a dark period of Lithuania's history.

As you enter, the giant stone images of a Soviet soldier and heroic partisan figures sit rather incongruously alongside a children's playground and a small zoo featuring ostriches, donkeys and goats. From the cafe, follow the loop trails anticlockwise, passing multiple Lenins, Stalins, prominent Lithuanian communists and freedom fighters. Inside the three exhibition buildings, look out for a Soviet-era poster featuring a smiling Yuri Gagarin, a rug depicting a 'come hither' Lenin, dramatic linocut prints portraying heroic Lenin scenes, a sobering map of deportee destinations around the Soviet Union, plus socialist-realist art with a pastoral bent, along with contemporary modernist pieces by Lithuanian painter Valerij Bodiaj.

BEST HOTELS IN DRUSKININKAI

Amberton Green Spa
Druskininkai's five-star option, with rooms and studios in smart greys and creams, an excellent restaurant and an award-winning spa offering innovative treatments. €€€

Aqua Hotel
Perfect for a family stay, this three-star hotel is part of the vast Aqua Park complex; good breakfast buffet. €€

Grand Spa Lietuva
Three buildings make up this epic health resort, from fully serviced apartments to spacious, bright rooms. Price includes Aqua Park access. €€

Art Hotel
Wooden mansion comprising spacious studios in soothing blues and whites, with bold contemporary art and high-beamed family apartments. €€

Beyond
Druskininkai

Traditional villages, a unique way of life, a settlement famous for its mushroom festival and a one-town republic await beyond Druskininkai.

East of Druskininkai lies Dzūkija National Park – Lithuania's largest at 560 sq km – that comprises continental dunes, pine forests, sandy plains, river valleys, dozens of lakes, forest trails and cycle paths, and visitor centres in the larger villages of Merkinė and Marcinkonys. Dzūkija's beautifully preserved settlements, part of ethnographic and cultural reserves and home to the Dzūkai – who practise the traditional crafts of woodcarving, weave linen and wool by hand and gather the harvest using scythes and sickles – are the best place to experience traditional Lithuania. The wooden-sculpture-lined Čiurlionis Way connects Merkinė to Varėna, the artist's birthplace and home of Lithuania's mushroom festival, while between the two lies the tiny breakaway republic of Perloja.

Dzūkija National Park

JONAS VEGELE/SHUTTERSTOCK ©

Places

Dzūkija National Park
p316

GETTING AROUND

To explore Dzūkija National Park on two wheels, rent a bicycle from one of several outlets in Druskininkai. The Druskininkai tourist office also has excellent free maps for cyclists. Buses from Druskininkai to Vilnius stop in Merkinė (30 minutes). Daily trains to/from Vilnius stop at Zervynos (1¾ hours), Marcinkonys (two hours) and Varėna (1½ hours). During the summer months, you can opt for a three-hour cruise to Liškiava Monastery from Druskininkai aboard the steamboat *Druskininkai* (gelme-druskininkai.lt).

☑ TOP TIP

Guides to the Black Potter Trail, homestays in traditional houses in Dzūkija's villages and tours in Čepkeliai Reserve must all be arranged in advance.

MANTAS_BAC/SHUTTERSTOCK ©

Čepkeliai Reserve, Dzūkija National Park

MUSHROOMING & BERRYING

There's a local saying in Dzūkija: 'If it weren't for the mushrooms and berries, Dzūkai girls would walk around naked.' Assist local women in their quest to clothe themselves by purchasing jars of chanterelles, boletus and brown-capped *baravykas* during the August to November mushrooming season from locals selling at roadsides, or attend Varėna's September **mushroom festival** (varena. lt). Alternatively, forage for Lithuania's 380 species of edible mushrooms yourself; note that mushrooming in the Čepkeliai Reserve is restricted to local villagers. Berrying is another big deal around Dzūkija National Park. Red bilberries only ripen in August and cranberries in September, but most other berries – wild strawberries, blueberries, buckthorn berries, sloe berries and raspberries – can be harvested whenever they are ripe.

Dzūkija National Park

Experience Lithuania at its most rural

They say Dzūkija's woodlands ring with song, as the Dzūkai who live in these parts are renowned for their singing voices and good humour in the face of a tough life of farming and foraging. To truly experience it, stay in farmstays in Merkinė, Marcinkonys and elsewhere, organised via the **national park directorate** (dnp.lrv.lt), exploring Dzūkija on foot, by 0ebicycle or canoeing on the Ūla and Grūda Rivers, and lingering in small villages to interact with woodcarvers, basketweavers and other artisans.

In the national park, there are nine designated hiking trails, ranging from 1km to 12km, departing from the villages of Marcinkonys, Margionys, Merkinė and Musteika, that take you through diverse natural ecosystems and introduce you to local crafts. Merkinė is the starting point for the 12km-long **Secrets of Black Clay** trail. Several pottery masters (particularly in Pelekiskes village) still practise the ancient ceramic art, whereby pots as black as soot are made from red clay using pine-wood resin. **Merkinė Visitor Centre** can arrange a guided visit to the kilns, including Lithuania's oldest; contact them in advance.

If you're short on time, get a taste for local woodcarving, weaving, basket-making and beekeeping at the **Ethnographic Homestead** in Marcinkonys, where the exposition explores the everyday life, traditions and material culture of Dzūkai people.

If you're interested in exploring the bogs, black alder swamps, Cladinoso-callunosa forest and lakes of the 112-sq-km **Čepkeliai Reserve**, home to more than 4000 species of animals and plants (including lynx and wolves), register in advance at the **Marcinkonys Visitor Centre** for a guided visit.

The best way to explore this unique corner of the country is on two wheels, and this loop from Druskininkai is best spread over two days.

From ❶ **Druskininkai**, pedal for 9km to ❷ **Liškiava**, a scenic little town on the bank of the Nemunas River renowned for its Dominican monastery with a gigantic cupola, seven rococo-style altars and a crypt with glass coffins. Carry on through the villages of Zeimiai and Panara to ❸ **Merkinė**, one of Lithuania's oldest formerly fortified settlements, sitting at the scenic confluence of the Merkys, Nemunas and Stange rivers. Its attractions include a small Museum of Lithuanian Freedom, Struggle and Suffering, and a compact Hill of Crosses commemorating the dead Forest Brotherhood (p71) members. Pedalling east along the A4, you'll pass sculpted wooden 'totem' poles and sculptures, erected in 1975 in commemoration of the 100th anniversary of the birth of artist and composer MK Čiurlionis (p262) in nearby ❹ **Varėna**, the mushroom capital of Lithuania. En route, tiny ❺ **Perloja** became a self-declared republic for five years in 1918, its armed guard of 50 men facing off against Germans, Russians, Poles and Lithuanian factions. From Varėna, take the quiet country road southwest to ❻ **Zervynos**, an old ethnographic village whose farmsteads have protected status. Further along, ❼**Marcinkonys**, a 16th-century forester village active in championing Lithuanian nationalism in defiance of the Russian tsar and then Poland, has been home to a locally famous folklore ensemble since the 1970s. Press on to 17th-century ❽ **Margionys**, known for its theatre productions since 1929. A little detour to the south, wild beekeeping ❾ **Musteika** is particularly appealing, with its 19th-century wooden houses and educational trail past hollow-tree beehives.

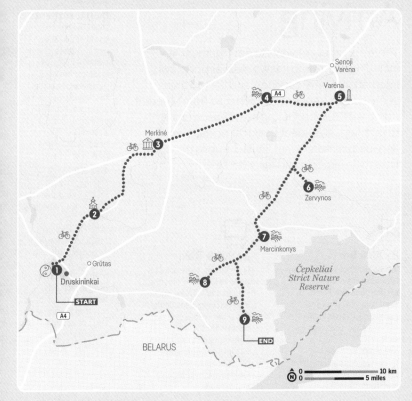

SERHII IVASHCHUK/SHUTTERSTOCK ©

Arriving

There's a variety of ways to get to Lithuania, including flights into its two main airports, two international ferry services, and limited train services and frequent bus services from different corners of Europe. During high season (June to late August) expect busier airports. Airport services are somewhat limited. Public transport links main airports and ferry port to city centres.

By Air & Boat

Vilnius and Kaunas airports are Lithuania's main flight hubs, serving numerous European destinations; Kaunas deals mainly with Ryanair flights. Palanga Airport receives seasonal summer flights. Klaipėda's ferry port has passenger and car ferry services to Kiel (Germany) and Karlshamn (Sweden).

By Bus & Train

From Vilnius, there are daily trains to Krakow (Poland) via Kaunas and Warsaw, and to Riga via Daugavpils. Train/bus services to Russia and Belarus are suspended until further notice. Lux Express, Ecolines and Eurolines buses connect Vilnius and Kaunas to Latvia, Estonia and beyond.

Money

Currency: euro (€)

CARD & CASH

Multilingual ATMs are ubiquitous in cities and towns; even villages are likely to have at least one. The majority accept Visa and MasterCard. American Express cards may be accepted at larger hotels and restaurants. It's worth carrying cash for small purchases (museum admission, bus tickets, market produce etc). Plan ahead if you're staying in small guesthouses, which are less likely to accept cards.

DIGITAL PAYMENTS

Digital payments have become the norm in hotels, restaurants, cafes and most businesses, particularly in bigger towns and cities and in touristy destinations. In smaller, rural destinations it's a good idea to carry cash, just in case.

TIPPING

Tipping 10% in restaurants is the norm; even if paying by card, tip with cash. In hotels, tipping is restricted to top-end establishments with room service and porters. Taxi drivers don't expect a tip, but it's common to round up the fare or add a couple of euros for assistance with baggage.

Getting Around

Lithuania is a compact country, covered by an extensive network of bus services as well as comfortable trains. Getting around is straightforward, whether you're traveling by bus or train. There's a certain amount of aggressive local driving, but the roads are in good condition, with little traffic along scenic country lanes. There are no internal flights.

BUS

The national bus network is extensive, linking all major cities to each other and smaller towns to regional hubs. Find most services on the Autobusų Bilietai (autobusubilietai.lt) website or app. Larger cities and towns are well covered by public transport networks.

BICYCLES, E-SCOOTERS & TAXI/RIDESHARE

In larger cities and towns there's an ever-growing number of cycling lanes and bicycle rental points, and a proliferation of electric scooters (Bolt or Lime). Bolt also operates as a cheaper taxi alternative. Taxis are relatively inexpensive and metered.

TRAIN

Operated by Lithuanian Rail (ltglink.lt), trains are comfortable, air-conditioned and an inexpensive, efficient way of getting around. Vilnius to Kaunas, Klaipėda or Šiauliai are handy routes. There are no direct trains between Kaunas and Klaipėda, so buses are a better option.

BOAT

There are two regularly scheduled year-round domestic ferry services between Klaipėda and Smiltynė on the Curonian Spit: a passenger ferry and a car ferry. In summer, regular boats connect Nida and Juodkrantė on the Curonian Spit with Dreverna, Ventė and Mingė.

CAR

Driving is the fastest way to visit remoter attractions. Car hire is offered in all the major cities. Spark (spark.lt) is Vilnius' and Kaunas' electric carshare service. Parking is occasionally problematic in historic city centres. Winter tyres are compulsory from mid-November through March.

DRIVING ESSENTIALS

Drive on the right side

Speed limit is 50km/h in cities, 70km/h to 90km/h outside cities, and 110km/h to 130km/h on motorways.

Blood alcohol limit: 0.4%.

TOOLKIT

The chapters in this section cover the most important topics you'll need to know about in Estonia, Latvia and Lithuania. They're full of nuts-and-bolts information and valuable insights to help you understand and navigate Estonia, Latvia and Lithuania and get the most out of your trip.

**Family Travel
p322**

**Accommodation
p323**

**Food, Drink
& Nightlife
p324**

**Responsible
Travel
p326**

**LGBTiQ+
Travellers
p328**

**Accessible
Travel
p329**

**Health & Safe
Travel
p330**

**Nuts & Bolts
p331**

Rīga (p162), Latvia

Family Travel

The Baltic countries are family-friendly by design. Governments are pressed to fight the depopulation crisis by creating an environment attractive for raising children. Modern playgrounds and accessible sports facilities are ubiquitous. It's culturally acceptable and deemed safe enough to let children roam around freely and walk to school unaccompanied from a relatively early age.

Sights

Most museums in the Baltic countries offer either discounted or free entrance for children as well as heavily discounted family tickets. For example, a regular ticket for the Latvian National Museum of Art costs €8, while a family ticket for one adult plus up to four children costs €5, and two adults with the same number of children pay €7.

Accommodation

The proliferation of cottages and apartments for rent allows families to organise holiday life in a way not entirely dissimilar to life back home, complete with kitchen facilities and washing machines. Many of these come with dedicated rooms for children, sometimes with bunk beds. Cities and towns have large playgrounds, sports facilities and adventure parks.

Eating Out

Many restaurants, especially those in main holiday destinations, have dedicated kids' menus. For simple, home-style comfort food that children like, head to fast-food chains such as Lido in Latvia, or lunchtime cafeterias in big cities.

Sea & Lakes

The shallow waters and sandy beaches, especially in the Gulf of Rīga, have long made the Baltic states a magnet for family travel. Popular sea beaches as well as lakes come with all sorts of child-oriented facilities and attractions.

KID-FRIENDLY PICKS

Seaplane Harbour, Tallinn (p74)

Step into a real 1930s submarine and climb on a steam-powered icebreaker.

AHHAA Science Centre, Tartu (p105)

A playful, interactive science museum brimming with physics experiments and perceptual illusions.

Sigulda (p190)

Fly in a stream of pumped air, take a ride in a (soft-version) bobsleigh and find more activities in Latvia's outdoors central.

Aqua Park, Druskininkai (p313)

Whiz down a plethora of exhilarating water slides and float around in the whirlpool.

CHILDREN'S CITY

Ventspils in Latvia has chosen to develop itself as a family-friendly beach destination, with most prime attractions geared towards children. A steam train runs through the manicured park by the picture-perfect white-sand beach and there's Latvia's largest playground nearby. A new addition to the cityscape is the bravely futuristic building of Vizium – a youth science centre, where children of all ages get to engage in a cross between a game and a scientific experiment. Using cutting-edge equipment, they learn about gravitation and anatomy, earthquakes and plant growth.

Accommodation

Manors & Castles

Baltic German, Polish and Russian aristocrats have left behind dozens of classy, old-world lodgings scattered around the countryside. Many of these have been converted into hotels that range from luxurious and expensive to pretty affordable. The quality of the restoration also varies – a magnificent old building may contain run-of-the-mill corporate-style rooms.

Guesthouses

A guesthouse in the Baltic countries mostly means a fully fledged stand-alone wooden cottage or a smaller single-bedroom cabin near the beach or somewhere in the woods, often by a lake. Amenities can range from spartan to exquisite, and some kind of catering scheme is often provided. On-site saunas are ubiquitous.

Campgrounds

There are numerous campgrounds along the seaside in all three countries and you'll find more by the key tourist sites, lakes and rivers in the hinterland. Conditions vary, but general standards are pretty high, with attractive cabins and common facilities for tent-dwellers. Many campgrounds are associated with various outdoor activities, such as rafting in the Gauja Valley.

Apartments

Apartments for rent are very common across all three countries, especially in coastal areas. These range from very personable and exquisitely designed to the bland Ikea and plastic variety. There's also unrefurbished Soviet-era apartments, which can be gems or a disaster depending on who looks after them.

HOW MUCH FOR A NIGHT IN...

a dorm bed
€20–30

a room in a manor house
€50

a hut in the forest
€40–100

Youth Hostels

Hostels are in good supply in the Baltic capitals, where you can always find one with a genuine community as well as modern comforts. Beyond that, it's only major cities and university centres, like Tartu, that might have one or two. Main Baltic hostels are listed on hostelworld. com.

QUIRKY ACCOMMODATION

Accommodation comes in more unusual (and sometimes jaw-dropping) forms in the Baltic countries than elsewhere in Europe. Boat sheds and yachts, old barns and fire-engine garages have all been turned into rooms by entrepreneurial owners. Concepts may also contain an element of irony or artistic expression, often on the folk-art side. Unexpected additional perks may come up, like your own rowing boat to explore the lake. Comforts differ – sometimes you may have no electricity or running water in an otherwise tastefully designed room. What you pay for is the 'wow' factor.

Food, Drink & Nightlife

What Do They Eat?

Brace for big portions and extra calories. Baltic cuisine is quintessentially Eastern European, with strong German, Russian and Nordic influences. Pork and potatoes rule, but fish and wild mushrooms are also major staples. The summer season enlivens the diet with a plethora of forest and garden berries, which also turn into jams consumed for the rest of the year.

Where to Eat

Words designating food establishments are often used interchangeably, which creates some confusion.

Restaurant *restoranas* (LT), *restorāns* (LV), *restoran* (EE)

Cafe *kavinė* (LT), *kafejnīca* (LV), *kohvik* (EE) – anything between a coffee shop and a fully fledged restaurant

---

Bistro *bistro* (LT, LV), *bistroo* (EE) – mostly a self-service restaurant or cafeteria

---

Bar *baras* (LT), *bārs* (LV), *baar* (EE) – often serves food

---

Pub/inn *smuklė* (LT), *krogs* (LV), *kõrts* (EE) – serves traditional food

---

Market *turgus* (LT), *tirgus* (LV), *turg* (EE)

MENU DECODER

LITHUANIA:
jautiena (beef)
kiauliena (pork)
vištiena (chicken)
silkė (herring)
grybai (mushrooms)
kiaušiniai (eggs)
sūris (cheese)
blyneliai (pancakes)
midus (mead)
alus (beer)
vynas (wine)

LATVIA:
zupa (soup)
kotletes (meatballs)
desa (sausage)
lasis (salmon)
siļķe (herring)
pelmeņi (dumplings)
pankukas (pancakes

stuffed with meat or veggies)
siers (cheese)
kvass (beverage made from fermented rye bread)
alus (beer)
vīns (wine)

ESTONIA:
sealiha (pork)
kana (chicken)
vurst (sausage)
heeringas (herring)
forell (trout)
lõhe (salmon)
kapsa (cabbage)
leib (black bread)
kama (thick milkshake-like drink)
õlu (beer)
hõõgvein (mulled wine)

HOW TO… Save Money on Food

With plenty of affordable apartments featuring kitchens or kitchenettes, self-catering is one way of cutting costs. Farmers markets selling Baltic fish, forest mushrooms and berries, as well as garden produce, make it all more interesting. Also look out for fruit and vegetable stands on the side of the road during harvest season. Makeshift signs with words like 'Zemenes' (strawberries in Latvian) point to farmsteads eager to sell their produce; the same goes for smoked fish in coastal villages. Another option is having lunches at cafeterias for office workers. These come in all shapes and sizes and mostly serve home-style, calories rich Eastern European comfort food, although there are many variations. A typical lunch cafeteria will have salad, hot and cold soups, and hot meals, including vegetarian options.

HOW MUCH FOR...

main course in a restaurant
€8–14

bottle of water
(0.5L)
€0.6

local strawberries
at a market
from €5–7/kg

cafeteria lunch
€5–10

forest mushrooms
at a market
€10–20/kg

cup of coffee
€2–3

beer
€3–4

WHAT IF...

I Am Invited to Someone's Home?

Inviting people, including those you barely know, home for dinner is an essential part of Baltic culture. It's also one of the best experiences you can have in the region. People are not only hospitable and curious about strangers, but they also enjoy cooking to the extent that long-time expats often prefer dining in someone's home than going to a restaurant. The local restaurant scene often pales in comparison with the imagination self-styled chefs can afford at home. Brace for a feast. The food you might be treated to varies widely – people like to experiment with international and fusion foods, so don't necessarily expect something traditionally Baltic. But if that's on offer (more likely around Christmas or Easter), you may expect mayo-rich salads with potatoes and meat as well as more meat or wild mushrooms for the main course. Vegetarianism is not stigmatised – just flag it in advance so that your hosts start thinking in that direction. As for the etiquette, the rule of thumb is to bring along at least one bottle of wine (or pack of beer). Flowers will most likely be appreciated and it's appropriate to ask what else to bring – people may need something they've forgotten to procure, like cheese or fruit.

Drinking Habits

Drinking habits vary from household to household. Wine is more likely to be served at dinner than beer. Strong liquors on offer will likely include vodka and schnapps-type homemade booze.

BALTIC MARKETS

Baltic societies, even in their current urbanised state, are deeply rooted in their agricultural history, so markets are an important part of life and not just entertainment for tourists. These range from hipster-ish deli food-court-like outfits to 1990s-style Eastern European markets selling industrial goods like clothing alongside farm produce to quaint small-town markets where local gardeners dispose of surplus veggies and a baker brings bread fresh from the oven. So what to look out for? Although northern climate isn't really conducive to growing juicy tomatoes or watermelons, the range of offer can be truly amazing. If you buy seasonal strawberries, raspberries, plums or apples, you will immediately feel the added value compared with their supermarket peers. Then comes everything people collect in the forest – blueberries, cranberries, cloudberries and wild mushrooms. Among the latter, porcini and chanterelles are the easiest to cook. Berry jams and pickled mushrooms are also an excellent buy, especially if you want to take them home. Baltic markets are famous for great dairy products, especially cottage cheese and sour cream. There is, of course, plenty of fish – eel, lamprey, sole, herring – which is mostly smoked or salted, rather than fresh. If you've never tried pickled herring with cottage cheese, here's your chance – it's a Baltic speciality. Baked bread is always on offer and so are various nonalcoholic drinks, the best ones being made of rhubarb, aronia (chokeberry) and cydonia (a type of quince).

Responsible Travel

Climate Change & Travel

It's impossible to ignore the impact we have when travelling, and the importance of making changes where we can. Lonely Planet urges all travellers to engage with their travel carbon footprint. There are many carbon calculators online that allow travellers to estimate the carbon emissions generated by their journey; try resurgence.org/resources/carbon-calculator.html. Many airlines and booking sites offer travellers the option of offsetting the impact of greenhouse gas emissions by contributing to climate-friendly initiatives around the world. We continue to offset the carbon footprint of all Lonely Planet staff travel, while recognising this is a mitigation more than a solution.

Arrive by Land or Sea

To avoid flights, you can use the railway link between Poland and Lithuania or arrive by bus. You can also catch a ferry going into Baltic ports from Germany, Sweden and Finland.

Walk & Cycle

The Baltic countries are ideal for long-distance walks and cycling. All three countries are criss-crossed by well-marked routes, with detailed descriptions available online and in local tourist information offices.

There are rental and carshare services specialising in electric cars in all three countries, such as ELMO Rent in Estonia, Fiqsy in Latvia and Spark in Lithuania.

Mushrooms are a major source of protein for Baltic people. Check celotajs.lv for tours, on which you can learn which mushrooms to pick and how to do it sustainably.

PICK YOUR ACCOMMODATION

Embrace the nature by choosing to stay in forest lodges and cottages that are heated by wood fire and have compost toilets. There are also plenty of campgrounds, especially along the coast.

Post-Soviet deindustrialisation left the Baltic states dotted with abandoned buildings and depopulated settlements. You can help revitalisation efforts by visiting areas like Kohtla-Järve in Estonia and Karosta district in Liepāja, Latvia.

Mind the Minorities

Ethnic minorities in the Baltics struggle to preserve their culture and often find themselves politically alienated. You'll help conservation and revival efforts by visiting Liv, Seto and Russian Old Believers' villages across the region.

Green Estonia

Six areas in Estonia made it into Green Destinations 100 Top Stories, a list of world's best sustainability projects, in 2023. These are Järvamaa, Lahemaa, Hiiumaa island, Pärnumaa, Rakvere and Saaremaa island.

Fast Train

Rail Baltica (p343), a high-speed railway line, will connect Tallinn, Rīga, Kaunas and Vilnius by 2030, giving a boost to interregional travel. You'll see new futuristic stations emerging in the capital cities.

Blue Flag

Latvia currently has 11, Lithuania nine and Estonia two Blue Flag beaches.

Pay to Drive

It costs €30 to drive around the Curonian Spit – a measure aimed at reducing the impact of cars.

Political debates can be toxic and involve multidimensional historical grievances. It helps when visitors avoid taking sides, especially when it comes to ethnic divisions, but instead try to listen, learn and grasp nuance.

Local tourist offices in the Baltic countries can often point you to local homesteads or farms engaged in traditional crafts or ways of farming. It's a fun way of learning and helping to preserve traditions.

Country Rankings

Estonia ranked 14, Latvia 15 and Lithuania 31 in the global Environmental Performance Index for 2022. The data-based ranking is developed by Yale and Columbia universities.

RESOURCES

greendestinations.org
Global organisation supporting sustainable destinations, businesses and communities.

fiqsy.com; spark.lt; elmorent.ee
Electric-car rental and carshare services in Latvia, Lithuania and Estonia respectively.

baltictrails.eu
Long-distance hiking trails through the Baltics – the Coastal Trail and the Forest Trail.

⬟ LGBTIQ+ Travellers

The Baltic countries are relatively open to the LGBTIQ+ community, but there are many long-standing issues and progress is being stalled by far-right politics. Estonia comes across as the most LGBTIQ+ friendly country and the staunchly Catholic Lithuania as the least friendly one, with Latvia somewhere in between. It's generally safe to be openly gay, but homophobia is present, too.

Stay on Guard

The Baltic countries are not where you travel for a great LGBTIQ+ scene, but they are quite safe to be in, and the general culture of not meddling in people's private lives helps travellers to remain unperturbed. That said, homophobic attitudes do exist – discretion is still advised. Pride parades, under the brand Baltic Pride, have been staged in all three capitals since the mid-2000s and generally proceed without incidents. But there are far-right forces, which periodically enter government coalitions, so LGBTIQ+ rights remain limited.

BARS & CLUBS

The gay scene is perfectly legalised but a tad subdued in all three capitals, with only a couple of clubs and bars in each of them catering squarely to the gay crowd, plus more bohemian places that are simply gay-friendly.

Marriage Debate

Estonia's parliament voted to recognise same-sex marriages in 2023. In Latvia, the Constitutional Court ruled that same-sex marriage is legal, but the parliament was yet to legislate it at the time of writing and the matter was the subject of a massive political fight with the far right trying to block it. In Lithuania, same-sex marriage is explicitly banned.

ACCOMMODATION

You're very unlikely to be discriminated against in any well-established hotels in the Baltic countries. Issues may potentially arise with small guesthouses in the countryside or rental flats, but this risk is also low. Some geographical areas can be more problematic than others; for instance' Latgale in Latvia with its mixture of Latvian Catholicism and Russian nationalism.

QUEER LEADER

In 2023, Edgars Rinkēvičs became the first openly gay president in Latvia and in the whole of the European Union. But despite publicly coming out back in 2014, he has no strong political identification with the LGBTIQ+ cause and no official partner.

Associations

Main LGBTIQ+ organisations in the Baltic countries are the ones responsible for Baltic Pride – Mozaika in Latvia, Lithuanian Gay League and Estonian LGBT Association.

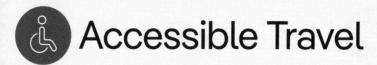# Accessible Travel

Travel in the Baltics won't be smooth for people with disabilities, but there has been progress with the removal of barriers, leading to greater accessibility.

Terrain Overview

It helps that terrain is mostly flat and pavements are largely asphalted. But Old Towns are made of cobblestoned streets and most residential buildings are not wheelchair-friendly.

Airport

All Baltic airports maintain a smooth procedure for passengers requiring wheelchair access or other forms of assistance. All require that you flag your needs at the time of booking.

Accommodation

Smaller hotels and guesthouses are unlikely to offer comprehensive assistance to people with special needs. Bigger hotels should have all the necessary facilities, but it's worth inquiring at the time of booking.

MUSEUMS

Wheelchair access in museums depends on whether the museum in question has been recently renovated. The main museums will qualify. In any case, it's worth asking local tourist information offices to list accessible museums.

TOILETS

When it comes to accessible toilets, shopping malls are the number-one choice. A few of the better restaurants and cafes will have them as well, but this is never guaranteed.

Public Transport

Baltic capitals have largely phased out services that don't provide wheelchair access, but some of the older buses and trams are still unsuitable. Soviet-era suburban trains in Rīga are slated for replacement any time now.

Taxis Services

Some of the taxi companies, such Tulika Takso AS in Tallinn and Red Cab in Rīga, provide services to people with special needs. Asistentinis Taxi, run by people using wheelchairs, can help you out in Lithuania.

RESOURCES

mapeirons.eu

Lists over a thousand accessible places of interest

accessibletourism. org

The website of the European Network for Accessible Tourism.

smartertravel.com/ disabled-travel

Links to a number of websites for travellers with a disability.

Rundāle Palace

The most opulent of Baltic palaces, Rundāle in Latvia (p200), has wheelchair access to all exhibitions as well as to the baroque gardens. Visitors using wheelchairs are also welcome to use a car park inside the palace.

Health & Safe Travel

INSURANCE

Travel insurance isn't mandatory for the Baltic countries if you don't need a Schengen visa. However, it's advisable that you have a comprehensive one, especially if you are planning outdoor activities that involve safety risks. EU citizens can get a free European Health Insurance Card (EHIC), which covers emergency medical treatments without charge.

Pickpockets

You should't worry about pickpockets as much as you would in large European cities, but it's worth being aware of the risk in crowded places like train stations or bigger markets. Watch for your belongings and don't carry your wallet in bags or pockets that a thief can easily access. If you need police assistance, call 112.

Road Safety

Traffic is relatively sparse in the Baltics, which reduces the risk of serious accidents. But dangerous and drunken driving is a problem, especially when it comes to overtaking on one-lane roads. Traffic cops are generally professional and not corrupt. Most roads are in good shape, but some of the secondary roads leave much to be desired.

TAP WATER

Despite all the filters people install in their houses, tap water in the Baltics is perfectly safe for drinking.

WINTER GEAR CHECKBOX

Winter jacket

Warm hat

Warm gloves or mittens

Extra-warm trousers and/or thermal underwear

Safe Swimming

Although Baltic beaches are generally quite safe for swimming, sea currents can be treacherous, particularly in the open sea beyond the Gulf of Rīga. The other source of danger is cold water, which can cause sudden cramps. Water temperature often changes abruptly as you walk over sand bars towards deeper sea.

MIND THE COLD

Winters usually have a few frosty spells and – from time to time – a lot of snow. You'll need proper warm clothing, especially if you are planning outdoor activities. Winter conditions greatly increase the risk of traffic accidents. It's compulsory to have snow tyres on your car during winter months in all three countries. Crucially, beware of longer braking distances.

Nuts & Bolts

OPENING HOURS

Hours vary widely depending on the season and the size of the town, but the following are fairly standard:

Banks 9am–4pm or 5pm Monday to Friday

Bars Noon–midnight Sunday to Thursday, to 2am or 3am Friday and Saturday

Cafes 9am–10pm

Post offices 8am–6pm Monday to Friday, 9am–2pm Saturday

Restaurants Noon–11pm or midnight

Shops 10am–6pm Monday to Friday, to 3pm Saturday

Supermarkets 8am–10pm

GOOD TO KNOW

Time zone
(GMT/UTC +2)

Country codes
+370 (LT), +371 (LV), +372 (EE)

Emergency number
112

Population
LT 2.8 million, LV 1.9 million, EE 1.3 million

Weights & Measures
The Baltic countries use the metric system.

Smoking
Smoking is not allowed in enclosed public spaces.

Electricity
220W/230W/50Hz

Type C
220V/50Hz

Type F
230V/50Hz

PUBLIC HOLIDAYS

New Year's Day
(LT, LV, EE) 1 January

Independence Day (LT)
16 February

Independence Day (EE)
24 February

Lithuanian Independence Restoration Day
(LT) 11 March

Easter Sunday & Monday
(LT) March/April

Easter Friday & Monday
(LV, EE) March/April

Labor/Spring Day (LT, LV, EE) 1 May

Restoration of Independence Day (LV)
4 May

Mothers' Day (LT) First Sunday in May

Pentecost
(EE) May/June

Fathers' Day (LT) First Sunday in June

Victory Day
(EE) 23 June

Midsummer's Eve (LV)
23 June

St John's Day
(LT, LV, EE) 24 June

Statehood Day
(LT) 6 July

Assumption Day
(LT) 15 August

Day of Restoration of Independence
(EE) 20 August

All Saints' Day
(LT) 1 November

Independence Day (LV)
18 November

Christmas
(LT, LV, EE) 25 and 26 December

STORYBOOK

Our writers delve deep into different
aspects of Estonia, Latvia & Lithuania life

Celebrating Uzgavenes (Mardi Gras), Vilnius (p238), Lithuania
MNSTUDIO/SHUTTERSTOCK ©

A HISTORY OF ESTONIA, LATVIA & LITHUANIA IN
15 PLACES

Reading into the history of the Baltics, you realise what a miracle it is that indigenous languages now prevail on the streets of the region's three capitals. It was never a given throughout the centuries of foreign domination and suppression of local cultures. By Leonid Ragozin

THE THREE BALTIC states display two distinctly different paths of history that ultimately converged after half a millennium. Baltic and Finno-Ugric tribes in present-day Latvia and Estonia had been subjugated by foreign invaders before they manage to form proper statehood. Lithuania is a different story. It built its own, uniquely multilingual and multiconfessional empire, and a confederation with Poland. But eventually it was also defeated and absorbed by even bigger and stronger entities.

Living between the rock and the hard place of the giant Germanophone and Russophone worlds has always been a feat of survival. This experience, which has involved brave resistance and reprisals, forced cultural assimilation and shameful collaboration, still profoundly affects the political psyche and the attitude to history in all three nations today. Talking about history is a minefield in the Baltics, so don't rush in with superficial generalisations and half-baked conclusions. It's better to listen and ponder, accepting the mind-boggling complexity and the presence of many competing historical 'truths'.

1. Kokenhausen, Latvia
FOUNDATION MYTHS

Events that took place before written history are steeped in mythology and folklore. The medieval Kokenhausen, or Koknese Castle, appears in the final scene of the Latvian nation-shaping epic, *Lāčplēsis*. The historical reality behind the legend of a man with bear's ears, which provide him with the strength of a bear who was aided by ancient Baltic gods in his struggle against German crusaders, pertains to the existence of Latgalian proto-states in the Daugava Valley during the late 12th century, when the Germans arrived in their relentless *Drang nach Osten* (Drive to the East). Without delay, they began subjugating Baltic and Finno-Ugric peoples in what they saw as a crusade in the name of Christ.

For more on Kokenhausen Castle, see p179

2. Ikšķile, Latvia
THE CRUSADE BEGINS

German colonisers built their first castle in what they called Üxküll – a Liv settlement, and now the small village of Ikšķile on the Daugava River where the remains of St Meynard's Church, Latvia's first, are preserved. But after a few years, in 1201, their third bishop Albert von Buxhovden moved his base to what is now Rīga, thus founding the Latvian capital. The now virtually extinct Finno-Ugric Livs, who occupied the coast and much of Vidzeme at the time, gave the name to the German warrior-monk state – the Livonian Order. Within a few decades, the knights conquered much of today's Latvia and Estonia.

For more on Ikšķile, see p178.

3. Toompea, Tallinn

COMMANDING HEIGHTS

It wasn't only the Germans who wanted a slice of the Baltic pie when the Pope called for a crusade against eastern heathens. The Danes under King Waldemar II waged an expedition into northern Estonia in 1219. They built a new castle on Toompea, or Cathedral Hill, and defeated Estonians in a decisive battle that took place under its walls. There was a 'divine intervention' moment in that battle when a banner allegedly fell from the skies; it became the current national flag of Denmark. The Danish rule in northern Estonia lasted until 1346, when the Danes sold the land to the Teutonic Order.

For more on Toompea, see p58.

Trakai Castle (p257)

KAP! NG/SHUTTERSTOCK ©

4. Gediminas Tower, Vilnius

FREE AND PAGAN

Wielding a sword and the Bible, the Livonian Order subjugated most Baltic peoples, but one stayed free and – for a while – staunchly pagan. The ancestors of modern Lithuanians, aided by their kin in the Latvian region of Zemgale, soundly defeated the knights in the battle of Saule in 1236. At the same time, power in Lithuania was consolidated by Duke Mindaugas as the Grand Duchy of Lithuania came into being. The duchy morphed into a major European power in the early 14th century under Grand Duke Gediminas, who founded Vilnius and expanded the realm all the way to Kyiv.

For more on Gediminas Tower, see p000.

5. Great Guild Hall, Tallinn

TRADE UNION

The monk knights of the Livonian Order were followed by German merchants and artisans as the Hanseatic League, a confederation of trade cities around the Baltics and the North Sea, came into being. The league created a trade thoroughfare stretching from Novgorod in Russia all the way to England. The tradesmen formed guilds and built brick houses in Hanseatic style. They are responsible for the outlook of Rīga's and Tallinn's (or Reval's, as it was then known) medieval cores. Tallinn's Great Guild Hall now houses a branch of the Estonian History Museum.

For more on the Great Guild Hall, see p57.

6. Trakai Castle, Lithuania

FROM SEA TO SEA

Lithuania's might peaked in the 15th century under Grand Duke Vytautas who ruled his multiethnic and multiconfessional realm, stretching all the way to the Black Sea, from his castle in Trakai. Fratricidal chaos and civil war didn't impede the expansion. Vytautas the Great fought against his cousin and predecessor Jogaila, who became the King of Poland, but at the end of the day they joined forces and defeated the Teutonic Knights in the epic battle of Grunwald. This period saw the convergence of Lithuania and Poland as well as the Christianisation of Lithuania, Europe's last pagan stronghold.

For more on Trakai Castle, see p257.

7. Cēsis Castle, Latvia
ENTER THE RUSSIANS

In the 16th century, the Livonian Knights' state went into decline and a scramble for its lands started between new actors – the Kingdom of Sweden and the Tsardom of Russia. This became known as the Livonian Wars. The troops of Russian Tsar Ivan the Terrible, who planned to install a Danish prince as his vassal in Livonia, initially prevailed, taking swathes of land in today's Estonia and Latvia. But then the Polish-Lithuanian Commonwealth came into play under its new king, Stephen Báthory. The Russians were soundly defeated under the walls of the Wenden (Cēsis) Castle, and eastern Baltic lands became an arena of struggle between Poles and Swedes.

For more on Cēsis Castle, see p197.

8. Jelgava, Latvia
DWARF EMPIRE

The Livonian Order formally ceased to exist as a result of the Livonian Wars. A peculiar German-dominated state emerged in its place in today's southwestern Latvia. For much of its existence, the Duchy of Courland was ruled out of Jelgava (then Mitava) by the family of the last Master of the Livonian Order, Gotthard Kettler. Its most successful ruler, Duke Jacob, was an industrious man who developed the economy and embarked on creating a mini-empire by colonising the Caribbean island of Tobago and the delta of the Gambia River. But in the 18th century, the duchy ended up being absorbed by Russia.

For more on Jelgava, see p202.

9. Narva Castle, Estonia
LEARNING FROM DEFEAT

Russia returned to the Baltics in 1700, when a young Peter the Great attacked the Swedish-controlled fortress in Narva in what became the opening scene of the Great Northern War. His badly equipped and disorganised army suffered a crushing defeat at the hands of Swedish King Charles XII. But he learned the lesson and embarked on creating a modern European-styled army. After defeating Charles XII at Poltava in Ukraine, he completely ousted the Swedes from the Baltics, which is how present-day Estonia and much of Latvia ended up under Russian control. Today, the fortress houses the Narva Museum tracing the history of the city.

For more on Narva Castle, see p88.

10. Rundāle Palace, Latvia
BALTIC TSAR-MAKERS

Under Russian rule, Baltic Germans remained the real overlords in Baltic provinces, retaining economic and political power, while continuing to call themselves 'knights' until the 20th century. They also became disproportionally influential in the government of the empire run by the heavily Germanised Romanov family. Duke of Courland Ernst Johann von Biron became Russia's éminence grise during the reign of his lover, Empress Anna Ioanovna. He built his palace at Rundāle, in an effort to rival the splendour of St Petersburg. Another Baltic German (of Scottish descent), Prince Michael Barclay de Tolly was Russian commander-in-chief in the war against Napoleon.

For more on Rundāle Palace, see p200.

Memorial to Nazi victims, Paneriai (p259)

RED_BARON/SHUTTERSTOCK ©

11. Liepāja Harbour, Latvia

REVOLUTIONARY CHAOS

The Russian Revolution of 1917 created a total mess in the Baltics, with the Bolsheviks and the monarchists, Germans and Poles getting involved in multidimensional warfare, while indigenous populations realised it was time to take their fate into their own hands. At one point after proclaiming independence, the government of Latvia found itself in control of nothing else but the deck of the warship *Saratov* moored in the harbour of Liepāja. All three Baltic nations eventually fought their way into becoming newly independent states, albeit not exactly within today's borders: Vilnius was grabbed by Poland, for example.

For more on Liepāja Harbour, see p216.

12. Handkerchief Memorial, Rīga

ENSLAVED AND EXILED

Two decades of independence ended with the deal between Hitler and Stalin, under which the USSR seized the Baltic countries in 1940. The occupation was preceded by the forced resettlement of Baltic Germans to Germany, on Hitler's insistence. The Soviets' rule began with the executions and mass deportations of 'class enemies' – members of elites, business owners and intelligentsia of all ethnicities. In Rīga's Old Town, a giant metal handkerchief, onto which a Latvian woman embroidered the signatures of her fellow Gulag inmates, is a tribute to all those who died on the multi-week journey east or from harsh conditions in Siberia.

For more on the Handkerchief Memorial, see p169.

13. Paneriai, Lithuania

KILLING FIELDS

Hitler attacked the USSR in June 1941 and quickly overtook the Baltic states. After Soviet atrocities, many locals welcomed the Nazis, whose propaganda conflated Soviet Bolsheviks with the Jews. Without delay, the occupiers, assisted by local collaborators, embarked on exterminating the sizeable Jewish community. At Paneriai, near Vilnius, anywhere between 70,000 and 100,000 people were executed, the majority of them Jews from the Vilnius ghetto but also Poles and Soviet prisoners of war. A solemn memorial commemorating the victims stands here today, and a small museum provides information about the atrocities that took place at the site.

For more on Paneriai, see p259.

14. Maskavas Forštate, Rīga

ALIEN SYSTEM

The return of the Soviet occupation started with a new wave of deportations and the destruction of pro-independence guerrilla movements in all three Baltic countries. Communist terror subsided after the death of Stalin in 1953, but the totalitarian system itself felt alien in Baltic states – just like the Latvian Academy of Science tower, a Stalinist skyscraper modelled on its siblings in Moscow that looms incongruously above Maskavas forštate (Moscow suburb) in Rīga. People's land and other property was confiscated and collectivised, all aspects of life were regimented, and a flow of migrants from Soviet republics threatened the national identity.

For more on Maskavas forštate, see p170.

15. Song Festival Grounds, Tallinn

SONGS OF FREEDOM

The winds of change blowing from Moscow after Mikhail Gorbachev launched his reforms in 1985 presented an opportunity for occupied Baltic countries. Cautiously in the beginning, they started demanding – and eventually proclaiming – independence. Tallinn's Song Festival Grounds turned into a venue of massive pro-independence gatherings, which became known as the Singing Revolution. Broad popular movements (known at the time as 'fronts') were formed in all three countries, drawing wide support across the ethnic divide. Finally, after the collapse of the coup in Moscow in August 1991, the Baltic states were set free.

For more on the Song Festival Grounds, see p75.

MEET THE PEOPLE OF THE BALTICS

If you arrive in a town in the Baltics, and there are no people in the streets, most likely everyone has left to enjoy uninterrupted tranquillity in the countryside. Solveiga Kaļva introduces her people.

PEOPLE LIVING IN the three Baltic states are quite different from each other. Estonians, in particular, represent a distinctive language group (Finno-Ugric), contrary to Latvians and Lithuanians who share the Baltic language branch. But there is something common to all of us – a deep and culturally rooted connection to nature, and the need for our own space and time.

Venturing alone into a deep forest, vast meadow or endless bog is nothing frightening for us. In fact, it's quite the opposite. It allows us to empty our minds, observe nature and fill our baskets with wild berries, plants for herbal tea mixtures, and mushrooms. When walking along the Baltic Sea, you can sometimes spot fishermen's boats swaying on the waves. Closeness to nature and respect for it runs in our blood. Our cherished folklore is rich with references to the natural world, but this connection also has very pragmatic reasons. We are practical people who like creating things with our own hands.

It seems that almost every family has a summer cottage or a countryside house that allows us to hide from the hustle and bustle of city life. Planting a garden, and later harvesting fresh and healthy vegetables, is a common activity in the Baltic countries. Even in some cities, you might find urban gardens, seed exchange points or human-made beehives on the roofs of theatres, town halls and four-star hotels.

The further north you go, the more reserved or introverted people might seem. Some even say – impolite. However, that's only on the surface. If you ask for help we won't turn you down, but you might need to be the first one initiating the conversation. Once you get to know us better, we'll become your lifelong friends who will go out of our way to serve you a meal of 12 dishes at our home, show you around the most beautiful places, and generally express the highest levels of hospitality. You just have to break the ice, or wait until it melts.

Don't worry, our love for nature and tranquillity doesn't mean that all we do is wallow naked in the dew, although you might encounter this during the summer-solstice celebration or after a sauna ritual. For example, in the 1920s and 1930s, Rīga was called 'Little Paris' due to its vibrant art world and bohemians, and it still serves as a cultural citadel of the Baltic countries. Tallinn, famous for its medieval Old Town, is reborn as a joyful hipster hotspot rich with modern architecture and the newest technologies. Vilnius even has its own self-proclaimed artists' republic – Užupis. So, we do love culture too. We just need some peace to restore our energy.

Small Nations

It might be hard to grasp, but fewer people live in the Baltic states than in London. There are approximately 2.8 million people in Lithuania, 1.8 million in Latvia, and 1.3 million in Estonia.

Clockwise from top left: summer solstice, Latvia (p157); traditional costumes, Kaunas (p260), Lithuania; cheese shop, Tallinn (p52), Estonia; celebrating Uzgavenes (Mardi Gras), Vilnius (p238), Lithuania

CONNECTED TO ALL THREE STATES

I was born in Rīga, Latvia, but I'm a quarter Lithuanian, as my grandfather was from Lithuania. I call it my hot-blooded side. I spent most of my childhood living in a neighbourhood where all the houses looked the same – grey Soviet block buildings with no soul. Back then, I thought that I didn't like living in Rīga, and going to our summer house in the countryside was my salvation, but now, since moving to the city centre, I find Rīga very charming. Yet I haven't lost my love for nature.

Kinship ties or not, it has always been easier for me to understand Lithuanians than Estonians. However, I decided to follow in the footsteps of many 19th-century Latvian cultural workers and study at the master's level in Tartu, Estonia. Moving between all three Baltic states for work or studies, as well as going on short weekend trips to our neighbours, is quite usual practice for locals.

339

Choral Synagogue (p250), Vilnius
©SERGIO DELLE VEDOVE/SHUTTERSTOCK ©

JEWS IN THE BALTICS

The achievements, demise and resurgence of Jewish communities in the Baltics over the centuries are interwoven with the history of their adoptive homelands. By Anna Kaminski

THE HISTORY OF Jews in the Baltics goes back many centuries. They came as traders and artisans; some at the express invitation of the rulers of the day, others taking advantage of the lifting of the Pale of Settlement, which had restricted Jewish settlement to specific regions of the Russian Empire. Jews settled across Lithuania and Latvia (and to a much lesser extent in Estonia), contributing considerably to their respective country's cultural and intellectual life, and living in relative harmony with their Christian neighbours, in spite of occasional pogroms. All this came to an abrupt end during WWII. The German occupation of the Baltic states was a tragedy of unparalleled proportions for Baltic Jews, the vast majority of whom perished at the hands of the occupiers and local collaborators. However, many decades on, Jewish culture is making a modest revival across Estonia, Latvia and Lithuania.

A Brief History of Litvaks

Lithuania's first Jewish community dates back to the 12th century, when Grand Duke Gediminas (1316–41) granted 3000 Ashkenazi Jews political and economic privileges in order to attract their migration to Vilnius from Germany and to expand Lithuania's trade with its neighbours.

The name 'Litvak' (meaning 'Lithuanian Jew') comes from 'Litva', the name for Lithuania in many Slavic languages; famous descendants of Litvaks include Leonard Cohen, Bob Dylan and actor David Suchet. Over the centuries, Jewish communities enjoyed a status similar to that of burghers and monks, and the right to reside alongside Christians while practising self-government based on Jewish law. Jews settled all over Lithuania, particularly in Vilnius and Kaunas. In spite of restrictions imposed on Litvaks when Lithuania was annexed by the Russian Empire in the late 1800s, Vilnius nevertheless replaced Brest (in present-day Belarus) as the Litvaks' spiritual centre. It flourished as a Yiddish-language centre until the city was forcibly incorporated into Poland in 1922.

During WWI, Litvak leaders actively participated in the creation of Lithuania as a fledgling independent state, fighting on the country's side and then lobbying for Lithuania to be recognised internationally. When Lithuania's 1922 constitution was drawn up, Jews and other minorities were granted a certain degree of autonomy, but this didn't last. The rise of right-wing parties and a pivot towards Lithuanian nationalism saw Jewish autonomy progressively reduced.

Jews in Latvia

Though trade existed between individual Jewish merchants and Latvians from the 14th century, when Latvia was under the jurisdiction of Knights of the Livonian Order, the first Jewish Latvian settlement appeared in Kurzeme only in the late 16th century. Jews emigrated to Latvia primarily from western Ukraine and Belarus, settling in Latgale and Rīga. They featured prominently in Latvia's grain and timber trade, and set up woodwork factories, flax mills and distilleries in the capital until the wave of antisemitism that swept the Russian Empire in 1881 dealt Latvia's Jews a massive blow. They found their path to higher education severely restricted, were banned from working for government organisations and forced to move back to the Pale of Settlement if their officially registered trade differed from the one actually practised.

Jewish emigration to the USA, South Africa and Great Britain was followed by the deportation of tens of thousands of Jews to Russia after being accused of spying for Germany. Nonetheless, when Latvia became an independent republic in 1918, Jewish soldiers fought for their homeland and by the mid-1930s, several Jewish representatives were elected to the Saeima (Latvian parliament). This ended when a bloodless coup in 1934, led by Kārlis Ulmanis, Latvia's first president, disbanded all political parties and public organisations and targeted Jewish businesses.

A Minority Within a Minority

Individual Jews settled in Estonia in the 14th century, though the first permanent Estonian Jewish community didn't exist until five centuries later. The lifting of the Pale of Settlement restrictions by Russia's Tsar Alexander II allowed demobilised Cantonists (Jewish soldiers drafted into the Russian army at a young age), merchants and Jews with higher education to put down roots in Estonia from 1865 onwards, with small communities springing up in Tartu, Valga, Võro, Viljandi, Pärnu and Tallinn.

When Estonia declared itself an independent republic in 1918, it was a watershed moment for Estonian Jews who, along with Estonia's other ethnic minorities, benefitted from the policies of the postwar government that sought to combat discrimination. Cultural, religious and political autonomy followed during the brief 'honeymoon' period of the 1920s.

WWII, the Holocaust & Beyond

The Baltics fell under Soviet rule in 1940. Of the hundreds of thousands deported from Lithuania, Latvia and Estonia to Siberia as 'dangerous social elements', Jews made up 5% to 10%. The advancing German army pushed back the Soviets and occupied the Baltics in the summer of 1941. While much of Estonia's 3000-strong Jewish community had managed to flee east, over 90% of Lithuania's and Latvia's Jews were killed at mass execution sites dotted around their respective countries, with only 14,000 Latvian Jews and fewer than 25,000 Lithuanian Jews surviving the war. These atrocities were often carried out with active local participation.

By the end of WWII, Lithuania's Jewish community was all but destroyed and during the mid-1980s perestroika years a further 6000 Jews left for Israel. Postwar Latvia, by contrast, became one of the centres for Jewish national movements, with activists pushing for the right to honour Holocaust victims (illegal in the Soviet Union) and to emigrate to Israel. Postwar Estonia saw much of its Jewish population return, and though Jewish cultural life remained largely dormant until 1989, Tartu University saw an influx of Jewish students from all over the USSR.

Post-Soviet Revival

The small but thriving Jewish community in Vilnius and a smaller, elderly one in Kaunas number around 6900 in total, while Latvia boasts the Baltics' largest Jewish community of 12,000. An ever-present blight in Lithuania, in particular, is the failure to come to terms with the willing participation of numerous locals in the Holocaust, with many celebrated as anti-Soviet heroes. Estonia's first synagogue since WWII opened in 2007 in Tallinn, and Jewish religious and cultural life is enjoying a rebirth across nine cities.

THE RAILWAY UNLINKING THE BALTICS FROM THEIR PAST

The Baltic nations have embarked on the largest infrastructure project of the past century, aimed at redefining European connectivity, reshaping politics and starting a new historical chapter. By Angelo Zinna

INTERNATIONAL RAIL TRAVEL across the European Union is about to get much easier. Estonia, Latvia and Lithuania, supported by the EU, have initiated the largest infrastructure project of the past 100 years – the construction of a new 870km railway line that will provide seamless connectivity between the three Baltic countries, Warsaw and Western Europe. The Rail Baltica project, planned for completion in 2030, is poised to transform the way people and goods move across the continent, reducing travel times between the Baltic states and key European destinations.

Historically situated at the crossroads of trade routes, the Baltic region is now reclaiming its central role in European affairs. The move towards improved con-

nections with the EU has obvious political implications that go well beyond the modernisation of transport infrastructure – the Baltic states are not just getting closer to their western neighbours but also cutting ties with Russia, whose influence remains especially visible in the railway network criss-crossing Estonia, Latvia and Lithuania.

Gauge Size Matters

Let's take a step back. In the early 19th century, the Industrial Revolution was transforming the way people travelled around the world. The first railway line appeared in England in 1825 and it didn't take long before the rest of the continent – and later the planet – adopted the revolutionary technology. Within three decades, railway lines had appeared on all five continents, and by the late 1870s more than 1.3 million passengers and 635 million tonnes of goods were moving across the globe aboard steam-powered carriages. Jules Verne's imagined trip around the world in 80 days had finally become a real possibility.

The Russian Empire was initially reluctant to enter the rail age. Building a network of lines that would effectively connect opposite corners of a barely industrialised empire covering a sixth of the world's landmass seemed unfeasible. Yet, as other European powers invested in speed, transport along often frozen water courses appeared as slow as ever. It would take a German engineer, Franz Anton von Gerstner, to convince Tsar Nicholas I to construct the first 23km railway line between St Petersburg, the capital, and Tsarskoe Selo, his summer residence, in 1837.

The initial test was a success and the tsar began work to expand the Russian railway network across Eurasia. In 1843, Nicholas I appointed an American engineer, George Whistler, as the supervisor for the construction of the new St Petersburg–Moscow line, the longest double-track railway in the world, measuring 644km. Whistler promoted the use of the 1524mm train gauge, invented in England and common in the USA, which would become the norm in the entire Russian Empire in the following decades. When Russia began constructing its first railways in the 19th century, there was no universally accepted standard gauge – different countries and regions all had their own rail gauges. But things were changing. In 1846, the United Kingdom introduced a new Railway Regulation Act that enforced the use of the narrower 1435mm gauge across Great Britain and Ireland. Since the UK was Europe's main exporter of trains, the 1435mm gauge became the standard in most of Western Europe (except for Spain and Portugal).

The main issue with different gauges is that trains cannot cross from one system to the other. When, in the 1860s, the Russian Empire started building railways in the Baltics, the two networks came clashing. After the collapse of the Russian Empire, sections of the Baltic railway network were re-gauged by Germans to the Western European standard, but after WWII and the absorption of Estonia, Latvia and

Rail Baltica, Rīga (p162), Latvia

PANDORA PICTURES/SHUTTERSTOCK ©

Lithuania within the USSR, the Soviets converted all the lines back to the broader 'Russian gauge' (adapted to 1520mm). It was a strategic move – by keeping the networks separated, the Soviet Union avoided the risk of enemy forces entering their territory via rail. To this day, the vast majority of rail lines within the former USSR continue to use the Russian gauge.

It's not just a matter of gauge size – the entire railway network of the three Baltic countries is oriented towards Moscow and St Petersburg. After the fall of the USSR, integration with the European Union happened relatively fast on an institutional level – the Baltics joined NATO and the EU in 2004 – but transport infrastructure maintained its iron ties with the East, favouring trade with Russia.

Switching Tracks Westward

Discussions on decoupling from the Russian system started soon after Estonia, Latvia and Lithuania regained their independence in 1991, although it would take over a decade before concrete proposals would be put on the table, due to the immense scale of the task at hand. Rebuilding the infrastructure to integrate it with the European rail network and shifting from an east–west to a north–south orientation is an unprecedented enterprise with clear geopolitical implications, which has received more pronounced support since the start of the war between Russia and Ukraine in 2014.

The conflict heightened concerns in the Baltic states and the wider European community about regional security and

REBUILDING THE INFRASTRUCTURE TO INTEGRATE IT WITH THE EUROPEAN RAIL NETWORK AND SHIFTING FROM AN EAST–WEST TO A NORTH–SOUTH ORIENTATION IS AN UNPRECEDENTED ENTERPRISE WITH CLEAR GEOPOLITICAL IMPLICATIONS, WHICH HAS RECEIVED MORE SUPPORT SINCE THE START OF THE WAR BETWEEN RUSSIA AND UKRAINE IN 2014

Rail Baltica arrives in Rīga (p162) from Vilnius (p238)

GINTS IVUSKANS/SHUTTERSTOCK ©

stability – the Rail Baltica project became a means to bolster regional resilience and reduce vulnerabilities. Initial predictions of the total cost of the project set the price tag for Rail Baltica at €5.8 billion, with the EU committed to funding the large majority of the railway's construction. Far from cheap, Rail Baltica would not repay itself in the short term, but Ernst & Young analysts estimated that the new transport infrastructure would bring in over €16 billion in indirect revenue into the Baltic countries, resulting from reduced air pollution and climate change mitigation, faster freight transport, and more accessible public transport for individual citizens.

Doubts about such estimated profits have emerged as the project moves forward, and exact calculations about short- and medium-term advantages remain ambiguous. In addition to the predicted benefits, Rail Baltica is expected to employ approximately 13,000 people in regions of Eastern Europe that have experienced heavy outward migration in recent decades.

The challenge, however, lies in keeping the costs within the estimated budget – a task that has already presented many obstacles. In 2022, Estonia made the news for being the eurozone country hit hardest by inflation, with price increases that surpassed 20% (compared to a 9% European average). Latvia and Lithuania followed at a short distance, with double-digit inflation measurements. The Baltic countries' dependency on exports made them highly vulnerable to the energy crisis that hit Europe following Russia's invasion of Ukraine – a blow reflected in increased costs of **345**

GIRTS RAGELIS/SHUTTERSTOCK ©

Rail Baltica, Tallinn (p52), Latvia

construction materials that slowed down the progress of Rail Baltica. In the summer of 2023, the EU's Connecting Europe Facility awarded an additional €928 million to the project, followed by the Latvian government, which allotted €18 million to complete the domestic section of the rail line. Yet, the Latvian Ministry of Transport has declared that funding is still falling short of covering two of Rail Baltica's key nodes, the Rīga Central Station and the Rīga International Airport.

The first section of the project, known as Rail Baltica I, was completed in 2015, covering the 120km distance between Kaunas and the Lithuania–Poland border. A year later, the first service between Kaunas and the Polish city of Białystok was inaugurated, allowing passengers to travel across the border without having to switch trains for the first time. Once completed, Rail Baltica will run from Tallinn to Pärnu via Rap-

la, to then continue along the Baltic coast all the way to Rīga. From there, trains will enter Lithuania to reach Panevėžys before reaching Kaunas, Vilnius and ultimately Warsaw. The line will avoid passing through Kaliningrad, the Russian exclave locked between Poland and Lithuania, and connected to Russia via a direct rail link. A proposal to extend the Rail Baltica line all the way to Helsinki via a tunnel that would run through the Gulf of Finland has also been presented, although at the time of writing Estonia, Finland and the EU were still studying the feasibility of the project. If approved, the 80km Tallinn–Helsinki line would become the longest rail tunnel in the world.

As the Rail Baltica project moves closer to completion, it promises to not only transform the transportation landscape of the Baltic region but also the political dynamics of Europe as a whole.

REINTRODUCING BEARS TO THE BALTICS

Why are there over 900 bears in Estonia, but (almost) no bears in Latvia and Lithuania? How decades of conservation efforts have brought back the big mammals from near-extinction. By Angelo Zinna

IN MAY 2020, the CCTV cameras of the Estonian Open-Air Museum on the outskirts of Tallinn recorded a brown bear crossing the road near the museum's entry gate. Spotting a bear so close to the capital was an exceptional event – the area's residents were advised by the Estonian Rescue Board to go into lockdown until the police could locate the city-dwelling predator, as news articles from the time report. Two years later, in September 2022, something similar happened in Tartu, Estonia's second city. In the early hours of the day a young bear was spotted roaming the Ropka area, south of the city, and later in Supilinn, northwest of the city, which left the authorities wondering whether the animal could have crossed through central Tartu during the night.

Close Encounters

In recent years, encounters between people and big mammals in Estonian urban areas seem to have become more frequent. While this is due in part to the reduced human presence outdoors during the COVID pandemic and the increased presence of video-recording devices active in the cities, experts agree that bear populations are growing together with urban areas, creating more and more overlaps between the habitats of humans and animals. With more than 2 million hectares of forests, accounting for over half of Estonia's surface, there appears to be no shortage of space for wildlife to thrive. Such encounters, however, tell a different story – according to experts, while older bears tend to be stable in the deeper reaches of Estonia's forests, members of the younger generation have a tendency to branch out in search of new territory to settle in, occasionally reaching human-inhabited areas. And with bear reproduction rates increasing over the past 100 years, young renegade bears are making the news with increased frequency.

As of 2023, the Estonian Environment Agency has counted between 900 and 950 bears on the country's territory, a number that has been expanding steadily over the past 15 years. Brown bears have long been a protected species in Estonia – in 2022 the Estonian Naturalists' Society even declared the brown bear 'animal of the year' – but the growing population comes with a set of problems that are still a matter of public debate. Besides the obvious panic produced by bears getting lost in the cities, the animals have caused damage on rural farms and in beekeeping operations, leading hunters' associations to call for an increase in the cull quota set each year by the Estonian Environment Agency. Strict rules determine when and how many bears can be hunted down. In 2022 and 2023, the quota was established at 96, a record high in line with the population growth and accounting for just over 10% of the bears currently living within the national borders.

How Did Bears (Almost) Disappear?

While bears appear to be thriving in Estonia, this is not the case for Latvia and Lithuania, where the large predator has been – until recently – considered extinct since the 1920s. Bears once roamed the forests of all three Baltic countries, but between the late 19th and early 20th centuries industrialisation and intensive hunting reduced their population, reaching the point where they disappeared from most of the region. Only in northeastern Estonia – where bears are believed to have lived since the early Holocene epoch – a small number of the animals survived. Bears were known to live in large numbers across the forests of northern Estonia until the 18th century, but by the start of WWI fewer than a dozen animals were known to exist in the country, primarily in the area of Alutaguse where the majority of Estonia's bear population continues to reside to this day.

In the mid-1930s, bears became a protected species in Estonia. The new hunting laws, which were upheld by the Soviet government after WWII, allowed the Estonian animal population to recover from the sharp decline and start growing steadily over the course of the following decades, multiplying from a few dozens to 150 in the 1970s. However, by the time such regulations were introduced in Estonia, logging and hunting had already eliminated all bears from Latvia and Lithuania. But even extinction can be temporary, if you wait long enough.

Back from Extinction

In a historical U-turn, bears are back where their count had long been down to zero. Conservation efforts have paid off and the largest predators of the Baltics have unexpectedly returned to both Latvia and Lithuania over the course of the past decade. Settling mainly in border zones, Latvia's population of migrant bears reached approximately 70 animals in 2021, according to the National Institute of Forest Science, which is responsible for the monitoring of the country's fauna. Thanks to a strict hunting ban, Latvia's bears have been spotted regularly roaming the country's vast forests bordering Estonia, Russia and Belarus since 2009, and only in the past few years, naturalists have observed the animals mating and hibernating within the national borders, a sign that a new permanent population is flourishing once again.

The most southern of the three Baltic states, Lithuania was long deemed unsuitable for hosting a permanent bear population – with forests too sparse to let them take root – but in recent years brown bears have been spotted roaming within the country's borders. It is commonly believed that the last Lithuanian bear was hunted down in 1883, but in 2019 and 2020 cameras recorded bears walking near the Ukmergė district in central Lithuania and through the Šimonių forest, 50km south of the Latvian border. As internationally travelling bears appear in Lithuania more and more often, the 'extinct' label that has defined the animal for over a century may soon require revision.

INDEX

Map Pages **000**

353

"Tallinn's Old Town is a gem of stone architecture and cobbled alleys, with the culturally vibrant capital extending well beyond its ancient borders."
– ANGELO ZINNA

"Latvia is painted in blue and green – the blue of the sea and a multitude of lakes, the green of the forest canopy that covers much of the hinterland."
– LEONID RAGOZIN

Mapping data sources:
© Lonely Planet
© OpenStreetMap http://openstreetmap.org/copyright

THIS BOOK

Destination Editor
Sandie Kestell

Production Editor
Graham O'Neill

Book Designer
Megan Cassidy

Cartographer
Valentina Kremenchutskaya

Assisting Editors
Imogen Bannister, Peter Cruttenden, Soo Hamilton, Clare Healy, Charlotte Orr

Cover Researcher
Fergal Condon

Thanks Ronan Abayawickrema, Sofie Andersen, Karen Henderson

MIX
Paper from responsible sources
FSC™ C021741
www.fsc.org

Paper in this book is certified against the Forest Stewardship Council™ standards. FSC™ promotes environmentally responsible, socially beneficial and economically viable management of the world's forests.

Published by Lonely Planet Global Limited
CRN 554153
10th edition – Jun 2024
ISBN 978 1 83869 736 5
© Lonely Planet 2024 Photographs © as indicated 2024
10 9 8 7 6 5 4 3 2 1
Printed in Malaysia